William Hughes

An Atlas of Classical Geography

Salzwasser

William Hughes

An Atlas of Classical Geography

1. Auflage | ISBN: 978-3-84604-754-5

Erscheinungsort: Frankfurt, Deutschland

Erscheinungsjahr: 2020

Salzwasser Verlag GmbH

Reprint of the original, first published in 1870.

AN ATLAS

OF

CLASSICAL GEOGRAPHY.

CONSTRUCTED BY

WILLIAM HUGHES,

AND EDITED BY

GEORGE LONG.

FORMERLY PROFESSOR OF ANCIENT LANGUAGES IN THE UNIVERSITY OF VIRGINIA

WITH

A SKETCH OF CLASSICAL GEOGRAPHY

AND OTHER ADDITIONS,

BY THE AMERICAN EDITOR.

CONTAINING

FIFTY-TWO MAPS AND PLANS ON TWENTY-SIX PLATES,
WITH AN INDEX OF PLACES.

NEW YORK:
SHELDON & COMPANY, PUBLISHERS,
498 & 500 BROADWAY.

1870.

AMERICAN PUBLISHERS' NOTICE.

In reproducing the present work, various additions have been thought desirable. For reasons adduced in his Preface, Mr. Long inserted no boundaries in the maps. Impossible as it may be, at this distance of time, to determine with absolute accuracy the limits of contiguous territories, it yet was felt that without some indication of their position, as generally received by classical scholars, the student would frequently feel the want of an assistance to which he had become accustomed; and they have accordingly been introduced from standard authorities.

The interest attaching to the gradual development of geographical knowledge among the ancients, has seemed to render desirable the introduction of the charts collected on Plate 1, showing at a glance the progress of information from the earliest times, and enabling the student to comprehend and appreciate the ideas of the writers of successive periods. Plate 26 has likewise been added, presenting topographical plans, on an enlarged scale, of various places of interest, which may serve to elucidate passages in numerous classical authors. These additions have been selected from leading authorities, such as Kiepert, Forbiger, and Johnston.

With the view of rendering the work a convenient text-book for the student, a condensed sketch of Classical Geography has been prefixed, compiled and adapted principally from the recent manual of Professor Pillans, of Edinburgh. In this the object has been, not to present a complete enumeration of places, but merely to furnish such supplementary information as cannot be embodied in the maps. No allusion has been made to Sacred Geography, a subject too extensive and too important to be dismissed within the limits necessarily assigned to the sketch. In revising the Index, the opportunity has occasionally been found of marking the quantity of a syllable left unaccented by Mr. LONG; and this has been done whenever practicable. In many instances, however, places of little note, whose names do not occur among the poets, are necessarily uncertain.

Every care has been taken throughout to obtain entire accuracy, in the most careful revision of both, maps and text by the gentleman who has made the additions and superintended the press. The publishers trust that their efforts have not been misdirected, and that they will be found to have succeeded in producing an Atlas in every way suited to the increasing requirements of the improved classical scholarship of the age.

PHILADELPHIA, *August*, 1856.

PREFACE.

THE MAPS in this Atlas have been constructed by WILLIAM HUGHES from the best authorities; and they have been engraved under his superintendence. The original drawings and the engraved maps have been revised by GEORGE LONG. No pains have been spared to make the maps correct; and though it is impossible to avoid some errors in a work of this kind, it is hoped that there are not many. Such as may be discovered will be corrected.

The distribution of the subject-matter of this ancient Atlas differs from that of other Atlases in several respects. The map of the Roman Provinces is one example of this; and there are several other maps which will not be found in the common Atlases. This Atlas is intended for the use of students both at schools and at college; and though it does not contain every name, it contains everything that a classical student can want.

No attempt has been made* to show the exact boundaries of the political divisions and subdivisions of countries, which cannot be done, in small maps at least, with sufficient accuracy; and in many cases it cannot be done at all. A student must learn what these boundaries are, so far as they can be ascertained, either from works on Ancient Geography, or from the instruction of a teacher. The best method of teaching Geography in schools is by oral instruction on the Map, followed by examination.

GEORGE LONG.

* See American Publishers' Notice.

(v)

LIST OF PLATES.

1. GEOGRAPHY ACCORDING TO THE ANCIENTS.
   THE WORLD ACCORDING TO HOMER (B. C. 900).
   THE WORLD ACCORDING TO HECATAEUS (about B. C. 500).
   THE WORLD ACCORDING TO HERODOTUS (about B. C. 440).
   THE WORLD ACCORDING TO ERATOSTHENES AND STRABO (from about B. C. 200 to A. D. 20).
   WESTERN EUROPE ACCORDING TO STRABO.
   THE WORLD ACCORDING TO PTOLEMY (about A. D. 160).
   INDIA ACCORDING TO PTOLEMY.
   GREAT BRITAIN ACCORDING TO PTOLEMY.

2. THE WORLD AS KNOWN TO THE ANCIENTS (WITH THE BOUNDARY OF THE PERSIAN EMPIRE UNDER CYRUS).

3. THE EMPIRE OF ALEXANDER THE GREAT, WITH THE ADJOINING REGIONS.

4. THE PROVINCES OF THE ROMAN EMPIRE, A. D. 119.

5 BRITANNIA.

6. GALLIA.

7. HISPANIA.

8. ITALIA (NORTHERN PART).

9. ITALIA (SOUTHERN PART).
   CORSICA AND SARDINIA

10. PLAN OF ROME.

11. PART OF ITALY, EMBRACING THE ROMAN TERRITORY, AND THE ADJOINING COUNTRY, on an enlarged scale.

12. SICILIA.

13. SYRACUSAE, on an enlarged scale.
   THE BAY OF NAPLES, and adjacent Part of Campania.
   THE TWO PORTS OF BRUNDUSIUM.

SKETCH

OF

CLASSICAL GEOGRAPHY.

ANCIENT GEOGRAPHY is almost exclusively confined to the countries around the *Mediterranean sea*, in the period of the power of *Greece* and of *Rome*, the shores of that ocean being the scene of the life and actions of classical antiquity. In the course of time, the centre of action moves from the eastern parts of the Mediterranean, or rather the seas adjoining it in the east, to regions farther west; and at the same time geographical knowledge follows the arms of victorious legions, radiating in all directions from the Mediterranean, as the centre. (MAP 2.)

In MAP 1 will be found a series of charts illustrating the geographical views entertained at different periods, as expressed by prominent authorities. Those rude sketches, besides their interest as manifesting the gradual extension of human knowledge, possess a value to the student when their progressive development is considered in connection with the march of historical events. Thus, with *Homer*, B. C. 900, the world is a circular plain, around which the river Oceanus flows. He is familiar with European and Asiatic Greece, as well as with Aegypt: in the west he places Elysium: on the edge of the plain dwell the Aethiopes and Pygmaei: beyond the Oceanus in the north are the Cimmerii. In *Hecataeus'* view of the world, about B. C. 500, the western countries of the Mediterranean have assumed form and proportion, while the eastern boundary of knowledge has made some progress.

Herodotus, the "Father of History," B.C. 440, also added largely to the stock of geographical knowledge, having travelled over a great part of the eastern world. *Democritus*, B.C. 300, shows an increase of geographical information, chiefly in the easternmost parts, produced by the conquests of Alexander. (See Empire of Alexander, MAP 3.)

Thus far, the history of geography shows an empirical aggregation of facts. After this, the scientific or systematic treatment of geography begins, the characteristic feature of which we may find in the use of astronomy for geographical purposes. *Hipparchus*, of Nice, about B. C. 230, stands first among those who combined geography with astronomy. He determined latitudes and longitudes of places from celestial observation, and was engaged in the measurement of the earth and in determining its figure.

The first who produced a whole geographical system was *Eratosthenes*, about B. C. 200. He attempted the measure of the earth's circumference, and introduced into his maps a regular parallel of latitude, the running of which was of course imperfect, and at variance with the actual positions of places.

Strabo, a Greek geographer, A. D. 20, endeavored, with but partial success, to collect and to systematize the geographical knowledge which flowed in upon the Romans from their military expeditions in so many parts of the then known world. (See Roman Empire, MAP 4.)

Ptolemy, A. D. 160, corrected old errors, gathered new information, (see his charts of India and Britain, MAP 1,) and gave ancient geography that final shape which it retained during the long period of the Empire of the Occident and of the Orient, and through the Middle Ages, until Columbus and Vasco de Gama struck out new and wider courses of geographical knowledge; and mathematics, combined with physical science, taught us the true positions and relations of geographical objects.

BRITANNIA.—(MAP 5.)

GREAT BRITAIN was known to the ancients under the names of *Britannia* and *Albion*. The coast of Cornwall and the *Cassiterides* (Scilly Isles) were visited by the Carthaginians. Among all the classical Greek writers, down to Alexander the Great, Aristotle alone makes any allusion to the British Isles. The Romans were indebted for their knowledge of the country to the wars of Caesar and his successors.

Julius Caesar made two hostile incursions into *Britain*, B. C. 58 and 55; but they were short in duration, and confined to the country between the strait of Dover and the Thames. The only localities he particularizes are *Tamĕsis* (Thames) and *Cantium* (Kent). Once, also, he simply enumerates six British tribes, without any data for fixing their boundaries. Strabo, who lived under Augustus and Tiberius, does little more than repeat the vague generalities of Caesar: his brief chapter on Britain concludes, after some inaccurate general description, without the mention of a single mountain, river, town, district, or people. He declares that the island is not worth the trouble of conquering. Pytheas, a merchant of the Greek colony of Massilia, (Marseilles), visited Britain about the time of Alexander, and gave an account of it, which, though very correct, was little credited by antiquity.

The MOUNTAINS of *Britain* are slightly noticed by the ancients. The chief PROMONTORIES on the east coast were *Ocellum*, or Spurn Head, some distance north of the Humber, and *Cantium Promontorium*, or North Foreland. On the south was *Ocrinum*, Lizard Point, and *Bolerium*, or *Antivestaeum*, Land's End. Upon the west coast were *Herculis Promontorium*, or Hartland Point, *Octapitarum*, or St. David's Head, *Canganorum Promontorium*, at the extremity of Carnarvonshire, and *Novantum*, or the Mull of Galloway.

The AESTUARIES, following the same order, were *Tava Aestu.*, the Tay, *Bodotria*, or the Firth of Forth, *Abus*, or the Humber, *Metaris Aestuarium*, or the Wash, and *Tamissa Aestuarium*, the mouth of the Thames. On the south, *Tamarus* was Plymouth Sound; and on the west, *Sabriana* or *Sabrina Aestuarium*, the Bristol Channel, *Segeia* or *Seteia*, the mouth of the Dee or the Mersey, *Belisama*, perhaps the Ribble, *Moricambe Aestuarium*, Morecambe Bay, *Ituna Aestuarium*, the Solway Firth, and *Clota Aestuarium*, the Clyde.

Most of the RIVERS have been named in the above enumeration of the aestuaries. We may, however, add *Alaunus*, the Tweed, *Tisa*, the Tees, *Antona*, the Nen.

Of TRIBES and PROVINCES, we find the *Cantii* in Kent: southwest of them the *Regni*. West of these were the *Belgae*, and further west the *Damnonii*. Further north we find the *Trinobantes*, in Essex and Middlesex, the *Brigantes*, in Yorkshire, Durham, Lancaster, Westmoreland, and Cumberland, the *Icĕni*, in Norfolk and Suffolk, the *Silŭres* and *Ordovices*, in Wales. North of Hadrian's wall, in what is to-day Scotland, were the *Otadeni*, *Gadeni*, *Selgovae*, *Novantae*, *Damnii*, and *Epidii*. *Mona* is the island of Anglesey: of TOWNS, we find the name *Camalodunum*, Colchester, *Verulamium*, near St. Albans, *Londinium*, which is described by Tacitus as a place of great wealth and traffic, though not a Roman colony, and by Ammianus Marcellinus, who wrote 300 years later, as an ancient town, which in later times had received the name of Augusta. Juvenal alludes to *Rutupiae*, (Richborough or Sandwich,) on the Kentish coast.

Of IRELAND, we learn nothing from the classics but the name, *Hibernia*, *Juverna*, or *Ierne*. Its relative position is incorrectly given.

Ptolemy is the first who gives any detailed account of the geography of Britain. He enumerates a variety of subdivisions, tribes, and towns, and attempts even a map of the island. (See MAP 1.)

BRITAIN was divided, under the Byzantine empire, into four provinces, the relative position of which it is difficult to determine. Perhaps we may place them thus: I. *Britannia Prima*, below the aestuaries of the Severn and the Thames: II. *Britannia Secunda*, comprising Wales: III. *Flavia Caesariensis*, extending from the Thames to the Humber on the east, and from the Lower Avon to the Mersey on the west: IV. *Maxima Caesariensis*, from the Humber and Mersey to the wall of Severus.

We will now briefly mention the Roman *walls*, *roads*, and *camps*, in Britain.

From Bowness on the Solway Firth, two lines of defence ran eastward, nearly parallel, and close to each other. We can trace them still as they cross the Irthing, and pass by Carlisle, (*Luguvallium*), Glenwhelt, Rowchester, and Newcastle, terminating on the north side of the Tyne, three and a half miles below the town last named. The distance from one extremity to the other is seventy-three Roman miles, equivalent to sixty-eight and a half English. Between the two lines of defence was a military way, and the whole three were crossed at right angles by at least one great road, Watling Street, near the modern village of Corbridge. Along the wall there were military forts (*castella*) and military stations (*castra stativa*), which are now generally named Chesters, e. g. *Hunnum*, Halton Chesters.

Between the Firths of Clyde and Forth, a rampart and ditch extended eastward from Douglass, on the Clyde, two miles west of old Kilpatrick, to Carriden, between Abercorn and Borrowstowness, on the Forth, a distance of thirty-four and three-fourths English miles. Along this line, the first defences were made (A. D. 81) by Agricola, who seems to have erected a *praetentura*, or chain of forts, between the two seas, at this narrowest part of the island, with a view to secure his conquests against the *Caledonians*, leaving· them to the enjoyment of their savage liberty in all the country beyond. Adrian contracted the limits of the empire, and erected about A. D. 120, the new line of defence between the Tyne and Solway; whilst Lollius Urbicus, the lieutenant of Antoninus

Pius, carried a rampart and ditch from sea to sea, to connect the forts of Agricola, and to complete the defensive works, A. D. 144.

Roman Britain, under the later empire, was penetrated in all directions by military roads. London was a point of intersection for many of them. The most remarkable were *Watling Street*, which, starting from Rutupiae, Richborough, in Kent, ran through Canterbury and, passing by Rochester and London, through St. Alban's, Dunstable, and Wroxeter, to the north, as far as the wall of *Agricola*.

Icknield Way ran across the island from a point near Great Yarmouth (country of Iceni) over the Thames at Streetly to the *Fosse Way*.

The *Fosse Way* extended from Moridunum, or Seaton, through Corinium, or Cirencester, and Ratae, to Lindum, or Lincoln, and thence to York.

From this, above Corinium, branched off *Ryknield Way*, passed Derbentia and Little Chester, and joined *Fosse Way* again below Danum, Dancaster.

The encampments, of which slender remains may still be traced, are numerous; but the remains are fast disappearing, with the exception of monuments, altars, coins, weapons, which are preserved in various collections.

GALLIA.—(MAP 6.)

GALLIA (*Gaul*) and the GALLI (*Gauls*) extended farther than France and the French of the present day. The Romans made the distinction of *Gallia Cisalpina* and of *Gallia Transalpina*. The first became, in later times, Upper Italy, (*Italia Superior*), and we speak of it as a part of Italy. *Gallia Transalpina* comprised, besides the present French territory, Rhaetia, (Switzerland,) large tracts of South-western Germany and Belgium.

The mountain ranges of Gaul which are lofty enough to deserve the name, are the following : 1. *Cevenna*, the Cevennes, stretching N.N.E. from the Pyrenees; 2. An extinct volcanic group in Auvergne, (*Arverni*,) the highest points of which are the Cantal, Mont Dor, and Puy-de Dôme; 3 *Vosĕgus*, the Vôges, running parallel with the Rhine from Bâle to Coblentz; 4. *Jura*, which formed the boundary between the *Helvetii* and *Sequăni;* and, 5. All that portion of the Alpine range which lies to the W. and S. of the Upper Rhine, and sends the waters produced in its summits and slopes either into the Rhine or into the Rhone.

GALLIA may be regarded as composed of the basins of the RHONE, the GARONNE, the LOIRE, the

SEINE, the MEUSE, and the RHINE. The basins of these rivers account for the whole superficial contents of *Gallia Transalpina*, except the country watered by the *Samăra* (Somme) and *Scaldis* (Scheld). We have then,

1. The basin of RHODANUS, the RHONE. This river, springing from the side of St. Gothard, makes its way between two lofty ranges of the Alps through the Valais, where it passes the city of the *Sedŭni*, now Sitten or Sion, and *Octodŭrus*, Martigny. Then, forcing its way through the gorge of St. Maurice, it expands into *Lacus Lemănus*,[1] and, having deposited there the soil of the melted glaciers, it re-appears at the city of GENEVA in the form of a majestic river of a deep transparent blue. In pursuing its course westward, it disappears and flows under ground for a quarter of a mile. Meeting at last with the obstruction of the Cevennes, it turns abruptly to the south. At the angle, it is joined from the north by *Arar*, the Saone. On this tributary stood *Cabillonum*, now Châlons-sur-Saone, and *Matisco*, now Mâcon, both towns of the *Aedui;* and on its feeder, *Dubis*, (Doubs,) was *Vesontio*, now Besançon. At

---

[1] Also Lemannus.

the point of junction of the *Arar* and *Rhodănus*, stood *Lugdūnum*, which gave name to the Augustan division of Gaul, *Lugdunensis*. From Lyons, the Rhone continues its rapid course directly south, passing various towns, among which may be mentioned *Avenio*, Avignon, at the junction of the *Druentia*, the Durance, and *Arelāte* (Arles).

2. The *Basin* of GARUMNA, the Garonne, a river which rises in the Pyrenees, and flows N. W. into the *Sinus Cantabricus*, the Bay of Biscay. This basin is bounded by the Pyrenees, the Cevennes, the mountains of Auvergne, and by the *dos* or high ground that extends thence to the sea. Within these limits, it includes the minor basin of *Atŭris* (the Adour). In descending the Garumna, we find *Tolōsa*, Toulouse; and farther down, on the left bank of the river, stood *Burdigăla*, the modern Bordeaux. It was the birthplace of the poet Ausonius. Lower down, the Garonne receives the Dordogne, and widens into an aestuary which is called La Gironde.

3. The *Basin* of LIGER, the LOIRE. The Loire rises in the Cevennes, flows first northward, then westward, and falls into the Atlantic after a course of 500 miles. Among the towns on its banks most worthy of mention was *Genăbum*, which owes its modern name of Orleans to the people *Aureliani*, whose capital it was. Farther down the Loire were the *Turŏnes* and *Andes* v. *Andegăvi*, tribes which give the modern names Tours, Angers, and Anjou. Near the embouchure of the Loire dwelt the tribe *Namnētes*, whence the name of the modern city of Nantes. On the Arroux, a tributary of the Loire, *Bibracte* v. *Augustodūnum*, Autun, capital of the *Aedui*.

4. The *Basin* of SEQUANA, the SEINE. This river rises in the table-land of the Gallic tribe *Lingŏnes*, now called the Plateau de Langres, and, soon after its junction with *Matrŏna*, (the Marne), encloses an islet called *Lutetia Parisiorum*, now in the very centre of the capital of France. Between Paris and the sea is Rouen (*Rotomăgus*). Near the source was *Alesia*, taken by Caesar after a long siege, which he describes minutely in the 7th book of his Commentaries.

The comparatively small and very flat Basin of *Samăra*, the Somme, was the seat of the tribe *Ambiăni*, whose chief place was *Samarobriva*, of which mention occurs in Caesar and Cicero, as well as in Ptolemy; but the name of the people survives only in that of the modern city Amiens.

5. We next arrive at the Basin of MOSA, (in Dutch, Maas or Maes—in French, Meuse,) on which, as we descend the river, we come to no place of note in ancient times.

6. The Basin of RHENUS, the RHINE. This river rises in the central Alps, and is enclosed in its early course between Alpine ranges, until it expands into *Lacus Brigantīnus* v. *Venĕtus*, the lake of Constance. Thence it flows westward (forming at Schaffhausen the most noted waterfall in Europe, and passing *Augusta Rauracorum*) till it reaches *Basilia* (Basel or Bâle). Meeting there with an obstruction in the high ground between Jura and the Vôges, it turns abruptly to the north. In the subsequent part of its course, it passes successively the walls, 1. of *Mogontiăcum*, the capital of *Germania Superior*, now Mainz in German, Mayence in French: 2. of *Confluentes*, corrupted into the modern Coblentz, at the confluence of the Rhine and *Mosa* or *Mosella* (Mosel or Moselle): and, 3. of *Colonia Agrippĭna*, capital of *Germania Inferior*, now Cöln or Cologne.

In the English Channel, on the N. W. coast of Gaul, over against Britain, are *Portus Itius*, whence Caesar first set sail for Britain, and the three islands, now belonging to Great Britain, *Ridūna*, Alderney, *Sarnia*, Guernsey, and *Caesarĕa*, Jersey: facing the Atlantic is *Portus Brivātes*, the harbor of Brest: at the mouth of the Adour, *Lapurdum*, Bayonne.

On the Southern or Mediterranean coast was *Narbo Martius*, Narbonne, which gave name to one of the divisions of Gaul, *Narbonensis*. Ten leagues east of the Rhone mouth was *Massilia*, (Marseilles,) said to have been founded at a very remote period by a colony from *Phocaea*, a city on the coast of Asia Minor. *Telo Martius*, Toulon, is the great naval station of the French on the Mediterranean, as Brest is on the Atlantic. Off Toulon are the *Stoechădes Insulae*, the Isles d'Hières, *Forum Julii*, birthplace of Agricola, now Frejus, *Nicaea*, the last Gallic city towards Italy, now Nice.

ANCIENT DIVISIONS AND TRIBES OF GAUL.

At the time of Caesar's invasion, there was already in Gaul a *Provincia Romana*, lying between the Cevennes and the Alps. The rest of Gaul is described by him as divided into three parts, according as it was inhabited by the *Aquitāni* in the south, *Belgae* in the north, and *Celtae* in the middle. But the truth is, that GALLIA COMATA (as all beyond the Roman province was then called) was occupied by numerous independent tribes or peoples, generally hostile to each other. Some of these have been already named—the *Lingŏnes* and *Parisii* in the Basin of the Seine, the *Aureliani* and *Namnetes* in that of the Loire, and the *Sedŭni* in the Valais. A few shall now be added as occurring most frequently in Caesar's narrative of his campaigns in Gaul; and the locality of each tribe named will be indicated by the river-basin in which they dwelt.

The *Aedui* occupied the territory between the Loire and the Saone: on a tributary of the former was *Bibracte*, their capital, subsequently called *Augustodŭnum* (Autun). The *Sequăni* dwelt in the upper part of the Basin of the Saone, and the whole of that of its feeder *Dubis*, the Doubs, a river which winds round their chief city *Vesontio* (Besançon).

In the Basin of the Seine, south side, lived the tribe *Carnŭtes:* near their chief city *Autricum*, (Chártres), was the residence of the Arch-druid of Gaul. The *Allobrŏges* dwelt between the Rhone and its left-hand tributary *Isăra*, the Isère. The *Trevĕri* or *Trevĭri* occupied the space between the Meuse and the Rhine, and the lower Basin of the Moselle. Their chief city was that now called from the name of the tribe, in German, Trier, in French, Trèves. Through their country ran the extensive *Silva Arduenna*, the forest of Ardenne. To the west of the *Trevĭri*, in the Basin of *Sabis*, the Sambre, and the upper course of the Scheld, dwelt the *Nervii*, a gallant people of German extraction, who fought a great battle against Caesar.

HISPANIA.—(MAP 7.)

SPAIN was called *Iberia* by the Greeks, and by the poets *Hesperia*, as the farthest land toward the west, with the addition of *ultima*, to distinguish it from Italy.

An elevated ridge of mountain and table-land extends from N. to S., forming the water-shed of the country, and giving origin to all the great rivers, some of which find their way to the Mediterranean, and others to the Atlantic. To this crest or back-bone, as it were, of the peninsula, are attached, on the side facing the west, ranges of mountains and high ground, running in a S.W. direction and nearly parallel to each other; and these enclose, on two sides, the basins or tracts of country through which the rivers and their tributaries flow.

The main rivers that rise on the western slope of the central ridge and fall into the Atlantic, are *four* in number: 1. DURIUS, the Duero, (in Spanish,) Douro, (in Portuguese,) the vast basin of which, bounded by the Cantabrian and Asturian mountains on the north side, and by those of Castille on the south, includes the less considerable valley of *Minius*, the Minho; 2. TAGUS, famed for the gold found in its sand; 3. ANAS, the Guadiana; and, 4. BAETIS, the Guadalquivir (*i. e.* in Arabic, "the great river.")

The main rivers that rise on the eastern slope of the water-shed and fall into the Mediterranean, are also *four*, but, excepting the last, of much shorter course: 1. TADER, the Segura; 2. SUCRO, the Xucar: 3. TURIA, the Guadalaviar; and, 4. IBĔRUS, the Ebro; and the basins of these rivers are enclosed in like manner by lateral ranges of hills which start off,

like spinal processes, from the side of the central range fronting the east.

In tracing the rivers just enumerated, from fountain-head to the mouth, we fall in successively with the following towns and localities :

1. On the DURIUS, near the source, and not far from the modern town of Soria, stood *Numantia*, which Florus calls *Hispaniae decus*. It sustained a fourteen years' siege against the Romans, and was taken at last by Scipio Africanus Minor. At the mouth stood *Cale*, or *Portus Calensis*, (Oporto,) whence the kingdom of Portugal derives its name.

In the Basin of the DURIUS were also, on the north side, *Asturica Augusta*, Astorga, and *Legio* VII *gemina*, Leon. On the south side of the basin, *Salmantica*, Salamanca, and *Segovia*, famed for an aqueduct said to have been the work of Trajan, and still, with its double tier of arches, in good preservation.

2. On the TAGUS, *Tolĕtum*, Toledo, *Norba Caesarea*, where was a famous bridge over the river, now Alcantara, *Scalăbis*, Santarem, *Olisĭpo*, now LISBON, the capital of Portugal.

In the Basin of the Tagus, north side, were *Complŭtum*, Alcala, on the Henares, where Cardinal Ximenes founded a university, and where he published, in 1515, the famous Polyglot Bible commonly called *Biblia Complutensia*.

3. On the ANAS, half-way down, *Metellīnum*, founded by Caecilius Metellus, now Medellin, birthplace of Fernando Cortez, *Emerita Augusta*, a settlement provided by Augustus for his disbanded

veterans, (*emeriti*,) once the capital of Lusitania, now Merida.

4. On the BAETIS, near the source, *Castulo*, of which Hannibal's wife Imilce was a native, now Cazlona; the forest-land around—the *saltus Castulonensis* of Livy—is part of *Mons Marianus*, the great table-land now called the Sierra Morena, the scene of the fabulous adventures of Don Quixote. Farther down the river *Cordŭba*, (Cordova), birthplace of Lucan and the two Senecas; *Italica*, birthplace of the Emperor Trajan, and, some think, of Hadrian also and the poet Silius Italicus; *Hispălis*, SEVILLE.

The Basin of the BAETIS was occupied in the Middle Ages by the Vandals, and was then called Vandalitia—a name which appears now in the altered form of Andalusia.

5. TADER, the Segura, (the farthest south of those main rivers which fall into the Mediterranean,) after passing the modern city of Murcia, flows through the *Campus Spartarius*, a plain so called from its abounding in *spartum*, (esparto), a reed much used by the ancients for the cordage of ships, and various economical purposes.

6. SUCRO, the Xucar, had at its mouth a city of the same name.

7. At the embouchure of TURIA, (Guadalaviar,) was *Valentia*, a Roman colony, now the capital of Valencia.

8. On the IBERUS, half-way down, stood *Saldŭba*, afterwards CAESARAUGUSTA, now ZARAGOZA. The broad Basin of the EBRO, lying between the Pyrenees and the Central Ridge, is watered, from the heights of both, by numerous tributary streams, the most remarkable of which are, on the north side, the *Sicŏris*, on which stood *Ilerda*, (Lerida,) where Caesar defeated Pompey's generals, Afranius and Petreius, A. U. C. 704, (B. C. 49,) and on the south side, *Salo*, (Xalon,) on which stood *Bilbĭlis*, the native town of the poet Martial.

After thus following the course of rivers, if we next take the line of coast for our guide, we shall come upon towns which have been indebted for their importance and notoriety, in ancient or modern times, to the convenience of harborage, and their facility of access and resort to commercial and colonizing foreigners.

In this tour of the coast, starting from Cape Finisterra, the N. W. angle of the Peninsula, and going south, we find the harbor of Corunna (*Portus Magnus*). 'Corunna' is thought to be a corruption of COLUMNA, from an ancient tower ninety-two feet high, still standing, said to have been built by Hercules. At the S. W. angle of the Peninsula, between the mouth of the *Baetis* and the *Fretum Herculeum*, (Strait of Gibraltar,) stood the very ancient town of *Gadir*, founded and so named by the Phoenicians. The Romans called it *Gades*, and considered it as the extreme point of the earth westward, in like manner as the Ganges was reckoned the farthest point eastward. *Gadir* is the modern town and harbor of Cadiz.

Within the strait is *Calpe*, (the Rock of Gibraltar,) which the poets feigned to be one of the pillars erected by Hercules as his *meta laborum*, and as the western *terminus* of the habitable globe.

Proceeding along the shore of the Mediterranean, we find, a little inland, *Munda*, where Caesar defeated the two sons of Pompey, B. C. 45, (A. U. C. 708). Then comes *Nova Carthago*, (Cartagena,) the capital of the Carthaginian possessions in Spain, till it was taken by Scipio Africanus Major, A. U. C. 542, B. C. 210. A little north of Valencia was *Saguntum*, the storming of which was Hannibal's first act of aggression in the second Punic war. Out of its ruins was built a modern town, thence called Murviedro, i. e. *Muri Veteres*. Between the mouth of the Ebro and Pyrenees were *Tarraco*, (Tarragona,) chief city of the Roman province *Tarraconensis*, and *Barcino*, (Barcelona,) with its citadel, *Mons Jovis*, (Monjuich,) said to have been built by Hamilcar Barcas, father of Hannibal.

Off the coast of Valencia is the group of *Baleares Insulae*, *Major* and *Minor*, famed for furnishing corps of slingers to the Roman armies; and the *Pityūsae*, *Ebūsus*, Iviça, and *Ophiūsa*, Formentera.

The capes of the Peninsula are—*Promontorium Trileucum*, (Ortegal,) the most northern point; on the W. coast, *Nerium*, (Finisterra,) *Magnum*, (Rock of Lisbon,) *Barbarium*, (Espichel,) *Sacrum*, (St. Vincent,) *Junonis*, (Trafalgar.)

The Peninsula, in the time of the Roman Republic, was divided into *Duae Hispaniae*, *Citerior* and *Ulterior*, by the river *Ibĕrus*: under Augustus, into three provinces: 1. TARRACONENSIS, comprising all the north and north-east parts, from the *Durius* and *Tader* to the Pyrenees, in which were the native tribes *Gallaeci*, *Astŭres*, *Cantăbri*, *Cosetăni*, *Carpetăni*, *Ilergĕtes*, *Celtibĕri*, etc.; 2. BAETICA, the southern extremity, as far north as the *Anas*, in which were the *Turdetăni*, *Bastŭli*, *Turdŭli*, etc.; and, 3. LUSITANIA, the western and central part, between the *Anas*, the *Durius*, and the Atlantic, in which division were the *Vettŏnes* and the country called *Cuneus*. Most of the tribes named above are mentioned by Livy.

The Phoenicians were the first civilized people who visited Spain, more than 1000 years before Christ: they founded *Gadir*, *Malăca*, etc. Afterwards the inhabitants of *Massilia*, in Gaul, built *Rhoda*, now Rosas, and *Emporiae*, now Ampurias, in the N. E. corner of the Peninsula. The Carthaginians, coming next, built *Tarrăco*, *Barcĭno*, and *Nova Carthago*, and held possession of a great part of the country till they were expelled by the Romans; who, after contending for the possession of Spain for a period of 200 years before Christ, remained masters of it during the first four centuries of the Christian era.

ITALIA.—(MAPS 8, 9, 10, 11, 12, 13.)

ITALY was called *Hesperia* by the Greeks, as being west of Greece. In poetry, it was sometimes called *Oenotria*, from an Arcadian prince named Oenotrus, son of Lycaon, who settled in Lucania; and *Ausonia*, from the Ausones, a people of Latium. The epithet *Saturnia* was applied to it, as the fabled residence of Saturn, after his expulsion from heaven by Jupiter. Its common appellation of *Italia* was supposed, by the natives, to be derived from a prince named Italus; but this name was confined by the Greeks originally to a small district at the southern extremity of the country, and was gradually extended to the whole territory, which is fenced off from the rest of Europe by the mountain-barrier of the Alps, and surrounded on all other sides by the sea.

Italy, when contemplated under its physical aspects, presents itself as composed of two portions, nearly equal in extent, but widely different in natural character. The one is the peninsula of *Italia Propria*, surrounded by the waters of the Mediterranean and Adriatic on all sides, except where a straight line drawn over land, and connecting the little streams *Macra* and *Rubicon* in lat. 44°, forms the isthmus. The other main portion of Italian soil is the great Basin of *Padus*, called also by the poets *Eridănus*, the Po. Between these two territories, the contrast is striking. In the northern division, throughout its whole length, we find a river flowing in the lowest level between the Alpine and Apennine heights, which are its boundaries. In the southern or peninsular portion, the reverse is the case. The central line of the peninsula is not, as in Northern Italy, the lowest, but the most elevated part; being, in fact, the crest of the lofty and continuous chain of the Apennines, while the boundary line on both sides is the lowest of all levels, the sea. The one region is penetrated by a single river, swollen by the contributions of innumerable streams from the opposite sides of the basin. The peninsula, on the other hand, has abundance of streams, but they are all, even the Tiber, of comparatively short course, having each its own little basin and lateral feeders, and falling directly and independently into the sea.

To begin with the *northern* section. The huge Basin of the Po was, during the republican times, no part of Italy, but known to the Romans as GALLIA CISALPINA and LIGURIA. If we trace the PADUS from its source in *Mons Vesŭlus* (Monte Viso) to its mouth, we shall find, on the river itself, *Augusta Taurinorum*, taken by Hannibal on his descent from the Alps, now Turin, (Torino,) capital of the kingdom of Sardinia, *Placentia*, a Roman colony, now Piacenza, and *Cremŏna*.

On the *north* side of the Basin of the Po, which, from its position in regard to Rome, was called *Gallia Transpadăna*, we find the river joined by numerous streams from the Alps, among which the most notable are, 1. the *Duria Minor*, on which was *Segusio*, Susa, and 2. *Duria Major*, on which were *Augusta Praetoria*, Aosta, and *Eporedia*, Ivrea; 3. the *Sessītes*, near which was *Vercellae*, where Marius defeated the *Cimbri*; 4. *Ticīnus*, (Tessino,) issuing from Lake *Verbănus*, Maggiore, on the banks of which Hannibal first defeated the Romans in a skirmish of cavalry; 5. *Addua*, (the Adda,) issuing from Lake *Larius*, (Lago di Como), W. of which was *Mediolănum*, MILAN; and, 6. *Mincius*, issuing from Lake *Benăcus*, (Lago di Garda,) and investing *Mantua*, a city which Silius Italicus calls *musarum domus*, as being the birthplace of Virgil, though it is believed that the poet was born at *Andes*, a neighboring village. At the southern extremity of Lake *Benăcus* was the peninsula *Sirmio*, the residence of the poet Catullus. *Athĕsis*, a river which the Germans call Etsch, and the French Adige, may be said to belong to the Basin of the Po, though it falls direct into the Adriatic. On this river are the towns of *Tridentum*, Trent, and *Verŏna*, birthplace of

Catullus, which retains its ancient name, with a Roman amphitheatre in tolerable preservation. To the north of Verona were the *Colles Euganei*, famed for wool. Farther along is *Meduácus*, Bacchiglione, on which is *Patavium*, birthplace of Livy, now Padua.

The *south* side of the Po basin, as being that nearest to Rome, was called *Gallia Cispadāna*. It is permeated by numerous streams from the Apennines, the most memorable of which are the *Trebia*, on whose banks the Romans sustained a second and more severe defeat from Hannibal, and *Rhenus*, Reno, on which was *Bononia*, Bologna. In an island on this 'little Rhine,' the second triumvirate, Antony, Lepidus, and Augustus, met to portion out among them the Roman world.

In the peninsula of ITALIA PROPRIA, the only rivers of considerable length are the *Arnus*, *Tibĕris*, *Liris*, *Vulturnus*, all falling into the *Mare Inferum* v. *Tyrrhenum*, and the *Aufidus* and *Aturnus*, which flow into the *Mare Superum* v. *Adriaticum*, v. *Hadria*, the Gulf of Venice.

1. In the Basin of *Arnus* (Valdarno and Vallombrosa) were, on the river itself, *Florentia*, now Florence, capital of Tuscany, and near the mouth, *Pisae* (Pisa). Three miles N. E. from Florence, *Faesŭlae*, where Galileo made his observations, and farther north, *Pistoria*, where Catiline was defeated and slain.

2. In the Basin of *Tiberis*, the Tiber, (in Italian, Tevere,) were, 1st, on the river itself, *Perusia*, near *Lacus Trasymĕnus*, (now the Lake of Perugia,) where, for the third time, Hannibal routed the Roman army under Flaminius; *Fidĕnae*, beyond *Mons Sacer*, between the *Tiber* and *Anio*, ROMA, *Princeps Urbium*, and at the mouth, *Ostia*, the port of Rome; 2d, on the *right* side of the Basin of the Tiber, *Clusium*, the city of Porsenna, upon the tributary *Clanis*, and on the left side, *Tibur* (Tivoli) on the *Anio* (Teverone). At Tibur, Maecenas had a villa, in which Horace (whose Sabine farm lay at no great distance on the *Digentia*, a feeder of the *Anio*) was a frequent guest.

In the Basin of *Liris* (Liri at first, and then Garigliano) were, on the left side, *Arpĭnum*, birthplace of Marius and Cicero, the famous *Duo Arpinātes*, *Aquĭnum*, birthplace of Juvenal: at the mouth, near the marshes where Marius took refuge, *Minturnae*. On the *right* side, the *Liris* was joined by the *Fibrĕnus*. On the banks of the latter, and on the little island at the junction which belonged to Cicero, was held the dialogue De Legibus.

4. In the Basin of the *Vulturnus*, on the left side of the river, stood the following towns; *Allifae*, famed for its pottery, CAPUA, chief city of the *Campāni*, and the rival of Rome itself (hence called 'altera Roma') till towards the close of the 2d Punic war, when, having sided with Hannibal, it fell with his falling fortunes, *Venāfrum*, famed for its olives, *Cales* (-*ium*), for its vines, (*Venafranum*, sc. oleum, and *Calēnum*, sc. vinum, signified oil and wine of the first quality). *Beneventum*, a town of *Samnium* on the *Via Appia*, stood at the point of junction of *Sabātus* and *Calor*, whose united stream falls into the *Vulturnus*. On that river itself stood *Casilĭnum*, (on the site of the modern Capua,) which gained credit with the Romans by its long and obstinate resistance to Hannibal. Between *Beneventum* and *Capua* lay *Furcae Caudĭnae*, a defile where a Roman army was hemmed in by the Samnites, and forced to pass under the yoke.

5. In the Basin of the *Aufĭdus*, not far from the *right* bank of the river, were *Canusium* and *Cannae*: near the latter was gained the last and greatest of Hannibal's victories, and to *Canusium* the remains of the Roman army retreated after the disastrous battle. Higher up the valley, at the foot of Mt. *Vultur*, was *Venusia*, birthplace of Horace, on the debatable land between APULIA and LUCANIA. Here also, not at Horace's farm, was the *Fons Bandusiae*.

6. In the Basin of the *Aternus*, on the river itself, was *Amiternum*, birthplace of Sallust the historian, and *Corfinium*, the rallying point of the League against Rome in the Social War. At some distance south from the bend of the river stood *Sulmo*, Sulmona, a town of the *Peligni*, birthplace of Ovid.

To the geographical position of other towns and localities not connected with the six main rivers, a clue will be found if we follow the line of coast, with special reference at the same time to the principal subdivisions or provinces of ITALIA ANTIQUA. These provinces were either maritime or inland. Of the former class, six bordered on the Mediterranean, viz.: LIGURIA, ETRURIA, LATIUM, CAMPANIA, LUCANIA, and the BRUTII, and five on the Adriatic, viz.: APULIA, including *Japygia*, *Daunia*, and *Messāpia*, PICĒNUM, FRENTANI, UMBRIA, GALLIA *Cispadana* and *Transpadāna*, the latter including *Venetia*, *Carnia*, and *Istria*. The inland provinces were SAMNIUM and the highland districts of the MARSI, PELIGNI, and SABINI.

1. On the coast of LIGURIA, proceeding eastward

from the small river *Varus*, which flows from *Alpes Maritĭmae*, we find, at the head of the bay called *Sinus Ligustĭcus*, *Genua*, a city more famous in history under its modernized name of Genoa.

2. Crossing the *Macra*, we enter ETRURIA, and arrive first at the town of *Luna* and its harbor *Portus Lunensis* (Gulf of Spezzia). Not far off are the quarries of Carrara, which still supply statuary marble to Europe. As we approach the mouth of the Tiber, we come upon the ancient *Agylla*, subsequently called *Caere*, a town rewarded with the honorary freedom of the city, for its fidelity to Rome at the time of the Gallic invasion.

3. On the coast of LATIUM, the towns we meet with on crossing the Tiber are, *Laurentum*, the city of King Latinus, *Lavinium*, and *Antium*, the capital of the Volsci. Over the *Antiătes* the Romans gained their first victory at sea, in memory of which they fixed the beaks (*rostra*) of the ships they had captured in front of the tribune from which the orators harangued the people. *Antium* was famed in Horace's time for a Temple of Fortune. Eight miles inland was *Ardea*, the city of the Rutuli and of Turnus, and *Coriŏli*, the taking of which gained for Caius Marcius the title of Coriolanus. Farther along the coast were *Palūdes Pomptĭnae*, the Pontine Marshes: beyond is *Anxur* v. *Terracĭna*. Next come the town and promontory of *Circēii*, the town *Amyclae*, the town, promontory, and harbor of *Cajēta*, which took that name, according to Virgil, from the nurse of Aeneas: near it was Cicero's *Formianum*, where he was murdered by order of Mark Antony. Here commences, and is continued into Campania, the district in which the choicest wines of ancient Italy were produced, the *Formiani Colles*, *Mons Massicus*, the *ager Falernus*, *Caecŭbus*, *Calēnus*, *Setĭnus*.

4. On the coast of CAMPANIA were *Cumae*, which Virgil makes the first landing-place of Aeneas in Italy, and the abode of the Sibyl who conducted him to the shade of his father Anchises, in the abodes of the dead, *Baiae*, a favorite watering-place, *Puteŏli*, (Puzzuoli,) and *Parthenŏpe*, subsequently *Neapŏlis*, (Napŏli, Naples,) one of the numerous Greek colonies planted along the southern shore of the peninsula, which procured for it the name of MAGNA GRAECIA. At a little distance across the bay on which Naples stands, is *Vesuvius*, a volcano, of which the first eruption upon record took place A. D. 79. At the base of Vesuvius, and overwhelmed by its eruptions, were the now buried cities of *Hercula-*

neum and *Pompeii*, discovered and partially disinterred within the last and present centuries. Not far off, inland, was *Nola*, at the siege of which Hannibal first received a check. It was at *Nola* that Augustus died.

5. On the coast of LUCANIA was *Posidonia* v. *Paestum*, famed for its roses and its ruined temples. On that part of the Lucanian coast which is in the *Sinus Tarentinus*, were *Metapontum*, the residence for a time of Pythagoras and of Hannibal, *Heraclĕa*, the place of assembly for the deputies from the states of MAGNA GRAECIA, *Sybăris*, proverbial for the luxury and effeminacy of its inhabitants. In the bay, but beyond the limits of Lucania, was *Tarentum*, on the brook *Galēsus*, famed for the fine quality of the wool raised on its banks.

6. In AGER BRUTTIUS, on the *Fretum Sicŭlum*, (Strait of Messĭna,) was a rock with a cave under it, supposed to be the residence of the fabled monster Scylla: farther along, in the narrow part of the strait, was the town of *Rhegium* (Reggio). Near the Lacinian promontory, *Croto*, where Pythagoras long resided, and taught his doctrines: the birthplace also of the famous wrestler Milo, hence called Crotoniătes.

7. On the Adriatic coast of APULIA, after doubling *prom. Japygium*, (C. Leuca), we find *Hydrūs* v. *Hydruntum*, (Otranto), the nearest transit to Greece, but less frequented for that purpose than *Brundusium*, (see plan on MAP 13), which had an excellent harbor, and was the terminus of the *Via Appia*, the great high road from Rome to Greece. *Brundusium* and *Dyrrhachium*, on the opposite coast, were the Dover and Calais of the ancient world. This part of the Apulian coast was inhabited by a people called *Calăbri*, whose town *Rhudiae* was the birthplace of the poet Ennius. Next comes the projection of the land occupied by Mt. *Gargănus* and its oak forests ('quercēta Gargani').

8. On the coast of PICENUM occurs a smaller projection of the land, which, from the form it takes, was likened to the human elbow, ἀγκων, and hence the town built on it received the name of *Ancon* v. *Ancōna*.

9. On the coast of UMBRIA were two towns of note, 1. *Sena*, to which the epithet *Gallica* was added, as well to denote the fact of its being originally a Gallic settlement, as to distinguish it from *Sena Julia*, an inland town in Etruria—the former is now Sinigaglia, the latter Sienna; and, 2. *Ariminum*, (Rimini,) the storming of which was Caesar's first

overt act of civil war after crossing the *Rubicon.* Between those Umbrian towns flows the small river *Metaurus,* where Asdrubal, the brother of Hannibal, was defeated and slain by the consuls Livius and Nero, A. U. C. 546, (B. C. 207.)

10, 11. On the coast of GALLIA *Cisalpina,* south of the Po, stood *Ravenna,* near which Augustus constructed a station for his fleet on the *Mare Superum,* as he did at *Misēnum,* near Naples, to guard the *Mare Inferum.* Ravenna is now four miles from the sea; and it may be observed, generally, that in the lower course of the Po, the *Colmata* (i. e. *cumulata,* successive deposits of soil in the channels of rivers, in consequence of floods and artificial embankments) has already raised the bed of the river thirty feet above the level of the adjoining plain.

North of the Po lay the districts called *Venetia,* (on the shore of which is the modern city of VENICE,) *Carnia,* and *Istria,* extending to the little stream *Arsia,* the eastern boundary of Italy. Along this coast, the chief ancient towns were *Aquileia, Tergeste,* now Trieste, and *Pola.*

ITALIAN ISLANDS.

Off the coast of Etruria lies *Ilva* v. *Aethalia,* (Elba,) famed of old for the richness of its iron ores, and not far W. is *Corsica.* Off the coast of Campania are the islands of *Prochўta,* (Procida), *Inarīme,* (Ischia); and on the opposite side of the bay, *Capreae,* the retreat of Tiberius; and on the other side of the *prom. Minervae,* the three rocky islets, *Sīrenūsae.* Directly S. of Corsica is *Sardinia,* called *Ichnūsa* by the Greeks, from its supposed resemblance to the impress of the human foot (ιχνος, *vestigium*).

To the S. E. of Sardinia, near the extremity of Italy, lies the group of volcanic islets called *Ins. Aeoliae* v. *Vulcaniae,* (Lipari Islands), of which one only, *Strongўle,* (Strombŏli,) is still active.

South of this group lies SICILIA, (MAP 12,) called also *Sicania, Trinacria* v. *Triquetra Tellus.* The three promontories (τρια αχρα, trina cornua, *Ov.*) at the three corners of the triangular island were, N. E. *Pelōrus,* S. E. *Pachўnus,* and W. *Lilybaeum.*

In the strait, *Fretum Sicŭlum,* which separates Italy from Sicily, the poets describe a whirlpool called *Charybdis,* opposite to *Scylla,* on the Italian side. These were the two dangers of ancient navigators, between which it was thought so difficult to steer, that in avoiding the one it was hardly possible not to fall a prey to the other. Hence came the

proverbial use of the modern line: 'Incidit in Scyllam, qui vult vitare Charybdin.' A little to the E. was the town of *Zancle,* afterwards *Messāna,* now Messina. We next pass *Catīna* v. *Catăna,* Catania, which has suffered much and repeatedly from the lava of AETNA—the burning mountain, equally famed in fable and in history; and crossing *Simaethus,* the river of longest course in the island, we arrive at SYRACUSAE, (see plan on MAP 13,) the renowned metropolis of ancient Sicily. In front of the harbor is the island of *Ortygia* v. *Nasos,* and in it the fountain *Arethusa,* of poetical celebrity.

On the coast between *Pachўnus* and *Lilybaeum* was *Agrigentum,* or in the Greek form, *Acrăgas,* the second city in ancient Sicily—an early rival of Carthage, and noted for a Temple of Jupiter, of which some gigantic fragments still remain. The ancient name survives in the modern Girgenti.

Between Lilybaeum and Pelorus, on the northern shore of the island, the notable localities are, *Drepănum,* (Trapăni,) *Eryx,* a town and mountain— the latter surmounted by a Temple of Venus Erycīna; and off the shore *Aegātes Insulae,* where the Romans gained a naval victory which put an end to the first Punic war. *Panormus,* now Palermo, the modern capital of Sicily, and S. W. from it *Segesta,* with its temple almost entire.

Before quitting Italy and the Italian islands, it may be well to add a few notes on the Alps, and on some other peculiarities of the country which have not come under our notice in the geographical detail, but with which it is proper the classical student should be acquainted.

The great range of mountains called the Alps (*Alpes*) extends nearly 600 miles in the form of a crescent, between 5° and 18° E. Long., and 44° and 47½° N. Lat., with various indentations and sinuosities, from the Var to the Adriatic, presenting generally an abrupt face towards Italy, and sloping more gradually on the other side. Its different parts were anciently distinguished by different epithets, most of which are still retained. These were: 1. *Alpes Maritimae,* the Maritime Alps, extending from the Mediterranean to *Mons Vesŭlus,* Monte Viso—the mountain, as we have seen, which gives origin to the Po. 2. Thence to the modern Mt. Cenis were *Alpes Cottiae,* including Mt. Genèvre. This portion of the chain took its name from a Gallic chief who had early made his peace with Augustus, and assisted him in subduing the Alpine tribes whose names are enumerated on the triumphal arch erected at Susa. 3. The *Alpes Graiae* extended from Mt. Cenis to Mt. Blanc. There is strong ground for believing that the pass of the little St. Bernard, which is in this portion of the Alps, was that by which Hannibal effected his march over the Alps. 4. From Mt. Blanc to St. Gothard (*Adŭlas*) were the *Alpes Penninae* v. *Summae*, the central and highest of the whole range. Then follow eastward *Alpes Rhaeticae, Carnicae, Juliae*, whose respective limits it is not easy to define, till they reach the *Sinus Flanaticus*, the gulf of Quarnero.

Of this huge mountain chain, *Adŭla* (St. Gothard) may be regarded as the centre or *nucleus*; for though not the loftiest summit, Mt. Blanc being higher, it occupies, with its surrounding group of mountains, the most elevated ground of the whole range, as plainly appears from the circumstance that the rivers which rise there flow towards every point of the compass.

The chief lines of Roman road in Italy were: VIA APPIA, (*regina viarum*,) leading at first from Rome to Capua, and continued onwards to *Brundusium*, the great high road to Greece : VIA FLAMINIA, by *Ocriculum* to *Arimĭnum*: VIA AURELIA, along the coast of Etruria to *Pisae*; continued afterwards to Savona, and at last to *Arelăte*, Arles : VIA AEMILIA, first from *Ariminum* to *Bononia*, then through *Placentia* to *Mediolanum, Verona, Patavium*, and *Aquileia*: VIA CASSIA, through Etruria, between the *Aurelia* and *Flaminia*: VIA VALERIA, through the country of the *Sabini, Aequi*, and *Marsi*, into that of *Peligni*: VIA LATINA, through *Tusculum, Anagnia, Venafrum*, and *Teănum Sidicini* to *Casilinum*, where it joined the VIA APPIA.

Italy so abounds in antiquities, that a few only of the most remarkable can be added here to those already mentioned. At Capua, Casĭnum, Puteŏli, and Verŏna, are ruins of amphitheatres : that of the last-named was built to accommodate 30,000 spectators, and has suffered so little from time as to have been used on several public occasions in modern times. It is 1416 feet in circumference : the Colisium at Rome is 1719. Numberless ancient remains have been uncovered and dug up at Herculaneum and Pompeii, two towns on the Bay of Naples, which were overwhelmed in an eruption of Mount Vesuvius, A. D. 79, the former by a stream of lava, the latter by a shower of hot ashes. At *Paestum*, twenty leagues from Naples, are the ruins of three beautiful temples, of the simplest Doric order, and of great antiquity. At *Narnia*, are the remains of a bridge built by Augustus. On the road from Naples to Puzzuoli is the *Crypta Neapolitana*, Grotto of Pausilippo, a gallery or tunnel through a hill, 2323 feet in length, described by Seneca, and of unknown antiquity.

The most remarkable ancient remains and localities are in ROME itself. (MAP 10.) To begin with the *seven* hills, viz. : the Capitoline, Palatine, Aventine, Caelian, Esquiline, Viminal, and Quirĭnal. 1. On the Capitol were the temples of Jupiter *Feretrius* and Jupiter *Capitolinus*, and the *Tabularium*, or register-office. 2. The Palatine, on which Rome was originally built, (thence called *Roma Quadrata*, from the form of that hill,) was afterwards almost entirely covered with the *palace* of Augustus and the Temple of Apollo, with the library attached to it: of all which nothing remains but a few substructions. 3. The Aventine, the seat of the robber Cacus, and long held unlucky from the fate of Remus, contained afterwards the Temple of Diana, built by Servius Tullius, the Temple of Juno, vowed by Camillus at Veii, whence the statue of the goddess was brought, and the Temple of Bona Dea, consecrated by the vestal Claudia : on the east slope of this hill were the Baths of Caracalla, the ruins of which still remain. 4. On the Caelian, called also *Querquetulanus*, stood the palace of the *Laterani* family, presented to the Church by Constantine, and now called the church of St. John *Lateran*: near which stood the statue of Marcus Aurelius, since removed to the Capitol. Here also is the remnant of a noble portico, supposed to be part of the *Curia Hostilia*. Between the Palatine, Esquiline, and Caelian, lies the amphitheatre of Vespasian, called the *Coliseum*. 5. On the Esquiline, the baths and palace of Titus, among the ruins of which was found the famous statue of Laocŏon, and the mansion and gardens of Maecenas, on what was once a burying-ground. 6. To the east of the Viminal Hill, which, from the levelling and filling up, it is more difficult to trace than any of the rest, stood the baths of Diocletian : still farther eastward, beyond the *Agger* of *Tarquinius*, was the Praetorian Camp. 7. On the Quirinal Hill, now Monte Cavallo, stood the temple of the deified Romulus, Sallust's house and gardens, which extended over the Pincian hill or *Collis Hortulorum*, the *Campus Sceleratus*. and baths of Constantine.

These seven hills were all on the *left* bank of the

Tiber: on the *right* or Etrurian side were the *Janiculum* and *Mons Vaticanus*.

Between the Quirinal and Capitoline was Trajan's Forum, in the centre of which stands the *Columna Trajana*, representing his Dacian conquests.

The *Campus Martius* was a plain inclosed by a bend of the Tiber, and bounded by the Capitoline and Quirinal hills. It was originally used as a place of exercise and for the meetings of the people, but towards the end of the republic it began to be occupied with buildings, and was enclosed by the Emperor Aurelian within the walls. Amongst those buildings were, 1. The mausolēum of Augustus, the first distinguished tenant of which was young Marcellus, son of Augustus' sister Octavia, and heir of the empire, whose premature death is so pathetically lamented by Virgil: 2. The Antonine pillar: 3. *Septa Julia*, or *Ovilia*, inclosures for the people to vote in—rude at first, and wattled with twigs, like *sheep*-hurdles; afterwards, when the people had no free voice, made of marble: 4. The Temple of Minerva, built by Pompey out of the spoils of thirty years' successful war: 5. The *Panthĕon*, Rotonda, the best preserved of all the ancient temples: 6. *Circus Agonalis:* 7. Pompey's theatre, whence were visible the *Janiculum* and *Mons Vaticanus*, on the Tuscan side of the Tiber. The latter hill was added to modern Rome by the popes, and contains the church and dome of St. Peter, and the Vatican library.

Other remarkable places in ROME were,

1. *Forum Romanum*, the great centre of business, commercial and political, lying between the Capitoline and Palatine hills. Here stood, 1. the temple of Jupiter Stator, of which three pillars still remaining are supposed to be part: 2. the Temple of Concord, where the Senate usually met: 3. the Temple of Jupiter Tonans, or rather of Saturn, at the foot of the *Clivus Capitolinus:* 4. the triumphal arch of Septimius Severus, still pretty entire: near which was the *Milliarium Aureum* (*umbilicus Romae*): and, 5. the *Comitium*. The *Via Sacra* led from the *Forum* towards the *Colisĕum:*

2. *Circus Maximus*, between the Capitoline and Aventine, for the exhibition of chariot races, and other contests of strength and agility:

3. *Velābrum*, the low ground between the Palatine and the river:

4. The *bridges* over the Tiber in Rome, seven in number: *Pons Sublicius*, called afterwards, when built of stone, *Aemilius; Fabricius* and *Cestius*, leading to and from *Insula Tiberina*, the island of Aesculapius; *Palatinus* or *Senatorius*, now Ponte Rotto; *Vaticanus* or *Triumphalis;* these five are more or less destroyed; *Janiculensis*, now Ponte di Sisto; and *Aelius*, built by Adrian to give access to his magnificent mausoleum, now the bridge and castle of St. Angelo.

MACEDONIA, THRACIA, ILLYRICUM, AND THE PROVINCES ON THE MIDDLE AND LOWER DANUBE.—(MAP 7.)

BETWEEN Italy and the Danube lay the countries of *Rhaetia, Noricum, Pannonia, Illyricum*.

RHAETIA occupied the Central Alps, together with their northern and southern valleys, from the sources of the *Rhone* to those of the *Dravus* (Drave) and *Plavis* (Piave). Rhaetia comprehended, therefore, the Grisons and great part of the Tyrol, besides some Italian valleys. The people seem to have been of Celtic origin.

Noricum extended from the Inn to the line of hills which abut upon the Danube above Vienna, called by the Romans *Mons Cetius*, a prolongation of the *Alpes Noricae*, or Styrian Alps; and from the Danube to the Carnian Alps and the river *Savus* (Save). It was watered by the *Iuvavus*, (Salza,) an affluent of the Inn, and the *Murus*, which flows into the Drave in Pannonia. Its principal cities were *Lauriacum*, (Lorch,) a Roman naval station on the Danube, *Iuvavum*, (Salzburg,) *Noreia*, (Neumarch,) near the Mur, and *Celeia*, (Cilli,) near the Save. This country was famous for its iron, and for the skill of the inhabitants in working it.

East of Noricum, lying along the Danube to the mouth of the Save, was PANNONIA, first reduced to a Roman province by Tiberius, and subsequently divided into *Superior* or Western, and *Inferior* or Eastern Pannonia. It occupied a part of Hungary and Croatia. *Mons Pannonius* (Bakonyer Wald) was the principal mountain range. The Danube, with its tributaries, the *Dravus* (Drave) and *Savus*

(Save), were the most important rivers. We should not omit to mention two great lakes in this country, *Peiso Lacus* (the Nensiedler See) and *Volcea Palus* (Lake Balaton)

In *Pannonia Superior* was *Vindobona* (Vienna); but its chief city was *Carnuntum*, (Altenburg,) near the modern Presburg, but on the right bank of the river. Roman fortresses on the Danube were *Arrabona* (Raab) and *Acincum* (Ofen or Buda). On the opposite side of the river here, lay *Contra Acincum* (Pesth). *Siscia* stood upon the Save, near the confines of Illyricum; and lower down, on the same stream, *Sirmium*, a place of great celebrity and importance in the latter ages of the Roman empire.

South of Pannonia, bounded on the west by the Adriatic and on the east by Moesia, lay ILLYRICUM, occupied by various tribes. The Dinaric Alps, under the names of *Mt. Albanus* and *Bebii Montes*, formed the principal range. The *Colapis* (Kulpa) and *Drinus* (Drino), tributaries of the Save and the *Naro* (Narenta), are the chief rivers. In Dalmatia was *Salona*, near the modern Spalatro, the birthplace and retreat of Diocletian; and below it *Epidaurus*, or old Ragusa. Below Epidaurus are *Scodra* and *Lissus;* the former was called Scutari, the latter Alessio.

MOESIA is bounded on the west by Pannonia and Illyricum; on the south, it was divided from Macedonia and Thrace by *Mt. Scordus* and *Haemus*, the ranges of Gliubotin and the Balkan; on the east, it reaches to the Euxine; and on the north, to the Danube—thus occupying the present *Servia* and *Bulgaria*. In *Moesia Superior* the principal river was the *Margus* (Morava). At the confluence of the Danube and Save was *Singidunum*, now Belgrade. Somewhat lower down the river was a ridge of rocks, forming a cataract in the Danube—the spot at which the river was reputed to change its name from *Danubius*, above, to *Ister*, below. A little above this spot was the famous stone bridge of Trajan. Below it is *Ratiaria*, the ancient metropolis of Dacia, and the station of a fleet upon the Danube. In the interior is *Naissus*, (Nissa,) the birthplace of Constantine the Great; and south-east is *Sardica*, the metropolis of Dacia, and celebrated for a Christian council. East of the river *Ciabrus* was *Moesia Inferior.*

North of the Danube was the vast province of DACIA, bounded by this river on one side and by the Carpathian mountains on the other. Its chief city was *Sarmizegetusa*, now Gradisca, the ancient residence of the Dacian kings.

South-east of Illyricum was MACEDONIA, situated between the countries just enumerated and Greece proper, and participating in the nature of both. *Macedonia* was bounded on the south by Thessalia, on the east by Thracia, from which it was separated by the river *Nestus*, on the north by Moesia and Dardania, on the west by the Adriatic; the Aegean bounded it on the south-east, running up into two great gulfs, the *Sinus Strymonicus* and *Thermaicus*, between which were the peninsulas of *Acte, Sithonia,* and *Pallène*. Near the Thessalian frontier and the sea is *Mons Pierius*, and in the peninsula of Acte, *Mons Athos*.

The chief rivers were the *Haliacmon* and *Axius*, (Vardar,) flowing into the Thermaic gulf; the *Strymon*, into the gulf which bears its name; and the *Nestus*, which falls into the Aegean.

Of cities, we have to mention *Pydna*, where Perseus was baffled in his last effort against the Romans, B. C. 168. Farther north, on a lake fifteen miles from the sea, was *Pella*, the capital of Macedon, where Philip, the father of Alexander, resided. Pursuing again the line of coast, we come to *Thessalonica*, at the head of the Sinus Thermaicus. It was to the Christians of that city that St. Paul addressed his two epistles to the Thessalonians. Near the mouth of the Strymon we find *Stageirus* or *Stageira*, the birthplace of Aristotle. In the country between the rivers Strymon and Nestus, at some distance from the sea, was the battle-field of *Philippi*.

On crossing the Nestus, we find ourselves in THRACIA, a country the coast of which extended from the Nestus along the shores of the Aegean, the Hellespont, the Propontis, the Thracian Bosporus, and the Euxine sea, as far north as Mt. Haemus, which was its northern boundary.

Along the seaboard, from the Nestus eastward, we come upon *Abdēra*, the inhabitants of which formed, on account of their alleged stupidity, the laughing stock of antiquity; it was the birthplace of Democritus.

Farther east, we reach the mouth of *Hebrus*, connected with the myth of Orpheus.

Next comes the Thracian peninsula called *Chersonēsus*, on the eastern side of which is the strait named *Hellespontus*. The Hellespont widens into the sea lake called *Propontis*, and at the side of *Byzantium*, it contracts again into that which was called the *Thracian Bospŏrus*, (Strait of Constantinople, MAP 26,) which, after keeping the two continents narrowly asunder, opens out again into *Pontus Euxinus* (the Euxine or Black sea). At the northern extremity of the strait are some rocky islets, known under the name of the *Symplegădes*. (Thracian Bosporus, Map 26.)

Among the Greek colonies on the shore of the Euxine, belonging to Thrace, we mention *Salmydessus* and *Apollonia*.

GRAECIA.—(MAPS 15, 16, 17, 18, 19.)

THE name *Graecia* was not used by the Greeks themselves. They called themselves, generally, *Hellenes*, and their country *Hellas*. From this generic name, the Macedonians and Epirotes were jealously excluded; it was with some hesitation that the Acarnanians, Aetolians, and Thessalians, were included under it, though among these last lay the original seat of the little tribe of Hellenes, from whom it was actually derived. Homer mentions the Hellenes once only, and then as a specific tribe of Greeks; when he speaks of the Greeks collectively, he calls them *Achaei*, (Lat. Achivi,) *Danai*, and *Argaei*, (Lat. Argivi,) names which also belong properly to particular tribes.

Taking Greece in its most extended sense, including all the northern semi-Greek countries, we may compare it to a triangle, having the mountain chain of Haemus for its base, the coast lines of the Aegean and Ionian seas for its sides, and Cape *Taenărum*, (Matapan,) the southern extremity of the *Peloponnesus*, for its apex. This triangular space is nearly bisected by the chain of PINDUS and its adjuncts, which constitute the water-shed of the whole country, separating the rivers on the eastern side, which flow into the Aegean, from those on the western, which flow into the Ionian sea.

PELOPONNESUS—MOREA.—(MAP 18.)

The leaf-shaped peninsula so called is almost entirely covered with mountainous elevations and the well-watered valleys between them. This is particularly the case with the central region, ARCADIA, which, on this account, was assigned to the god of shepherds, and is identified in our language with images of pastoral life and rural simplicity.

Among the MOUNTAINS, the most noted were, 1. *Cyllĕne*, reputed by ancients and moderns to be the highest of them all, and fabled to have been the birthplace of Mercury: 2. *Lycaeus*, and, 3. *Maenălus*, both favorite haunts of Pan: 4. *Tăygĕtus*, the resort of Spartan maidens, a range of mountains now called, from its five peaks, Pentedactylon, which runs from N. to S., till it terminates at the bluff promontory of *Taenărum*, (Matapan,) the southern point of Greece, where Virgil places one of the approaches to the infernal regions: 5. *Stymphălus*, a mountain, town, and lake, where dwelt the voracious birds *Stymphalīdes*, that fed on human flesh, the destruction of which was one of the twelve labors of Hercules: 6. *Erymanthus*, the haunt of the boar, to destroy which was another of the prescribed tasks of Hercules.

The chief RIVERS of Peloponnesus were the two following: 1. ALPHEIUS, by much the largest and longest. On its right bank, not a great way from the embouchure, was the town of Pisa, and near it, the plain of *Olympia*, where the most famous of the Greek games were celebrated the first month of every fifth year—a period of time which was called an Olympiad, and formed the basis of Greek chronology. Here also was the sacred grove *Altis*, planted by Hercules, and adorned with the renowned statue of Jupiter by Phidias. The Alpheius, in its course, disappears under ground for a time, which gave rise to the fiction of the river-god making his way under the sea to meet his Arethusa in the Sicilian island Ortygia. The Alpheius is joined, on the right side, by the *Helisson*, on which was *Megalopŏlis*, birthplace of the historian Polybius and of Philopoemen, 'the last of the Greeks;' and by the *Ladon*. Among the mountains where Alpheius rises, was *Mantineia*, (MAP 26,) the scene of the second great victory of the Theban Epaminondas over the Lacedaemonians, and of his death:

2. The other river of note was the *Eurŏtas*. It rises not far from the Alpheius, on the opposite slope of the water-shed, and flows through a basin bounded on the W. by *Tăygĕtus*, on the E. by Mts. *Parnon* and *Zarax*. On its banks was the city of SPARTA v. LACEDAEMON, the great rival of Athens, not in arts, but in arms.

The other localities in the Peloponnesus worth noting will be best learned in connection with the *six* little departments—*five* maritime and *one* inland

—into which it was divided, viz. : 1. ACHAIA, bounded on the N. by *Sinus Corinthiăcus*, (Gulf of Lepanto,) and including *Corinthia* and *Sicyonia;* 2. ELIS; 3. MESSENIA; 4. LACONIA; 5. ARGŎLIS; and, 6. ARCADIA.

1. In *Achaia*, on the *Isthmus*, was *Corinthus*. It had a port on each side of the Isthmus, *Lechaeum* on the Corinthian gulf, and *Cenchrĕae* on the Saronic—hence the epithet *bimaris*. The Citadel was on the summit of a rock called *Acrocorinthus*, whence sprang the fountain *Pirĕne*.

2. In *Elis*, besides Pisa and Olympia, on the *Alpheius*, was *Pylus*, one of three towns of that name which claimed to be the city of Nestor, the sage of the Iliad.

3. In MESSENIA, in the basin of the stream *Pamĭsus*, was *Messēne* and its citadel *Ithŏme*, called by Philip of Macedon one of the 'horns of the Peloponnesus,' *Acrocorinthus* being the other.

4. On the Laconian coast were the two promontories, *Taenărum*, already mentioned, and *Malĕa*, or Malēa, a cape dangerous to mariners.

5. In *Argolis* were *Argos* v. *Argi*, a favorite city of Juno, and *Mycēnae*, the city of Agamemnon, *Tiryns*, the reputed birthplace of Hercules, *Lerna* and its marsh, the abode of the many-headed Hydra, which it was one of the twelve labors of Hercules to destroy, and *Nemĕa*, the haunt of the Nemean lion, the killing of which was another of those labors.

6. In the inland ARCADIA, besides the places mentioned above, was the town *Tegĕa*. *Cleitor* with its fountain, said to render those who drank of it averse to wine.

GRAECIA PROPRIA.—(MAP 16.)

The isthmus of Corinth connects *Peloponnesus* with Greece proper, the notable localities of which will be best indicated by referring each to the ancient division, as well as to the river, where there is one, on which it was situated. These divisions were ATTICA, MEGARIS, BOEOTIA, PHOCIS, DORIS, LOCRIS, AETOLIA, and ACARNANIA.

1. In *Attica* stood ATHENAE, with her *Acropŏlis* and its *Parthĕnon*, and her triple harbor (*Peiraeus, Munychia*, and *Phalĕrum*); *Eleusis;* the plain of *Marăthon*, memorable for the defeat of the Persians, B. C. 490, (A. U. C. 263,) (MAP. 26); Mt. *Pentelĭcus*, (Mendeli,) which furnished marble for the building of the Parthenon; the silver-mines of *Laurium;* and the southern promontory *Sunium*, crowned with the temple of Minerva Sunias, the pillars of which still standing give name to the modern Cape Colonne.

2. In BOEOTIA the low country was proverbial for its thick atmosphere and the *pingue ingenium* of its inhabitants; but the mountains *Cithaeron* and *Helicon*, with its fountain *Hippocrĕne*, and the hills which enclose the plain, were all of a character so opposite, that, under the general name of *Aonĭa*, they were celebrated by the poets as the favorite haunts of the Muses, who were hence called *Aonĭdes*, *Aoniae puellae*, and *Heliconĭdes* v. *Heliconĭădes*. In BOEOTIA were the towns of THEBAE, the capital, birthplace of Epaminondas and Pindar; south of it, *Plataeae*, (MAP 26,) where the confederated Greeks defeated the Persians under Mardonius; and *Leuctra*, (MAP 26,) where Epaminondas gained his first victory over the Lacedaemonians, B. C. 371, (A. U. C. 383). On the narrow strait called *Eurĭpus*, which separates Boeotia from Euboea, was *Aulis*, where the Grecian fleet destined for Troy was detained by contrary winds, till Agamemnon consented to the required sacrifice of his daughter Iphigenĭa.

3. Of PHOCIS, the remarkable features were, 1. The fountain-head and early course of the *Cephissus*, (major,) whose lower basin formed the northern portion of Boeotia: 2. Mt. *Parnassus*, sacred to Apollo. Between the two peaks was *fons Castalius*, and farther down, on the *Pleistus*, of which the Castalian spring is a feeder, stood the Temple of Apollo, and in it the Tripod of the Pythia, and the Delphic Oracle.

4. AETOLIA was famous in early Greek story as the country ravaged by the Caledonian boar, which was slain at last by Meleager. *Achelŏus*, the longest and largest of Grecian rivers, and fabled by the poets to have been the first created, forms the boundary between Aetolia and

5. ACARNANIA, (MAP 15,) a district which lies between Achelŏus and the Ambracian gulf. At the entrance of this gulf, near the promontory *Actium*, the naval battle was fought between Augustus and Marc Antony, which secured to the former the undisputed sovereignty of the Roman world, B. C. 31.

6. Between the Ambracian gulf and the Acroceraunian promontory lay the extensive region of EPIRUS, famed for its breed both of horses and of watch-dogs,—the latter called Molossian, from *Molossis*, a district of Epirus,—and still more famous for the most ancient of all the Greek oracles, *Dodŏna*

Having now reached the western limits of Greece, we return eastward to the Aegean shore, and find (lying to the N. of Greece proper, and separated from it by Mt. *Oeta*, which is an offset from the Pindus chain) the country called by the ancients

THESSALIA.—(MAP 15.)

Physically considered, THESSALIA is made up of the basin of the river *Peneius*. It is a territory containing 4000 square miles of surface, and is singular in being encompassed on all the *four* sides, even the side facing the sea, by ranges of mountains; on the west by *Pindus*; on the north by *Montes Cambunii* and M. *Pierus*; on the south by M. *Othrys*; and on the east and north-east by *Pelion, Ossa*, and *Olympus*, the three hills by the piling of which, one upon the other, the fabled giants attempted to scale the heavens. To the continuity of this mountain-chain there is but one interruption—a rent in the rocky barrier between Olympus and Ossa, and through it the single main river of Thessaly proper finds its way to the Aegean. This outlet of the *Peneius* bore the name of *Tempe*, a valley which in some places is so narrow as barely to allow the river to pass between the opposite cliffs.

On one of the tributaries of the Peneius called *Apidănus*, where it is joined by its feeder *Enīpeus*, lies the field where the battle of *Pharsalus* was fought between Caesar and Pompey, B. C. 48, (A. U. C. 705). On the *Peneius* itself, below the point where the *Apidănus* falls into it, stood *Larissa*, which some describe as the city of Achilles; but that honor belongs rather to another *Larissa*, not within the limits of the great basin, but in that south-eastern portion of Thessaly called *Phthiōtis*, the country of the *Dolŏpes* and the *Myrmidŏnes*.

Owing to the deep indentations, numerous projections, and great irregularity of the line of coast, the headlands and bays make an important feature of the geography of Greece.

Of the former, *Taenărum, Malea, Sunium*, and *Caphăreus*, have been already mentioned; to which may be added *prom. Rhium* (south) and *Antirrhium* (north), which nearly block up the entrance of the *Sinus Corinthiăcus; Araxus*, the north-west point of Peloponnesus; *Chelonates*, the farthest west, and *Acrītas* in Messenia.

The bays and gulfs connected with Peloponnesus were *Sinus Corinthiăcus, Messeniacus, Laconĭcus, Argolĭcus*, and *Saronĭcus:* in the last of these were the islands of *Calauria*, where Demosthenes

died; *Aegīna*, once the rival of Athens at sea; and in front of the harbor of Athens, *Salămis*, off the east end of which the fleet of Xerxes was defeated by the Athenians, B. C. 480. In continental Greece were the *Sinus Maliăcus*, (Zeitoun); *Pagasaeus*, (Volo,) so called from the town *Pagăsae;* and along the coast of Macedonia, *Sinus Thermaicus*, (Salonichi,) *Toronaicus, Singitĭcus*, and *Strymonĭcus*.

The most noted islands pertaining to Greece are:

I. In the Ionian sea—1. *Corcȳra*, (Corfu,) thought to be the Homeric *Scheria*, the island of the Phaeacians, where lived the suitors of Penelope: 2. *Ithăca*, the home of Ulysses: 3. *Zacynthus*, (Zante,) a colony from which is said to have peopled and given name to Saguntum: 4. Off the west coast of Peloponnesus the rocks called *Strophădes*, (Strivali,) the haunts of the harpies. To the south of the Laconian promontory *Malea*, was *Cythĕra*, an island sacred to Venus: still farther south is CRETA, with the cities of *Cnossus*, the capital of King Minos, *Gortȳna*, and *Cydonia*, all three famed for archery. Of its mountains, *Ida* was the loftiest, and on *Dicte* Jupiter was said to have been reared, and fed upon honey and the milk of the goat Amalthēa. The sea around the island was called *Creticum*.

II. Of the islands lying to the east of Greece and in the Aegean sea, we shall name first those worthy of mention which are situated to the north of the 38th parallel of latitude. They are,

1. *Euboea*, an island stretching 150 miles along the coast of Boeotia and Attica, and approaching so near the continent in the channel called *Eurīpus*, that a bridge is said to have been at one time thrown across. On this channel was the chief city of the island, *Chalcis*, opposite to *Aulis* in Boeotia. In doubling *Caphăreus*, a promontory at the south-east extremity of Euboea, the Grecian fleet on its return from Troy was overtaken by a storm, which partly destroyed and partly dispersed it:

2. *Samothrăce*, where the Corybantes practised the rites and mysteries of Cybĕle:

3. *Lemnos*, an island sacred to Vulcan:

4. *Tenĕdos*, an island in sight of Troy:

5. Directly south is *Lesbos*, birthplace of Alcaeus and Sappho, the two great lyric poets of Greece:

6. *Chios*, (Scio,) one of the seven places which contended for the honor of giving birth to Homer. *Chios* was also noted for its wines.

The numerous islets in the Aegean, in latitudes lower than 38°, are generally classed under two denominations, *Cyclădes* and *Sporădes*.

I. The CYCLADES, a group which cluster round DELOS—that floating island which Neptune fixed with his trident as a resting-place for Latona to give birth to Apollo and his twin-sister Diana.

Of this group the most noted, after *Delos*, were,

1. *Paros*, famed for its statuary marble, and the birthplace of Phidias, the sculptor who made the noblest use of it:

2. *Ceos*, off the promontory of *Sunium*, birthplace of the elegiac poet Simonides:

3. South of Delos, *Naxos*, an island that figures in the history of Bacchus and Ariadne:

II. The *scattered* islets to the east and south-east of the Cyclädes were called from that circumstance SPORADES. They extended as far E. as *Icaria*, which took its name, as did the sea around it, from the fabled fate of Icarus, the son of Daedalus, and as far S. E. as *Carpäthos*, (Scarpanto,) which in like manner gave to the waters round it the name of *Carpathium Pelagus*. Between Icaria and the continent was *Samos*, birthplace of Pythagoras, and a favorite island of Juno.

GENERAL OBSERVATIONS ON GREECE.

The chain of Pindus, of which we have already spoken as dividing the waters that fall into the Aegean from those that fall into the Ionian sea, has numerous lateral branches, which on the *east* side go off nearly at right angles, like ribs from the spine: such are the mountains of Argŏlis, of Attica, and those which form the northern and southern boundaries of Thessaly; while on the *west* side these offsets are disposed in ridges nearly parallel to Pindus itself.

The lateral branches which are on the *east* side of PINDUS inclose a great number of *basins*, the most remarkable of which are as follows, beginning from the north:

1. The Basin of the Strymon, including the Macedonian plain of Serres, distinguished by the fertility of its soil and the abundance of its products, particularly of cotton:

2. The Basin of the Peneius, forming the country of Thessaly. Being nearly circular, and not opening wide to the sea, like most other basins, it has every appearance of having once been a great lake, whose waters were at last discharged, either by the sudden disruption, or by the gradual wearing down, of the narrow ravine called the Vale of Tempe:

3. The valley of the Sperchius, inclosed by the mountain ranges of Othrys and Oeta:

4. The Basin of the northern Cephissus, which

4

includes a great part of DORIS and BOEOTIA. The river, arriving at low and spongy ground, spreads out into the lake *Copäis*, now Topolias, whose waters find their way to the Aegean sea by subterranean passages:

5. The Basin of the Alpheius, in the Peloponnesus, though the course of the river is westward, may be enumerated as a fifth. The Alpheius, rising on the confines of Laconia, collects in its course all the streams produced on the interior summits and sides of the mountain chain that encircles Arcadia.

The basins on the *west* side of PINDUS are longer and narrower, and, owing to the position of the mountain ridges, extend generally in a north-east and south-west direction. In Greece proper are the Basins of the Achelöus and Evēnus: those farther to the north are less memorable.

The Mountains of Greece are almost entirely lime·stone, which assumes the shape, in some places, of long, sharp, continuous ridges; in others, of round craggy summits, with strata highly inclined. It is to this physical conformation of the soil and surface of Greece that she owes many of her natural features and peculiarities—such as, the numerous caverns, fountains, *katabothra*, or under-ground river coursse, hot springs, stalactitic incrustations, and gaseous exhalations, which, among a people of lively fancy and abounding with traditionary story, served to nourish, if they did not give birth to, much of the popular superstition and beautiful mythology of the Greeks.

The height of the principal mountains has not been accurately ascertained. Orbēlus, now Argentaro, is covered with perpetual snow, and must therefore, being in the latitude of 42°, have at least 8000 feet of perpendicular elevation. The range of Pindus is considerably lower, probably from five to six thousand feet at the highest. Mount Athos rises to the height of 4350 English feet.

The Rivers of Greece, with the exception of those that form the basins enumerated, and some of their tributaries, are of short course, and often little more than winter torrents, ($\chi \epsilon \iota \mu a \rho \rho o \iota$,) whose channels are dry in summer. Such, for example, is the famed Ilissus at Athens.

A distinguishing feature of Graecia Propria and Peloponnesus, and one which had a considerable influence in the first moulding of its political condition, is the frequent occurrence of rich plains, overlooked and commanded by abrupt insulated rocks rising in the middle or at one end of them, and bounded at no great distance by mountains. These plains and natural fortresses, presenting facilities for subsistence, defence, and retreat, attracted population, and encouraged the forming of small independent communities. Such were Thebes, Argos, Messene, and Corinth.

Antiquities. — Some curious specimens of the colossal architecture called Cyclopean, much more ancient than the classical times of Greece, still remain at Mycēnae, Argos, Tiryns, etc.: it is rude in its form and gigantic in its dimensions, and probably the work of the same people, who have left still more numerous and striking examples of it in Italy. Of the classical age, the remains are principally temples, and the most remarkable of these are in and about Athens. On the *Acropolis* are still to be found the ruins of the *Propylaea*, the *Parthĕnon*, or Temple of Minerva, that of Victory, the united Temples of Neptune, Erechtheus, and Minerva Polias, built on the spot where the contest between Minerva and Neptune was supposed to have taken place, the *Pandroseion*, in honor of Pandrŏsos, daughter of Cecrops On the plain below the Acropolis, the Temple ot Theseus, *Theseion;* and near it, the comparatively modern arch of Hadrian, and the Temple of Jupiter Olympius, *Olympieion*, begun by Pisistratus, and dedicated 700 years after by the Empcror Hadrian.

In the city of Athens and its suburbs, (MAP 17,) the most remarkable points were — the *Areopăgus*, the *Pnyx*, where the assemblies of the people were held, the theatre of Bacchus, the *Ceramīcus*, including the *Agŏra* or *Forum*, *Prytanĕum*, the Schools, viz., the *Lycĕum* of Aristotle, the *Academia* of Plato, the portico called Στοα Ποικιλή, in Latin, *Poecile*, where Zeno the *Stoic* taught, and *Cynosarges*, frequented by Antisthĕnes and the Cynics.

ASIA MINOR.—(MAP 20.)

THE country which we call *Asia Minor* was called by the ancients *Asia* simply, and has now the name of *Anatolia*. Surrounded on three sides by the sea, it has something of the character of a peninsula. It is bounded on the north by the Pontus Euxinus (Euxine or Black Sea) and the Propontis; on the west by the Aegean; and on the south by the Mediterranean. On the east, it is separated from the main continent of Asia by the river Euphrates and the range of the Taurus.

Commencing in the north-east, we find the following towns and localities of interest:

The town *Trapēzūs -untis*, a Greek settlement of great antiquity, which, under the modern form of Trebizond, was a place of considerable note during the Eastern Empire;

Cerăsūs, whence Lucullus transplanted the tree which bears its name in Latin (cherry);

The mouth of the river *Thermŏdon*, whose basin and town, *Themiscŷra*, were assigned as the dwelling-place of the fabled race of female warriors called Amazons;

The river *Halys*, eastern boundary of the Lydian kingdom of Croesus, the crossing of which proved fatal to him in his contest with Cyrus, king of Persia;

Sinŏpe, on a peninsula that juts into the sea, said to have been as old as the Argonautic expedition, at one time capital of the kingdom of Pontus, till taken by Lucullus, and birthplace of Diogenes the Cynic;

Carambis, a promontory opposite to another in the Crimea called *Criumetopon*, (ram's forehead,) at the distance of 150 miles across the Euxine;

Heraclĕa, — surnamed *Pontica* to distinguish it from numerous cities of similar name in the ancient world — chief town of the *Mariandȳni*, and said, like the others, to have been founded by Hercules;

The mouth of the *Sangarius* v. *Sagăris*, which rises in Mt. *Dindȳmon;*

All these localities are in the provinces of ASIA MINOR called *Pontus*, *Paphlagonia*, and *Bithynia*. The other *maritime* provinces of the peninsula are six in number. Of these, three are on the Asiatic shore of the Aegean, viz.: 1. MYSIA, including *Phrygia* Minor and the TROAD (MAP 26); 2. LYDIA v. MAEONIA, including IONIA, which was the seaboard of Lydia, and thickly planted with Greek colonies; and, 3. CARIA, including the district of *Doris*. The other *three* are on the Mediterranean. 1. LYCIA; 2 PAMPHYLIA, including *Pisidia* and *Isauria;* and, 3. CILICIA. In all these six provinces, there are lo alities with whose names and positions every student ought to be made familiar. For example:

1. In MYSIA, it is sufficient to name TROJA or ILION, situated on an eminence between the *Simois* and *Scamander*. The city was overlooked by Mt. *Ida*, and itself overlooked the plain of Troy. Here

also was the river *Granĭcus*, on whose banks Alexander the Great gained his first victory over Darius, B. C. 324, (MAP 26).

2. In LYDIA flowed the river *Hermus*, famed for the gold found in the sand of its channel: near it was the site of *Sardis*, at the foot of Mt. *Tmolus*, the capital of Croesus, king of Lydia. A little way S. of the Hermus was *Smyrna*, on the *Meles*, one of the cities which contended for being the birthplace of Homer. Among the twelve cities that formed the Ionian league, besides *Smyrna*, were *Teos*, birthplace of Anacreon, and *Ephĕsus*, birthplace of the weeping philosopher Heraclĭtus, and of the painter Parrhasius. It was situated at the mouth of the *Caijstrus*, famed among the poets for its swans. Farther south is Mt. *Mycăle*, off which the Greeks gained a signal victory over the Persians, the same day, it is said, on which Mardonius was defeated at *Plataeae*. We next cross the *Maeander*, a river of great length, and so remarkable for its windings as to have furnished an English word descriptive of a similar character in other streams. South of the Maeander, but still to be reckoned an Ionian city, was *Milētus*, from which went most of the Greek colonies that fringed the border of the Euxine Sea. It was noted also for its wool, and was the birthplace of Thales, the earliest of the Greek philosophers.

3. On the coast of CARIA stood *Halicarnassus*, a city memorable as the birthplace of the great historians Herodotus and Dionysius, and for the sepulchral monument of Mausŏlus, reared by his queen Artemisia. On the opposite side of the bay stood *Cnidus*, where was a statue of *Venus*, reckoned the master-work of Praxitelès; and at the entrance of this bay, mid-way between *Halicarnassus* and *Cnidus*, lay the island *Cōs*, birthplace of the famous physician and medical writer Hippocrates, and of Apelles, the most celebrated of Grecian painters. Cos was noted also for its wines, and for the manufacture of fine cloth. Off the coast of Caria is another island much larger and more noted than Cos, viz., *Rhodos*, Rhodes, in the capital of which, of the same name, was the brazen statue of the sun, called *Colossus*, 70 cubits high, which bestrode the entrance of the harbor.

4. Moving eastward, along the Carian shore, we enter LYCIA, and pass under the wooded *Cragus*, one of the extremities of Mt. TAURUS, and a favorite resort of Diana. Having crossed the *Xanthus*, we arrive at *Patăra*, the winter residence, according to the poets, of Apollo, as *Delos* was his favorite dwelling-place in summer. Farther east, after

rounding the *Prom. Sacrum*, we find *Mons Chimaera*.

5. In PAMPHYLIA, the only point of interest is the town *Phasēlis*.

6. CILICIA extends from the eastern limit of Pamphylia to the *Sinus Issĭcus* and Mt. *Amānus*, and has the mountain chain of *Taurus* for its northern boundary. The western portion of Cilicia is *rough* and hilly, and was thence called *Tracheia:* the eastern, being more level and fertile, was called *Pedias*. On the coast of the latter, as we approach the river *Cydnus*, we pass through *Soli*. We then come to the *Cydnus*, by ascending which we arrive at *Tarsus*, the capital of the province, and the birthplace of St. Paul. The last town in Cilicia, situated at the head of the *Sinus Issĭcus*, was *Issus*, (MAP 26,) where Alexander gained his second great victory over the Persians, and made prisoners of war the wife, mother, and infant son of Darius. In this neighborhood were also the *Pylae Amanĭcae* and *Pylae Syriae*, narrow passes or gorges in *Amānus*, the mountain range which runs north-east from the bay of Issus till it joins Mt. *Taurus*. Fronting the bay of Issus is *Cyprus*, the favorite island of Venus, and hence the numerous epithets applied to the goddess which are derived from towns and temples therein —such, for example, are *Cypria, Paphia, Idalia, Amathuntia* v. *-thusia,* and *Salaminia.*

The *inland* provinces of Asia Minor were:

1. PHRYGIA, in the centre of which was *Synnăda*, noted for its quarries of variegated marble, which was a costly article of ornamental architecture at Rome. In this province, on the confines of Caria, and not far from the sources of *Maeander,* were also the cities of *Laodicēa* and *Colossae*, the seats of early Christian churches, and *Celaenae*, where mythological history places the scene of the flaying of Marsyas by Apollo:

2. GALATIA v. GALLOGRAECIA, (both terms alluding to the fact of the invasion and settling there of a body of Gallic emigrants,) comprehended the upper portions of the river-basins of *Halys* and *Sangarius,* and the cities of *Pessĭnūs, Ancȳra,* (Angora,) and *Gordium.* 1. The first of these towns, situated at the foot of Mt. *Dindȳmon,* was noted for the worship of Cybĕle. 2. At *Ancȳra,* a temple was erected to Augustus during his lifetime. 3. *Gordium,* before the invasion of the Gauls, was the capital of Phrygia,—the city of Gordius, the father of Midas,—and famous for the story of the Gordian knot:

3. In CAPPADOCIA, the point of greatest interest

is Mt. *Argaeus*, with *Mazăca*, the capital of the province, at the foot of it:

4. West of Cappadocia was the province of LYCAONIA, with its capital *Iconium*, the scene of the labors of St. Paul and Barnabas, as recorded in the Acts of the Apostles:

5. To the N.E. of Cappadocia lay ARMENIA *minor*, in which Pompey founded a city which he called *Nicopŏlis*, in memory of a decisive victory he gained there in the Mithridatic war.

Physical Aspects. — The mountain range called *Amānus* forms the S.E. boundary of Asia Minor, separating it from SYRIA, in like manner as the *Euphrātes* and part of Mt. *Taurus* separate it on the N.E. from *Armenia major*. The Asiatic peninsula— of which we have done little more than trace the seaboard of low rich land that skirts the shores of the Euxine, Propontis, Aegean, and Mediterranean seas —exhibits a central belt of elevated land, abutting on mountain ranges, which slope downward to the respective seas that form its northern and southern boundary. The southern chain is so marked and uninterrupted, that it was early designated by a general name. All ancient geographers agree in calling it TAURUS; but some trace it eastward from Cape *Trogilium* and Mt. *Mycăle* on the Aegean; while Strabo, whose authority is high in what concerns this peninsula, of which he was himself a native, makes it commence from a precipitous and lofty ridge which runs northward from *Prom. Sacrum* and Mt. *Climax* in Lycia. Thence making a sweep to the E., and taking, in one part of its course, the name of *Antitaurus*, it proceeds in a N.E. direction until, as it approaches the Euphrates, it sends off the branch called *Amānus* to the south west, and skirts the course of that river, of which it alters the direction. Another branch of Taurus runs more directly E., bounding to the N. the maritime provinces of Pamphylia and Cilicia. The northern chain connected with Antitaurus, and running W. parallel with the Black Sea, is more broken and scattered than Taurus, and has not therefore been distinguished by a general appellation, but it may be traced westward in the successive ranges of *Paryadres*, *Olgassys*, the two *Olympi* and *Ida*. The central *plateau*, comprehending the four inland provinces already mentioned, is distinguished by a number of lakes without issue, most of them salt, and of rivulets that never reach the sea—facts which attest the general levelness of the surface. That part of Phrygia called anciently *Katakecaumĕne*, (i. e. combusta,) abounds in appearances of scorching and sterility, which Strabo considers as indications of frequent earthquakes and volcanic eruptions.

Antiquities.—Although Asia Minor, especially the coast of the Aegean, was in ancient times the seat of many noble cities, adorned with splendid monuments of art, time and barbarism have either entirely destroyed even the ruins, or left them in such shapeless, scattered, and mutilated masses, as to convey but little information. Not only are there no remains of the famous Temple of Diana at Ephesus, but the very site of the town is disputed. The existence of former civilization is attested by fragments, curious and interesting indeed, but not singly of importance enough to be enumerated in so general an outline as this.

PALAESTINA.—(MAP 21.)

PALAESTINA, PHOENICIA, and JUDAEA, were parts of what was, in classical times, called SYRIA, the tract of land which forms the eastern boundary of the Mediterranean, between Asia Minor and Aegypt.

The physical characteristic of this country is an almost continuous range of MOUNTAINS, stretching from north to south in a direction parallel to the eastern shore of the Mediterranean, and nowhere far distant from it. Though it assumes different local appellations, the chain may be called by the general name of *Libănus*, (the Lebanon of Scripture,) and the highest part of the range is where it diverges into two branches, *Libănus* and *Antilibanus*. To that point, the Hermon of Holy Writ, and the high ground adjoining, may be traced the sources of the three principal, and. indeed only RIVERS, the *Orontes*, *Leontes*, and *Jordānes*.

1. The *Orontes*, (see Map 20,) after flowing northwards during the greater portion of its course, makes a bend to the west, traversing a wide valley between *Mons Pierius* on the north (the termination of *Amānus*) and *Mons Cassius* on the south (the commencement of *Libănus*). On the left bank, twenty miles from the mouth, stood ANTIOCHEIA, long the capital of Syria, and celebrated for the luxury of its inhabitants.

2. The *Leontes*, rising at the point of divergence of *Libănus* and *Antilibanus*, flows south through a widening basin, enclosed between these two ranges, which, from its physical aspect, was called *Coele-Syria.*

3. *Jordānes*, the Jordan, springing from Mt. Hermon, near *Paneas*, afterwards *Caesarēa Philippi*, flows almost due south, forming in its course successively, 1. the Lake *Samochonītis;* 2. the Lake *Tiberias*, known also in the New Testament as 'the Sea of Tiberias,' 'Galilee,' or 'Gennesaret,' on which was situated the city of *Tiberias* (now Tabarieh), so named by Herod Antipas in honor of Tiberius Caesar; and, 3. the *Lacus Asphaltītes*, or Dead Sea, a bituminous lake without issue, in which the Jordan is lost. The banks of this lake are the lowest inhabited land known, being 1312 feet below the level of the Mediterranean.

About half-way between the head of the Dead Sea and the Mediterranean, on the brook Kedron, stood *Hierosolўma*, JERUSALEM, (see plan MAP 21,) the metropolis of Palestine, northeast of which is *Jericho.* To the east of the Jordan, in the valley of the *Jabbok*, were *Gerasa* and *Philadelphia.*

Proceeding from the north along the coast, and passing *Berytus*, (Beirût,) — a Roman colony in the reign of Augustus, — we find ourselves, as we approach the mouth of the *Leontes*, in SIDON, and soon after crossing it, in TYROS, both of which cities are in PHOENICIA. They were the earliest, most enterprising, and wealthiest of all ancient states. Nearly on the same parallel of latitude as Sidon, but considerably to the east beyond the chain of *Antilibănus*, was *Damascus.* Farther south, on the coast, was the town called *Accho* in Scripture, afterwards *Ptolemais*, and the modern St. Jean d'Acre.

The last memorable point in Phoenicia is *Carmelus M.*, soon after passing which we enter PALAESTINA, and reach the town and port of *Caesarēa*, so named in honor of Augustus, more anciently *Turris Stratonis*, the capital of Samaria under the Romans: south-eastward we find *Sebaste*, the old *Samaria;* and returning to the coast, we pass successively *Joppa* and *Ascalon*, places of note during the Crusades. The last point of classical interest near the coast was *Gaza*, which had a port on the sea.

The connection of Palestine with Sacred History not coming within the scope of the present sketch, no allusion has been made to the innumerable points of interest which it presents in relation to the Scriptures—a subject too important to be treated in so limited a space.

ASSYRIA.—(MAP 22.)

WITH regard to the vast continent of Asia, which stretches eastward beyond that peninsular portion of it that we have been examining, it was so imperfectly known to the ancients in the brighter periods of their literary history, that but few notices of it are requisite. The great basins of the *Euphrātes* and *Tigris*, embracing part of ARMENIA and of MEDIA, and the whole of MESOPOTAMIA, ASSYRIA, SUSIANA, and BABYLONIA, are important in themselves, and contain points of considerable interest. Both these rivers rise in *Armenia*, the Euphrates in *Abus*, and the *Tigris* in *Niphātes*, the two eastern terminations of the range of *Taurus* and *Antitaurus;* and after a course, the Euphrates of 1530 miles, the Tigris of 1000, having run nearly parallel to each other, they unite their waters and fall into the *Sinus Persicus.*

1. ARMENIA *major* was chiefly composed of the Basin of the *Araxes*, a river which rises in *Antitaurus*, a few miles from one of the sources of the Euphrates, and after joining the *Cyrus*, which is the northern boundary of Armenia, they flow with united stream into the *Mare Caspium v. Hyrcānum.* On the *left* side of the Araxes, and overlooked by Mt. Ararat on the *right*, was the capital *Artaxăta.*

2. In MESOPOTAMIA, whose name indicates the nature of a country formed by the alluvial deposits of the two large rivers that enclose it on either side, were *Carrhae*, memorable for the defeat and death of Crassus, and *Nisibis*, on the tributary *Mygdonius*, a frontier city of Imperial Rome.

3. ASSYRIA is the left side of the Basin of the *Tigris* during the latter part of its course. On the river itself stood NINUS, Nineveh, the metropolis of the Assyrian Empire. The site and vicinity of this ancient city have been the scene of recent excavations and discoveries, which promise to throw light upon the early records of our race. A little eastward were *Gaugamēla* and *Arbēla*, the scene of the battle with Alexander which sealed the fate of Darius and of the Persian monarchy.

4. BABYLONIA and CHALDAEA occupied the lower part of the Basin of the Euphrates down to its junction with the Tigris, and onward to its mouth in the *Sinus Persicus.* The most noted localities were the following: on the Euphrates, and bisected by it,

BABYLON, one of the most renowned among the cities of remote antiquity. In the latest period of its annals, it was the scene of the death of Alexander the Great. Farther up the river was the plain of *Cunaxa*, where the younger Cyrus was defeated and slain by his brother Artaxerxes; and whence, in consequence of that defeat, began the retreat of the Ten Thousand Greeks, described by Xenophon. (MAP 26.)

The Basin of the *Choaspes*, a tributary of the Euphrates, was the country called *Susiana*, from its capital SUSA, on the river itself.

East of Assyria is Media.

AFRICA.—(MAP 23.)

THE northern coast of Africa extends westward about 2000 miles, from the frontiers of Egypt to the Pillars of Hercules, that is, from long. 25° east, to 6° west: bounded on the north by the Mediterranean; on the south by the deserts of Libya and Sahăra, and by the mountain range of ATLAS. Mauritania Tingitana stretches further to the southwest, beyond the Pillars of Hercules, to where the Atlas M. approaches the Atlantic Ocean.

As we advance westward from *Alexandria*, we arrive at *Paraetonium*, the frontier town of Egypt, two degrees south of which is the most famed of the *oases* which rise like islands, at rare intervals, out of the ocean of arid sand that stretches across the continent of Africa. In this *oasis* was the Temple of Jupiter Ammon, which Alexander the Great went to consult. Returning to the coast, we meet with nothing of classical interest except the *Catabathmus*, or great declivity, which Sallust improperly describes as the boundary between Egypt and Africa, till we reach *Cyrēne*. In the latter days of Greece, *Cyrēne* was a flourishing colony, where art and philosophy were cultivated; but at the present day not a vestige of it remains. Farther along, *Berenīce* is mentioned as a town near which were the Gardens of the *Hesperīdes;* but Virgil places them in *Mauritania*. This brings us successively to the shallows and whirlpools called *Syrtes, major* and *minor*. Near the *Syrtis minor* was the Lake *Tritōnis*, obscurely connected with the mythological history of Minerva, who is often called Tritonia Virgo.

From this point commences a region of great natural fertility, which was long the 'granary' of Rome, and rich in historical recollections. First, we have Africa *propria*, the proper domain of CARTHAGO, (Carchedon,) the great rival of ROME; and twenty-seven miles west, on the *Bagrădas*, was *Utĭca*, where the second Cato, rather than submit to Caesar, put a period to his life, and hence he is distinguished from Cato Major by the epithet *Uticencis*. In the interior is *Zama*, where the elder Scipio defeated Hannibal. We then enter *Numidia*, the country of Jugurtha, and the scene of the first exploits of Metellus *Numi-*dicus, which prepared the way for Marius to finish the war and carry Jugurtha prisoner to Rome. The last western division of this African coast was *Mauritania*, the kingdom of Bocchus and of Juba; bounded on the N. by the Mediterranean, on the W. by the Atlantic, and on the S. by the lofty range of Mt. *Atlas*, which protects it from the encroachments of the ocean of sand that lies beyond. As we approach the Atlantic, we come in sight of *Abȳla* (Rock of Ceuta) and *Calpe* (Rock of Gibraltar), the two Pillars of Hercules, on opposite sides of the *Fretum Herculeum*.

GENERAL OBSERVATIONS ON NORTHERN AFRICA.

The two most remarkable features of this country are, the Great Desert, and the mountain range of Atlas. The former, the largest continuity of barren surface in the known world, extends, under different names, from the shores of the Atlantic to the banks of the Nile, interrupted only by a few *oases*.

The mountain range of ATLAS, which is the northern boundary of the desert called Sahăra or Zaara, stretches from Fezzan to the Atlantic. It rises in successive terraces from the most northern, which does not exceed 580 or 600 yards in height, to the farthest south, which, if it be covered with perpetual snow in lat. 32°, as some travellers affirm, cannot be less than 11,000 feet high. The lower elevations are calcareous; and among them was found the Numidian or Gaetulian marble, an article of luxury in great request among the Romans. The successive gradations are connected by transverse branches running north and south, among which are plains and valleys, watered by streams without issue, and constituting the 'Country of Dates.' Atlas extends eastward from the Atlantic to the *Regio Syrtica*, forming a bulwark against the moving sands of the southern desert.

The streams that descend from the northern side of Atlas water that belt of land, from 60 to 160 miles broad, which was long the granary of the Roman empire, and is now the country of Tunis, Algiers, and Morocco.

AEGYPTUS.—(MAP 24.)

EGYPT is the north-east portion of the great peninsular continent of AFRICA, situated between the Tropic of Cancer (23° 30′) and 31° 30′ N. latitude, and between 30° and 35° E. longitude.

There is perhaps no part of the world, out of Italy and Greece, to which allusion is more frequently made by the poets and orators of antiquity than to Egypt; but no ancient writer who is not a professed geographer goes much into detail, or mentions more than one or two of its towns and localities. The singular nature of the country, the immemorial existence of the pyramids, the dim traditions of a very remote antiquity, the absence of rain, the mighty cataracts and periodical inundations of the river, and, above all, the unexplored and, as the ancients thought, inexplorable fountain-head of the Nile—all combined to throw a charm of sublimity and interest over the whole.

Of the towns so thickly planted on the banks of the Nile, we only mention *Memphis*, on the left bank of the Nile, with the pyramids in its immediate neighborhood. Fifteen miles farther down, the Nile separated into different channels, by all of which its waters found their way to the sea. Of these channels the ancients enumerated seven : the most noted are the two extreme ones, the *Ostium Canopĭcum* W. and *Pelusiăcum* E. These two diverging branches, with the sea-coast line between them, form the sides and base of the triangular space Delta, so called from its resemblance to the capital form of that letter in the Greek alphabet; and by these two channels alone the water of the Nile is now discharged. Twelve miles west from the Canopic embouchure was *Alexandria*, so named after Alexander the Great, who founded it on his way back from the Oasis and Temple of Jupiter Ammon—a great city in ancient times, as it is now under the same name. (MAP 26.)

The annual overflow of the Nile, and the deposit by this of a rich stratum of earthy matter, was the chief cause of the great fertility of Egypt. There were artificial canals, sluices, and a large receptacle called Lake *Moeris*, for the distribution of the water. *Arsinoe* was the capital of the richest portion of Egypt, and near it was the celebrated *Labyrinth*.

GERMANIA.—(MAP 25.)

GERMANIA, in the most extended sense of the term, reached from the Alps to the North and Baltic Seas, and from the Rhine to the Vistula. Viewed physically, this vast parallelogram may be divided into two nearly equal portions—of which the southernmost comprises the great valley of the Danube, and the other is watered by the rivers which flow into the northern seas. We have spoken already of the tribes between the Danube and the Alps, and consider here only the other part.

Of mountains, we find, besides the *Alps, the Jura*, Mt. *Abnŏba*, or the Black Forest, the *Montes Sudeti*, or Riesengebirge, and the Carpates M. From the Jura to the Carpathians, that is, from the Rhine to the sources of the Vistula, this northern range was covered in ancient times by a vast forest, under the general name of the *Silva Hercynia*, which, according to Caesar, extended sixty days' journey in length. Its breadth was, in some parts, nine days' journey. From its northern flanks issued the waters of the *Moenus* (Main) and *Nicer* (Neckar), which fall into the Rhine—of the *Amisia*, (Ems,) *Visurgis*, (Weser,) *Viadrus*, (Oder,) and *Vistula*, (Weichsel). The *Albis*, (Elbe,) rising in the Sudeti Montes, and receiving the *Sala* or Saale on the left, divided ancient Germany north of the Danube into two nearly equal portions, east and west.

The chief political divisions of Germania *north* of the Danube were these : of the tribes adjacent to the Danube, the principal were the *Quadi*, the *Marcomanni*, and the *Hermunduri*. All these, together with the *Suevi*, (who formerly lived in the eastern parts of Germany—in later times, in the south-western,) are comprised under the general name of *Hermiones*. The *Istaevones* inhabited the western regions bordering on the Rhine, and the *Ingaevones* occupied the low countries from the mouth of that river to the Cimbric Chersonesus. The *Lygii* seem to have been a considerable people, between the Viadrus and the Vistula.

Between the Rhine and the North Sea we find the *Frisii:* their country was intersected by a canal made by Drusus, which carried a portion of the waters of the Rhine into the *Lacus Flevo* (now Zuyder Zee). The channel of Drusus is now the Yssel. North-west of the Frisii were the *Chauci:* beyond the mouth of the Elbe were the *Angli, Saxones,* and *Cimbri*—the two first of whom crossed over in a later time into Britain. South of the Chauci were the *Angrivarii* and *Cherusci,* who, under *Arminius,* overthrew Varus and his three legions in the *Silva Teutobergiensis,* near the sources of the Lippe and Ems.

Ascending the Rhine from the coast of the Frisii, we arrive at the *Bructeri,* on the Yssel, and the *Marsi,* on the Lippe. The *Usipetes* and *Tenctheri* were driven across the Rhine by more powerful neighbors. On the *Luppia,* (Lippe,) the *Rura,* (Ruhr,) and *Sigus,* (Sieg,) lived the *Sicambri.* The *Mattiaci* lay between the Sieg and the *Moenus,* (Main,) and occupied the *Mons Taunus.* Southward from hence, the district between the Rhine, the Main, and the Upper Danube, was called by the Romans *Agri Decumates,* from the tithe which they had to pay to the Romans. In this region we find afterward the *Alemanni,* which was probably only a new league of

the old tribes of these regions. Behind the Sicambri, about the sources of the Visurgis, lay the *Chatti,* (Hessians,) a tribe of the Hermiones.

Passing eastward from the valley of the Upper Rhine, we come to the Hermunduri : east of them, on the bank of the Danube, were the *Narisci,* about Ratisbon : north-east of these, the *Boii,* or Boiohemi, in Bohemia, whose country was seized by the *Marcomanni.* North-east of them were the *Osi, Gothini,* and *Buri,* in Silesia : north-west of whom were the *Marsigni,* and farther to the north-west, the *Semnones.*

Among the Lygian tribes between the Viadrus and Vistula, we mention the *Arii, Helvecones, Manimi, Elisii,* and *Naharvali.*

On the shores of the Baltic, and to the south of it, we find Vandal tribes—as the *Varini, Rugii, Lemovii, Reudigni,* and the *Langobardi.*

The Baltic Sea was known to the Romans as *Sinus Codānus,* or *Mare Suevicum.* Tacitus mentions the *Suiones* and *Sitones* (in Sweden and Norway). All the country east of the Vistula was comprised under the name of *Sarmatia.*

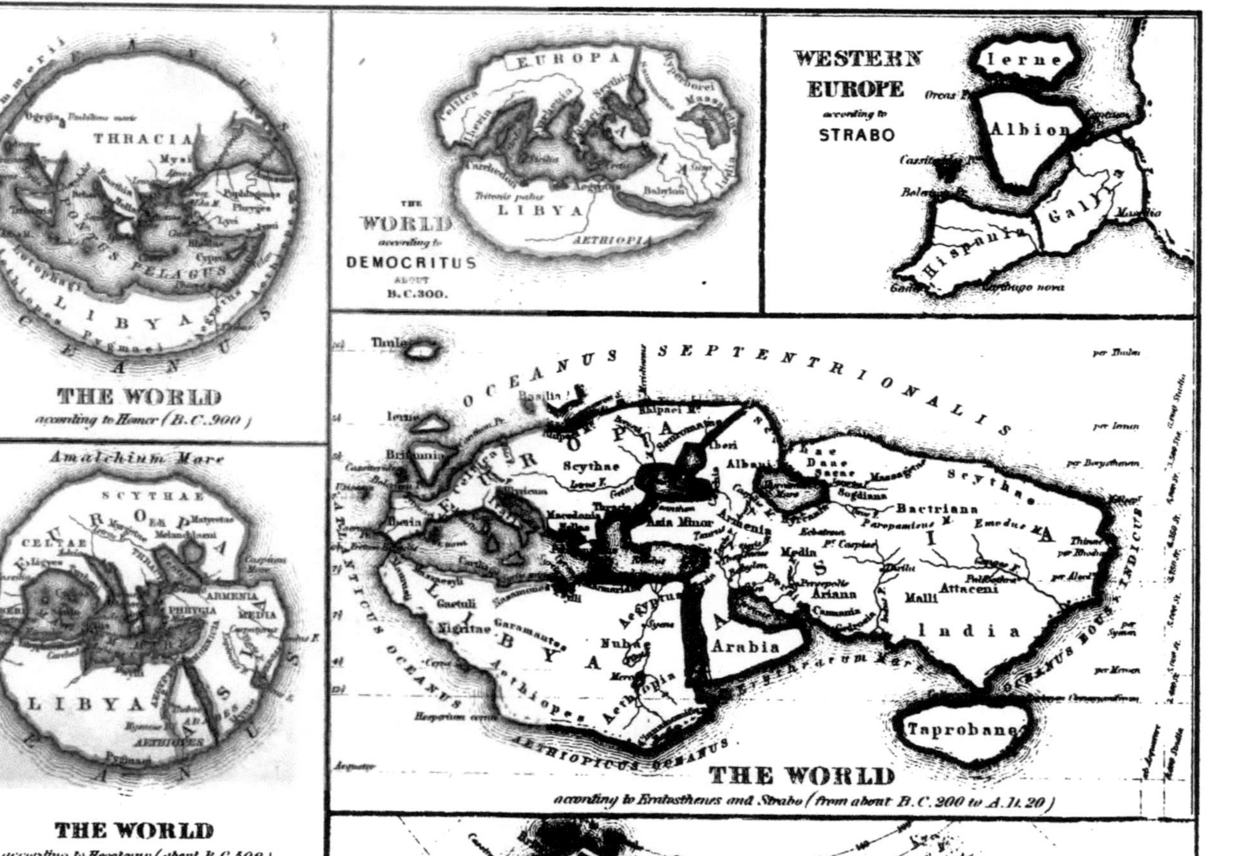

WESTERN EUROPE according to STRABO
Ierne
Albion
Hispania
Galic
THE WORLD according to Homer (B.C. 900)
THRACIA
LIBYA
EUROPA
THE WORLD according to Democritus about B.C. 300.
EUROPA
LIBYA
AETHIOPIA
Amalchium Mare
THE WORLD according to Hecataeus (about B.C. 500)
SCYTHAE
ARMENIA
MEDIA
THRACIA
LIBYA
THE WORLD according to Eratosthenes and Strabo (from about B.C. 300 to A.D. 20)
OCEANUS SEPTENTRIONALIS
EUROPA
Scythae
Bactriana
India
Taprobane
ASIA
Arabia
AEGYPTUS
LIBYA
Aethiopes
ATLANTICUS OCEANUS

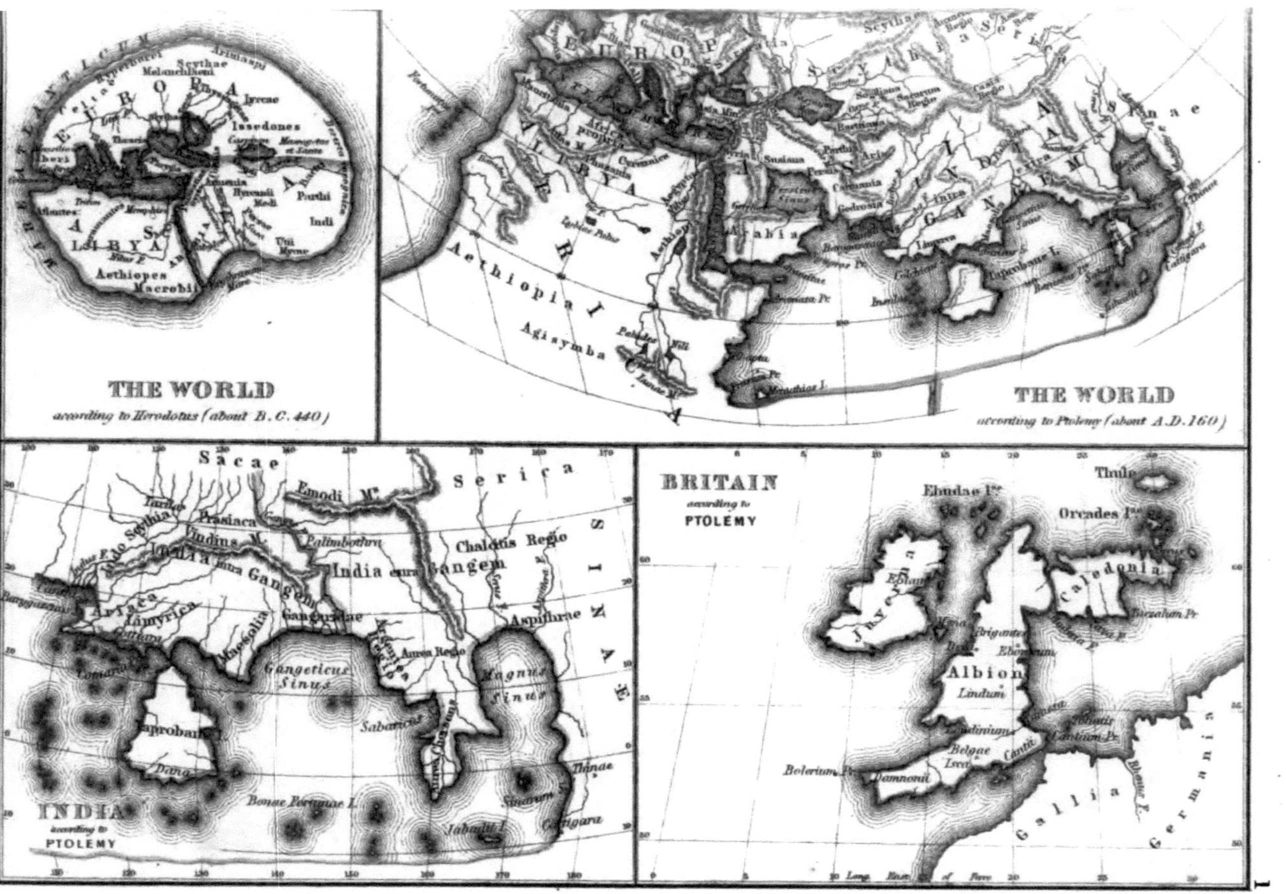

THE WORLD
according to Herodotus (about B.C. 440)
THE WORLD
according to Ptolemy (about A.D. 160)
INDIA
according to PTOLEMY
BRITAIN
according to PTOLEMY

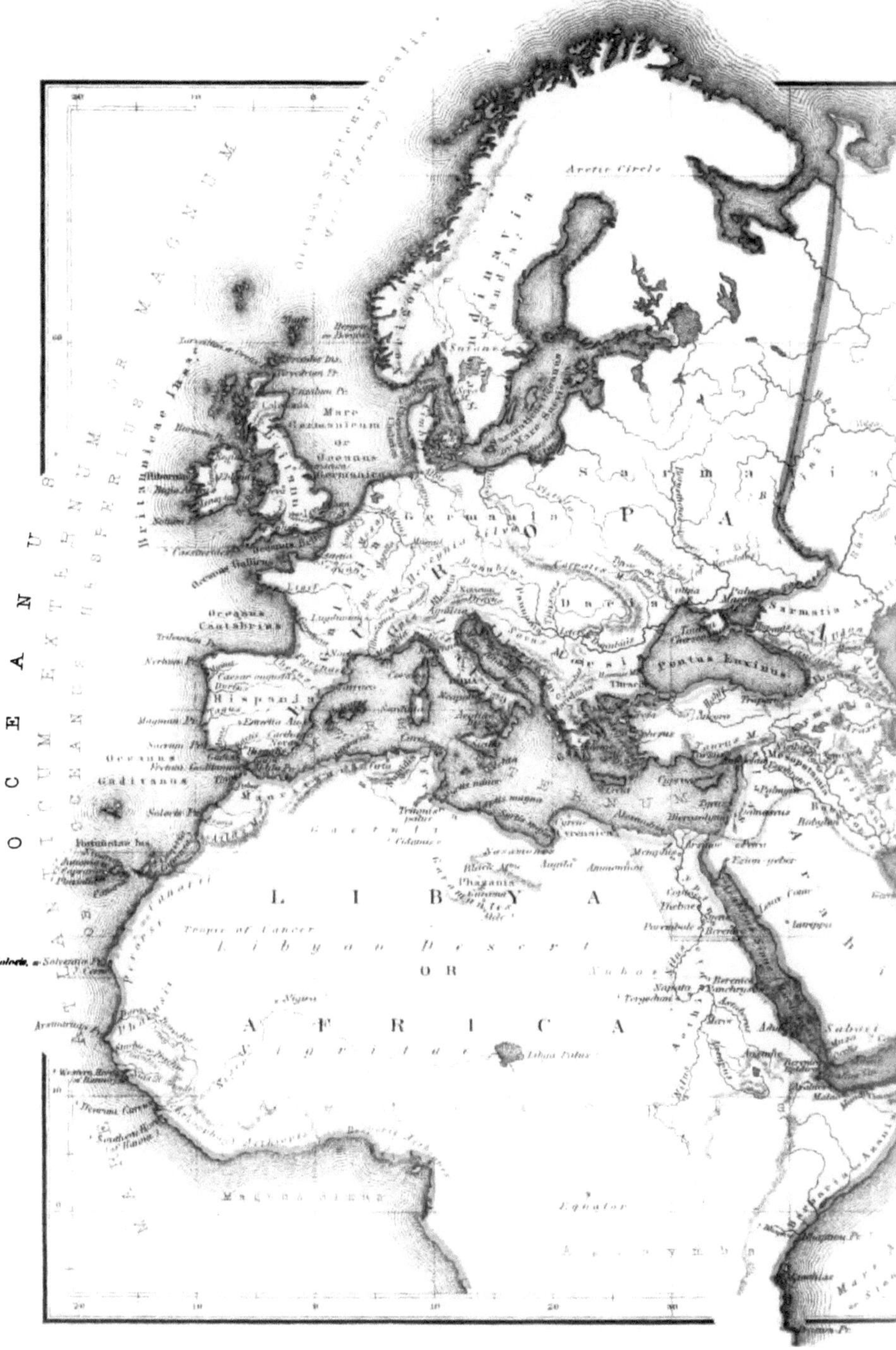

Arctic Circle
OCEANUS EXTERNUS or OCEANUS SEPTENTRIONALIS
Oceanus Septentrionalis
SARMATIA
EUROPA
Scandinavia
Mare Germanicum or Oceanus Germanicus
Britannicae Insulae
Hibernia
Oceanus Cantabricus
Germania
Dacia
Sarmatia
Pontus Euxinus
Hispania
Gaditanus
LIBYA
Tropic of Cancer
Libyan Desert
OR
AFRICA
Equator
Fortunatae Ins.
Magnum Prom.

THE WORLD
AS KNOWN TO THE ANCIENTS
...... Boundary of the Persian Empire under Cyrus.
Hyperborei
SCYTHIA
EXTRA IMAUM
Jaxartes
Massagetae
Oxus
Sogdiana
Maracanda
Bactra
Bactriana
Parthia
Aria
Arachosia
Drangiana
Gedrosia
Patala
SCYTHIA
EXTRA IMAUM
SERICA
SINA
Ganges
Palimbothra
INDIA INTRA GANGEM
INDIA EXTRA GANGEM
Cattigara
MARE ERYTHRAEUM
INDICUS OCEANUS
Longitude East of Greenwich

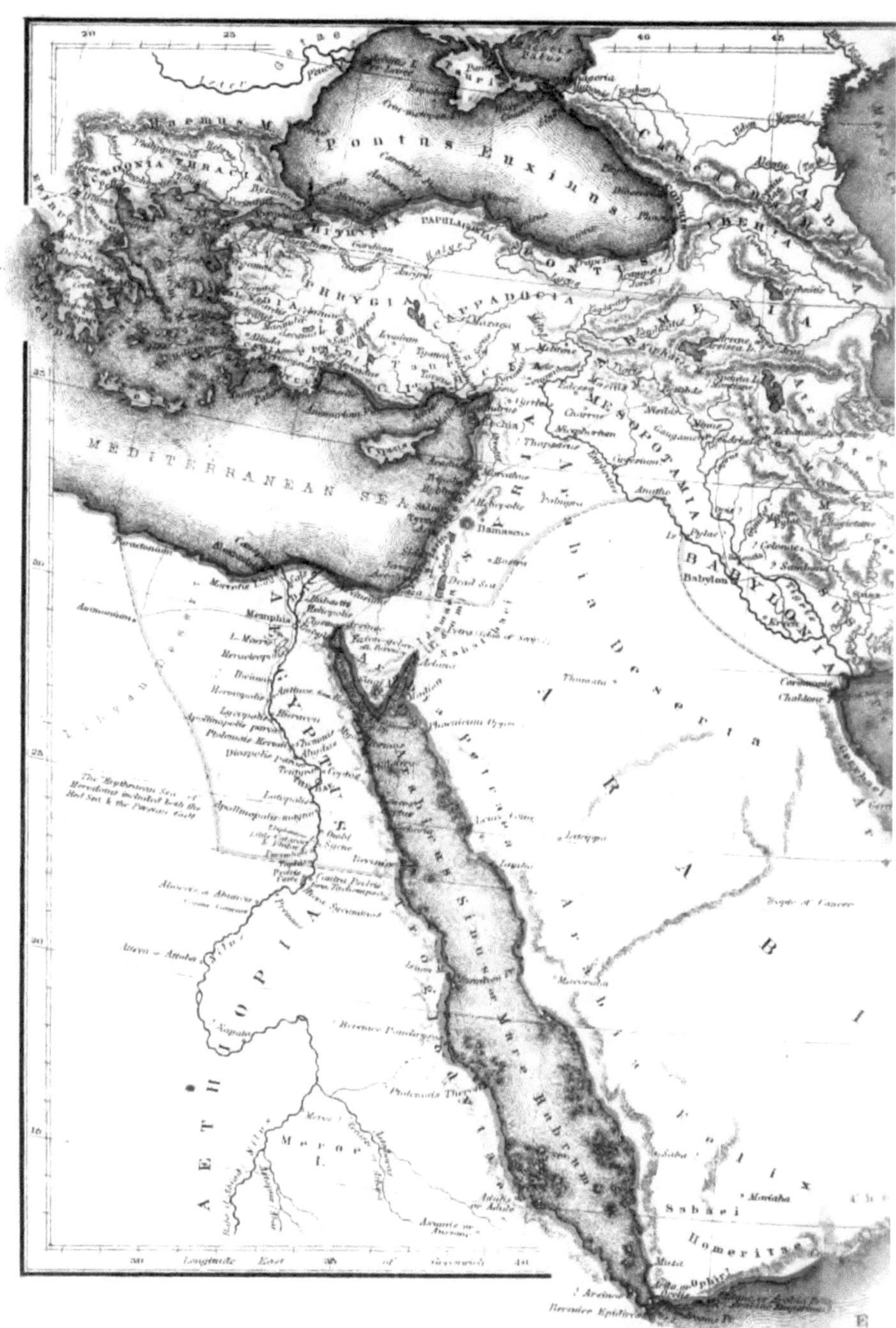

Empire of Alexander

THE GREAT;

WITH THE ADJOINING REGIONS.

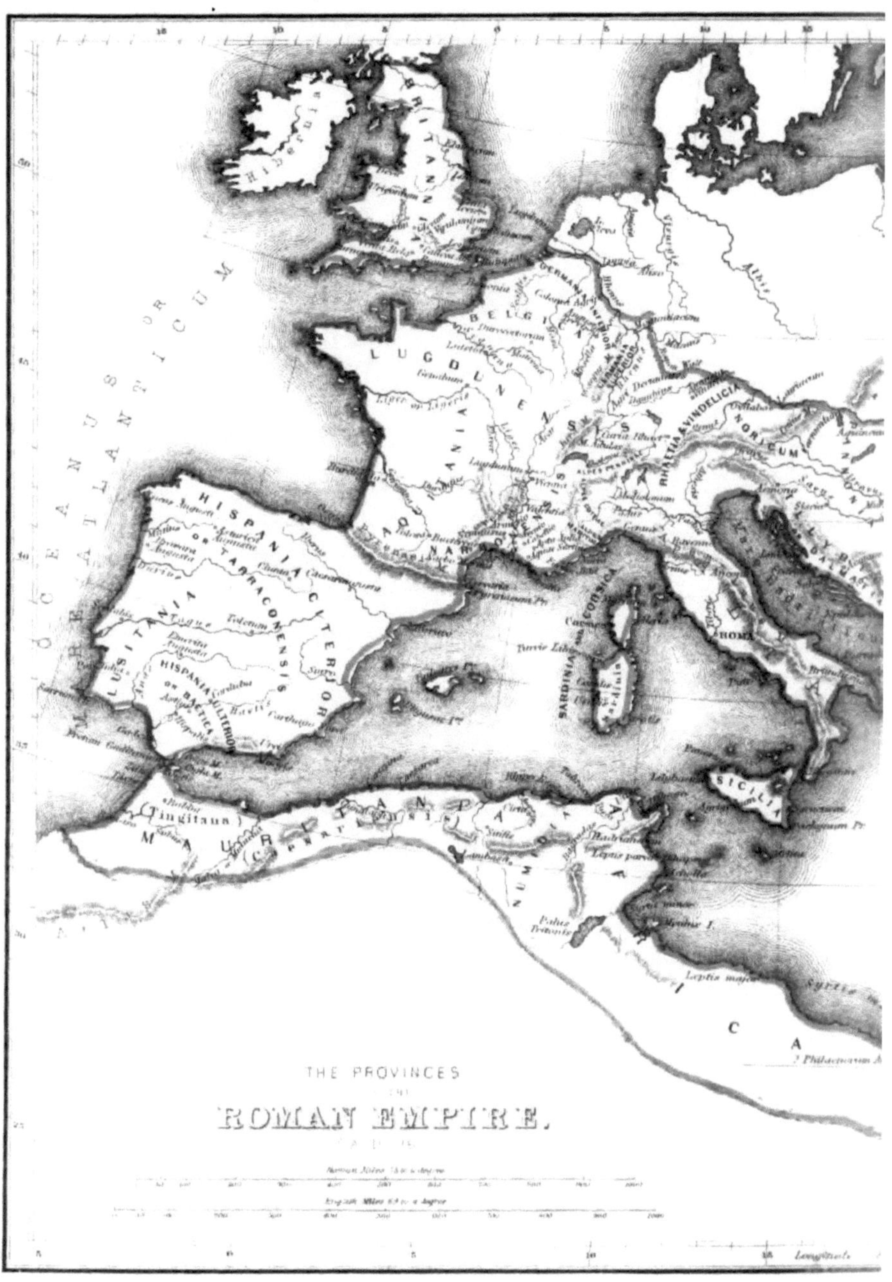

THE PROVINCES
OF THE
ROMAN EMPIRE.

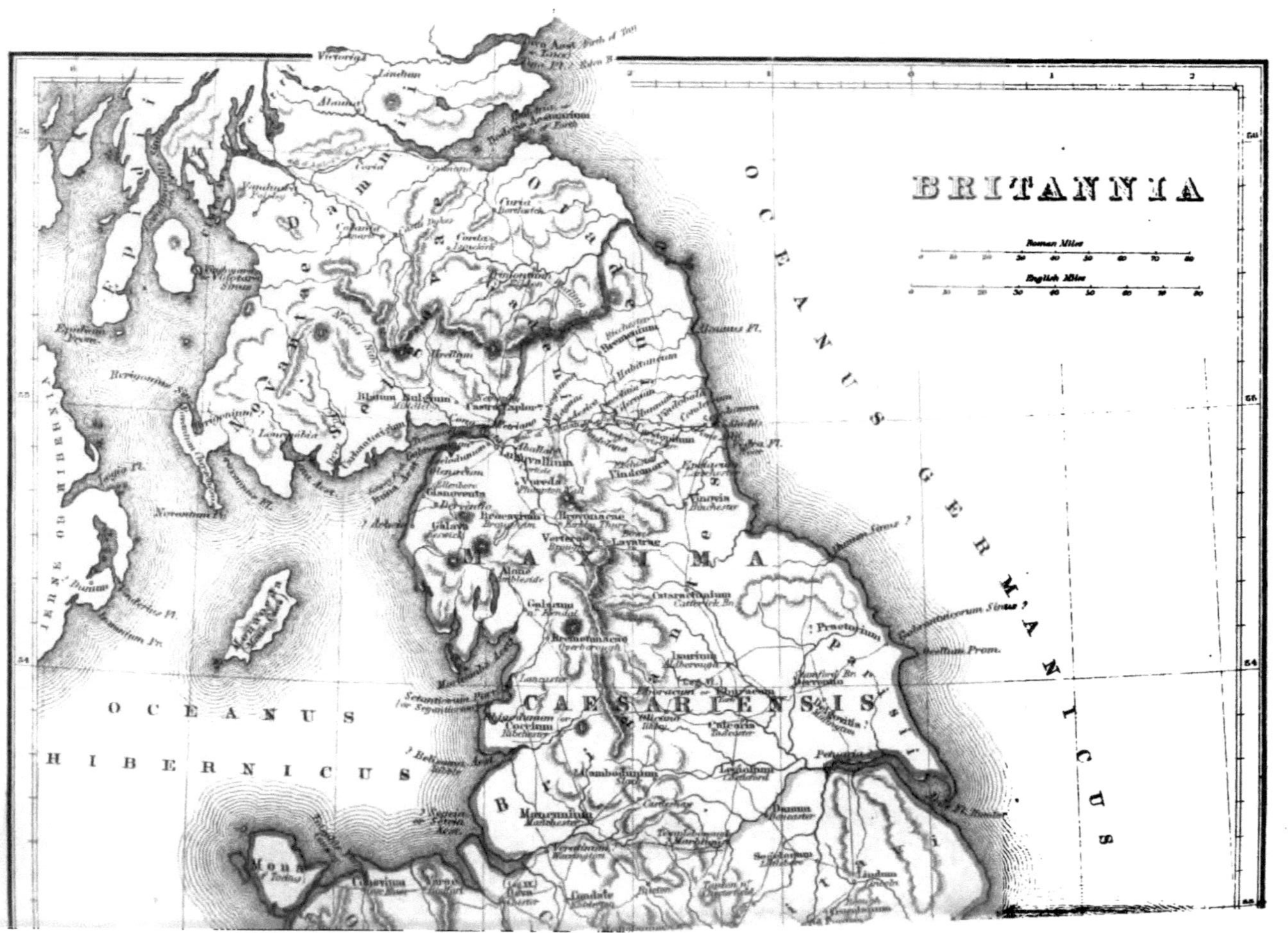

BRITANNIA
Roman Miles
English Miles
OCEANUS GERMANICUS
OCEANUS HIBERNICUS
INSULÆ OR HIBERNIA
MAXIMA
CAESARIENSIS

FLAVIA
CAESARIENSIS
BRITANNIA SECUNDA
BRITANNIA PRIMA
Iceni
Simeni
Trinobantes
Regni
Cantii
Durotriges
OCEANUS VERGINIUS
OCEANUS BRITANNICUS
GALLIA
Londinium Augusta
Camulodunum
Venta Icenorum
Verulamium St. Albans
Calleva Atrebatum Silchester
Venta Belgarum Winchester
Aquae Solis Bath
Durnovaria Dorchester
Portus Lemanis Lympne
Dubris Dover
Regnum Chichester
Longitude West of Greenwich

GALLIA
Pictones
or Pictavi
HISPANIA
Gallicus Sinus
Cantabri
Varduli
Vascones
Lacetani
Petrocorii
Roman Miles
Gallic Leagues
English Miles
Longitude East of Greenwich
6.

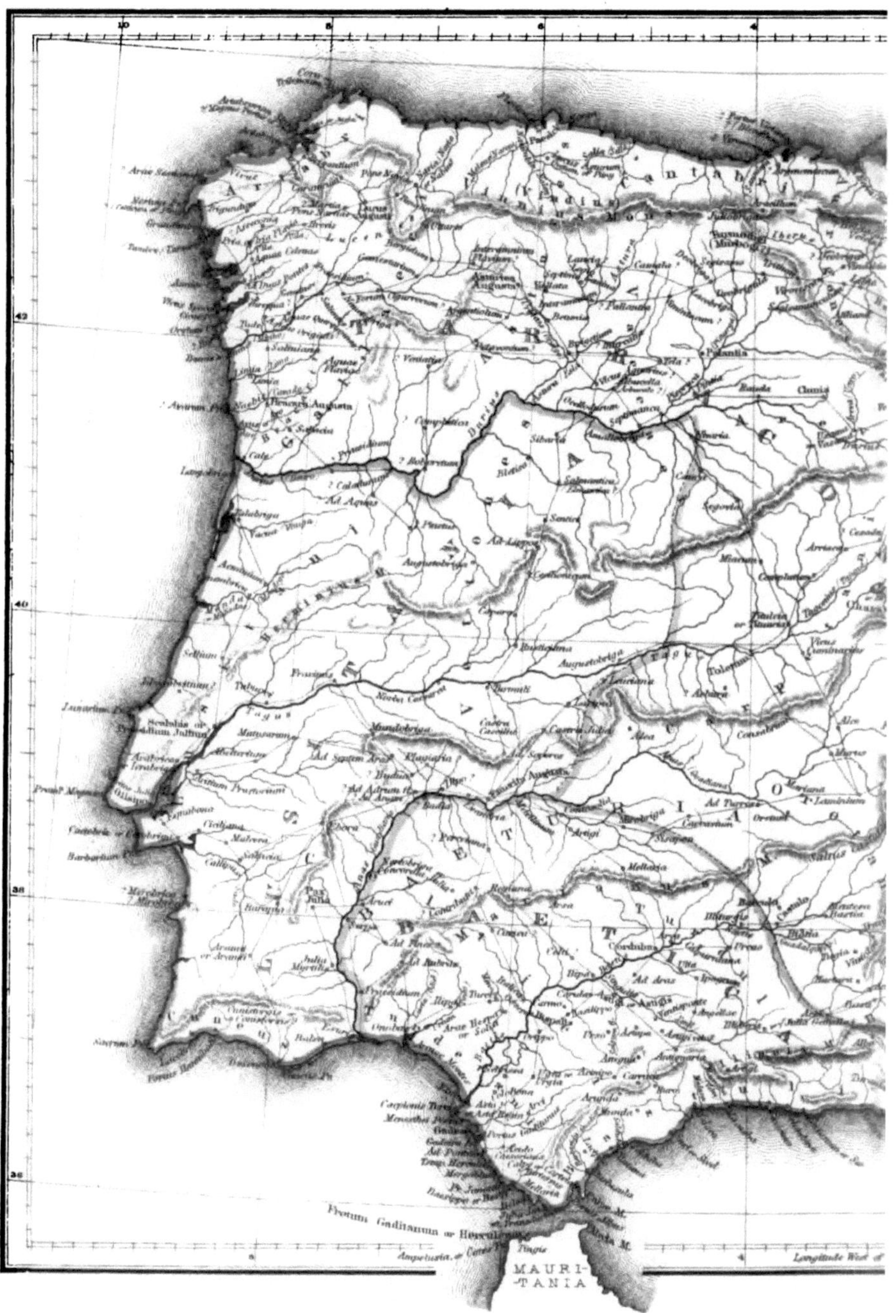

MAURI-
-TANIA
Cantabri
VARDULI
ASTURIA
TARRACO
LUSITANIA
BAETICA
Tagus
Frenum Gaditanum or Herculeum
Longitude West of

7.
GALLIA
Gallicus Sinus
Mare Balearicum
BALEARES INSULAE or GYMNESIAE
Balearis Minor or Nura
Balearis Major or Columba
PITYUSAE INS.AE
Sucronensis Sinus
HISPANIA.
MAURITANIA
Roman Miles
English Miles
Longitude East of Greenwich

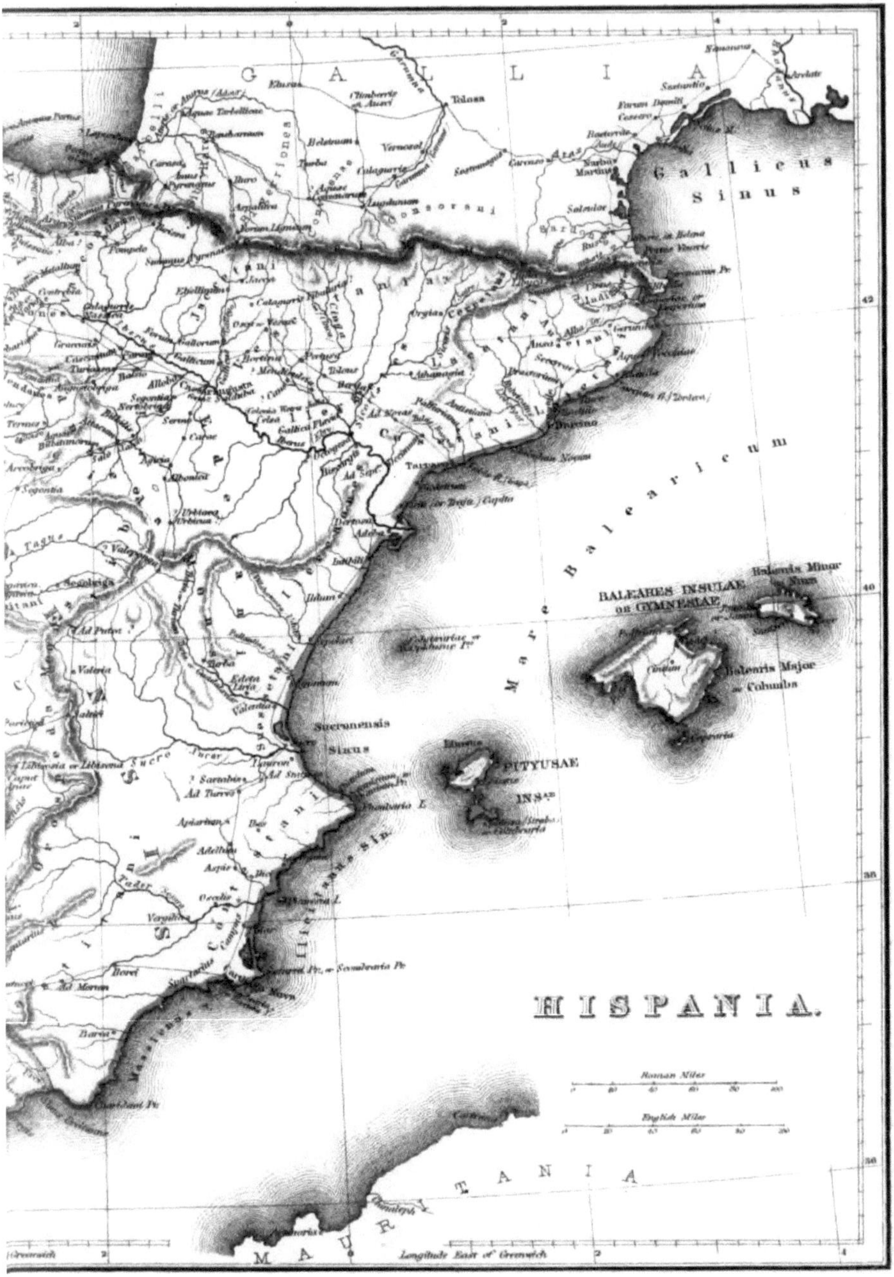

ITALIA.
(NORTHERN PART.)
Roman Miles
English Miles
LIGUSTICUM MARE
CYRNOS,
OR
CORSICA
Longitude East

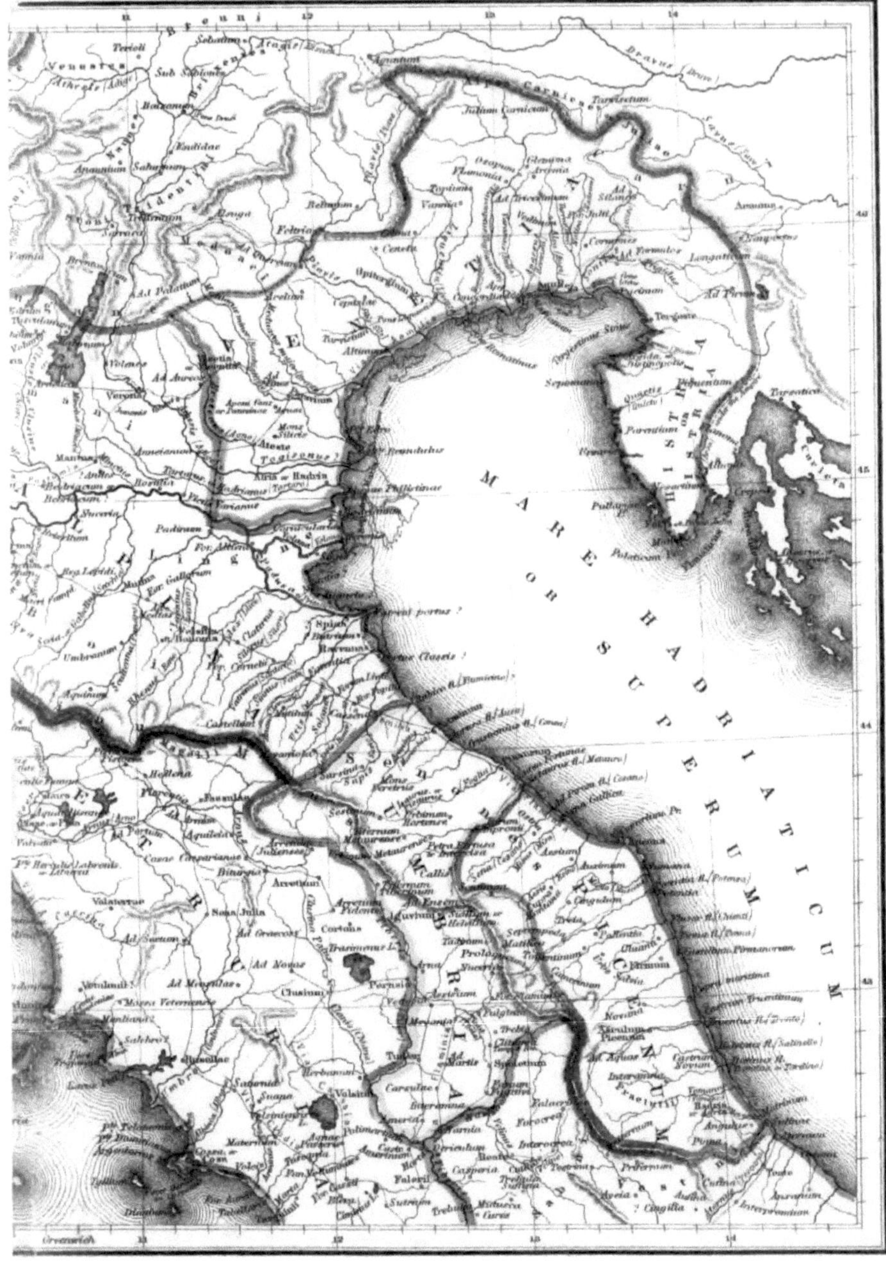

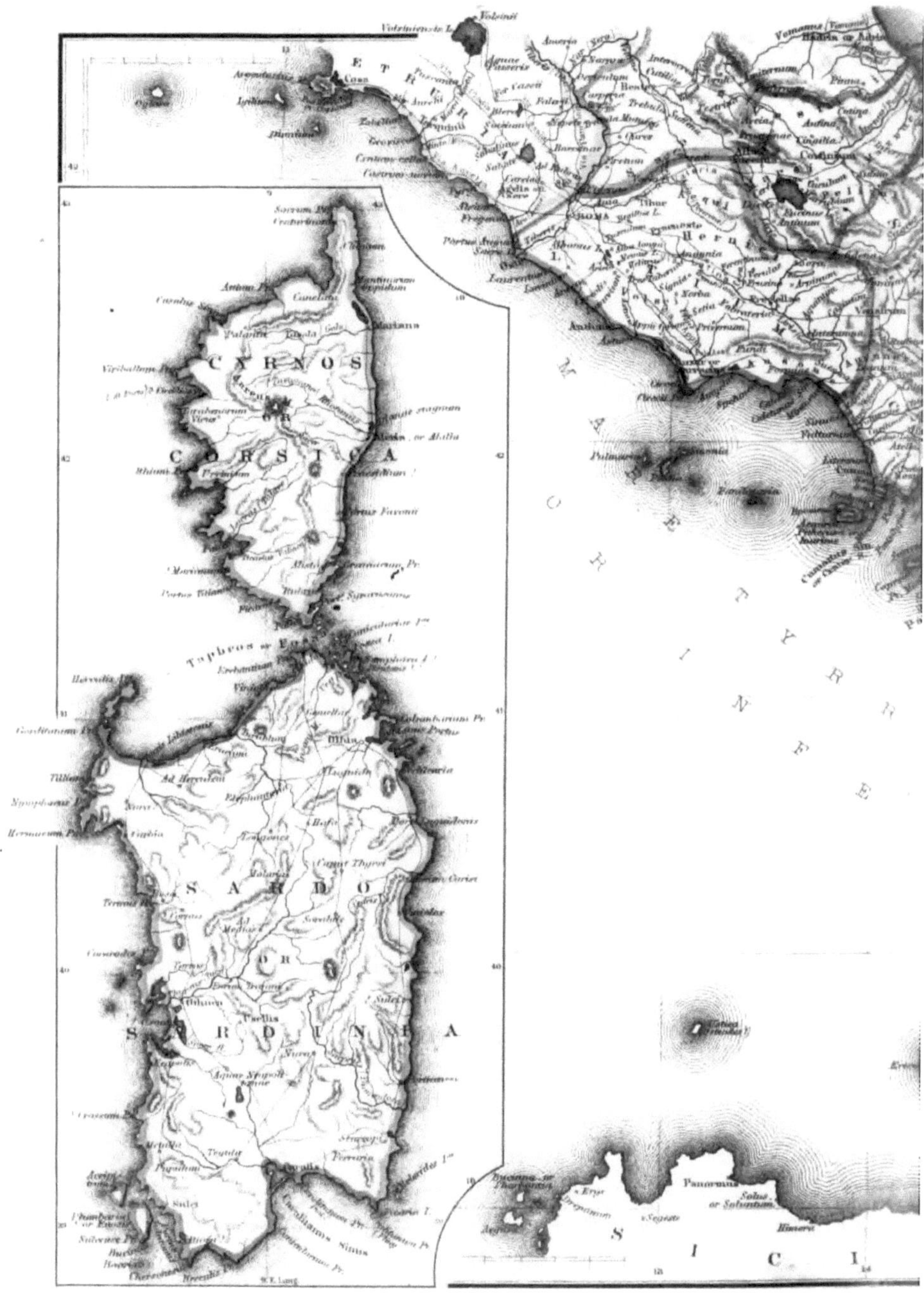

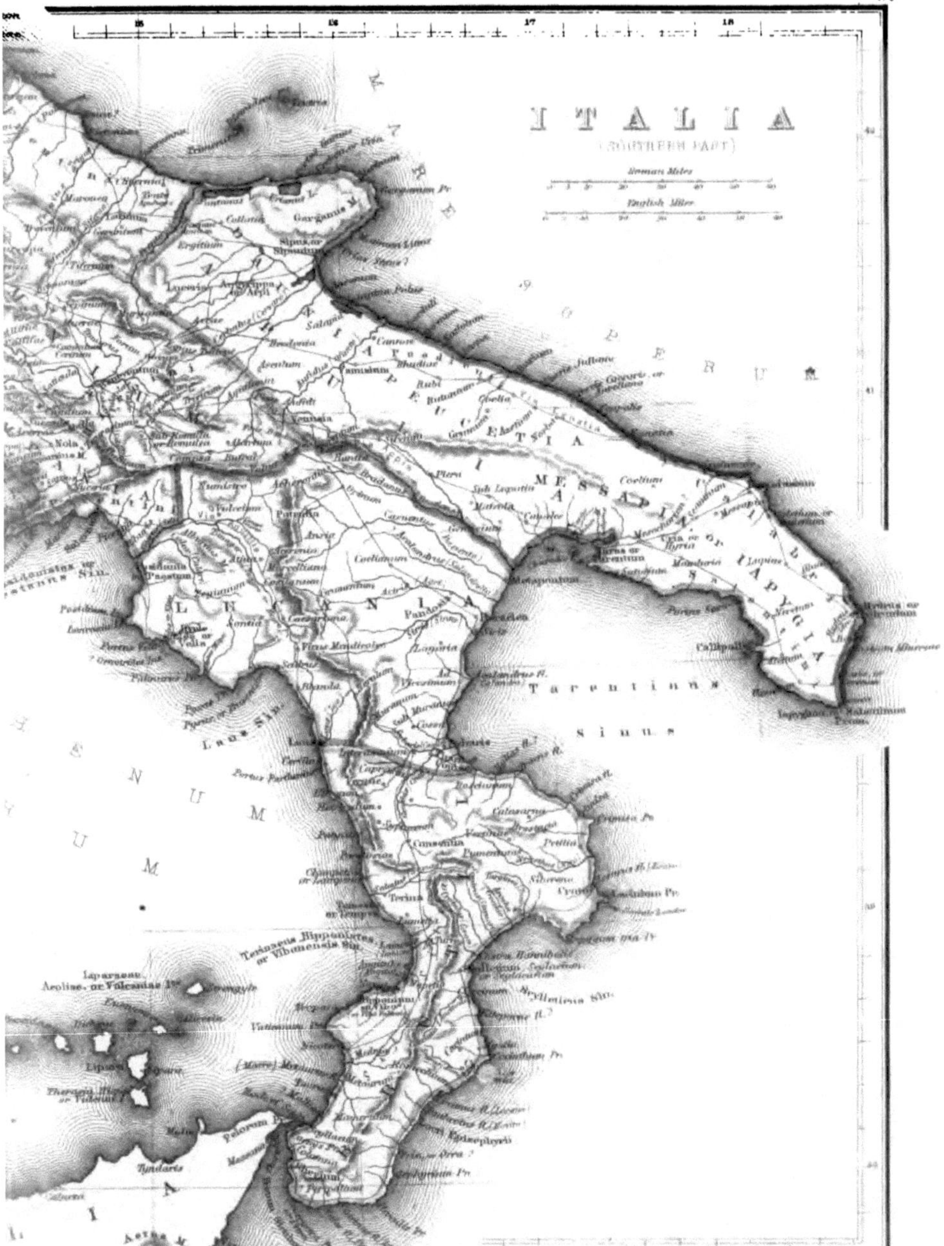

ITALIA
(SOUTHERN PART)

Roman Miles

English Miles

MESSAPIA

CALABRIA or IAPYGIA

LUCANIA

BRUTIUM

Tarentinus Sinus

Laus Sin.

Liparaeae, Aeoliae or Vulcaniae Iⁿ

Tyndaris

Longitude 17 East of Greenwich

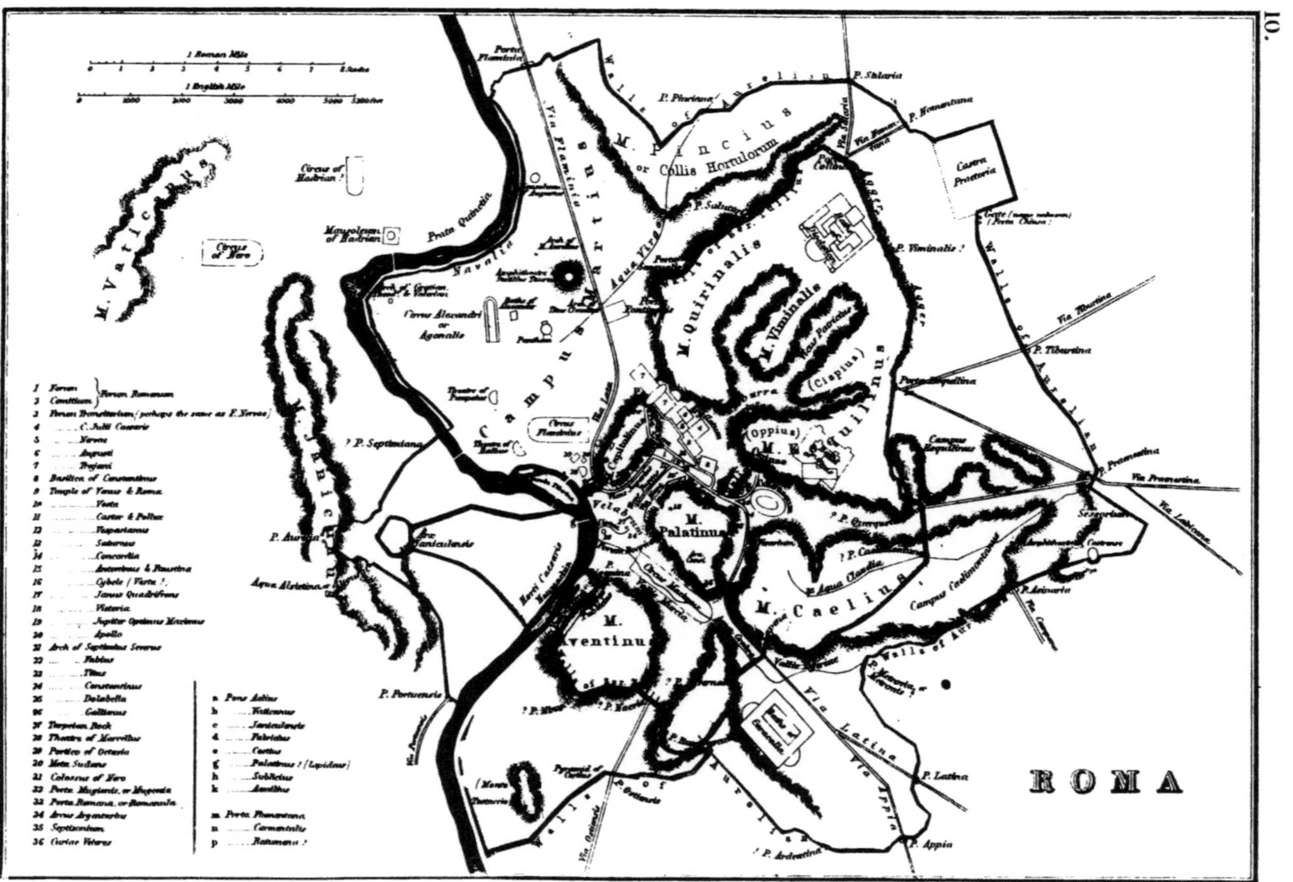

ROMA
1 Foum   } Forum Romanum
2 Comitium }
3 Forum Transitorium (perhaps the same as F. Nervae)
4 .... C. Julii Caesaris
5 .... Nervae
6 .... Augusti
7 .... Trajani
8 Basilica of Constantinus
9 Temple of Venus & Roma
10 .... Vesta
11 .... Castor & Pollux
12 .... Vespasianus
13 .... Saturnus
14 .... Concordia
15 .... Antoninus & Faustina
16 .... Cybele / Vesta ?
17 .... Janus Quadrifrons
18 .... Victoria
19 .... Jupiter Optimus Maximus
20 .... Apollo
21 Arch of Septimius Severus
22 ..... Fabius
23 ..... Titus
24 ..... Constantinus
25 ..... Dolabella
26 ..... Gallienus
27 Tarpeian Rock
28 Theatre of Marcellus
29 Portico of Octavia
30 Meta Sudans
31 Colossus of Nero
32 Porta Misqueris, or Magonia
33 Porta Romana, or Romanula
34 Arcus Argentarius
35 Septizonium
36 Curiae Veteres

a Pons Aelius
b ..... Vaticanus
c ..... Janiculensis
d ..... Fabricius
e ..... Cestius
g ..... Palatinus ? (Lapideus)
h ..... Sublicius
k ..... Aemilius

m Porta Flumentana
n ..... Carmentalis
p ..... Ratumena ?

1 Roman Mile
1 English Mile

M. Vaticanus
Circus of Nero
Circus of Hadrian
Mausoleum of Hadrian
Prata Quinctia
Navalia
Campus Martius
Circus Alexandri or Agonalis
Theatre of Pompeius
Circus Flaminius
M. Janiculus
P. Septimiana
P. Aurelia
Aqua Alsietina
Ara Janiculensis
Velabrum
M. Palatinus
M. Aventinus
M. Caelius
M. Esquilinus
(Oppius)
(Cispius)
M. Viminalis
M. Quirinalis
M. Pincius or Collis Hortulorum
Castra Praetoria
Agger
Walls of Aurelian
Via Flaminia
Porta Flaminia
P. Pinciana
P. Salaria
P. Nomentana
P. Viminalis ?
Via Salaria
Via Nomentana
P. Collina
Porta Esquilina
Via Tiburtina
P. Tiburtina
Campus Esquilinus
Via Praenestina
P. Praenestina
Via Labicana
Amphitheatrum Castrense
P. Asinaria
Via Campana
Campus Castrensis
Aqua Claudia
? P. Caelia
? P. Querq.
Via Latina
P. Latina
Via Appia
P. Appia
? P. Ardeatina
Walls of Aurelian
P. Portuensis
Pyramid of Cestius
(Monte Testaccio)
? P. Navalis
? P. Minor
Aqua Virgo
Forum
Capitolinum
Circus Maximus

PART OF ITALY
showing
THE ROMAN TERRITORY
AND THE NEIGHBOURING COUNTRY
Roman Miles
English Miles

8

SICILIA.

Scale Stadia
Greek Stadia
Roman Miles
English Miles

Longitude East of Greenwich

Aeoliae, Vulcaniae, or Liparenses Ins.

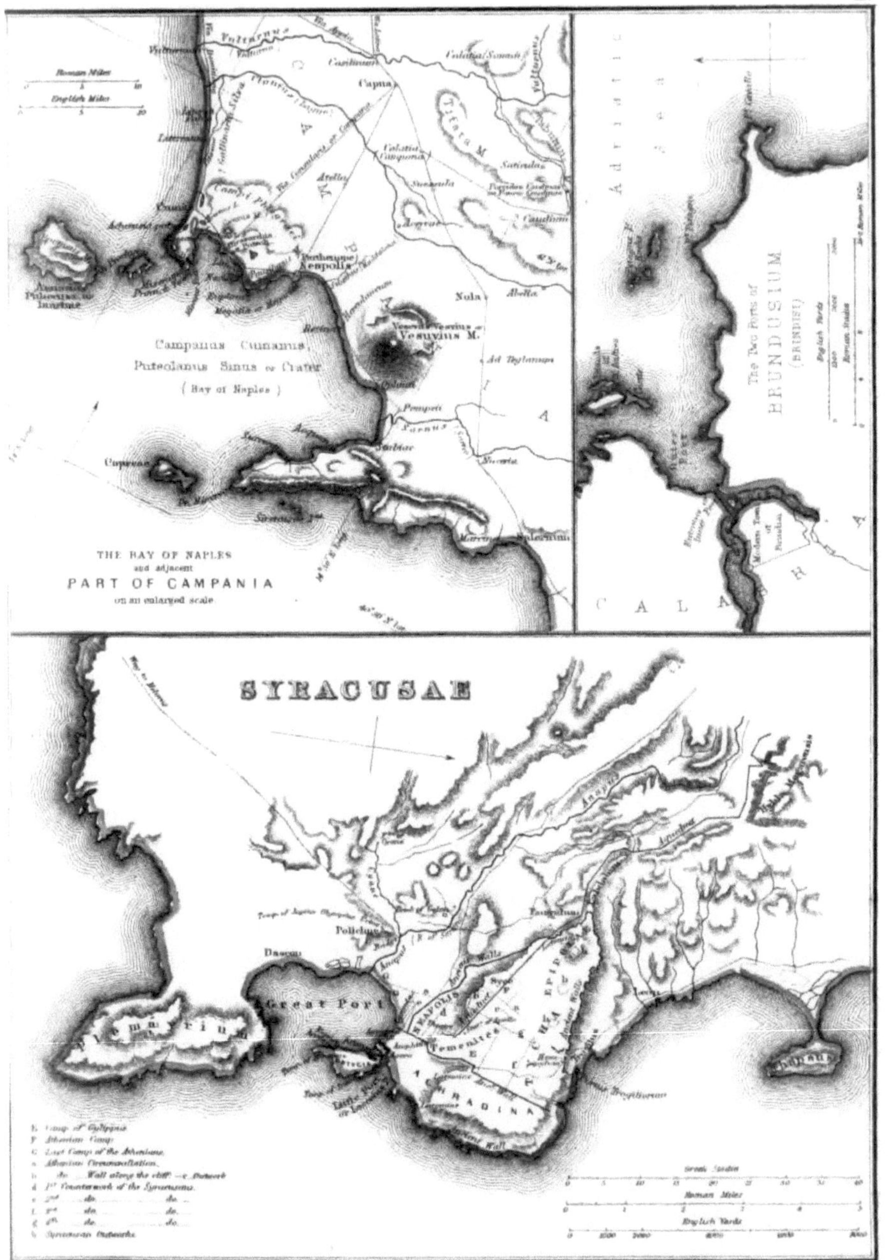
Roman Miles
English Miles
THE BAY OF NAPLES
and adjacent
PART OF CAMPANIA
on an enlarged scale
Campanus Cumanus,
Puteolanus Sinus or Crater
(Bay of Naples)
Vesuvius M.
Neapolis
Capua
Nola
Abella
Pompeii
Capreae
The Two Ports of
BRUNDUSIUM
(BRINDISI)
Adriatic Sea
CALAB
SYRACUSAE
Great Port
Greek Stadia
Roman Miles
English Yards

MACEDONIA
THRACIA, ILLYRICUM
AND THE
PROVINCES of the MIDDLE & LOWER DANUBE
Roman Miles
English Miles

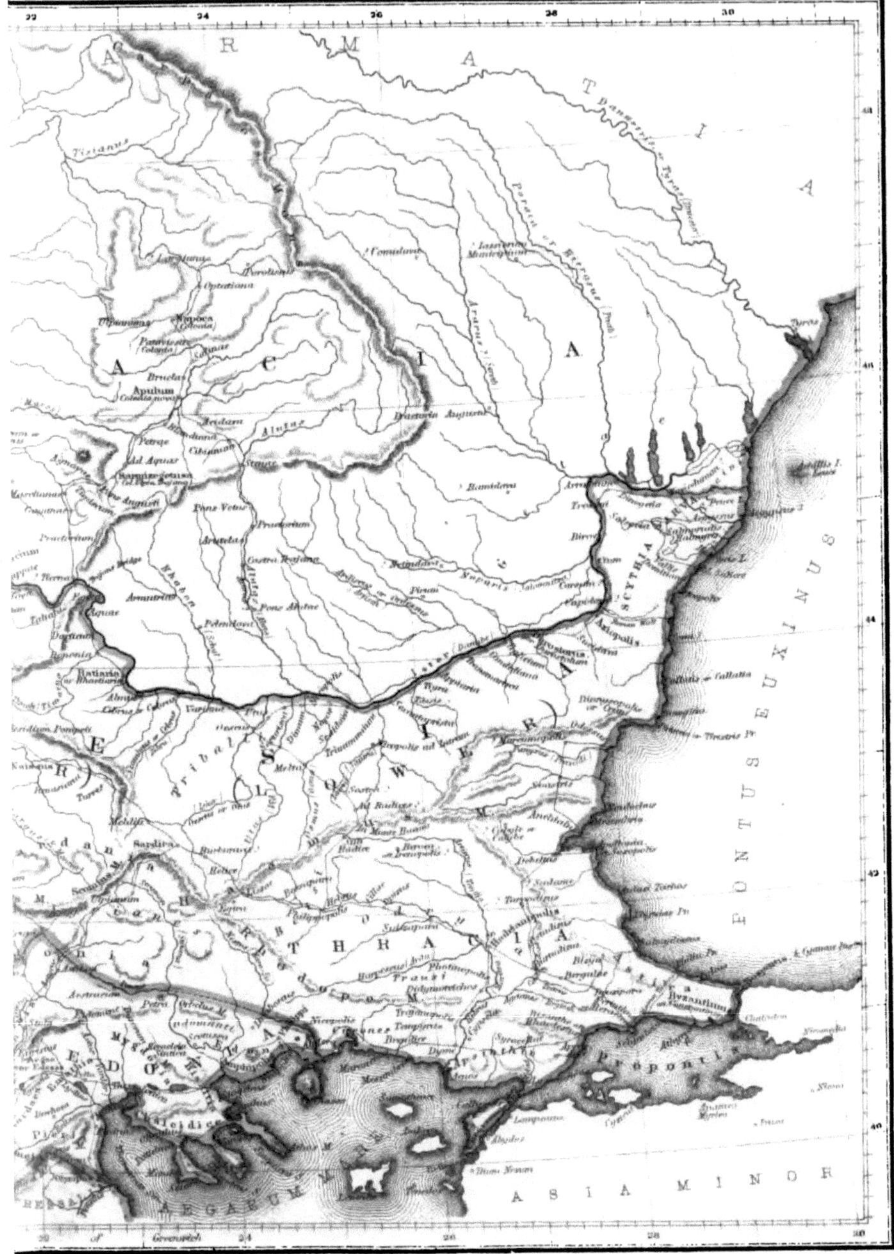
SARMATIA
DACIA
PONTUS EUXINUS
SCYTHIA
THRACIA
ASIA MINOR
AEGÆUM MARE
Propontis
Byzantium
Greenwich

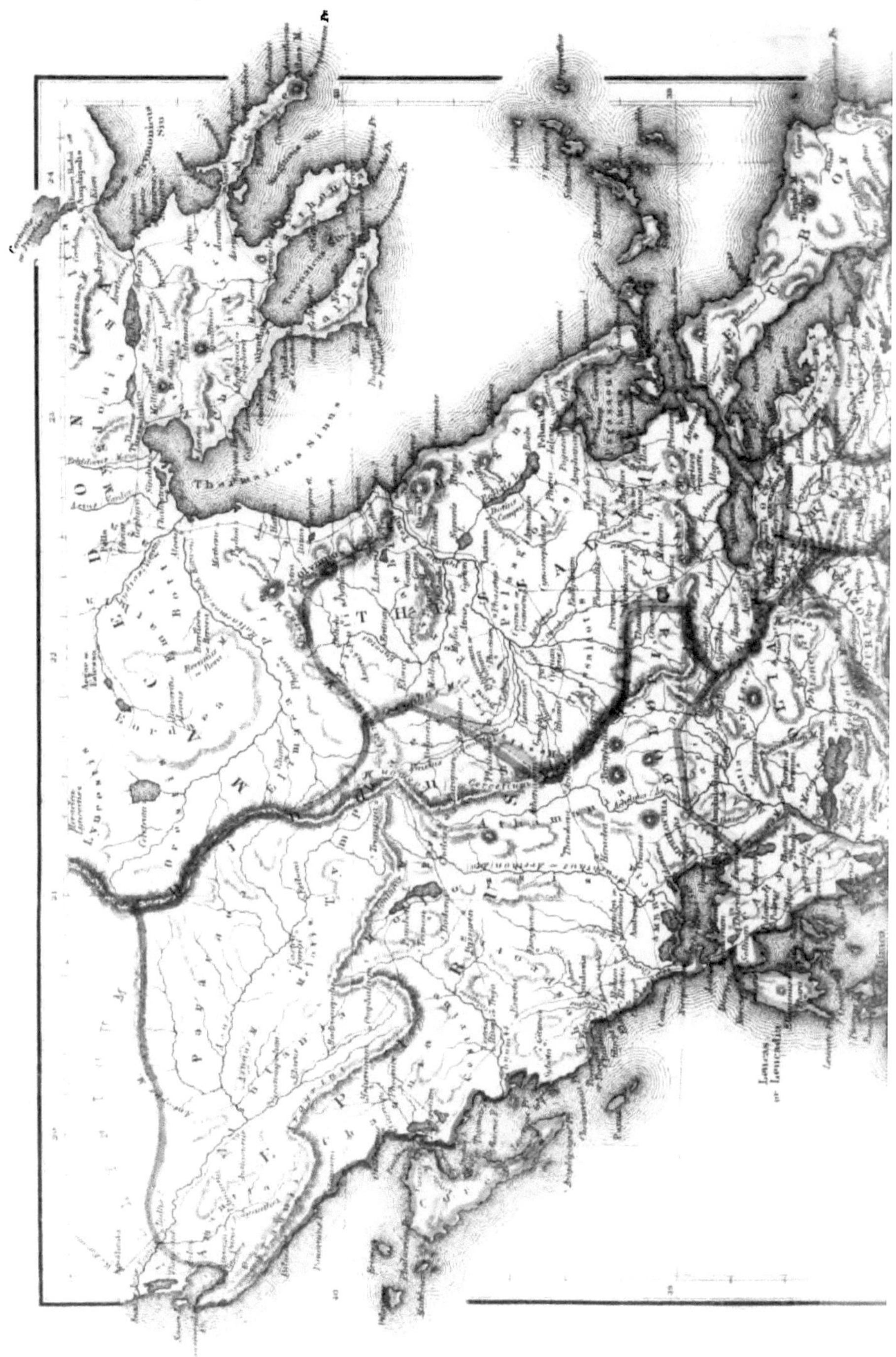

GRAECIA
INCLUDING
EPIRUS AND THESSALIA
WITH PART OF MACEDONIA
Grear Stadia
Roman Miles
English Miles
Longitude East of Greenwich
Corinthiacus Sinus
Samos sec Cephallenia
Zacynthus
Cyparissius Sinus
MESSENIA
ARGO
MESSENIACUS SIN
Laconicus Sin
PELOPONNESUS
Cythera
15.

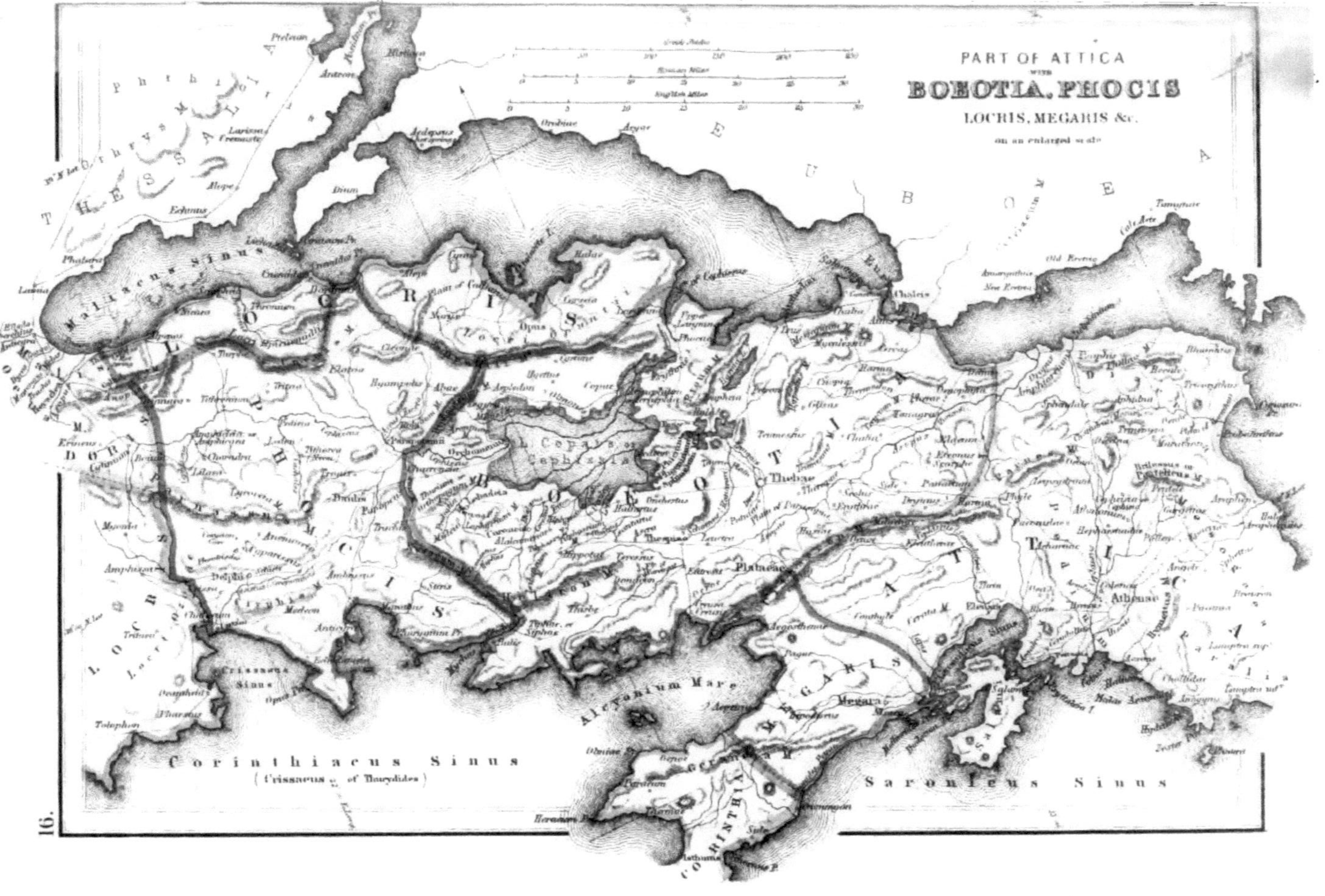

PART OF ATTICA
WITH
BOEOTIA, PHOCIS
LOCRIS, MEGARIS &c.
on an enlarged scale
Corinthiacus Sinus
(Crissaeus ... of Thucydides)
Saronicus Sinus
Alcyonium Mare
Maliacus Sinus
Corinthia
Megaris
Phocis
Boeotia
Doris
Locris
Thessaly
Phthiotis
Euboea
Megara
Plataeae
Thebae
Athenae
Chalcis
Copais or Cephissis

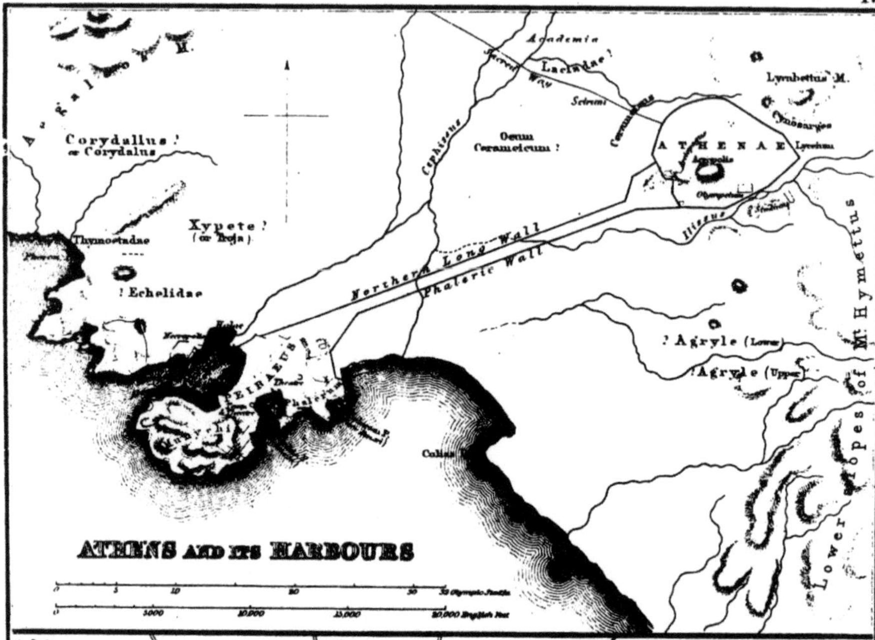

Academia
Lacladae
Oenum Cerameicum?
ATHENAE
Lymbettus M.
Cynosarges
Corydallus? or Corydalus
Xypete? (or Troja)
Thymoetadae
Echelidae
PEIRAEUS
Northern Long Wall
Phaleric Wall
Agryle (Lower)
Agryle (Upper)
Lower Slopes of Mt. Hymettus
Colias
ATHENS AND ITS HARBOURS
0 5 10 20 30 Olympic Stadia
5000 10,000 15,000 20,000 English Feet

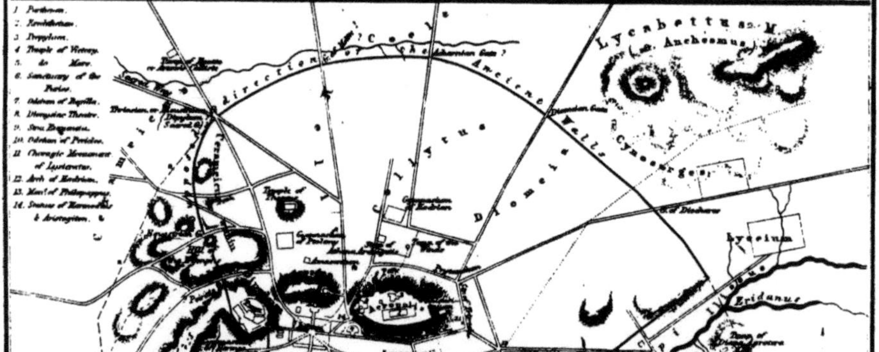

1. Parthenon.
2. Erechtheum.
3. Propylaeum.
4. Temple of Victory.
5. do. Mars.
6. Sanctuary of the Furies.
7. Odeium of Regilla.
8. Dionysiac Theatre.
9. Stoa Eumenia.
10. Odeium of Pericles.
11. Choragic Monument of Lysicrates.
12. Arch of Hadrian.
13. Mon. of Philopappus.
14. Statues of Harmodius & Aristogiton.
Lycabettus M. (or Anchesmus)
Ancient Walls
Cynosarges
Lyceum
Eridanus
ATHENAE
Olympic Stadia
English Feet
0 500 1000 2000

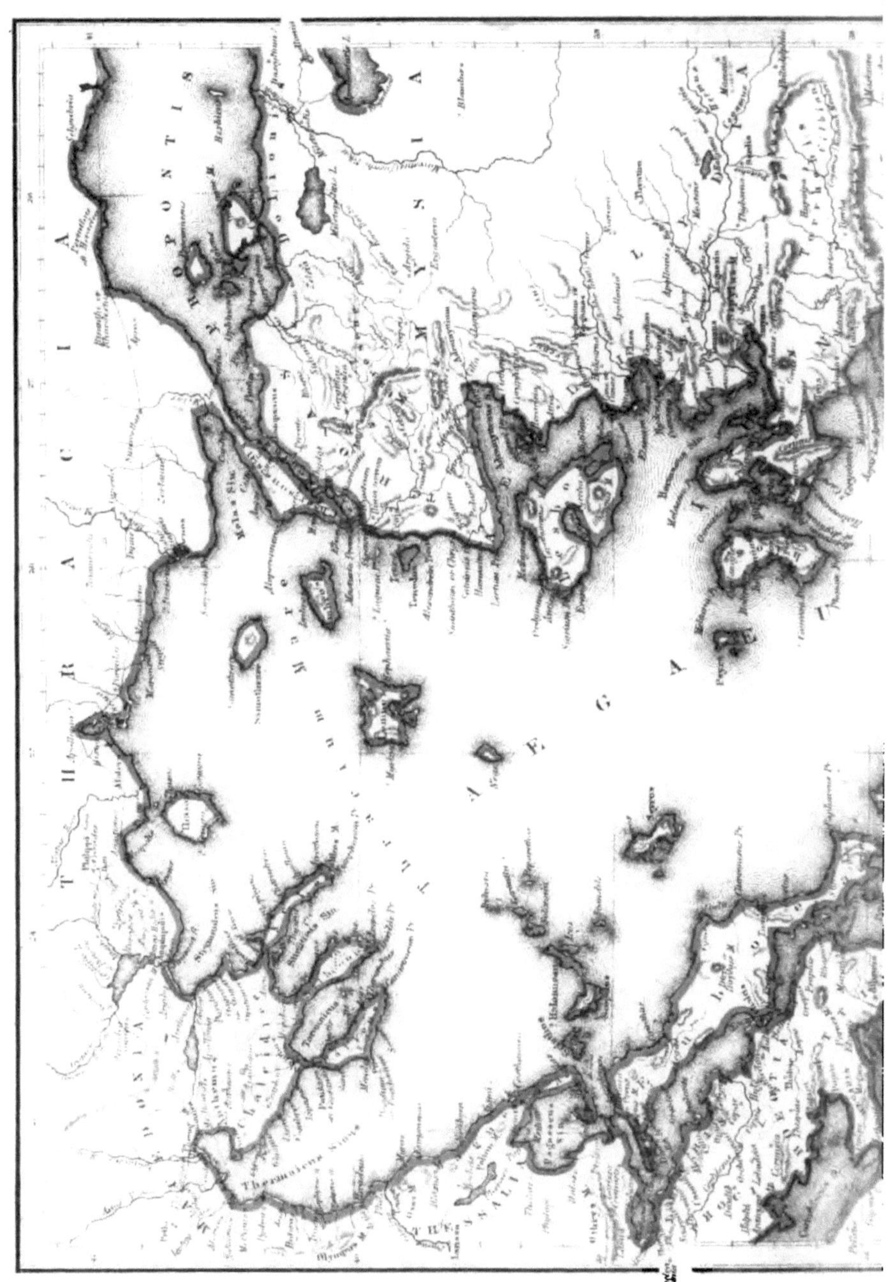

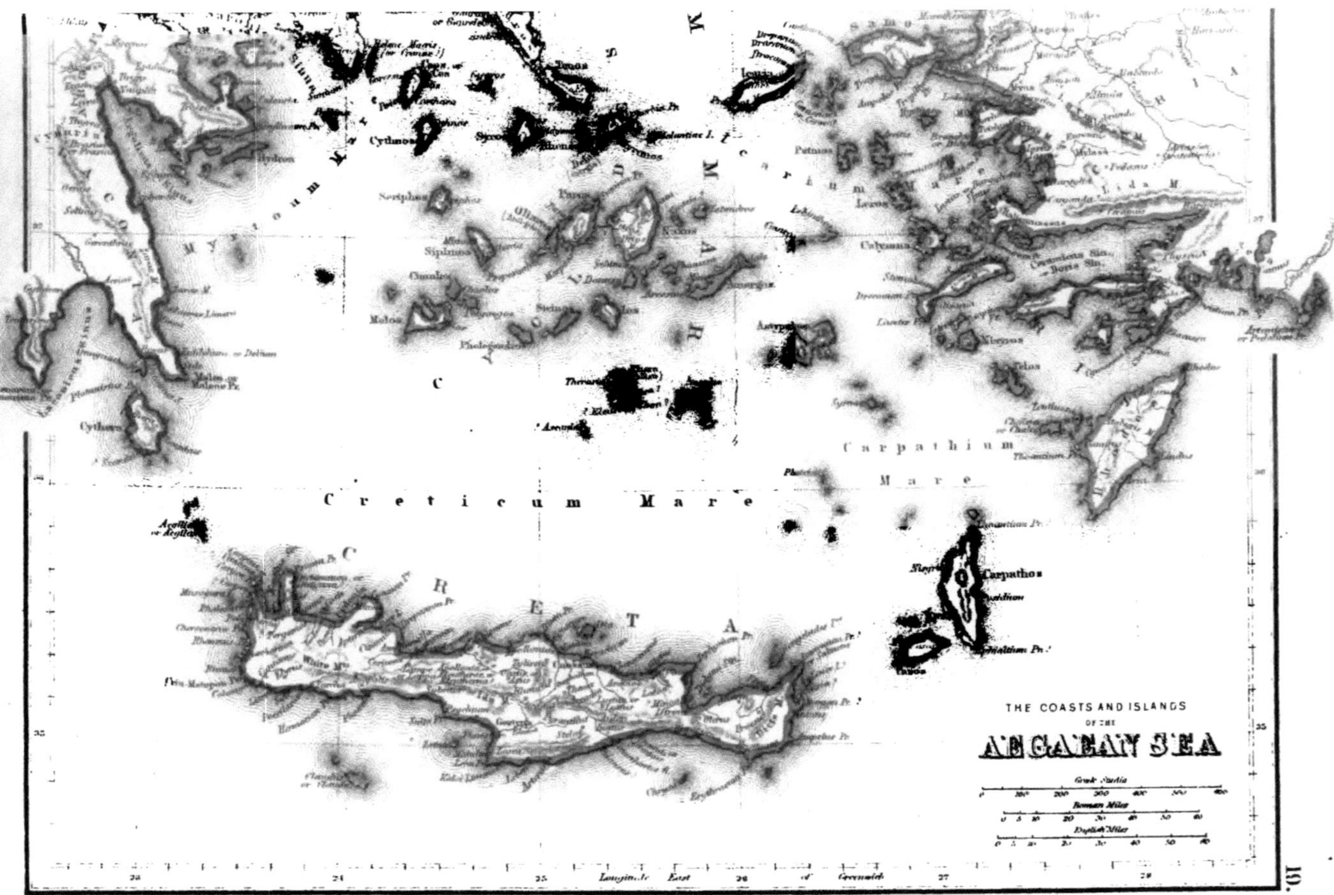
THE COASTS AND ISLANDS
OF THE
AEGEAN SEA
Greek Stadia
Roman Miles
English Miles
Creticum Mare
Carpathium Mare
Carpathos
Longitude East of Greenwich

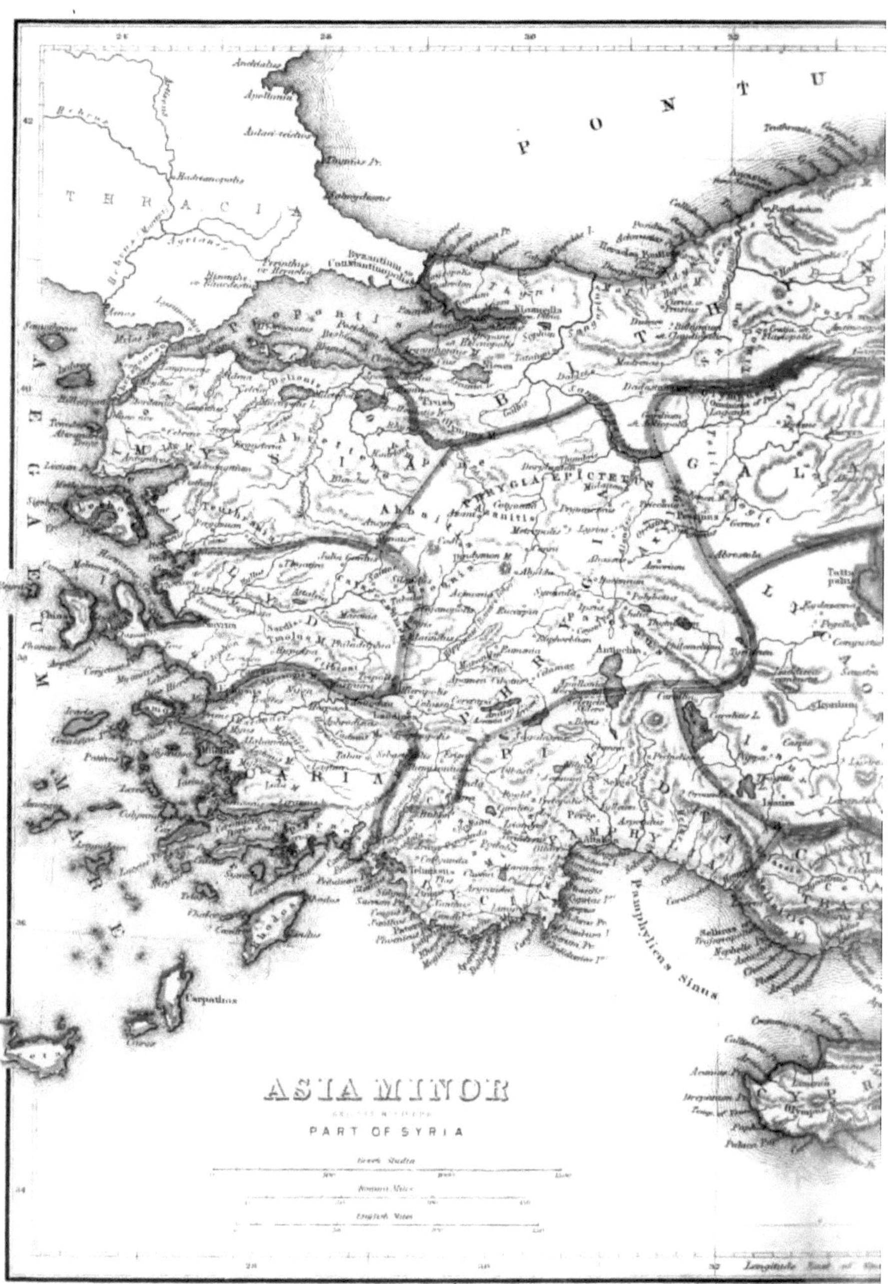

ASIA MINOR
PART OF SYRIA
PONTU
THRACIA
BITHY
GALATIA
MYSIA
PHRYGIA EPICTETUS
LYDIA
PHRYGIA
PISIDIA
PAMPHYLIA
LYCIA
CILICIA
Pamphylius Sinus
Byzantium seu Constantinopolis
Carpathus

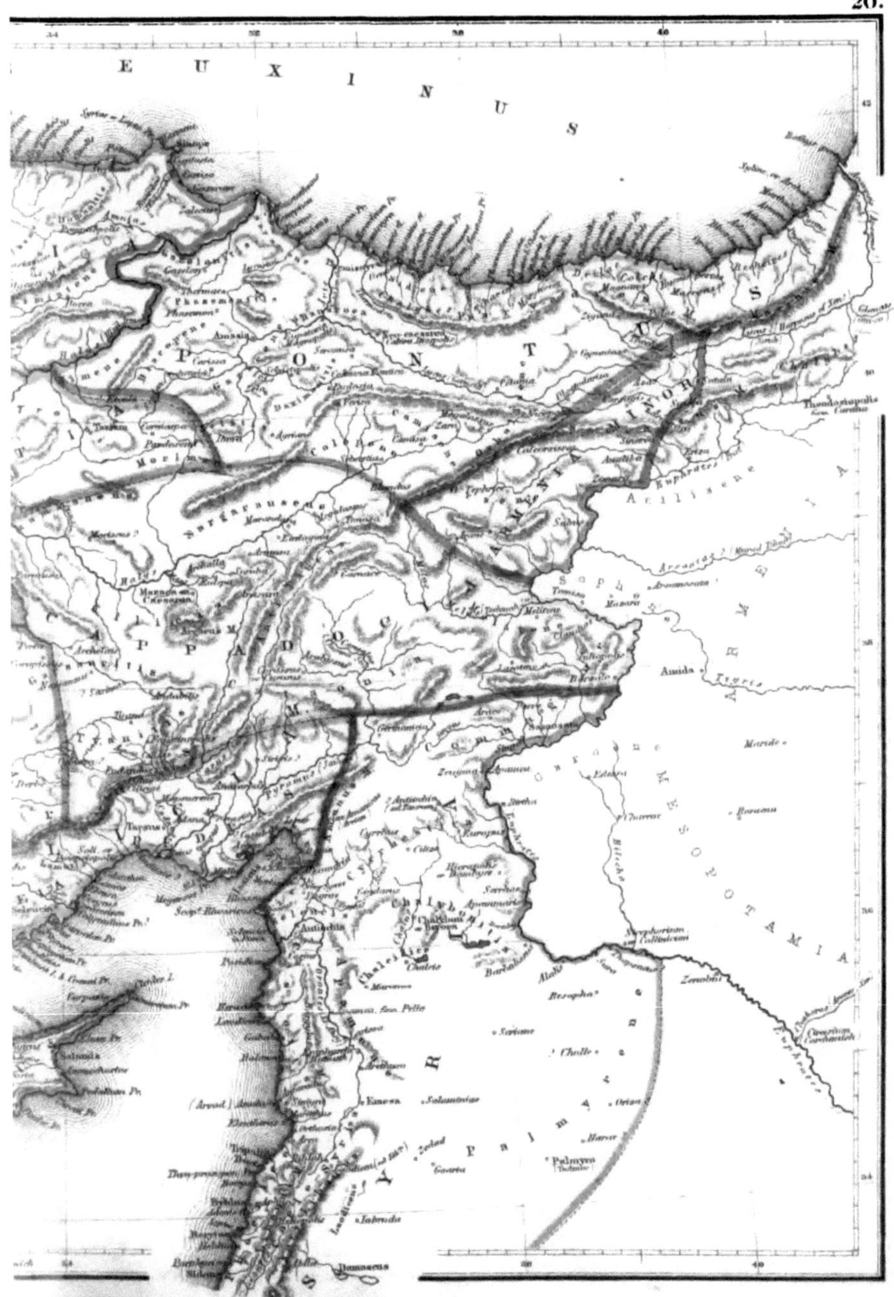
E U X I N U S
PONTUS
ARMENIA MINOR
CAPPADOCIA
CILICIA
MESOPOTAMIA
SYRIA
Amisus
Amasia
Melitene
Amida
Palmyra
Tadmor
Damascus
Euphrates
Zenobia

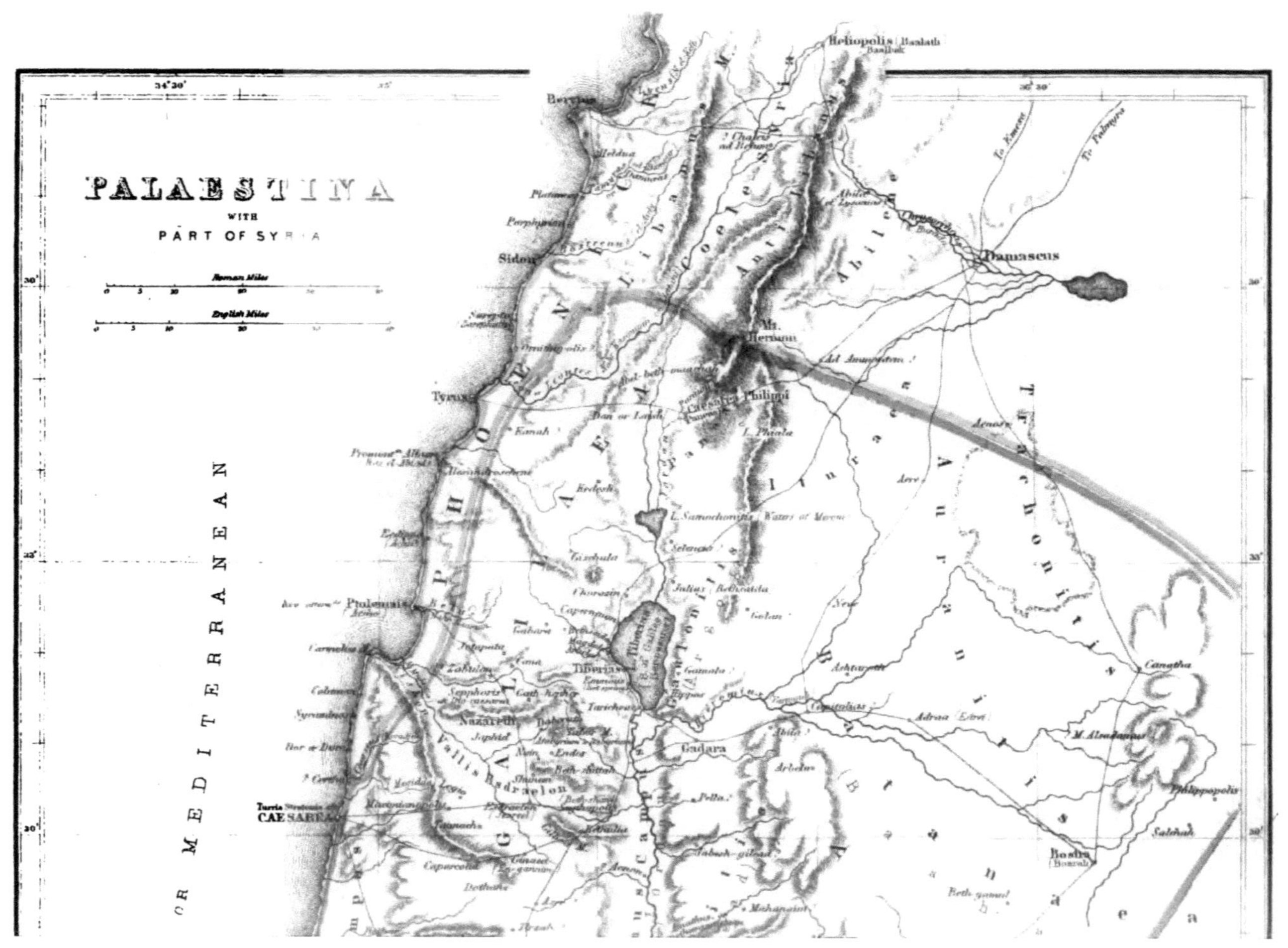

PALAESTINA
WITH
PART OF SYRIA
Roman Miles
English Miles
OR MEDITERRANEAN
Heliopolis (Baalath)
Damascus
Sidon
Tyrus
Ptolemais
Caesarea Philippi
Mt. Hermon
Nazareth
Tiberias
Gadara
CAESAREA
Bostra
Canatha
Philippopolis
Salchah
Trachonitis

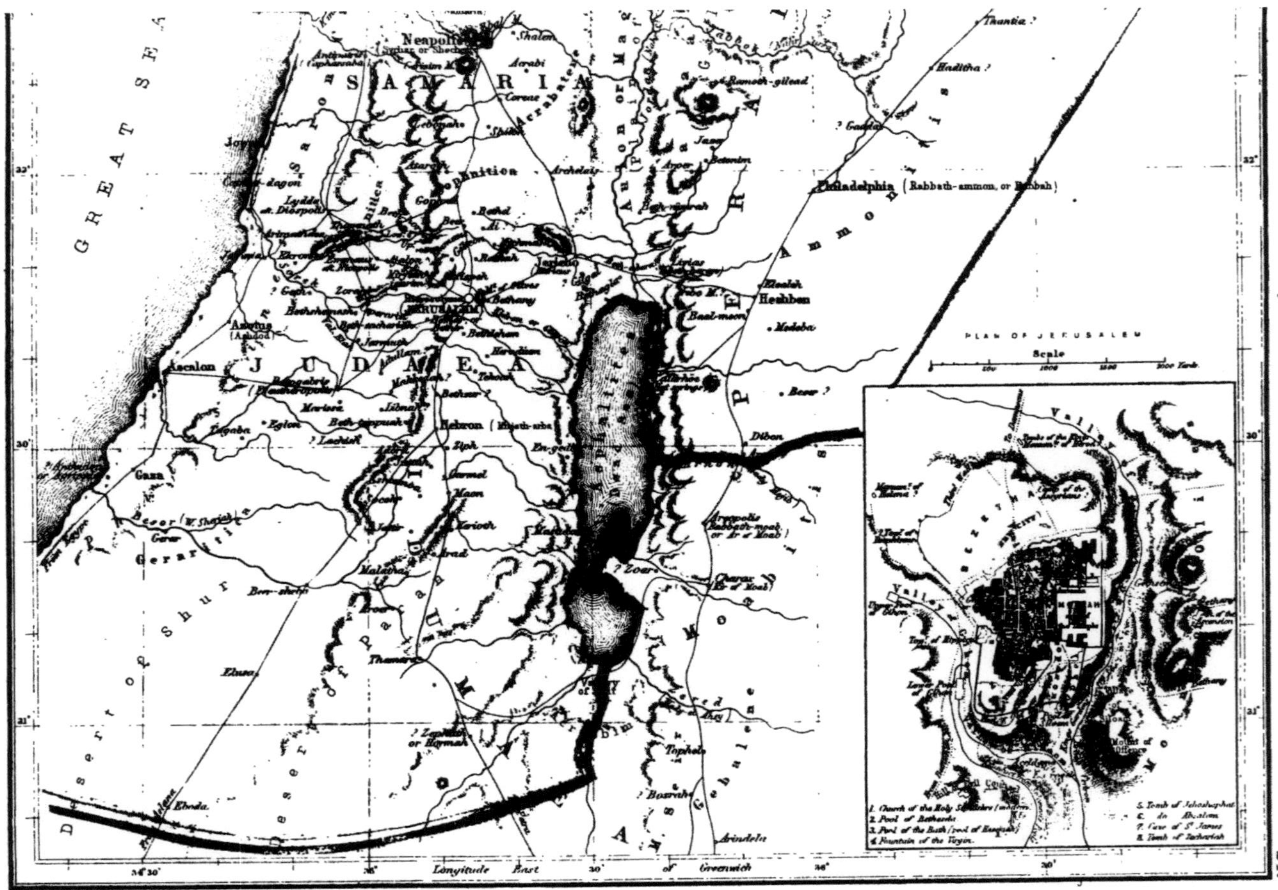
GREAT SEA
SAMARIA
JUDÆA
IDUMEA
PEREA
Neapolis (Sychar or Shechem)
Philadelphia (Rabbath-ammon, or Rabbah)
Heshbon
Ascalon
Gaza
Hebron (Kirjath-arba)
Desert of Shur
Longitude East of Greenwich
PLAN OF JERUSALEM
Scale
Valley of Jehoshaphat
1. Church of the Holy Sepulchre (modern).
2. Pool of Bethesda.
3. Pool of the Bath (pool of Hezekiah).
4. Fountain of the Virgin.
5. Tomb of Jehoshaphat.
6. do. Absalom.
7. Cave of S. James.
8. Tomb of Zacharias.

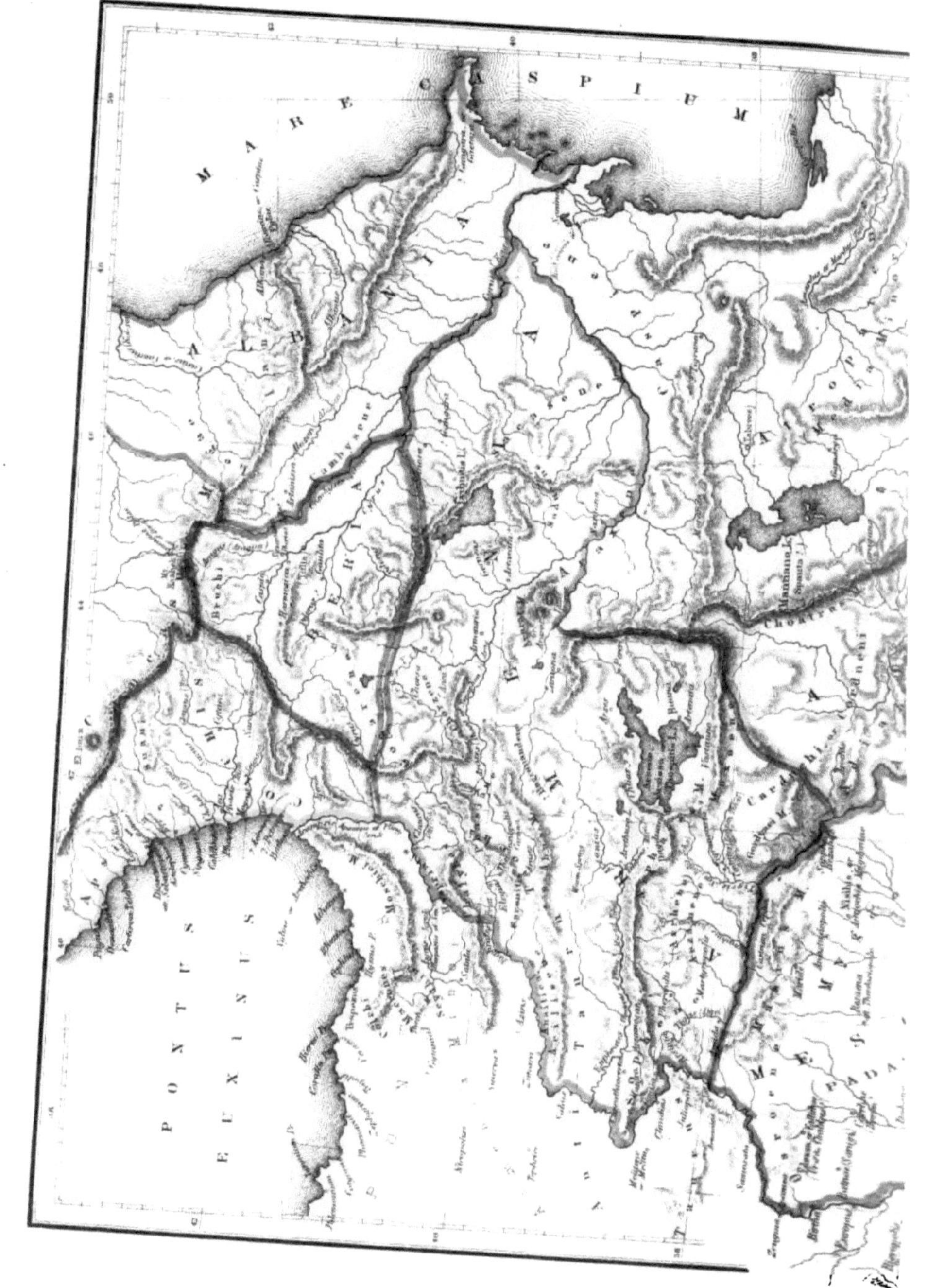

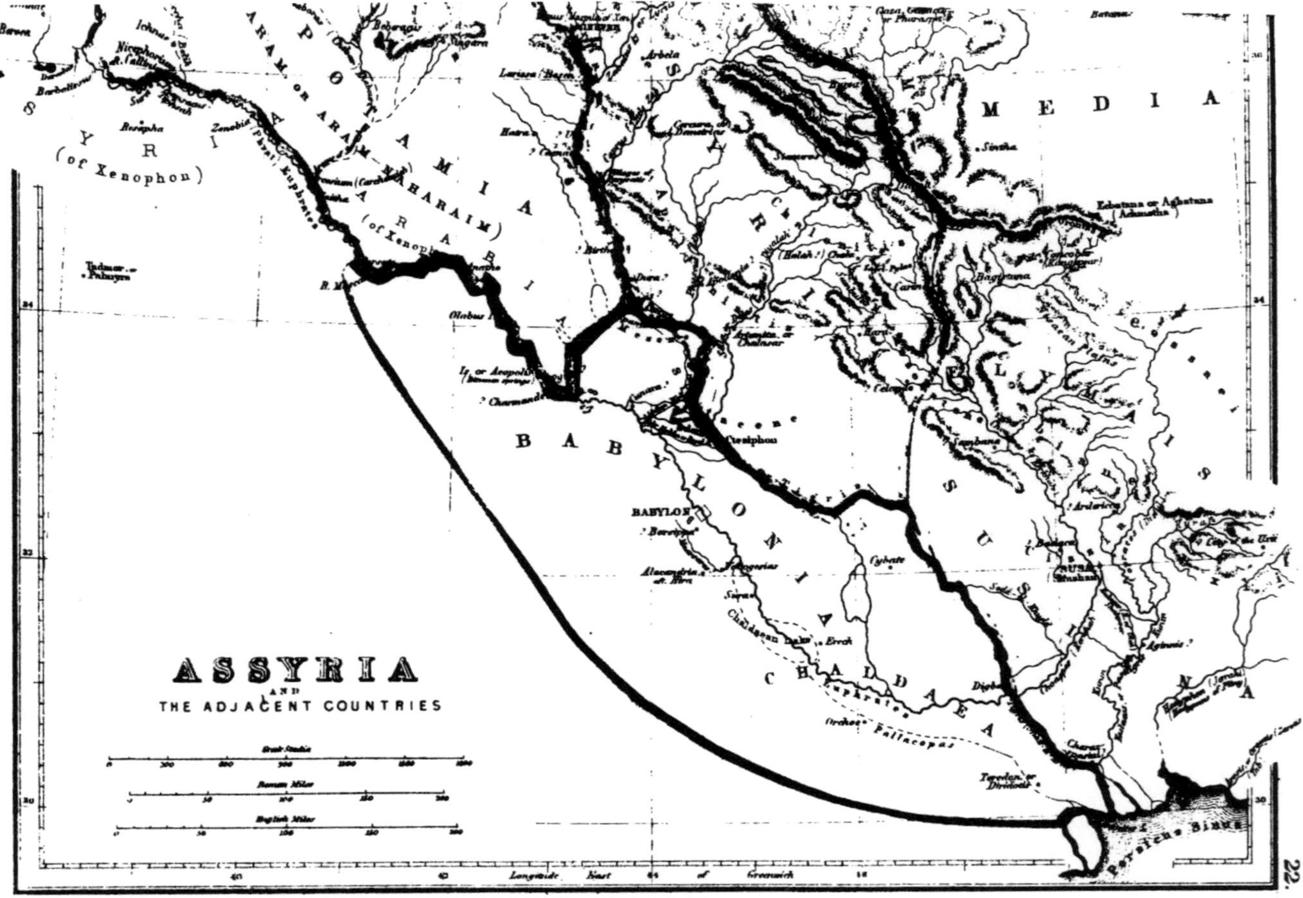
ASSYRIA
AND
THE ADJACENT COUNTRIES
MEDIA
MESOPOTAMIA
ARAM or ARAM NAHARAIM (of Xenophon)
SYRIA (of Xenophon)
ARABIA
ASSYRIA
BABYLONIA
CHALDAEA
SUSIANA
BABYLON
Persian Gulf
Euphrates
Tigris
Ctesiphon
Ecbatana or Aghatana (Achmetha)
Tadmor or Palmyra
Longitude East of Greenwich
Greek Stadia
Roman Miles
English Miles

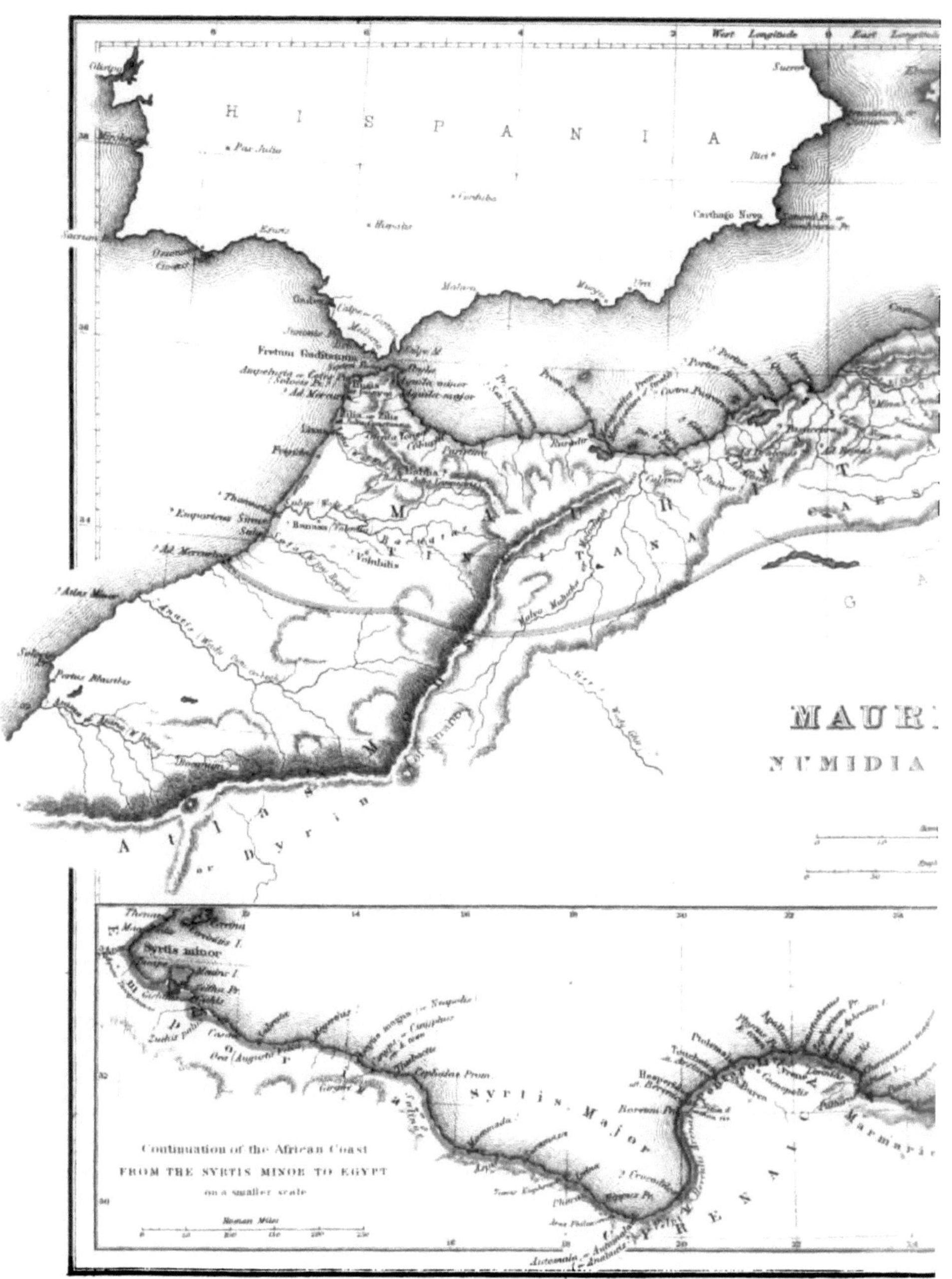

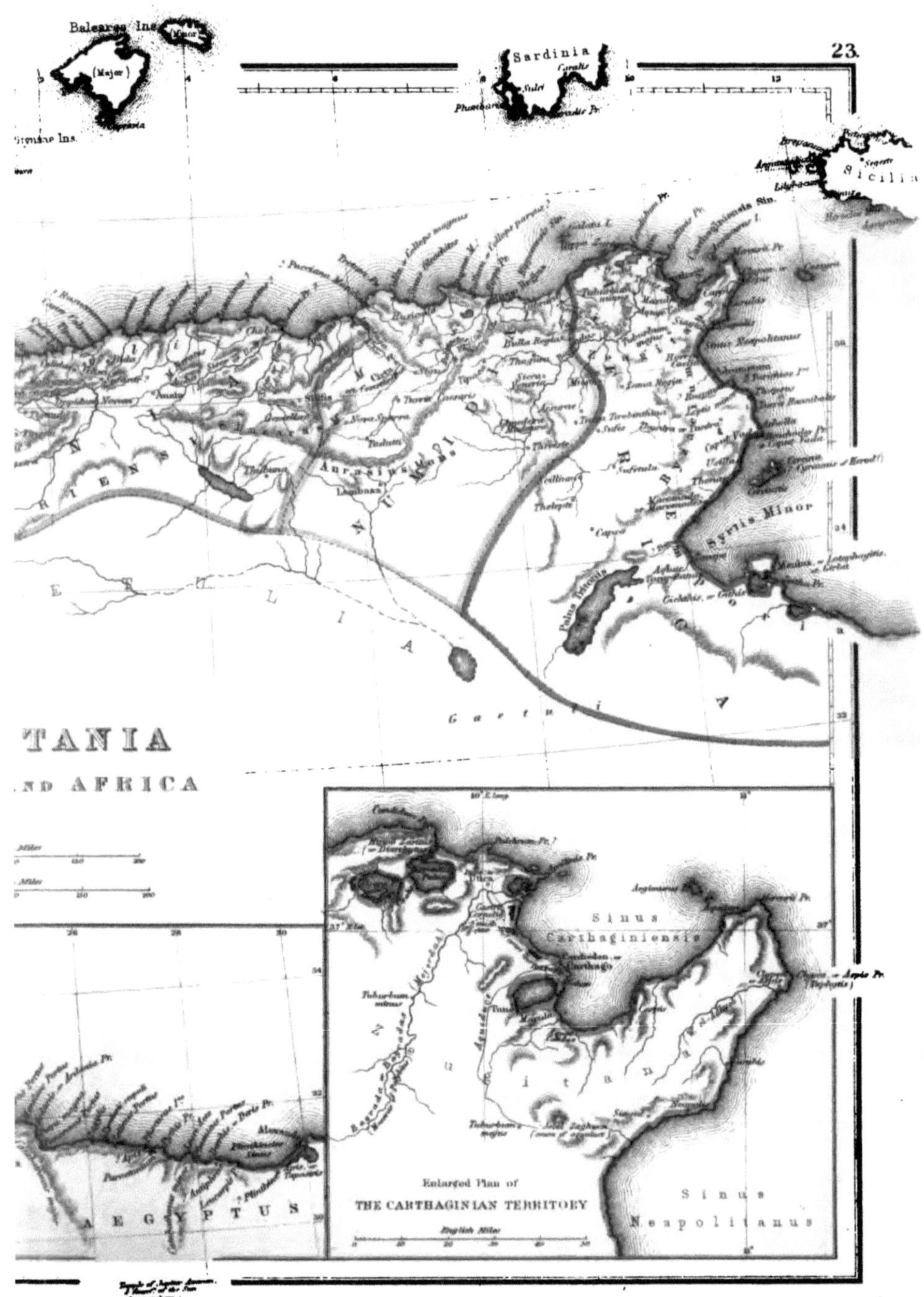

23.
Balearas Ins.
(Major)
(Minor)
Sardinia
Caralis
Sulci
Phaubaris
Sicilia
Lilybaeum
TANIA
AND AFRICA
Miles
Abrasinni Mons
Syrtis Minor
Gaetuli
Sinus Neapolitanus
Sinus Carthaginiensis
Carthago
AEGYPTUS
Enlarged Plan of
THE CARTHAGINIAN TERRITORY
English Miles
Sinus
Neapolitanus

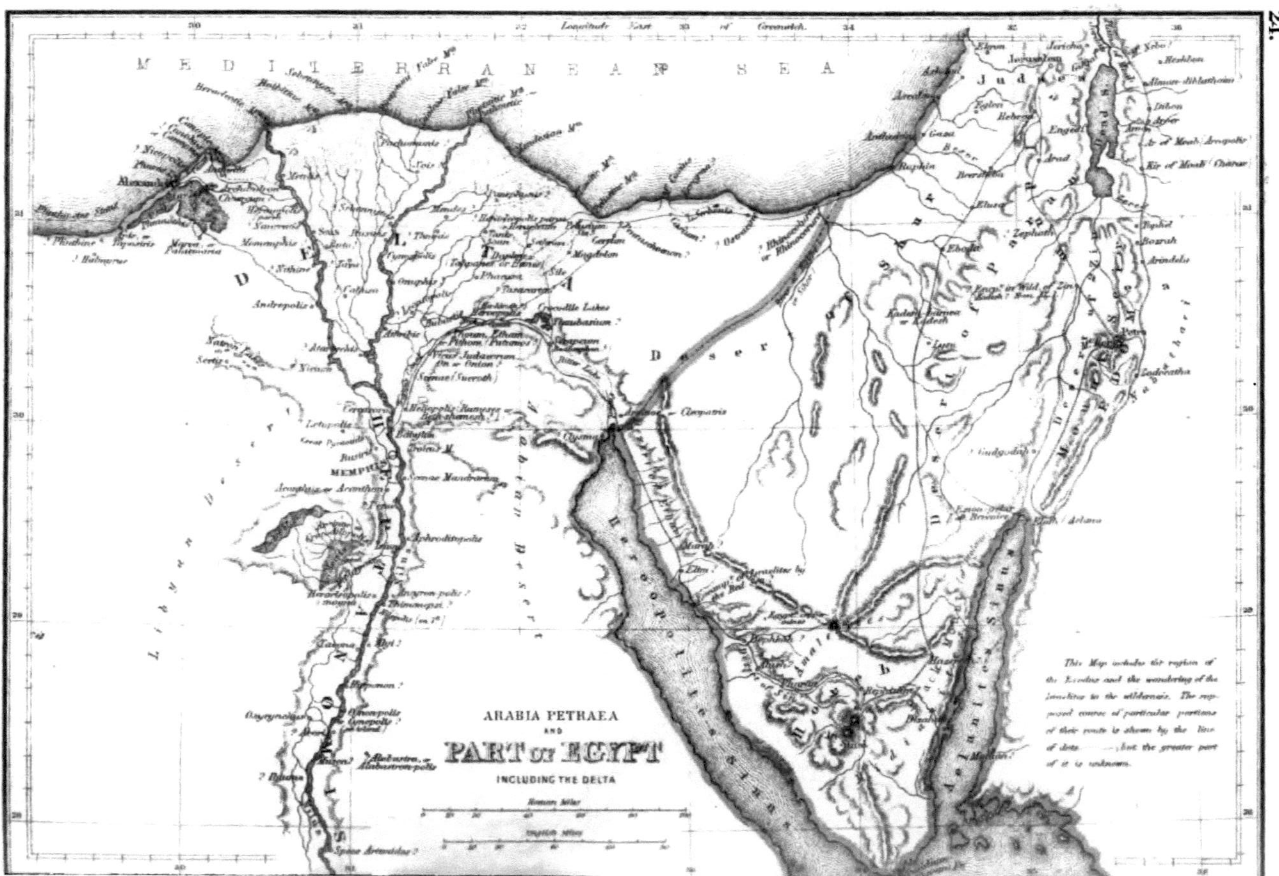
MEDITERRANEAN SEA
ARABIA PETRAEA
AND
PART OF EGYPT
INCLUDING THE DELTA
Roman Miles
English Miles
Longitude East of Greenwich
Alexandria
MEMPHIS
DELTA
Libyan Desert
Arabian Desert
Desert
Heroopolites Sinus
Aelanites Sinus
Crocodile Lakes
Bitter Lake
Judaea
This Map includes the region of
the Exodus and the wandering of the
Israelites in the wilderness. The sup-
posed course of particular portions
of their route is shown by the line
of dots ——— but the greater part
of it is unknown.

GERMANIA MAGNA
WITH THE
PROVINCES ON THE UPPER DANUBE
Roman Miles
English Miles
Oceanus Germanicus
Mare Suevicum
Cimbri
Anglia Angli
Saxones
Varini
Rugii
Lemovii
Gothones
Vistula
SARMATIA
Langobardi
Vithones or Nuithones
Semnones
Mani
Naharvali
Helvecones
Elisii Helisii
Arii Harii
Buri
Marsigni
Gothini
Carpi
Boiohemum
Boii. olt. Marcomanni
Quadi
Bastarnae
Narisci
RHAETIA
NORICUM
DACIA
GERMANIA
GALLIA
Langobardi
Chauci
Chamavi
Ubii
Marsi
Angrivarii Fosi
Elbe
Albis
Danubius
Longitude East of 20 Greenwich

HELLESPONTUS
CAPUS
Sigeum
Sigeion
Agamia
ILIUM vel TROJA
TROJA
THERMOPYLAE
Heraclea
Alpenos
Callidromus M.
PONTUS EUXINUS
Salmydessus
Perinthus
Paphlagonia
Mysia
Pergamum
Amisia
Cappadocia
Sardis
Phrygia
Colossae
Caria
Lycia
Pisidia Cilicia
Cyprus
MARE INTERNUM
SYRIA
Mantinea
Hippodromus
Peloponnesii
Thebae
Ophis
MANTINEA
ROUTE OF XENOPHON
and the Ten Thousand Greeks
Parium M.
Pylae Ciliciae
Pylae Amanicae
Issus
Alexander
ISSICUS SINUS
Alexandria
Myriandrus
Pylae Syriae
Pieria
Antiochia
Cohoenus
Leuctra
Thespiae
Thebae
Lacedaemonii
Katronis
LEUCTRA
ISSUS
Gordyaei M.
Aturia
Ninivah (Ninus)
Mespila
Gaugamela
Alexander
Darius
Larissa
Arbela
ARBELA

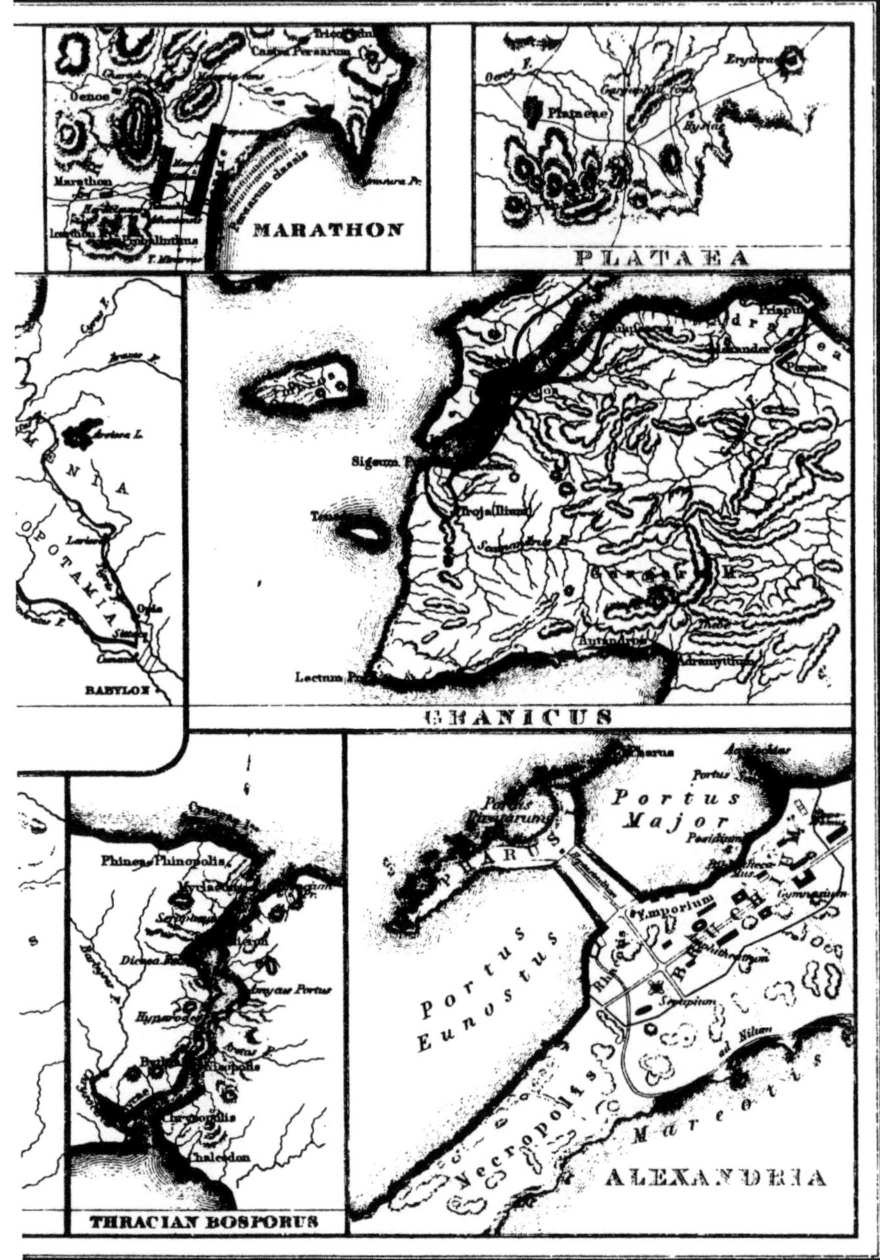

Trioonon
Castra Persarum
Oenoe
Marathon
MARATHON
Oeot. F.
Plataeae
Erythrae
Hysiae
PLATAEA
Canal L.
NIA
MESOPOTAMIA
Corcura L.
Opis
Sittace
BABYLON
Priapu
Alexander
Sigeum Pr.
Troja (Ilium)
Scamander F.
Antandrus
Adramyttium
Lectum Pr.
GRANICUS
Phineus Phinopolis
Mydacum
Scyropinga
Dicaea Port.
Hynacos
Chrysopolis
Chalcedon
THRACIAN BOSPORUS
Pharus
Portus
Portus
Major
Portus
Piratarum
Posidium
PHAROS
Emporium
Gymnasium
Portus
Eunostus
Serapium
ad Nilum
Necropolis
Mareotis
ALEXANDRIA

INDEX.

The abbreviation F. is used for Fluvius—I. or Ins. for Insula—M. for Mons—P. for Portus—Pr. or Prom. for Promontorium—S. for Sinus—n. for Near—r. for Ruins—G. for Gulf—B. for Bay—for. for Formerly.

Names of Countries, Districts, etc., are distinguished by Capitals—Names of Tribes or People by an Asterisk prefixed. The Modern Names are in Italics. The note of interrogation attached to a name signifies that the site is uncertain.

The latitudes are in all cases North, unless otherwise distinguished: the longitudes, East of the meridian of Greenwich, excepting where the letter W. (West) is attached. In the case of Rivers, the latitude and longitude given is that of the place where the name happens to be written on the Map.

NAMES.	LAT.	LONG.	MAP.
Ad Dracŏnes?	35°.8'	0°.41' w	23
Addua F., *Adde.*	45.40	9.30	8
Ad Duos Pontes, *Ponte-vedra*	42.24	8.38 w	7
Adĕba	40.43	0.40	7
Adellum, *Eldu*	38.32	0.51 w	7
Ad Ensem, *Scheggia.*	43.24	12.41	8
Ad Fines, *Fino.*	43.26	10.25	8
Ad Fines, *Arlesega.*	45.27	11.43	8
Ad Fines, *Avillano*	45.4	6.21	8
Ad Fines? *Paymago.*	37.49	7.5 w	7
Ad Formŭlos, *Verlosa.*	45.53	13.42	8
Ad Gallĭnas (Saxa Ru-bra), *Prima Porta.*	42.1	12.9	11
Ad Graecos, *Tojano.*	43.18	11.48	8
Ad Hercŭlem? *Sassari*	40.44	8.33	9
Ad Horrea? *Napoule.*	43.32	0.56	6
ADIABĒNE	36.45	43.20	22
Ad Ladios? *Banialouka*	44.46	17.12	14
Ad Lamĭnas	42.2	12.57	11
Ad Lippos.	40.39	5.52 w	7
Ad Malum?	45.34	14.17	14
Ad Martis, *Oulx.*	45.2	6.49	8
Ad Martis, *Massea.*	42.46	12.33	8
Ad Matrices, *Mostar.*	43.20	17.53	14
Ad Medias, *Samoggia.*	44.34	11.9	8
Ad Medias (Carbantia)? *Cabiano*	45.6	8.25	8
Ad Medias, *Sedilo.*	40.10	8.55	9
Ad Medias, *Mesa.*	41.23	13.6	11
Ad Mensŭlas, *Monte Al-cino*	43.5	11.30	8
Ad Mercŭri?	35.34	5.58 w	23
Ad Mercurios? *Al-Man-soriah.*	33.46	7.16 w	23
Admedera (Madaura)? *Ayedrah.*	35.30	8.27	23
Ad Morum, *Velez Rubio*	37.35	2.19 w	7
Ad Nonas, *n. Lago Morto*	42.6	12.10	11
Ad Nonum.	43.28	1.33	6
Ad Nonum, *Annone.*	44.53	8.18	8
Ad Novas	41.29	0.49	7
Ad Novas, *Monte Pul-ciano*	43.8	11.48	8
Ad Octăvum, *Rivoli.*	45.4	7.30	8
Ad Palatium, *Ala.*	45.48	11.1	8
Ad Pictas	41.46	12.52	11
Ad Pirum F., *Cesano.*	43.45	13.9	8
Ad Pirum, *Adelsberg.*	45.47	14.13	8
Ad Pontem	36.25	6.10 w	7
Ad Pontem, *Farndon, n. Newark.*	53.3	0.52 w	5
Ad Portum, *Empoli.*	43.43	10.57	8
Ad Publicănos, *L'Hôpi-tal.*	45.41	6.22	8
Ad Punĭcum, *Santa Ma-rinella*	42.2	11.51	11
Ad Putea? *Cuença.*	40.4	2.11 w	7
Ad Quercum.	45.55	11.56	8
Ad Quintănas, *n. Co-lonna*	41.52	12.46	11
Adraa (Edrei), *Draa.*	32.43	36.13	21
Ad Radices? *n. Ka-brova*	42.50	25.19	14
*Adramītae, *Coast of Hadramaut.*	15.0	50.0	3
Adramyttēnus Sinus.	39.30	26.40	19
Adramyttĭum, *Adramyti*	39.35	27.3	19
Adrana F., *Eder.*	51.10	8.45	25
Adrana, or Adrans, *St. Oswald.*	46.10	14.49	14
Adranum, or Hadranum, *Aderno*	37.38	14.49	12
Adranus F., *Aderno.*	37.45	14.48	12
Adrapsa, or Drapsaca, *Inderaub.*	35.43	69.25	3
Ad Regias? *Mofhan,* or *Afkan.*	35.15	0.5 w	23
Adria, or Hadria, *Atri.*	42.34	14.1	8
Ad Rubras, *Cabezas Ru-bias.*	37.42	6.54 w	7
Ad Rubras? *Madroma.*	35.1	1.45 w	23
Adrumētum, *Susah.*	35.50	10.35	23

NAMES.	LAT.	LONG.	MAP.
Ad Salices, *Kara Ker-man.*	44°.33'	29°.0'	14
Ad Septem Aras, *Arron-ches.*	39.9	7.5 w	7
Ad Septimum Declmum	41.20	1.0	7
Ad Sextum.	43.37	0.42	6
Ad Sextum, *Filette.*	43.16	11.14	8
Ad Silănos, *Cighigno.*	46.9	13.42	8
Ad Silănum, *Anglars, n. Estaign.*	44.36	2.46	6
Ad Sorōres.	39.14	6.7 w	7
Ad Statuas, *Xativa S. Felipe.*	38.59	0.33 w	7
Ad Taum, *Taesburgh.*	52.31	1.14	5
Ad Toglănum, *n. Palma*	40.51	14.33	13
Ad Tricesĭmum, *Trice-simo.*	46.9	13.13	8
Ad Turres.	41.57	12.5	11
Ad Turres Albas.	41.18	13.1	11
Ad Turres, *Torre Olc-vola.*	41.14	13.9	11
Ad Turres, *Olleria.*	38.56	0.45 w	7
Ad Turres?	38.53	3.54 w	7
Ad Turres, *Maida.*	38.56	16.21	9
Ad Turres.	45.11	14.42	14
Ad Turrim, *Tources.*	43.24	5.55	8
Aduatŭca, *Tongres* or *Tongern*	50.47	5.27	6
*Aduatuci	50.45	4.30	6
Adulas Mons, *Mt. St. Gothard.*	46.33	8.34	8
Adulĭcus S., *G. of Zulla*	15.15	29.45	3
Adūlis, or Adūle, *Zulla*	15.10	39.42	3
Adullam?	31.38	35.1	21
Ad Vicesĭmum, *n. Monte della Guardia.*	42.12	12.29	11
Ad Vicesĭmum, *Amen-dolara.*	39.58	16.32	9
Ad Vicesĭmum.	43.28	1.45	6
Aea, *Poti.*	42.12	41.44	22
*Aeae.			1
Aeantium Prom., *Tri-keri Point.*	39.5	23.3	15
Aeas, or Aōus F., *Vo-yussa.*	40.37	19.25	15
Aebūra? *Cuerva*	39.41	4.11 w	7
Aecae, *Troja.*	41.21	15.19	9
Aeculănum, or Eclănum, *Le Grotte, n. Mira-bella.*	41.1	13.0	9
Aedepsus, *Lipso.*	38.51	23.3	15
*Aedui	46.50	4.0	6
Aegae, or Edessa, *Vod-hena.*	40.47	22.2	15
Aegae (Euboea), *Limni*	38.45	22.20	16
Aegae (Achaia), *Akrata*	38.10	22.19	18
Aegae, *Guzel-hissar.*	38.46	27.3	19
Aegae, *Ayas.*	36.45	35.46	20
Aegalĕos M., *Skarman-ga,* or *Skaramanga.*	37.58	23.30	16
Aegalion M.? *Aghia,* or *Malia.*	37.10	21.41	18
Aegātes, or Aegŭsae Ins.	38.0	12.10	12
Aege?	39.59	23.39	15
Aegeira, *n. Mavra Li-tharia.*	38.7	22.23	18
Aegeirus.	38.4	23.9	16
Aegiae, *Limni.*	36.47	22.32	18
Aegiăle	36.54	26.0	19
Aegida, aft. Justinopŏ-lis, *C. d'Istria.*	45.32	13.44	8
Aegilia I., *Stoura.*	38.10	24.9	15
Aegilia, or Aegīla I., *Cerigotto.*	35.50	23.18	19
Aegilia, *Tzurela.*	37.45	23.55	18
Aegīlon, or Capraria I., *Cupraja.*	43.2	9.50	8
Aegimūrus I., *Zembra.*	37.8	10.48	23
Aegīna I., *Eyhina,* or *Egina.*	37.44	23.30	18
Aegīna, *Eyhina.*	37.45	23.26	18
Aeginetos, *Apana.*	40.59	34.3	20

NAMES.	LAT.	LONG.	MAP.
Aeginium, *Stagus.*	39°.40'	21°.41'	[illegible]
Aegithallus, or Aegitha-rus, Pr., *C. S. Teodora*	37.57	12.27	[illegible]
Aegitium, *n. Varnakova*	38.29	22.1	[illegible]
Aegium, *Vostitza*	38.15	22.5	[illegible]
Aegonia.	38.48	22.10	[illegible]
Aegos-potămi.	40.20	26.33	[illegible]
Aegosthĕnn, *Ghermano.*	38.9	23.14	[illegible]
Aegūsa I., *Favignana.*	37.57	12.16	[illegible]
Aegys, *Kamara.*	37.15	22.13	[illegible]
Aegyssus, or Aegypsus?	44.57	30.0	11
Aelāna (Elath), *Akaba*	29.31	35.1	[illegible]
Aelanītes Sinus, *G. of Akaba*	29.0	34.45	[illegible]
Aeminium, *Penacova.*	40.18	8.16 w	[illegible]
Aemōna, or Emōna (aft. Julia Augusta), *Lay-bach.*	46.4	14.31	14
Aenaria, Pithecūsa, or Inarīme I., *Ischia.*	40.44	13.54	11
Aeneia, *on C. Karaburnu*	40.28	22.50	15
*Aeniānes	39.0	22.10	15
Aenon?	32.26	35.36	21
Aenona, *Nona.*	44.14	15.10	14
Aenos, *El-Musmeih.*	33.16	36.26	21
Aenos, *Enos.*	40.42	26.5	[illegible]
Aenus, or Oenus F. *Inn*	47.30	12.0	[illegible]
Aenus M., *Monte Nero,* or *M. Elato.*	38.8	20.41	15
Aenyra?	40.37	24.42	[illegible]
Aeoliae, Liparaeae, or Vulcaniae Ins., *Li-pari Islands.*	38.30	15.0	[illegible]
AEŌLIS	39.0	27.0	15
Aepĕa? (Corōne), *Peta-lidhi.*	36.57	21.56	[illegible]
Aequana, *Vico Equense*	40.40	14.26	[illegible]
*Aequi, or Aequicŭli.	42.0	13.10	11
Aequinoctium, *Fischa-ment*	48.3	16.38	14
Aequum?	43.41	16.59	14
Aere, *Es-Sunamein.*	33.9	36.15	[illegible]
Aeropus M., *Mt. Tomoros*	40.35	20.10	14
Aesărus F., *Esaro.*	39.8	17.9	[illegible]
Aesēpus F.	40.0	27.30	19
Aesernia, *Isernia*	41.35	14.12	9
Aesĭca, *Great Chesters.*	55.0	2.27 w	[illegible]
Aesis F., *Esino.*	43.30	13.10	[illegible]
Aesium, *Jesi*	43.32	13.15	[illegible]
Aeson F.	40.16	22.33	[illegible]
Aestraeum, *Ostromja.*	41.28	22.43	14
Aestria I., *Lagosta*	42.45	16.53	[illegible]
Aesūla, *Mt. Afiano*	41.56	12.51	11
Aethalia or Ilva I., *Elba*	42.47	10.15	[illegible]
*Aethiopes.			1
AETHIOPIA	20.0	31.0	[illegible]
Aetna? *Castro*	37.35	14.55	[illegible]
Aetna Mons, *Etna,* or *Mongibello.*	37.44	15.0	[illegible]
AETOLIA	38.40	21.40	[illegible]
Aexōne, *Asani*	37.54	23.44	[illegible]
Affilae, *Affile*	41.54	13.6	[illegible]
AFRICA	36.0	9.30	[illegible]
Agamea.	39.50	26.10	[illegible]
Agaricus Sinus.			[illegible]
Agātha, *Agde.*	43.18	3.25	[illegible]
Agathyrna, or Agathyr-num? *San Marco.*	38.2	14.40	13
Agbatăna, or Ecbatăna, *Hamadan*	34.48	48.33	[illegible]
Agendicum, or Agedin-cum, aft. Senones, *Sens.*	48.11	3.17	[illegible]
Aginnis? *Hawas.*	31.20	48.50	[illegible]
Aginnum. *Agen.*	44.14	0.37	[illegible]
Agiria, *Daroca.*	41.13	1.17 w	[illegible]
AGISYMBA?	4.05	30.0	[illegible]
Aguavae	45.29	22.43	14
*Agraei	38.57	21.30	[illegible]
Agri Decumātes.	48.10	9.0	[illegible]
Agriăne.	39.52	35.1	[illegible]
*Agrianes	42.0	23.0	[illegible]
Agrianes F., *Erginch.*	41.20	27.0	[illegible]

NAMES.	LAT.	LONG.	MAP.
Agrigentum, or Acrăgas, *Girgenti*	37°.16'	13°.35'	12
Agrinium?	38.48	21.29	15
Agrippias, or Anthēdon?	31.27	34.25	21
Agrippína, or Colonia Agrippinensis, *Cologne*	50.56	6.57	6
Agrȳle(Upper and Lower)? *R. at foot of Hymettus*	37.57	23.44	17
Aguntum, *Innichen*	46.44	12.18	14
Agylla, aft. Caere, *Cervetri*	42.1	12.3	11
Agyrium, *S. Filippo d'Argiro*	37.38	14.32	12
Ai?	31.54	35.16	21
*Aii	10.0	77.0	2
Ajalon, *Yalo*	31.51	35.2	21
Alăba, or Allăva?	37.27	13.12	12
Alabanda, *Arab Hissar*	37.36	27.57	19
Alabastra, or Alabastron-polis?	28.21	31.7	24
Alăbus F., *Lo Cantaro, or Molinello*	37.15	15.5	12
Alaesa, or Halēsa, n. *Tusa*	37.57	14.14	12
Alaesus, or Halēsus, F., *Pettineo*	37.55	14.16	12
Alagonia? *Zarnata*	36.55	22.12	18
Alalcomēnae (Boeotia), *Sulinari*	38.22	22.59	16
Alalcomēnae (in Ithăca)?	38.22	20.41	18
Alalia, or Aleria, *Aleria*	42.7	9.31	9
Alalis, *Abu Herarah*	35.50	38.31	20
Alander F.	39.20	31.10	20
*Alāni	42.0	47.0	22
Alanton, *Lete*	42.50	1.49 w	7
Alatrium, or Aletrium, *Alatri*	41.46	13.24	11
Alauna, *Kier*	56.10	3.58 w	5
Alauna, *Alaume*, n. *Valognes*	49.31	1.27 w	6
Alaunium	43.53	5.50	6
Alaunus F.? *Alne*	55.24	1.36 w	5
Alaunus F., *Axe*	50.43	3.3 w	5
Alāzon F., *Alasan*	41.40	46.0	22
Alba, *Abla*	37.14	2.55 w	7
Alba?	42.50	2.14 w	7
Alba F., *Ter*	42.0	2.35	7
Alba Fucentia, or Fucentia, *Colle di Albe*	42.4	13.26	11
Alba Helviōrum, *Aps, or Alps*	44.33	4.36	6
Alba Longa	41.46	12.41	11
Alba Pompeia, *Alba*	44.41	8.2	8
Albāna, *Derbend*	42.5	48.12	22
*Albani			1
ALBANIA	41.30	47.30	22
Albaniae or Caspiae Pylae, *Pass of Derbend*	42.0	48.16	22
Albānus F., *Seamour*	41.28	48.0	22
Albānus L., *Lago di Albano*	41.45	12.41	11
Albānus M., *Monte Cavo*	41.45	12.44	11
Albānus, or Albius M.	44.30	17.0	14
Albianum, *Kufstein*	47.35	12.11	14
*Albici	43.50	6.0	6
Albiga, *Alby*	43.57	2.9	6
Albinia F., *Albeyna*	42.34	11.24	8
Albion			1
Albis F., *Elbe*	53.20	10.30	25
Albium Intemelium, *Vintimiglia*	43.45	7.40	6
Albium Ingaunum, *Albenga*	44.4	8.12	8
Albius, or Albānus M.	44.30	17.0	14
Albona, *Albona*	45.5	14.7	8
Albonica, *Puerta da Daroca*	41.7	1.20 w	7
Albucella (Arbucale, or Arbacala)?	41.46	5.25 w	7
Album Pr., *Ras el-Abiad, or White C.*	33°.12'	35°.8'	21
Alburnus Mons, *Monte Alburno, or Di Postiglione*	40.30	15.20	9
Albus Portus, n. *Algesiras*	36.6	5.26 w	7
Aloe, *Alcazar de S.Juan*	39.25	3.14 w	7
Alcīmus	37.56	23.38	17
Alcyonium Mare, *B. of Livadostro*	38.7	23.5	18
Alea, *Alia*	39.24	5.3 w	7
Alea	37.46	22.29	18
Aleius Campus	36.45	35.10	20
Alele? *Mourzouk*	25.50	14.12	2
Aleria, or Alalia, *Aleria*	42.7	9.31	9
Alesia, *Alise*	47.37	4.23	6
Alesiae	37.3	22.27	18
Alesius M	37.38	22.26	18
Aletrium, *S. Maria della Lizza*	40.0	18.6	9
Aletrium, or Alatrium, *Alatri*	41.46	13.24	11
Aletrium, *Calitri*	40.33	15.26	9
Alexandreia Troas, *Eski Stamboul*	39.45	26.10	19
Alexandria ultIma, *Khojend*	41.21	68.30	3
Alexandria, aft. Hira	32.0	44.30	22
Alexandria? n. *Mittunkote*	29.0	69.28	3
Alexandria (ad Caucasum), *Ghoorbund*	34.50	68.40	3
Alexandria (ad Issum), *Iskenderoon*	36.35	36.9	20
Alexandria (in Ariis), *Herat*	34.22	62.10	3
Alexandria, *Iskenderich, or Alexandria*	31.11	29.55	24
Alexandroschene, *Iskenderoona*	33.11	35.8	21
Algidus	41.44	12.49	11
Aliassus, *Karaketscheli*	39.38	33.26	20
Alicanum, *Martyancz*	44.31	16.27	14
Alinda, *Demirji Dereh*	37.33	27.50	19
Aliphēra	37.31	21.53	18
Aliso, *Elsen*	51.45	8.45	25
Alista, *Porto Vecchio*	41.36	9.17	9
Allaria, *Monteforte*	35.10	26.0	19
Allăva F.? *Caltabellotta*	37.30	13.14	12
*Allemanni	48.40	9.0	25
Allia F.? *Scolo del Casale*	42.4	12.35	11
Allia F.? *Di Conca*	42.0	12.32	11
Allifae, *Alife*	41.20	14.18	9
Allobo, *Alagon*	41.51	1.8 w	7
*Allobrōges	45.30	5.30	6
Alma F., *Alma*	42.50	10.50	8
Almo F., *Aequataccia*	41.52	12.30	11
Almus, n. *Smorden, or Smordini*	42.47	23.5	14
Alōne, *Ambleside*	54.26	2.57 w	5
Alonta F., *Terek*	43.40	45.0	3
Alōpe (Locris)	38.43	22.56	16
Alōpe (Phthiotis)	38.54	22.46	16
Alopeconnēsus	40.18	26.15	19
Alōrus, *Paleakhora*	40.31	22.31	15
Alos, or Halos, *Kefalosi*	39.9	22.47	15
Alpēnos	38.47	22.32	16
Alpes Carnicae, or Juliae, *Carnic or Julian Alps*	46.32	13.20	8
Alpes Cottiae, *Cottian Alps*	45.0	6.42	8
Alpes Graiae, *Grecian, or Graian, Alps*	45.30	7.0	8
Alpes Maritīmae, *Maritime Alps*	44.10	7.20	8
Alpes Noricae, *Noric Alps*	47.20	14.0	14
Alpes Pennīnae, *Pennine Alps*	46.0	8.0	8
Alpes Rhaeticae, *Rhaetian Alps*	46°.25'	10°.0'	8
Alpheius F., *Rufia*	37.36	21.45	19
Alpis Cottia, *Mont Genévre*	44.56	6.42	8
Alpis Graia, *Little St. Bernard*	45.40	6.51	8
Alpis Pennīna, *Great St. Bernard*	45.53	7.9	8
Alsa F., *Ausa*	46.0	13.16	8
Alsadamus Mons? *Kelb Hauran*	32.41	36.46	21
Alsietīnus L., *Lago di Martignano*	42.8	12.17	11
Alsium, *Palo*	41.56	12.3	11
Alsuga, *Borgo di Valsugana*	46.5	11.23	8
Altīnum? *Batazzek*	46.11	18.45	14
Altīnum, *Altino*	45.34	12.22	8
Aluntium? *S. Filadelfo*	38.2	14.34	12
Alush?	28.47	33.25	24
Alutas F., *Aluta*	44.30	24.15	14
Alydda	38.53	30.4	20
Alyi?	28.55	31.6	24
Alyzia, *Kandili*	38.42	20.59	15
*Amalekites	29.0	34.0	24
Amallobriga, *Tordesillas*	41.31	5.2 w	7
AMANTIA	40.23	19.40	15
Amantia, *Livissa*	40.21	19.41	15
Amānus Mons, *Jawur Dagh, etc.*	37.0	36.20	20
Amanus Portus, aft. Flaviobriga, *Portugalete*	43.20	3.3 w	7
Amardus, or Mardus F., *Kisil Uzen, or Sejred Rood*	37.30	48.0	22
Amarynthus	38.23	23.51	16
Amasēnus, *Amaseno*	41.26	13.13	11
Amasia, *Amasia*	40.36	35.54	20
Amastris, for. Sesāmus, *Amasserah*	41.45	32.24	20
Amāthus, *Old Limasol*	34.43	33.9	20
Amāthus, or Betharamathum, *Amateh*	32.19	35.40	21
Ambacia, *Amboise*	47.24	1.0	6
*Ambarri	46.16	5.0	6
Ambastus F.			1
*Ambiāni	49.48	2.0	6
Ambiāni, *Amiens*	49.54	2.17	6
*Ambivareti	47.15	3.20	6
Amboglanna, *Burgoswald*	54.59	2.37 w	5
AMBRACIA	39.5	21.0	15
Ambracia, *Arta*	39.8	21.0	15
Ambracius S., *G. of Arta*	38.57	20.55	15
Ambrācus, *Fidho-Kastro*	39.2	20.57	15
Ambre, *Dachau*	48.16	11.28	25
Ambrȳsus, *Dhistomo*	38.26	22.40	16
Ameria, *Amelia*	42.33	12.26	8
Amestrătus, *Mistretta*	37.55	14.21	12
Amīda, *Diyarbekr*	37.55	39.54	22
Amilus? *Aghia Triada*	37.45	22.21	18
Amisia F., *Ems*	52.40	7.20	25
Amīsus, *Samsoon*	41.20	36.21	20
Amiternum, *San Vettorino*	42.23	13.22	8
Ammochostos, *Famagousta*	35.7	33.58	20
AMMONITIS	32.0	36.12	21
Amnias F., *Kostambul Tchai, or Gok Irmak*	41.30	34.30	20
Amorgos I., *Amorgo*	36.50	26.0	19
Amorium, *Hergan Kaleh*	39.0	31.27	20
Ampēlos M.	37.45	26.52	19
Ampēlos Pr., *C. Pseudo*	39.57	24.1	15
Ampēlos Pr., *C. Colonni*	37.38	26.53	19
Ampēlus Pr., *C. Sacro*	35.1	26.16	19
Ampelusia, or Cotes Pr., *C. Spartel*	35.47	5.56 w	23
Amphanae	39.20	22.55	15
Ampheia	37.15	22.5	18

NAMES.	LAT.	LONG.	MAP.
Amphiareium, *Mavro-Dhilissi*	38°.17'	23°.50'	16
Amphicleia, or Amphi-caea, *Dhadhi*	38.38	22.35	16
AMPHILOCHIA	39.4	21.15	15
Amphimalla	35.21	24.18	19
Amphipăgus Prom.? *C. Bianco*	39.21	20.7	15
Amphipŏlis, *Neokhorio*	40.48	23.51	15
Amphissa, *Solona*	38.32	22.22	16
Amphitrŏpe, *Metropista*	37.47	24.0	18
Amphītus F.	37.16	22.0	18
Amphrȳsus F.	39.10	22.47	15
Ampsaga F., *Wady el-Kebir*	36.45	6.10	23
Amsanctus Lacus, *Le Mofete*	40.59	15.1	9
Amyclae	41.16	13.20	9
Amyclae, *Agios Kyriaki*	37.2	22.27	18
Amyrus F.	39.34	22.44	15
Amȳrus? *Kastri*	39.34	22.41	15
Amȳzon	37.34	27.42	19
Anabucis (or Automa-lax?)	30.16	19.14	23
Anactorium	38.54	20.50	15
Anaea, *Arnear*	37.47	27.19	19
Anagnia, *Anagni*	41.46	13.10	11
Anagyrus, *Vari*	37.50	38.48	16
ANAITICA, or ACILISĒNE	39.20	40.0	22
Analiba, *Herhemeh*	39.31	39.16	20
Anamis F., *Ibrahim*	27.10	57.20	3
*Ananes	44.50	10.0	8
Anăphe I. and Town, *Anafi*	36.22	25.48	19
Anaphlystus, *Anavyso*	37.43	23.56	18
Anăpus F. (Acarnania)	38.35	21.14	15
Anăpus F., *Anapo, or Fiume di Sortino*	37.5	15.10	13
Anas F., *Guadiana*	38.27	7.10 w	7
Anassus F., *Revonchi*	46.0	13.13	8
Anastatiopŏlis, *Dara*	37.10	40.57	22
Anătho, *Annah*	34.30	42.3	22
Anatis F.? *Wady Oom-er-begh*	33.10	8.0 w	23
Anaua L. (or Ascania?) *L. of Chardak, or Hadji Tous Ghieul*	37.53	30.0	20
Anaunium, *Non*	46.18	•10.57	8
Anazarbus, *Ain Zarba*	37.18	35.51	20
*Ancalites	51.20	1.50 w	6
Anchesmus M. (Lyca-bettus), *Hill of St. George*	37.59	23.45	17
Anchiăle? *Mound n. Karaduwar*	36.48	34:43	20
Anchiălus, *Ahiolou*	42.34	27.40	14
Anchisa M., *Armenia*	37.42	22.25	18
Ancon Pr., *C. Tchalti*	41.22	36.40	20
Ancŏna, *Ancona*	43.37	13.31	8
Ancȳra	39.11	28.58	20
Ancȳra, *Angora*	39.56	32.56	20
Ancyron-pŏlis?	29.9	31.15	24
Andabĭlis, *Eski Andaval*	37.56	34.50	20
Andaca? *Valley of Lughman*	34.38	70.25	3
Andania, *Eliniko-kastro*	37.17	22.1	18
Andecavi, *Angers*	47.28	0.33 w	6
Andematūnum, *Langres*	47.51	5.21	6
Anderida? *Pevensey*	50.49	0.21	5
Anderitum, *Anterrieux*	44.50	3.4	6
*Andes, or Andecavi	47.30	0.30 w	6
Andes, *Pistola*	45.7	10.50	8
Andretium	43.43	16.15	14
Andriăce, *Andraki*	36.13	30.2	20
Andrius F.	39.52	26.45	19
Andropŏlis	30.37	30.46	24
Andros, *Palaeopolis*	37.49	24.50	19
Andros I., *Andro*	37.50	24.55	19
Anemo F., *Lamone*	44.10	11.43	8
Anemoreia?	38.27	22.38	16
Anemurium, *Anamour*	36.1	32.51	20
Angĕle? *Papa Anghe-lati*	37.58	23.53	16

NAMES.	LAT.	LONG.	MAP.
Angellae, *Rute*	37.25'	4.25' w	7
Angites F., *Anghista*	40.50	24.0	19
Angitŭla F., *Angitola*	38.10	16.16	9
*Anglii, or Angli	54.20	10.0	25
*Angrivarii	52.15	9.0	25
Angularia, *Anguillara*	42.7	12.14	11
Angŭlus, *S. Angelo*	42.30	12.8	8
Anigrus F., *Mavropo-tamo*	37.30	21.38	18
Anio F., *Teverone*	41.56	12.40	11
Annamatia, *Adony*	47.7	18.54	14
Anneisnum, *Legnago*	45.11	11.20	8
Anopaea	38.44	22.28	16
Anopŏlis	35.13	24.6	19
Ansa Paullīni, *Anse*	45.56	4.43	6
*Ansibarii	53.10	7.15	25
Antandros, *Antandro*	39.34	26.50	19
Antarădus, *Tartoos*	34.52	35.55	20
Antemnae	41.57	12.30	11
Anthĕdon (Boeotia), *Paleo-kastro*	38.28	23.27	16
Anthĕdon, or Agrip-pias?	31.27	34.25	21
Anthĕla	38.48	22.28	26
ANTHĔMUS	40.32	23.10	15
Anthĕmus	40.31	23.13	15
Anthĕmus F?	42.50	41.18	22
Anthĕne? *Ellinico*	37.23	22.41	18
Anthylla	31.15	30.12	24
Anticȳra (Locris)?	38.24	22.0	18
Anticȳra (Malis)	38.51	22.22	16
Anticȳra (Phocis), *As-pra Spitia*	38.23	22.38	16
Antigonĕa, or Psaphăra	40.20	23.6	15
Antigoneia? *Tepedelen*	40.20	20.0	15
Anti-Libănus, *Jebel esh-Shurky*	34.10	36.10	20
Antinŏe, for. Besa, *Sheikh Abadeh*	27.48	30.54	3
Antinoopŏlis, *Cherkesh*	40.43	32.56	20
Antīnum, *Civita d'An-tino*	41.53	13.27	11
Antiocheia (ad Maean-drum)	37.52	38.33	19
Antiochīa (ad Taurum)? *Aintab*	37.4	37.25	20
Antiochīa, *Antakia*	36.12	36.9	20
Antiochīa Mygdoniae, or Nisibis, *Nisibin*	37.1	41.10	22
Antiochīa (ad Cragum)	36.8	32.30	20
Antiochīa (Pisidia), *Ya-lobatch*	38.16	31.17	20
Antiochīa? *Merv*	37.30	62.0	3
Antipatreia, *Arnaoud Berat*	40.44	19.49	14
Antipătris (Capharsa-ba), *Kefr Saba*	32.13	34.59	21
Antiphellus, *Andifilo*	36.12	29.41	20
Antīphrae? *Kasr Jam-memeh*	31.7	28.22	23
Antipŏlis, *Antibes*	43.35	7.7	6
Antipyrgos Portus, *Mar-sa Toubrouk*	32.2	24.3	23
Antiquaria, *Antequera*	37.9	4.35 w	7
Anti-Rhium Pr., *Kastro-Roumeli*	38.20	21.46	18
Antissa, *Kalas Limneo-nas, n. Sigri*	39.13	25.52	19
Antistiăna, *Llacuneta*	41.27	1.28	7
Anti-Taurus, *Dujik Dagh, &c*	39.15	40.0	22
Antium, *Porto d'Anzo*	41.25	12.40	11
Antivestaeum, Bole-rium, or Belerium, Prom., *Land's End*	50.4	5.42 w	20
Antona F., *Nen*	52.25	0.32 w	5
Antron, *Fano*	38.58	23.0	16
Antunnacum, *Ander-nach*	50.26	7.24	6
Anurogrammum, *Ana-rajahpoora*	8.18	80.31	2
Anxănum (Apulia), *Torre di Rivoli*	41.29	15.56	9

NAMES.	LAT.	LONG.	MAP.
Anxānum (Frentano-rum), *Lanciano Vec-chio*	42°.14'	14.°23'	8
Anxia, *Anzi*	40.29	15.54	8
Anxur, or Tarracina, *Terracina*	41.16	13.15	11
Aornos ?	34.25	73.0	:
Aornos (Bactriana)?	36.40	68.35	3
Aotis, or Aeas F., *Vo-yussa*	40.37	19.25	15
Apamĕa	37.17	37.53	20
Apamĕa, for. Pella, *Famieh*	35.29	36.24	20
Apamĕa Cibŏtus, *Di-neir*	38.3	30.13	20
Apamĕa Myrtĕa, *Mou-dania*	40.22	28.54	20
Apameia, *Jibbarah*	34.2	44.3	22
APAMĒNE	35.30	36.30	24
Apammaris	36.16	38.12	20
Apelaurus M.	37.50	22.28	18
Apenninus Mons, *Apen-nines*	44.0	11.0	8
APERANTIA	38.50	21.27	15
Aperopia I., *Dhoko*	37.20	23.20	18
Aperrhae	36.9	29.52	20
Apĕsas M., *Fouka*	37.51	22.45	18
Aphĕtae, *Trikeri*	39.5	23.5	15
Aphidna, *Kotroni*	38.11	23.54	16
Aphrodisias (Caria), *Geira*	37.43	28.45	20
Aphrodisias (Cilicia)	36.10	33.41	20
Aphrodisias (Laconia)?	26.34	22.57	18
Aphrodisium (Latium)?	41.35	12.29	11
Aphrodisium (Cyprus)	35.24	33.50	20
Aphroditŏpolis, *Atfieh*	29.27	31.20	24
Aphȳtis, *Athyto*	40.6	23.27	15
Apiarium	38.42	0.51 w	7
Apicilia, *Latisana*	45.46	13.0	8
Apidănus F., *Fersaliti*	39.25	22.10	15
Apīla, or Apilas, F., *R. of Platamona*	39.57	22.35	15
Apis?	31.24	27.2	22
Apis?(Taposiris?) *Arab's Tower*	30.47	29.34	24
*Apodŏti	38.31	21.50	15
Apollīnis Lucus, *Pol-lone*	45.37	7.59	8
Apollīnis Pr., *C.Gobeah, or Farina*	37.11	10.14	22
Apollinopŏlis Magna, *Edfou*	24.59	32.54	3
Apollinopŏlis Parva	27.0	31.22	3
Apollo Corynthus, *Tem-ple of*	36.51	21.56	11
Apollonia, *Paleo-kastro, n. Armyro*	35.23	25.4	19
Apollonia, aft. Sozopŏ-lis, *Sizeboli*	42.26	27.44	14
Apollonia, *Arsouf*	32.18	34.51	21
Apollonia, *Marsa Sousa*	32.54	21.56	23
Apollonia, *Abulliont*	40.9	28.42	20
Apollonia, *Pollina*	37.57	14.8	12
Apollonia (Assyria)?	34.22	44.24	22
Apollonia (Acte)	40.13	24.20	15
Apollonia (Chalcidice), *Polighero*	40.24	23.22	15
Apollonia, Eleuthĕrae, or Eleutherna?	35.19	24.41	19
Apollonia (Illyria), *Pol-lina, or Pollona*	40.40	19.25	15
Apollonia (Lydia)?	38.59	27.31	19
Apollonia Mordiaeum, *Oluburlu*	38.6	30.38	20
Apollonia (Mygdonia), *Pollina*	40.36	22.30	15
Apollonia (Siphnos), *Kastro*	36.58	24.44	19
Apollonia (Thracia)?	41.7	25.6	19
APOLLONIĀTIS	34.20	44.30	22
Apolloniātis L., *L. of Abulliont*	40.10	28.35	20
Apollŏnis	38.46	27.37	19

(86)

NAMES.	LAT.	LONG.	MAP.
Agōni fons, or Patavī-nae Aquae, *Bagni d'Albano*	45°.22'	11°.46'	8
Apostāna?	27.5	53.2	3
App aria, *Taban*	43.55	26.14	14
Appii Forum, *Foro Appio*	41.28	13.1	11
Appiōla? *n. Ponte delle Streghe*	41.47	12.36	11
Apros, or Apri, *Ainad-jik*	40.54	27.11	14
Aprusa F., *Ausa*	44.2	12.38	8
Apsārus F. (Acampsis?) *Joruk Su*	41.0	41.46	20
*Apsilae	43.0	41.10	22
*Apsinthii	40.50	26.30	14
Apsus F., *Chervesta*	40.50	19.35	14
Apta Julia, *Apt*	43.52	5.25	6
Aptēra, *Palevkastro*	35.27	24.7	19
*Apuāni?	44.27	10.0	8
APULIA	41.0	16.0	9
Apulum (ColoniaNova), *Karlsburg*	46.5	23.35	14
Aqua Crabra, *Marrana*	41.53	12.32	11
Aqua Viva, *Majerje*	46.21	16.11	14
Aqua Viva, *Acquaviva*	42.18	12.25	11
Aquae, *Beran-Palanka*	44.27	22.30	14
Aquae, *Baaden*	48.1	16.11	14
Aquae Albūlae	41.59	12.44	11
Aquae Apollināres, *Bag-ni di Stigliano*	42.11	12.1	11
Aquae Augustae, or Tar-bellīcae, *Dax*	43.43	1.2 w	6
Aquae Balissae?	45.33	17.20	14
Aquae Bilbitanōrum, *Alhama*	41.20	1.54 w	7
Aquae Borbōnis, *Bour-bonne-les-Bains*	47.57	5.45	6
Aquae Bormōnis, *Bour-bon l'Archambault*	46.36	3.2	6
Aquae Caeretānae, *Bag-ni di Sapo*	42.4	11.59	11
Aquae Calīdae, *n. Chift-lik Khan*	37.27	34.46	20
Aquae Calīdae, *Ham-mam Merigah*	36.25	2.22	23
Aquae Calīdae, *Ham-mam l'Enf, n. Tunis*	36.42	10.18	23
Aquae Calīdae, *Vichy*	46.7	3.25	9
Aquae Celenae, *Caldas de Rey*	42.34	8.38 w	7
Aquae Convenārum, *Bagnères de Bigorre*	43.4	0.9	6
Aquae Ferentīnae, *n. San Rocca*	41.47	12.41	11
Aquae Flaviae, *Chaves*	41.55	7.30 w	7
Aquae Gratiānae, *Aix*	45.42	5.54	6
Aquae Mattiācae, *Wies-baden*	50.5	8.15	25
Aquae Neapolitānae, *n. Sardara*	39.37	8.47	9
Aquae Neri, *Neris*	46.16	2.40	6
Aquae Nisineii, *Bour-bon l'Anci*	46.37	3.46	6
Aquae Origīnis?	42.10	8.27 w	7
Aquae Passēris, *Ba-cucco*	42.27	12.3	8
Aquae Pisānae, *Bagni di Pisa*	43.46	10.26	8
Aquae Populoniae	42.58	10.38	8
Aquae Querquennae?	42.12	8.12 w	7
Aquae Segeste, *Fer-rières*	48.2	2.35	6
Aquae Segeste?	45.25	4.18	6
Aquae Sextiae, *Aix*	43.32	5.27	6
Aquae Statiellae, *Acqui*	44.40	8.27	8
Aquae Solis, *Bath*	51.23	2.21 w	5
Aquae Tacapitānae, *El-Hammat-el-Khabs*	33.50	9.45	23
Aquae Vetuloniae, *Ve-tulia*	43.6	10.33	8
Aquae Voconiae, *Caldas (n. Gerona)*	41.53	2.51	7
Aquīla major, *n. Te-touan*	35°.37'	5°.17' w	23
Aquīla minor, *Castillejo*	35.45	5.21 w	23
Aquilaria, *Awariyeh*	37.4	10.58	23
Aquileia, *Aquileia*	45.46	13.22	8
Aquileia, *Incisa*	43.41	11.29	8
Aquilonia, *Lacedogna*	41.4	15.25	9
Aquincum, or Acincum, *Alt-Buda*	47.30	19.3	14
Aquīnum, *Aquaria*	44.16	10.44	8
Aquīnum, *Aquino*	41.30	13.41	9
*Aquitāni	44.0	0.30 w	6
AQUITANIA	45.0	1.0	4
Ar of Moab, or Rab-bath-moab (Areopo-lis,) *Rabba*	31.22	35.45	21
Ara Augusti, or Lugdu-nensis	45.46	4.50	6
Ara Jani, *Riano*	42.7	12.32	11
Ara Ubiōrum, *Godes-berg*	50.40	7.9	6
ARABIA	25.0	45.0	3
ARABIA DESERTA	32.0	40.0	3
ARABIA FELIX, *Yemen*	17.0	45.0	3
ARABIA PETRAEA	29.0	34.0	3
Arabiae Empōrĭum, or Adane, *Aden*	12.46	45.8	3
Arabīcus S., or Mare Rubrum, *Red Sea*	20.0	39.0	3
*Arabii	36.30	66.30	3
Arābis F., *Purali*	25.40	66.25	3
Arabissus, *Howschin*	38.7	36.42	20
Arabrica, or Ierabriga, *Alenquer*	39.2	8.56 w	7
Arace, *Beheeneh*	37.40	37.57	20
Araceli, *Huarte Araquil*	42.53	2.5 w	7
Arachnaeus M., *Arna*	37.39	23.2	18
ARACHOSIA	32.0	66.0	3
Arachōtus, *Urghundaub*	32.12	66.22	3
Arachthus or Arethon F., *Arta*	39.20	21.7	15
Aracillum, *Aradillos*	43.3	3.55 w	7
Aracynthus M., *Zygos*	38.30	21.25	15
Arad, *Tell Arad*	31.19	35.9	21
Arādus (Arvad), *Ruad I.*	34.50	35.52	20
Arādus I., *Maharag*	26.14	50.43	3
Arae Hespēri, or Solia, *S. Lucar la Mayor*	37.24	6.2 w	7
Arae Mutiae, *Monte Musino*	42.7	12.25	11
Arae Philenōrum	30.20	18.54	23
Arae Sestiānae? *C. Vil-lano*	43.8	9.8 w	7
Araegenus, *Argentan*	48.44	0.1 w	6
Aragus F., *Aragua*	42.20	44.46	22
ARAM NAHARAIM, or PADAN ARAM (MESO-POTAMIA), *Al Jezireh*	36.0	41.0	22
Arandi, or Aranni, *Ou-rique*	37.41	8.10 w	7
Arane?	39.1	37.49	20
Aranni, or Arandi, *Ou-rique*	37.41	8.10 w	7
Arāphen, *Rafina*	38.1	24.0	16
Arar, or Sauconna F., *Saône*	46.20	4.50	6
Arārat M., *Agridagh*	39.41	44.16	22
Ararus F.? (Alutas), *Aluta*	44.30	24.15	14
Ararus F.? *Sereth*	46.30	26.50	14
Arasaxa, *Seresek*	38.42	35.40	20
Araurāca	39.55	39.35	20
Arauris F., *Herault*	43.40	3.30	6
Arausio, *Orange*	44.8	4.49	6
*Aravisci	47.30	17.30	25
Araxa, *Oren*	36.45	29.25	20
ARAXĒNE	39.15	45.0	22
Araxes F., *Aras*	39.15	47.10	22
Araxes F., *Bendamir*	29.40	53.0	3
Araxes F. (of Xeno-phon), *Khabour*	35.17	40.40	22
Araxus Prom., *C. Kalo-gria*	38.13	21.22	18
Arbe I., *Arbe*	45°.47'	14°.45'	14
Arbeia? *Moresby*	54.36	3.32 w	5
Arbēla, *Irbid*	32.38	36.0	21
Arbēla, *Kalat Ibn Ma'an*	32.50	35.30	21
Arbēla, *Arbil*	36.12	43.56	22
ARBELITIS	36.12	43.56	26
Arbor, *Arbon*	47.31	9.25	6
Arca, *Tell Arca*	34.34	36.2	20
ARCADIA	37.35	22.0	18
Arcadia, *Arkhadi*	35.11	25.7	19
Arcesine	36.47	25.46	19
Arcesīne, *Arkassa*	35.31	27.8	19
Archābis, or Xylēne, *Arkava*	41.21	41.16	20
Archalla, *Erkelet*	38.49	35.14	20
Archandron?	31.12	30.22	24
Archelāis, *Ak-serai*	38.19	34.5	20
Archelāis, *El-Aujeh*	32.0	35.25	21
Arci, *Arcos*	36.51	5.49 w	7
Arcidava? *Werschitz*	45.6	21.24	14
Arcītis I., *Arki*	37.23	26.46	19
Arcobriga, *Arcos*	41.10	2.19 w	7
Arconnēsus I., *Orak*	36.58	27.30	19
Arconnēsus I., or Aspis, *Hypsili*	38.2	26.54	19
Arctus	41.	29.3	20
Ardanis, or Ardania Pr., *Ras el-Milhr*	31.53	25.5	23
Ardea, *Ardea*	41.36	12.34	-11
Ardelica, *Peschiera*	45.27	10.42	8
Ardericca? *Kir Ab*	32.23	48.36	22
*Ardiaei	43.50	17.0	14
Ardiscus, or Ordessus F., *Arjisch*	44.23	26.0	14
Ardobrica, *Corunna*	43.23	8.21 w	7
Arduenna Silva, *Arden-nen, &c.*	50.0	5.30	6
Arebrigium, *St. Didier*	45.46	6.58	8
Arelāte, *Arles*	43.41	4.37	6
Arenacum, *Arnhem*	51.58	5.55	6
Arēnae Montes	37.0	6.30 w	7
Arēon F., *Congoon*	28.0	52.15	3
Areopōlis (Ar of Moab, or Rabbath-moab), *Rabba*	31.22	35.45	21
Arethon, or Arachthus, F., *Arta*	39.20	21.7	15
Arethūsa	40.39	23.39	15
Arethūsa fons (Ithaca)	38.20	20.44	18
Arethūsa L.? *Nazuk Ghieul*	38.56	42.10	22
Arethūsa (Syria), *Rus-tan, or Restun*	35.5	36.38	20
Aretias I. (Chalcerītis), *Kerasunt Ada*	40.56	38.27	20
Areva F., *Ucero*	41.40	3.4 w	7
*Arevaci	41.30	3.0 w	7
Argaeus M., *Erdjish Dagh*	38.32	35.11	20
Arganthonius M., *Sa-manlu Dagh*	40.30	29.26	20
Argantomagus, *Argen-ton*	46.35	1.31	6
ARGEIA	37.40	22.38	18
ARGEIA (AMPHILOCHIA)	38.55	21.15	15
Argennum Pr.? *C. S. Alessio*	37.52	15.20	12
Argennum Pr., or Argi-num, *C. Bianco, or Aspro Kavo*	38.16	26.15	19
Argenomescum? *Argo-medo*	43.23	3.48 w	7
Argentarius M.	37.55	2.56 w	7
Argentarius Mons, *M. Argentaro*	42.22	11.10	8
Argenteus, *Argens*	43.30	6.16	6
Argentia? *Argenta*	44.37	11.51	8
Argentia, *Gorgonzola*	45.33	9.25	8
Argentiōlum, *Torneros*	42.15	6.13 w	7
Argentorātum, aft. Stra-taeburgus, *Strasbourg*	48.35	7.45	6
Argentovaria, *Artzen-heim*	48.5	7.30	6

NAMES.	LAT.	LONG.	MAP.
Argīda?	39°.48'	27°.32'	19
Argilas	40.45	23.44	15
Arginūsae Ins.	39.0	26.49	19
Argithēa, *Knisovo*	39.25	21.26	15
Argob (Gaulonitis), *Jaulan*	32.54	35.45	21
Argolicus S., *G. of Nauplia*	37.20	23.0	18
Argōlis	37.40	23.0	18
Argos, *Argos*	37.38	22.43	18
Argos Amphilochicum, *Neokhori*	38.55	21.12	15
Argos Oresticum?	40.33	21.10	14
Argȳra	38.18	21.47	18
*Argyrini	40.7	21.10	15
Argyrippa, or Arpi, *Arpa*	41.31	15.33	9
Aria	35.0	62.0	3
Ariaca, *Concan*	18.0	73.20	2
Ariāna	32.30	65.0	3
Ariaspae?	31.0	63.30	3
Ariassus	36.55	30.35	20
Aricia, *Lariccia*	41.43	12.41	11
Ariconium, *Weston, n. Ross*	51.55	2.31 w	5
Arigaeum? *Nawugee, or Naaghi*	34.47	71.16	3
*Arii, or Harii	51.0	20.30	25
Arimathaea? *Ramleh*	31.55	34.52	21
Arimazes (Rock of)? *Kokeetun, n. Derbend*	38.59	67.40	3
Ariminum, *Rimini*	44.4	12.34	8
Ariminus F., *Marecchia*	44.0	12.25	8
Arindela, *Ghurundel*	30.47	35.46	24
Ariolica? *Arc-sous-Cicon*	47.3	6.24	6
Ariolica, *between Roure and La Cartelas, n. St. Just en Chevalet*	45.54	3.47	6
Arisbe	40.10	26.30	26
Aristēra I	37.26	23.32	18
Aristonautae, *n. Kamari*	38.5	22.36	18
Aritium Praetorium, *Benevente*	38.58	8.47 w	7
Arlape, or Arelate? *Moelk*	48.13	15.22	14
Armauria, *Tapadevi, or Amavir*	40.6	44.1	22
Armaxa, *Pallass*	39.0	35.48	20
Armēne, *Artaschin*	41.12	41.0	20
Armenia	40.0	44.0	22
Armenia Minor	40.0	39.30	20
Armeniae Pylae, *Gergen Kalak-si*	37.58	39.8	22
Armenium, *Magula*	39.27	22.37	15
Arminia F., *Fiore*	42.25	11.38	8
Armorica	48.20	1.30 w	6
Armutria, *Motru*	44.32	23.29	14
Arna, *Civitella d'Arno*	43.8	12.29	8
Arnae	40.27	23.45	15
Arne (Cierium), *Mataranga*	39.23	22.3	15
Arnon (River), *Wady Mojib*	31.29	35.45	21
Arnus F., *Arno*	43.40	10.40	8
Aro F., *Arone*	42.0	12.16	11
Aroanius M., *Khelmos*	37.58	22.13	18
Aroanius, or Olbius, F.	37.57	22.20	18
Aroanius F.	37.54	21.56	18
Aroanius F., *Katsana*	37.52	22.9	18
Arocha F., *Crocchio*	39.0	16.45	9
Aroer, *Ararah*	31.13	35.3	21
Aroer, *Ara'ir*	31.29	35.50	21
Aroer, *Aireh*	32.1	35.44	21
Aromāta Prom. (Notu Keras?) *C. Gerdafoon (Guardafui)*	11.41	51.12	2
Arōsis, or Oroatis F. (Zarotis), *Tab*	30.20	49.52	22
Arpi, or Argyrippa, *Arpa*	41.31	15.33	9
Arpinum, *Arpino*	41.39	13.38	11
Arrabo? *Kormönd*	47.0	16.38	14
Arrabo F., *Raab*	47.18	17.0	14
Arrabona, *Raab*	47.41	17.38	14
Arretium, *Arezzo*	43°.30'	11°.56'	8
Arretium (Julienses), *Subliano*	43.37	11.54	8
Arretium (Fidentes), *Castiglione*	43.22	12.0	8
Arrhēne (Arzanēne)	38.20	41.0	22
Arriaca, *Guadalaxara*	40.39	3.10 w	7
Arriani Prom.			1
Arrubium	45.18	28.13	24
Arsa, *Aznaga*	38.11	5.41 w	7
Arsamosāta	38.35	39.29	22
Arsanias F.? *Murad Tchai*	39.5	41.30	22
Arsen E.	37.43	22.3	18
Arsēne, Arsissa, or Thospitis L.? *L. of Van*	38.40	42.40	22
Arsia F., *Arsa*	45.5	14.2	8
Arsinaria, *Arzaw*	35.50	0.15 w	23
Arsinia, *Arghana Maden*	38.19	39.40	22
Arsinoe (Aethiopia)?	12.50	42.57	3
Arsinoe (Cilicia), *Softa Kalassi*	36.6	33.5	20
Arsinoe (Creta)?	35.16	25.28	19
Arsinoe (Cyprus), *Polikrusoko*	35.6	32.30	20
Arsinoe, for. Teucheira (*Taukra*)	32.32	20.32	23
Arsinoe, or Crocodilopōlis	29.25	31.4	24
Arsinoe, or Cleopātris	30.3	32.34	24
Arsissa, or Arsēne L., *L. of Van*	38.40	42.40	22
*Artābri	43.20	8.0 w	7
Artabrōrum S., *B. of Ferrol*	43.25	8.20 w	7
Artāce, *Erdek*	40.24	27.46	19
Artacoāna? *Aowbah, or Obeh*	34.18	63.8	3
Artagera?	40.5	43.0	22
Artanes, *Tschileh*	41.10	29.38	20
Artanissa? *Thelawi*	41.54	45.29	22
Artaxāta? *Ardaschad*	39.58	44.35	22
Artēmis, Proscoa, Tem. of, *n. C. Amoni*	39.1	23.19	15
Artemisium	39.0	23.15	15
Artemisium, or Pedalium Pr., *C. Suvela*	36.35	28.53	19
Artemisium, or Dianium Pr., *C. St. Martin*	38.46	0.14	7
Artemisius M., *Malevo*	37.37	22.32	18
Artemisius M., *Monte Arriano*	41.43	12.48	11
Artemīta, *Artemid*	38.25	43.7	22
Artemīta, or Chalasar, *Sheriban*	33.58	44.56	22
Artena Veientum? *Buccea*	41.58	12.16	11
Artena Volscorum? *n. Monte Fortino*	41.44	15.57	11
Artenia, *Artegna*	46.13	13.11	8
Artigi, *Alhama*	37.0	4.10 w	7
Artigi, *Castuera*	38.40	5.34 w	7
Artiscus F., *Tondja*	42.20	26.20	14
Artolica, *La Tuille*	45.42	6.56	8
Aruci? *Moura*	38.7	7.18 w	7
Arunda, *Ronda*	36.50	5.5 w	7
Arupium? *Josephsthal*	45.12	15.17	14
Arutela	44.58	24.15	14
Arva, *Alcolea*	37.55	4.39 w	7
Arvad (Arādus), *Rund I.*	34.50	35.52	20
*Arverni	45.40	3.30	6
Arverni (Nemossus), *Clermont*	45.47	3.4	6
*Arvii	48.0	0.30 w	6
Arvisia	38.35	26.0	19
Arx, *Arce*	41.36	13.37	11
Arx Carventūna, *Rocca Massima*	41.41	12.58	11
Arycanda, *Arouf*	36.31	30.9	20
Arzanēne (Arrhēne)	38.20	41.0	22
Arzes, *Ardjish*	39.3	43.15	22
Asama, or Asana F.? *Wady Tensift*	32.0	9.0 w	23
Asamum? *Melonta*	42°.28'	18°.27'	14
Ascālon, *Askulan*	31.39	34.32	21
Ascania I.? *Christiani*	36.15	25.13	19
Ascania L. (or Anaua)? *L. of Chardak, or Hadji Tous Ghieul*	37.53	30.0	20
Ascania L., *L. of Iznik*	40.20	29.30	20
Asciburgium, *Asburg*	51.28	6.38	6
Ascra, *Pyrgaki*	38.18	23.6	18
Ascūlum, *Ascoli*	41.11	15.34	11
Ascūlum Picēnum, *Ascoli*	42.52	13.37	9
Ascuris L., *Esero*	39.54	22.26	15
Asēa, *n. Frango Vrysi*	37.25	22.17	18
Aser?	32.23	35.21	21
Ashdod (Azōtus), *Esdood*	31.45	34.41	21
Ashtaroth, *Tell Ashtereh*	32.48	36.4	21
Asido (Caesariāna)? *Medina Sidonia*	36.27	5.55 w	7
Asinaeus (or Messeniacus) S., *G. of Kalamata*	36.45	22.5	18
Asinārus F., *Fiume di Noto, or Falconara*	36.55	15.0	12
Asīne, *Tolon*	37.32	22.52	18
Asīne, *Koroni, or Coron*	36.48	21.59	18
Asīnes, Acesīnes, or Onobālas F., *Cantara*	37.50	15.10	12
Asmiraxa			1
Asnaus M., *Mertzika*	40.19	20.20	15
Asōpus, or Cyparissia, *Blitra*	36.41	22.51	18
Asōpus F. (Boeotia), *Vurieni*	38.16	23.35	16
Asōpus F. (Malis), *Karvunaria*	38.47	22.23	16
Asōpus F. (Peloponnesus), *St. Gheorgios*	37.52	22.39	18
*Aspaciacae	40.0	60.0	3
Aspaluca, *Pont l'Esquit*	43.3	0.36 w	6
Aspendus	36.58	31.16	20
Asphaltītes L. (Dead Sea), *Dead Sea, or Bahr Lūt*	31.30	35.30	21
Aspithra F.			1
Aspis, *Aspe*	38.22	0.49 w	7
Aspis, *Marsa Zaffran*	31.14	16.43	23
Aspis, or Clypēa, *Kulibia*	36.50	11.8	23
Aspis, or Clypēa, Pr., *Ras el-Melhr*	36.52	11.9	23
Aspis I., or Aroonnesus, *Hypsili*	38.2	26.54	19
Asplēdon, *Avrokastro*	38.32	23.0	16
Assa, *Paleokastro*	40.21	23.45	15
Asseconia? *Santiago de Compostella*	42.49	8.28 w	7
Assisium, *Assisi*	43.4	12.38	8
Assorus, *Asaro*	37.36	14.25	12
Assos, *Beiram Keui*	39.29	26.22	19
Assurae, *Zanfour*	35.39	8.51	23
Assus F., *Kineta*	38.34	22.50	16
Assyria	36.0	44.0	2
Asta, *Asti*	44.53	8.11	8
Asta, aft. Asta Regia? *Xeres de la Frontera*	36.40	6.7 w	7
Astabōras F., *Tecazze, or Atbara*	17.0	'35.0	3
Astacēnus S., *G. of Ismid*	40.45	29.40	20
Astācus	40.45	29.58	20
Astācus, *on Port Platia*	38.29	21.7	15
Astāpa, *Estepa*	37.19	4.55 w	7
Astapus F., *Abai*	15.0	33.5	3
Astelephus F., *Markula*	42.45	41.23	22
Astēris I., *Daskaglio*	38.26	20.36	18
Asterusia, *Astrizzi*	34.57	25.2	19
Astibon, *Istip*	41.47	22.10	14
Astīca	41.20	28.10	14
Astigi, or Astigis, *Ecija*	37.31	5.5 w	7
Astigi vetus, *Alameda*	37.16	4.43 w	7

NAMES.	LAT.	LONG.	MAP.
Astura, *Torre di Astura*	41°.23'	12°.49'	11
Astūra F., *Conca*	41.30	12.46	11
Astūra F., *Esla*	41.45	6.0 w	7
*Astūres	43.0	5.50 w	7
Asturica Augusta, *Astorga*	42.28	6.10 w	7
Astycus F., *Vravnitza*	41.40	22.10	14
Astypalaea I., *Astropalaea, or Stampalia*	36.35	26.25	19
Astypalaea Pr	37.43	23.55	18
Astyra	40.1	26.38	19
Astyra ?	39.36	26.53	19
Atabyris M., *Atairo, or Attayard*	36.12	27.54	19
Atabyrium, or Itabyrium (Mt. Tabor), *Jebel et-Toor*	32.42	35.25	21
*Atacini	43.0	2.30	6
Atagis F., *Eisach*	46.47	11.50	8
Atalante I., *Talanta*	38.39	23.6	16
Atarbēchis ?	30.21	31.4	24
Atarneus, *Dikili Keui*	39.4	26.54	19
Ataroth, *Atara*	32.1	35.11	21
Atax F., *Aude*	43.14	2.30	6
Atella, *S. Maria di Atella*	40.58	14.14	13
Aternum, *Pescara*	42.27	14.15	8
Aternus F., *Pescara*	42.14	14.0	8
Ateste, *Este*	45.13	11.39	8
ATHAMANIA	39.24	21.20	15
Athanagia? *Agramunt*	41.47	0.58	7
Athēnae, *Athens (Athina)*	37.58	23.44	16
Athēnae (Pontus), *Atina*	41.9	40.55	20
Athenaeum, n. *Apano Porta*	39.27	21.35	15
Athenaeum ?	36.31	22.59	18
Athēnas Teichos, *Psatho Pyrgo*	38.19	· 21.53	18
Athenopōlis? *Napoule*	43.32	6.56	8
Athēsis F., *Adige*	45.15	11.17	8
Athmōnum, *Marusi*	38.4	23.49	16
Athos M., *Agion Oros, or Monte Santo*	40.10	24.20	15
Athribis, *Tell Atrib*	30.30	31.11	24
Athyras F	41.0	28.35	14
Atiliāna, *Calzada*	42.22	2.57 w	7
Atina, *Atena*	40.27	15.34	9
ATINTANIA	40.15	20.15	15
Atlanticum, Externum, or Magnum Mare, or Oceānus Hesperius, *Atlantic Ocean*	40.0	20.0 w	2
Atlas Minor ? *C. Blanco (North)*	33.9	8.34 w	23
Atlas Mons, or Dyrin, *Mt. Atlas*	31.20	7.0 w	23
Atrax, *Sidhiro-peliko*	39.39	22.12	15
*Atrebates	50.20	2.40	6
*Atrebatii	51.30	1.20 w	5
Atria, or Hadria, *Adria*	45.3	12.3	8
ATROPATĒNE, or MEDIA MINOR	37.0	47.0	22
*Attaceni			1
*Attacotti	56.10	4.40 w	5
Attacum, *Ateca*	41.24	1.44 w	7
Attaleia, *Adala*	38.36	28.20	19
Attaleia, *Adalia*	31.53	30.44	20
Attea, *Ayasma*	39.13	26.48	19
Attegua, *Teba*	37.6	4.53 w	7
Attelebūsa I., *Raschat Ada*	36.47	30.39	20
ATTĒNE	25.0	50.30	3
Atteva, or Attoba, *Osbe, or Doshi*	20.30	30.16	3
ATTICA	38.0	23.50	18
Attoba, or Atteva, *Osbe, or Doshi*	20.30	30.16	3
ATURIA	36.30	43.10	22
Aturia, *Oria*	43.10	2.0 w	7
Atūris F., *Adour*	43.44	1.0 w	6
Atudum Pr.? *C. Carbon, or Ras Metzukoub*	36.46	5.10	23

NAMES.	LAT.	LONG.	MAP.
Audus F.? *Adous, or Sumeim*	36°.14'	4°.0'	23
Aufidēna, *Alfidena*	41.44	14.3	9
Aufidus F., *Ofanto*	41.11	16.0	9
Aufina, *Ofena*	42.14	13.49	8
Augīla, *Aujelah*	29.15	21.54	2
Augusta?	44.36	12.3	8
Augusta Felix (Oea), *Tripoli*	32.54	13.11	23
Augusta Fossa	44.28	12.13	8
Augusta, for. Londinium, *London*	51.31	0.6 w	5
Augusta Praetoria, *Aosta*	45.44	7.18	8
Augusta Rauracōrum, *Augst*	47.32	7.44	6
Augusta Suessionum, *Soissons*	49.24	3.20	6
Augusta Taurinōrum, *Turin*	45.4	7.40	8
Augusta Trevirōrum, *Treves*	49.46	6.40	6
Augusta Tricastinōrum, *Aouste-en-Diois*	44.44	5.4	6
Augusta Vagiennorum, n. *Bene*	44.33	7.51	8
Augusta Verumanduōrum, *St. Quentin*	49.51	3.17	6
Augusta Vindelicorum, *Augsburg*	48.22	10.56	25
Augustana, *Straubing*	48.53	12.36	25
Augustobōna, aft. Tricasses, *Troyes*	48.17	4.6	6
Augustobriga, *Puente del Arzobispo*	39.51	5.8 w	7
Augustobriga, *Agreda*	41.50	1.56 w	7
Augustobriga, *Ciudad Rodrigo*	40.31	6.26 w	7
Augustodūnum, *Autun*	46.57	4.18	6
Augustodūrus, *Bayeux*	49.17	0.42 w	6
Augustomāgus, aft. Silvanectes, *Senlis*	49.12	2.35	6
Augustomāgus ?	46.10	1.22	6
Augustonemētum, *Clermont*	45.47	3.4	6
Augustoritum, aft. Lemovices, *Limoges*	45.50	1.16	6
Augustum, *Aoste*	45.37	5.33	6
Aulaei Teichos, *Kurudereh*	42.2	27.58	14
*Aulerci-Cenomani	48.10	0.40	6
*Aulerci-Diablintes	48.25	0.40 w	6
*Aulerci-Eburovices	49.9	1.0	6
Aulis, n. *Vathy*	38.24	23.37	16
Aulon M	40.31	17.12	9
Aulon (Creta), *Auli*	35.6	25.17	19
Aulon (Illyricum), *Avlona, or Valona*	40.28	19.26	15
Aulon (Mygdonia)	40.39	23.35	15
Aulon, or Magnus Campus (Plain of Jordan), *el-Ghor*	32.20	35.35	21
Aunos I., *Ons*	42.21	8.55 w	7
AURANĪTIS, *Haurân*	32.50	36.20	21
Aurasius Mons, *Jebel Auress*	35.15	6.0	23
Aurea Chersonēsus, *Malay peninsula*	8.0	100.0	2
Aureliāni, *Orleans*	47.54	1.55	6
Aureus Mons?	45.54	18.33	14
Aureus Mons, *Stolnatz, or Grotzka*	44.40	20.51	14
Aureus Mons	42.15	9.0	9
*Aurunci	41.20	14.0	9
Ausa, *Vich*	41.55	2.17	7
Ausara? *Ras-al-Sair, or Ras Seger*	16.45	53.43	3
*Ausci	43.39	0.35	6
Auser F., *Serchio*	43.50	10.26	8
*Ausetāni	41.55	2.30	7
*Ausōnes	41.18	13.35	9
*Autariātae	42.20	20.0	14
Autesiodūrum, *Auxerre*	47.48	3.34	6

NAMES.	LAT.	LONG.	MAP.
Automala, or Automalax (or Anabucis ?)	30°.16'	19°.14'	23
Autricum, aft. Carnūtes, *Chartres*	48.26	1.29	6
*Autrigōnes	43.0	3.20 w	7
Auxacii M			1
Auximum, *Osimo*	43.30	13.28	8
Auzia, *Sour el-Rezlan,* n. *Hamza*	36.9	3.22	23
Avalītes, *Zeilah*	11.22	43.31	2
Avalītes S., *G. of Aden*	12.0	45.0	2
Avara F., *Eure*	47.5	2.20	6
Avaricum, aft. Bituriges, *Bourges*	47.5	2.25	6
Avarum Pr.?	41.28	8.40 w	7
Avedonacum, *Aunay*	46.2	0.20 w	6
Aveia, *Acra*	42.14	18.30	9
Avendo, *Jezerana*	45.4	15.14	14
Avenio, *Avignon*	43.56	4.49	6
Aventia F., *Lavenza*	44.2	10.5	8
Avernus L., *Lago Averno*	40.51	14.5	13
Avesica? n. *Senosetsch*	45.44	13.59	14
*Aviones	53.25	11.0	25
Avisio Portus? *Eza*	43.43	7.23	8
Avus, or Avo F., *Aye*	41.24	8.30 w	7
Axelodūnum, *Burgh-on-the-Sands*	54.55	3.3 w	5
Axima, *Aime*	45.33	6.38	8
Axiopōlis, *Rassova*	44.16	27.58	14
Axius F., *Vardar*	41.5	22.30	14
Axōna F., *Aisne*	49.25	3.30	6
Axuenna	49.24	3.55	6
Axuenna?	49.18	4.50	6
Axūmis, or Auxume, *Axoum*	14.8	38.52	3
Axus, or Oaxus, *Axus*	35.16	24.50	19
Axylis	32.40	23.0	22
AXŸLOS	39.20	31.30	20
Aza, *Kalkit Chiftlik*	40.7	39.40	20
Azāni, *Tchavdour Hissar*	39.16	29.43	20
AZANIA, or BARBARIA, *Ajan*	5.0	47.0	2
AZANĪTIS	39.16	30.0	20
Azanium Mare, or S. Barbaricus	0.0	50.0	2
Axenia	37.40	24.0	19
Azetium, *Rutigliano*	41.0	17.2	9
Aziris? *Erzingan*	39.32	39.46	22
Azochis, *Zakhu*	37.13	42.37	22
Azōrus, *Vuvala*	40.0	22.1	15
Azōtus (Ashdod), *Esdood*	31.45	34.41	21

B.

Names.	Lat.	Long.	Map.
Baetis F., *Guadalquivir*	38°.0'	4°.0' w	7
Baetŭlo, *Castle of Mongat*	41.30	2.16	7
Baetŭlo F., *Besos*	41.30	2.12	7
BAETURIA	38.40	6.0 w	7
Bagacum, *Bavay*	50.18	3.47	6
Bagis, or Bage, *Sirghis*	39.34	29.5	20
Bagisara? *Ras Arubah*	25.14	64.31	3
Bagistāna, *Baghistan, or Besitun*	34.16	47.33	22
Bagrada, or Bagradas F. (Macaras), *Mejerdah*	36.22	9.0	23
Bagradas F., *Nabon*	27.45	53.0	3
BAGRAUANDĒNE	39.45	42.40	22
Baiae, *Baiae*	40.49	14.4	13
Baiae, *Bayae*	36.45	36.12	20
*Baiocasses	49.10	0.40 w	6
Balanea, *Baneas*	35.11	36.0	20
Balbūra, *Katara*	36.56	29.34	20
Baleāres Insulae, or Gymnesiae, *Majorca, &c*	37.30	3.0	7
Balearicum Mare	40.0	2.0	7
Baleāris Major, or Columba, *Majorca*	39.30	3.0	7
Baleāris Minor, or Nura, *Minorca*	40.0	4.0	7
Baletium, or Valetium	40.33	18.5	9
Balŏmus, *Ras Shemaul Bunder*	25.12	62.55	3
Balsa, *Tavira*	37.7	7.31 w	7
Balsio, *Borja*	41.55	1.31 w	7
Balyra F., *Mavrozumono*	37.15	21.54	18
Balzānum, *Botzen*	46.31	11.18	8
Bambyce, or Hierapolis, *Membidj, or Bambouj*	36.32	37.57	20
Banasa (Valentia)? *Mamora*	34.16	6.13 w	23
Bandusiae Fons, *Fontana Grande*	40.52	40.58	9
Bantia, *Banzi*	40.50	16.0	9
Baphȳras F	40.8	22.31	15
Barace I., *Peninsula of Cutch*	23.0	70.0	3
Barbalissus, *Kalaat Balis*	35.59	38.11	20
Barbana F., *Moratsha*	42.30	19.30	14
BARBARIA, or AZANIA, *Ajan*	5.0	47.0	2
Barbariāna, *S. Martin de Berberana*	42.12	2.26 w	7
Barbaricus S., or Mare Azanium	0.0	50.0	2
Barbārium Prom., *C. Espichel*	38.24	9.24 w	7
Barbesūla F., *Guadiaro*	36.30	5.25 w	7
Barbesūla, *r. on R. Guadiaro*	36.18	5.18 w	7
Barbosthenes M.	37.2	22.30	18
Barbyses F.	41.10	28.56	26
Burca, *El-Medinah*	32.31	21.0	23
Barcino, *Barcelona*	41.22	2.10	7
Barderāte, *Bra*	44.42	7.52	8
Bardŭlī, *Barletta*	41.19	16.18	9
Barca, *Vera*	37.13	1.53 w	7
Bargāsa? *Port Giova*	37.3	28.23	19
Bargylia	37.12	27.37	19
Bargyliētes S., or Iasius, *G. of Mendelyah*	37.15	27.25	19
Bargȳlus Mons, *Jebel Nusairiyeh*	35.15	36.15	20
Baris? *Isbarta*	37.46	30.39	20
Baris, or Verētum, *S. Maria di Vereto*	39.52	18.21	9
Barium, *Bari*	41.8	16.52	9
Barna? *Gwadel*	25.10	62.14	3
Barygaza, *Baroche*	21.42	73.3	2
Barygazēnus S., *G. of Cambay*	21.0	72.30	3
Barza, *Berozeh*	36.1	46.7	22
Barxalo, *Gerger*	37.58	39.7	20

Names.	Lat.	Long.	Map.
Basante, or Bassianae, *r. n. Debrincae*	44°.45'	20°.0'	14
Basilia, *Bâle, or Basel*	47.35	7.36	6
Basilippo	37.25	5.30 w	7
Bassae	37.26	21.54	18
Bassiana, *Ivany Egereseg*	47.19	15.58	14
Bassianae, or Basante, *r. n. Debrincae*	44.45	20.0	14
Basta, *Vaste*	40.3	18.21	9
*Bastarnae, or Peucini	48.30	21.0	25
Basti, *Baza*	37.29	2.53 w	7
*Bastitāni	38.0	2.0 w	7
*Bastŭli	36.50	4.30 w	7
Batĭna?	36.30	48.35	22
BATANAEA (BASHAN)	32.30	36.15	21
Batāva Castra, *Passau*	48.34	13.27	14
*Batăʹvi	51.55	5.0	6
Bathy-*Colpos*	40.12	29.10	26
Bathys F.	39.40	31.11	20
Bathys F.? *Fiati, or Iati*	38.0	13.5	12
Bathys Portus, *Batoum*	41.37	41.38	20
Batinus F., *Trontino, or Tordino*	42.44	14.0	8
Batnae (Saruji), *Saruj*	36.57	38.25	22
Bauli	40.48	14.5	13
Bautae, *Vieux Annecy*	45.55	6.7	6
Bautisus F.			1
Bazira? *Bajour*	35.4	71.25	3
Beberacus L., *L. of Katuniyʼk*	36.16	41.12	22
Bebiāna, *n. Torrimpetra*	41.56	12.12	11
Bebii M.	42.30	20.0	14
Bebriacum, or Bedriacum? *Cividale*	45.3	10.30	8
*Becheires	40.50	40.45	20
Bedesis F., *Ronco*	44.2	12.0	8
Bedriacum, or Bebriacum? *Cividale*	45.3	10.30	8
Beer, *Bireh*	31.55	35.12	21
Beer-sheba, *Beer es-Seba*	31.16	34.21	21
Begorrītis L., *L. of Kitrini*	40.31	21.43	15
Belbīna I., *S. Georgio*	37.28	23.55	18
Belbīna, or Belemina, *r. on Mt. Khelmos*	37.16	22.16	18
Belca	47.48	2.25	6
Beleia, or Veleia?	42.49	2.50 w	7
Belemina, or Belbīna, *r. on Mt. Khelmos*	37.16	22.16	18
Belerides I., *Serpentaria I*	39.8	9.37	9
Belerium, Bolerium, or Antivestaeum Pr., *Land's End*	50.4	5.42 w	5
*Belgae (Britannia)	51.0	2.0 w	5
*Belgae (Gallia)	49.55	4.0	6
BELGICA	50.0	4.0	4
Belisama Aest.? *Mouth of Ribble*	53.43	3.0 w	5
*Bellovaci	49.30	2.0	6
Bellovaci (Caesaromagus), *Beauvais*	49.27	2.4	6
Belon, *Tower of Bolonia*	36.5	5.48 w	7
Belsinum, *Masseure*	43.24	0.35	6
Belunum, *Belluno*	46.7	12.14	8
Belus F., *Nahr Naaman*	32.55	35.10	21
Benācus L., *Lago di Garda*	45.35	10.40	8
Benaventa, or Isannavatia, *Burrow Hill, n. Daventry*	52.16	1.8 w	5
Beneharnum, *Castelnon*	43.27	0.40 w	6
Beneventum, *Benevento*	41.8	14.45	9
Berenice	23.55	35.28	3
Berenice Epidīres	12.20	43.20	3
Berenice (Ezion-geber)	29.33	34.58	24
Berenice, for. Hesperides, *Benghazi*	32.7	20.3	23

Names.	Lat.	Long.	Map.
Berenīce Panchrȳsos? *Souakin*	19°.6'	37°.20'	3
Bergĭdum, *Perez*	42.48	6.58 w	7
Bergintrum, *St. Maurice*	45.37	6.46	8
Bergŏmum, *Bergamo*	45.42	9.41	8
Bergon, or Bergos, *Bergen*	60.21	5.19	3
Bergŭlae, *Tchatal Burgas*	41.25	27.18	14
Bergusium, *Bourgoin*	45.35	5.16	6
Bermius M. (or Bora), *Verria*	40.26	22.0	14
Beroea, or Chalȳbon, *Aleppo*	36.12	37.11	20
Beroea, aft. Irenopŏlis? *Eski Sagra*	42.30	25.44	14
Beroea, or Berrhoea, *Verria*	40.29	22.8	14
*Berŏnes	42.20	2.30 w	7
Berrhoea, or Beroea, *Verria*	40.29	22.8	15
Bersovia, *Osakova*	45.29	21.16	14
Berȳtus, *Beirout*	33.50	35.28	21
Berziminium	42.26	19.19	14
Besa, or Antinŏe, *Sheikh Abadeh*	27.48	30.54	3
Besbīcus I., *Kalolimno*	40.31	28.21	20
Besidiae, *Bisignano*	39.30	16.17	9
Besippo, or Baesippo, *r. n. Porto Barbato*	36.11	5.55 w	7
Besor, Brook, *Wady Sheriah*	31.21	34.30	21
Bessapara, *Tatar Bazardjik*	42.5	24.30	14
*Bessi	42.0	24.40	14
Beste, *Bost*	31.29	64.10	3
Besunga? *Bassain*	16.35	94.52	3
Besunga F., *Irawady*	20.0	95.0	3
Beth-abara?	31.49	35.36	21
Beth-gamul, *Um-el-Jemāl*	32.23	36.26	21
Beth-haran (Livias), *Er-Rameh*	31.49	35.39	21
Beth-horon, Upper, *Beitoor el-Foka*	31.53	35.6	21
Beth-horon, Lower, *Beitoor et-Tahta*	31.54	35.5	21
Beth-nimrah, *Nimreen*	31.56	35.36	21
Beth-shittah, *Shutta*	32.38	35.29	21
Beth-tappuah, *Teffuh*	31.33	35.5	21
Beth-zachariah, *Tell Zakariyeh*	31.43	34.57	21
Bethagla, *Ain Hojla*	31.48	35.34	21
Bethany, *El-Aziriyeh*	31.46	35.16	21
Bethar? *Bareen*	32.19	35.0	21
Bethar, or Bether, *Beitoer*	31.44	35.7	21
Bethbaramthum, or Amāthus, *Amateh*	32.19	35.40	21
Bethel, *Beiteen*	31.55	35.15	21
Bothlehem, *Beitlahm*	31.43	35.13	21
Bethsaida (of Galilee)?	32.53	35.31	21
Bethsaida (Julias), *Et-Tell*	32.58	35.40	21
Bethshemesh, *Ain Sheme*	31.45	34.58	21
Bethshemesh, or Rameses (Heliopolis), *Matarieh*	30.8	31.20	24
Bethulia, *Beit Ilfah*	32.31	35.28	21
Bethzur? *Ed-Dirweh*	31.36	35.9	21
Betogabris (Eleutheropolis), *Beit Jibreen*	31.36	34.55	21
Betonim? *Batneh*	32.2	35.45	21
Betunia, *Oebrones*	42.15	5.53 w	
Bezabde, or Sapphe, *Jezireh Ibn Omar*	37.17	41.59	21
Bezer?	31.36	35.56	21
Bias F., *Djane*	36.59	21.50	18
Biatia, *Baeza*	37.58	3.29 w	7
Bibium?	45.20	15.30	14
Bibracte, aft. Augustodūnum, *Antun*	46.57	4.18	6

NAMES.	LAT.	LONG.	MAP.
Bibrax? *Bièvre*	49°.32'	3°.37'	6
*Bibroci	51.20	1.0 w	6
Blida, *Blida*	36.29	2.49	23
Bidaium, *Altenmarkt*	48.0	12.32	14
Bidis? *S. Giovanni di Bibino*	37.5	15.2	12
Pienna, or Biennus, *Vianos*	35.3	25.28	19
Bienum	35.16	23.31	19
*Bigerriones	43.10	0.10 w	6
Bigestae, *Gabella*	43.5	17.40	14
Bilbilis, *Calatayud Vieja*	41.25	1.35 w	7
Bilecha F., *Belik*	36.20	39.0	22
Bilitio, *Bellinzona*	46.13	8.58	8
Billaeus F., *Filiyas*	41.7	32.0	20
Bingium, *Bingen*	49.57	7.55	6
Bioia? *Porto Pino*	38.57	8.35	9
Biroe	44.52	28.3	24
Birtha, *Birehjik*	37.2 ·	38.0	20
Birtha? *Tekreet*	34.36	43.40	22
BISALTIA	40.50	23.30	15
Bisanthe, aft. Rhaedestus, *Rodosto*	40.59	27.31	14
Biscargis, *Berrus*	41.18	0.26	7
Bisto'nis Lacus, *L. Bourou*	41.4	25.8	19
BITHYNIA	41.20	33.0	20
Bithynium, aft. Claudiopōlis? *Boli*	40.42	31.47	20
Bitter Lake	30.17	32.20	24
Biturgia, on *River Ambra*	43.32	11.39	8
Bituriges, *Bourges*	'47.5	2.25	6
*Bituriges-Cubi	47.0	1.40	6
*Bituriges-Vivisci	45.0	0.50 w	6
Bizya, *Viza*	41.36	27.44	14
Black Mountains, *Jebel Soudan*	29.0	15.0	2
Black Mountains	29.0	34.40	24
BLAENE?	41.20	33.40	20
Blanda, *Blanes*	41.40	2.50	7
Blanda, *Maratea*	39.56	15.44	9
Blandiana	45.56	23.25	14
Blandōna? *Vrana*	43.58	15.34	14
Blandus	39.24	37.8	20
Blariacum, *Blerick*	51.21	6.7	6
Blatum Bulgium, *Middleby*	55.5	3.13 w	5
Blaundus? *Bolat*	39.33	28.36	20
Blaundus, *Suleimanly*	38.24	29.22	20
Blavia, *Blaye*	45.7	0.39 w	6
Blendium? *Santander*	43.10	3.43 w	7
Blera, *Bieda*	42.18	12.1	11
Blestium, *Monmouth*	51.49	2.42 w	5
Bletisa, *Ledesma*	41.17	6.2 w	7
Boactes F., *Vara*	44.12	9.48 ·	8
Boagrius F.	38.45	22.41	16
Boaria, *Toro*	38.52	8.23	9
Bocanum? *Morocco*	31.40	7.37 w	23
Boderia (or Bodotria), Aestuarium, *Firth of Forth*	56.0	3.0 w	5
*Bodiontici	44.10	6.10	6
Bodotria (or Boderia), Aest., *Firth of Forth*	56.0	3.0 w	5
Boeae?	36.31	23.2	18
BOEATICE	36.30	23.5	18
Boeaticus S., *Vatika Bay*	36.30	23.2	18
Boebe	39.29	22.50	15
Boebeis L., *Karla*	39.30	22.41	15
BOEOTIA	38.20	23.15	16
*Boii	44.20	11.6	8
*Boii	46.40	3.30	6
*Boii, aft. Marcomanni	49.30	14.30	25
Boii, *Bouges*	44.35	0.46 w	6
Boiodūrum, *Innstadt*	48.34	13.29	14
BOIOHEMUM, *Bohemia*	49.40	14.30	25
Boium, r. n. *Mariolates*	38.39	22.29	16
Bola, *Poli*	41.53	12.55	11
Bolax, *Volantza*	37.38	21.33	18
Belbo L., *Besikia*	40.40	23.25	15

NAMES.	LAT.	LONG.	MAP.
Bolbitine Mouth (of Nile)	31°.32'	30°.45'	24
Bolerium, Belerium, or Antivestaeum Prom., *Land's End*	50.4	5.42 w	5
Bolinaeus F.	38.18	21.52	18
Bolissus, *Volisso*	38.29	25.56	19
*Bomienses	38.43	22.0	15
Bomium, *Ewenny*	51.29	3.34 w	5
Bonconica, *Oppenheim*	49.51	8.23	6
Bonna, *Bonn*	50.44	7.4	6
Bononia, *Ulok*	45.13	19.27	14
Bononia, *Bregova*	44.6	22.38	14
Bononia, for. Felsina, *Bologna*	44.30	11.22	8
Boon, *Vona Liman*	41.4	37.47	20
Boon, or Genetaea Pr., *C. Vona*	41.5	37.48	20
Bora, or Bermius M., *Verria*	40.26	22.0	15
Borbetomagus, *Worms*	49.38	8.23	6
Borcovicus, *Housesteads*	55.1	2.19 w	5
Boreium M., *Kravari*	37.26	22.20	18
Boreum Prom., *Malin Head*	55.22	7.23 w	2
Borsippa? *Bira Nimroud*	32.21	44.26	22
Bortina, *Almudevar*	42.0	0.30 w	7
Borysthěnes F., *Dnieper*	53.6	30.10	2
Bosa, *Bosa*	40.18	8.30	9
Bospŏrus Cimmerius, Strait of Kertsch, or *Jenikaleh*	45.15	36.30	3
Bospŏrus Thracius, Channel of Constantinople	41.5	29.4	14
Bostra (Bozrah), *Bosra*	32.27	36.38	21
Bostrēnus F., *Nahr el-Auly*	33.35	35.30	21
BOTTIAEA	40.35	20.25	15
Boviānum, *Bojano*	41.30	14.28	9
Bovillae, n. *Palaverde*	41.46	12.38	11
Bovium, *Bangor*	53.0	2.54 w	5
Bozrah? *El-Busaireh*	30.52	35.43	21
Bozrah (Bostra), *Bosra*	32.27	36.38	21
Bracăra Augusta, *Braga*	41.34	8.23 w	7
Brachōdes Prom. (or Caput Vada), *C. Kapoudiah*	35.10	11.10	23
Bradanus F., *Bradano*	40.40	16.20	9
Branchĭdae, or Didymi	37.21	27.18	19
Brannogenium (or Bravinnium?) *Leintwardine*	52.22	2.52 w	5
*Brannovices	46.10	4.20	6
Branodūnum, *Brancaster*	52.58	0.39	5
Brasiae, or Prasiae? *St. Andreas*	37.22	22.47	18
Brattia I., *Brazza*	43.20	16.40	14
Bratuspantium? *Breteuil*	49.38	2.17	6
Brauron, *Vraona*	37.56	23.57	16
Bravinnium (Brannogenium?) *Leintwardine*	52.22	2.52 w	5
Bregetio, or Bregentium, r. n. *Szony*	47.45	18.9	14
Bremenium, *Riechester*	55.17	2.15 w	5
Bremetonacae, *Overborough*	54.11	2.35 w	5
Brendice	40.57	25.45	14
Brenthe, *Karytena*	37.29	22.4	18
Brentonicum, *Brentonico*	45.51	10.56	8
*Breuni	46.52	11.30	8
Breviodūrum, *Pont Authon*	49.20	0.36	6
Brevis, *Burres*	42.49	8.10 w	7
*Brigantes	54.0	2.0 w	5
Brigantia, or Brigantium, *Bregens*	47.30	9.45	25

NAMES.	LAT.	LONG.	MAP.
Brigantīnus L., *L. of Constance*	47°.40'	9°.20'	6
Brigantio, *Briançon*	44.55	6.36	6
Brigantium? *Betanzos*	43.18	8.12 w	7
Brige, *Broughton*	51.6	1.33 w	5
Brigetium, *Benavente*	42.0	5.40 w	7
Brigiosum, *Briou*	46.10	0.9 w	6
Brilessus, or Pentelicus M., *Penteli, or Mendeli*	38.7	23.53	16
*Briniates	44.24	9.40	8
BRITANNIA, *England*	53.0	2.0 w	2
Britannicae Ins., *British Islands*	55.0	2.0 w	2
Briva Isărae, *Pontoise*	49.3	2.5	6
Brivates Portus? *Brivain, n. Croisic*	47.20	2.30 w	6
Brivates Portus, or Gesocribate? *Brest*	48.24	4.29 w	6
Brivodūrum, *Villeneuve, n. Bonny*	47.35	2.52	6
Brixellum, *Brescello*	44.54	10.30	8
*Brixentes	46.40	11.30	8
Brixia, *Brescia*	45.33	10.13	8
Brizana F., *Bunder Dilem*	30.2	50.20	8
Brocavium, *Brougham*	54.39	2.41 w	5
Brocomagus, *Brumath*	48.44	7.42	6
Bromagus, *Promasens*	46.36	6.50	6
Bromiscus? *Stavros*	40.38	23.41	15
Brovonacae, *Kirkby Thure*	54.37	2.32 w	5
*Bruchi	42.21	44.15	22
Brucla	46.16	23.41	14
*Bructeri	52.0	7.0	25
Brundusium, *Brindisi*	40.38	18.0	9
*Brutii	38.37	16.20	9
Brygias, *Prespa*	41.5	21.4	14
Bryseae, *Sinanbey*	37.1	22.26	18
Brystacia, *Umbriatico*	39.22	16.56	9
Buana, *Van*	38.29	43.10	22
BUBACENE?	37.30	71.0	8
Bubassus, Dulopŏlis, or Acanthus	36.46	28.11	19
Bubastis, *Tel Basta*	30.34	31.26	24
Bubon	36.59	29.26	20
Buca? *Punta della Penna*	42.11	14.42	9
Bucephăla? *Jeloum*	32.55	73.37	8
Bucephăla Prom., *C. Skyli*	37.26	23.31	18
Bucephălus Prom.	37.51	23.7	18
Buchetium? *Port St. John*	39.16	20.31	15
Bucina I., *Vacca*	38.56	8.25	9
Budinna, or Phorbantia I., *Levanzo*	38.3	12.19	12
Bucra Pr., *C. Scalambri*	36.46	14.31	12
*Budini?	53.0	40.0	2
Budōrum Pr.	37.57	23.25	16
Budōrus F.	38.46	23.25	15
Budua? *Campo Mayor*	39.2	6.54 w	7
Bulis	38.17	22.50	16
Bulla Regia, *Boul.*	36.25	8.44	23
Bullaeum (or Burrium?), *Usk*	51.42	2.53 w	5
Bumădus F., *Khazeir*	36.30	43.25	22
Buphagium, *Papadha*	37.37	21.56	18
Buphăgus F., *River of Papadha*	37.36	21.55	18
Buporthmus Prom., *C. Muzaki*	37.21	23.16	18
Buprasium?	38.5	21.24	18
Bura	38.10	22.10	18
Buraïcus F., *Kalavryta*	38.3	22.8	18
Burbida? *Parada*	42.7	8.47 w	7
Burburaca? n. *Yenikhan*	42.30	23.45	14
Burdigăla, *Bordeaux*	44.51	0.33 w	6
Burginatium, *Schenkenschanz*	51.50	6.8	6
*Buri	50.30	19.0	25
Burnum?	44.5	16.0	14

NAMES.	LAT.	LONG.	MAP.
Baetis F., *Guadalquivir*	38°.0'	4°.0' w	7
Baetulo, *Castle of Mongat*	41.30	2.16	7
Baetulo F., *Besos*	41.30	2.12	7
BAETURIA	38.40	6.0 w	7
Bagacum, *Bavay*	50.18	3.47	6
Bagis, or Bage, *Sirghis*	39.34	29.5	20
Bagisara? *Ras Arubah*	25.14	64.31	3
Bagistana, *Baghistan, or Besitun*	34.16	47.33	22
Bagrada, or Bagradas F. (Macaras), *Mejerdah*	36.22	9.0	23
Bagradas F., *Nabon*	27.45	53.0	3
BAGRAUANDENE	39.45	42.40	22
Baiae, *Baiae*	40.49	14.4	13
Baina, *Bayas*	36.45	36.12	20
*Baiocasses	49.10	0.40 w	6
Balanea, *Baneas*	35.11	36.0	20
Balbura, *Katara*	36.56	29.34	20
Baleares Insulae, or Gymnesiae, *Majorca, &c*	37.30	3.0	7
Balearicum Mare	40.0	2.0	7
Balearis Major, or Columba, *Majorca*	39.30	3.0	7
Balearis Minor, or Nura, *Minorca*	40.0	4.0	7
Baletium, or Valetium	40.33	18.5	9
Balomus, *Ras Shemaul Bunder*	25.12	62.55	3
Balsa, *Tavira*	37.7	7.31 w	7
Balsio, *Borja*	41.55	1.31 w	7
Balyra F., *Mavrozumono*	37.15	21.54	18
Balzanum, *Botzen*	46.31	11.18	8
Bambyce, or Hierapolis, *Membidj, or Bambouj*	36.32	37.57	20
Banasa (Valentia)? *Mamora*	34.16	6.13 w	23
Bandusiae Fons, *Fontana Grande*	40.52	40.58	9
Bantia, *Banzi*	40.50	16.0	9
Baphyras F.	40.8	22.31	15
Barace I., *Peninsula of Cutch*	23.0	70.0	3
Barbalissus, *Kalaat Balis*	35.59	38.11	20
Barbana F., *Moratsha*	42.30	19.30	14
BARBARIA, or AZANIA, *Ajan*	5.0	47.0	2
Barbariana, *S. Martin de Berberana*	42.12	2.26 w	7
Barbaricus S., or Mare Azanium	0.0	50.0	2
Barbarium Prom., *C. Espichel*	38.24	9.24 w	7
Barbesula F., *Guadiaro*	36.30	5.25 w	7
Barbesula, r. on R. Guadiaro	36.18	5.18 w	7
Barbosthenes M.	37.2	22.30	18
Barbyses F.	41.10	28.56	26
Barca, *El-Medinah*	32.31	21.0	23
Barcino, *Barcelona*	41.22	2.10	7
Barderate, *Bra*	44.42	7.52	8
Bardulf, *Barletta*	41.19	16.18	9
Barea, *Vera*	37.13	1.53 w	7
Bargasa? *Port Giova*	37.3	28.23	19
Bargylia	37.12	27.37	19
Bargylietes S., or Iasius, *G. of Mendelyah*	37.15	27.25	19
Bargylus Mons, *Jebel Nusairiyeh*	35.15	36.15	20
Baris? *Isbarta*	37.46	30.39	20
Baris, or Veretum, *S. Maria di Vereto*	39.52	18.21	9
Barium, *Bari*	41.8	16.52	9
Barna? *Gwadel*	25.10	62.14	3
Barygaza, *Baroche*	21.42	73.3	2
Barygazenus S., *G. of Cambay*	21.0	72.30	3
Barza, *Berozeh*	36.1	46.7	22
Barzalo, *Gerger*	37.58	39.7	20
Basante, or Bassianae, r. n. *Debrincze*	44°.45'	20°.0'	14
Basilia, *Bâle, or Basel*	47.35	7.36	6
Basilippo	37.25	5.30 w	7
Bassae	37.26	21.54	18
Bassiana, *Ivany Egerszeg*	47.19	15.58	14
Bassianae, or Basante, r. n. *Debrincze*	44.45	20.0	14
Basta, *Vaste*	40.3	18.21	9
*Bastarnae, or Peucini	48.30	21.0	25
Basti, *Baza*	37.29	2.53 w	7
*Bastitani	38.0	2.0 w	7
*Bastuli	36.50	4.30 w	7
Batana?	36.30	48.35	22
BATANAEA (BASHAN)	32.30	36.15	21
Batava Castra, *Passau*	48.34	13.27	14
*Batavi	51.55	5.0	6
Batby-Colpos	40.12	29.10	26
Bathys F.	39.40	31.11	20
Bathys F.? *Fiati, or Iati*	38.0	13.5	12
Bathys Portus, *Batoum*	41.37	41.38	20
Batinus F., *Trontino, or Tordino*	42.44	14.0	8
Batnae (Saruji), *Saruj*	36.57	38.25	22
Bauli	40.48	14.5	13
Bautae, *Vieux Annecy*	45.55	6.7	6
Bautisus F.			1
Bazira? *Bajour*	35.4	71.25	3
Beberacus L., *L. of Katuniyah*	36.16	41.12	22
Bebiana, *n. Torrimpetra*	41.56	12.12	11
Bebii M.	42.30	20.0	14
Bebriacum, or Bedriacum? *Cividale*	45.3	10.30	8
*Becheires	40.50	40.45	20
Bedesis F., *Ronco*	44.2	12.0	8
Bedriacum, or Bebriacum? *Cividale*	45.3	10.30	8
Beer, *Bireh*	31.55	35.12	21
Beer-sheba, *Beer es-Seba*	31.16	34.21	21
Begorritis L., *L. of Kitrini*	40.31	21.43	15
Belbina I., *S. Georgio*	37.28	23.55	18
Belbina, or Belemina, r. on *Mt. Khelmos*	37.16	22.16	18
Belca	47.48	2.25	6
Beleia, or Veleia?	42.49	2.50 w	7
Belemina, or Belbina, r. on *Mt. Khelmos*	37.16	22.16	18
Belerides I., *Serpentaria I*	39.8	9.37	9
Belerium, Bolerium, or Antivestaeum Pr., *Land's End*	50.4	5.42 w	5
*Belgae (Britannia)	51.0	2.0 w	5
*Belgae (Gallia)	49.55	4.0	6
BELGICA	50.0	4.0	4
Belisama Aest.? *Mouth of Ribble*	53.43	3.0 w	5
*Bellovaci	49.30	2.0	6
Bellovaci (Caesaromagus), *Beauvais*	49.27	2.4	6
Belon, *Tower of Bolonia*	36.5	5.48 w	7
Belsinum, *Masseure*	43.24	0.35	6
Belunum, *Belluno*	46.7	12.14	8
Belus F., *Nahr Naaman*	32.55	35.10	21
Benacus L., *Lago di Garda*	45.35	10.40	8
Benaventa, or Isannavatia, *Burrow Hill, n. Daventry*	52.16	1.8 w	5
Beneharnum, *Castelnon*	43.27	0.40 w	6
Beneventum, *Benevento*	41.8	14.45	9
Berenice	23.55	35.28	3
Berenice Epidires	12.20	43.20	3
Berenice (Ezion-geber)	29.33	34.58	24
Berenice, for. Hesperides, *Benghazi*	32.7	20.3	23
Berenice Panchrysos? *Souakin*	19°.6'	37°.20'	3
Bergidum, *Perez*	42.48	6.58 w	7
Bergintrum, *St. Maurice*	45.37	6.46	8
Bergomum, *Bergamo*	45.42	9.41	8
Bergon, or Bergos, *Bergen*	60.21	5.19	2
Bergulae, *Tchatal Burgas*	41.25	27.18	14
Bergusium, *Bourgoin*	45.35	5.16	6
Bermius M. (or Bora), *Verria*	40.26	22.0	15
Beroea, or Chalybon, *Aleppo*	36.12	37.11	20
Beroea, aft. Irenopolis? *Eski Sagra*	42.30	25.44	14
Beroea, or Berrhoea, *Verria*	40.29	22.8	15
*Berones	42.20	2.30 w	7
Berrhoea, or Beroea, *Verria*	40.29	22.8	15
Bersovia, *Osakova*	45.29	21.16	14
Berytus, *Beirout*	33.50	35.28	21
Berziminium	42.26	19.19	14
Besa, or Antinoe, *Sheikh Abadeh*	27.48	30.54	3
Besbicus I., *Kalolimno*	40.31	28.21	20
Besidiae, *Bisignano*	39.30	16.17	9
Besippo, or Baesippo, r. n. *Porto Barbato*	36.11	5.55 w	7
Besor, Brook, *Wady Sheriah*	31.21	34.30	21
Bessapara, *Tatar Basardjik*	42.5	24.30	14
*Bessi	42.0	24.40	14
Beste, *Bost*	31.29	64.10	3
Besunga? *Bassain*	16.35	94.52	2
Besunga F., *Irawady*	20.0	95.0	2
Beth-abara?	31.49	35.36	21
Beth-gamul, *Um-el-Jemal*	32.23	36.26	21
Beth-haran (Livias), *Er-Rameh*	31.49	35.39	21
Beth-horon, Upper, *Beitoor el-Foka*	31.53	35.6	21
Beth-horon, Lower, *Beitoor et-Tahta*	31.54	35.5	21
Beth-nimrah, *Nimreen*	31.56	35.36	21
Beth-shittah, *Shutta*	32.38	35.29	21
Beth-tappuah, *Teffuh*	31.33	35.5	21
Beth-zachariah, *Tell Zakariyeh*	31.43	34.57	21
Bethagla, *Ain Hajla*	31.48	35.34	21
Bethany, *El-Aziriyeh*	31.46	35.16	21
Bethar? *Bareen*	32.19	35.0	21
Bethar, or Bethor, *Beiteer*	31.44	35.7	21
Betharamathum, or Amathus, *Amateh*	32.19	35.40	21
Bethel, *Beiteen*	31.55	35.15	21
Bethlehem, *Beitlahm*	31.43	35.13	21
Bethsaida (of Galilee)?	32.53	35.31	21
Bethsaida (Julias), *Et-Tell*	32.58	35.40	21
Bethshemesh, *Ain Shems*	31.45	34.58	21
Bethshemesh, or Rameses (Heliopolis), *Matarieh*	30.8	31.20	24
Bethulia, *Beit Ilfah*	32.31	35.28	21
Bethzur? *Ed-Dirweh*	31.36	35.9	21
Betogabris (Eleutheropolis), *Beit Jibreen*	31.36	34.55	21
Betonim? *Batneh*	32.2	35.45	21
Betunia, *Cebrones*	42.15	5.53 w	7
Bezabde, or Sapphe, *Jezireh Ibn Omar*	37.17	41.59	22
Rezer?	31.36	35.56	21
Bina F., *Djane*	36.59	21.50	18
Biatla, *Baeza*	37.58	3.29 w	7
Biblum?	45.20	15.30	14
Bibracte, aft. Augustodunum, *Autun*	46.57	4.18	6

NAMES.	LAT.	LONG.	MAP.
Fibrax ? *Bièvre*	49°.32'	3°.37'	6
*Bibroci	51.20	1.0 w	6
Bida, *Blida*	36.29	2.49	23
Bidaium, *Altenmarkt*	48.0	12.32	14
Bidis ? *S. Giovanni di Bibino*	37.5	15.2	12
Bienna, or Biennus, *Vianos*	35.3	25.28	19
Bienum	35.16	23.31	19
*Bigerriones	43.10	0.10 w	6
Bigestae, *Gabella*	43.5	17.40	14
Bilbilis, *Calatayud Vieja*	41.25	1.35 w	7
Bilēcha F., *Belik*	36.20	39.0	22
Bilitio, *Bellinzona*	46.13	8.58	8
Billaeus F., *Filiyas*	41.7	32.0	20
Bingium, *Bingen*	49.57	7.55	6
Bioia ? *Porto Pino*	38.57	8.35	9
Biroe	44.52	28.3	24
Birtha, *Birehjik*	37.2	38.0	20
Birtha ? *Tekreet*	34.36	43.40	22
BISALTIA	40.50	23.30	15
Bisanthe, aft. Rhaedestus, *Rodosto*	40.59	27.31	14
Biscargis, *Berrus*	41.18	0.26	7
Bistonis Lacus, *L. Bourou*	41.4	25.8	19
BITHYNIA	41.20	33.0	20
Bithynium, aft. Claudiopōlis ? *Boli*	40.42	31.47	20
Bitter Lake	30.17	32.20	24
Biturgia, on *River Ambra*	43.32	11.39	8
Bituriges, *Bourges*	47.5	2.25	6
*Bituriges-Cubi	47.0	1.40	6
*Bituriges-Vivisci	45.0	0.50 w	6
Bizya, *Viza*	41.36	27.44	14
Black Mountains, *Jebel Soudan*	29.0	15.0	2
Black Mountains	29.0	34.40	24
BLAENE ?	41.20	33.40	20
Blanda, *Blanes*	41.40	2.50	7
Blanda, *Maratea*	39.56	15.44	9
Blandiana	45.56	23.25	14
Blandōna ? *Vrana*	43.58	15.34	14
Blandus	39.24	37.8	20
Blariacum, *Blerick*	51.21	6.7	6
Blatum Bulgium, *Middleby*	55.5	3.13 w	5
Blaundus ? *Bolat*	39.33	28.36	20
Blaundus, *Suleimanly*	38.24	29.22	20
Blavia, *Blaye*	45.7	0.39 w	6
Blendium ? *Santander*	43.10	3.43 w	7
Blera, *Bieda*	42.18	12.1	11
Blestium, *Monmouth*	51.49	2.42 w	5
Bletisa, *Ledesma*	41.17	6.2 w	7
Boactes F., *Vara*	44.12	9.48	8
Bougrius F.	38.45	22.41	16
Boaria, *Toro*	38.52	8.23	9
Bocanum ? *Morocco*	31.40	7.37 w	23
Boderia (or Bodotria), Aestuarium, *Firth of Forth*	56.0	3.0 w	5
*Bodiontici	44.10	6.10	6
Bodotria (or Boderia), Aest., *Firth of Forth*	56.0	3.0 w	5
Boeae ?	36.31	23.2	18
BOEATICE	36.30	23.5	18
Boeaticus S., *Vatika Bay*	36.30	23.2	18
Boebe	39.29	22.50	15
Boebēis L., *Karla*	39.30	22.41	15
BOEOTIA	38.20	23.15	16
*Boii	44.20	11.6	8
*Boii	46.40	3.30	6
*Boii, aft. Marcomanni	49.30	14.30	25
Boii, *Bougè*	44.35	0.46 w	6
Boiodūrum, *Innstadt*	48.34	13.29	14
BOIORHMUM, *Bohemia*	49.40	14.30	25
Boium, r. n. *Mariolates*	38.39	22.29	16
Bola, *Poli*	41.53	12.55	11
Bolax, *Volantza*	37.38	21.33	18
Belbo L., *Besikia*	40.40	23.25	15

NAMES.	LAT.	LONG.	MAP.
Bolbitine Mouth (of Nile)	31°.32'	30°.45'	24
Bolerium, Belerium, or Antivestaeum Prom., *Land's End*	50.4	5.42 w	5
Bolinaeus F.	38.18	21.52	18
Bolissus, *Volisso*	38.29	25.56	19
*Bomienses	38.43	22.0	15
Bomium, *Ewenny*	51.29	3.34 w	5
Bonconica, *Oppenheim*	49.51	8.23	6
Bonna, *Bonn*	50.44	7.4	6
Bononia, *Ulok*	45.13	19.27	14
Bononia, *Bregova*	44.6	22.38	14
Bononia, for. Felsina, *Bologna*	44.30	11.22	8
Boon, *Vona Liman*	41.4	37.47	20
Boon, or Genetaea Pr., *C. Vona*	41.5	37.48	20
Bora, or Bermius M., *Verria*	40.26	22.0	15
Borbetomagus, *Worms*	49.38	8.23	6
Borcovicus, *Housesteads*	55.1	2.19 w	5
Boreium M., *Kravari*	37.26	22.20	18
Boreum Prom., *Malin Head*	55.22	7.23 w	2
Borsippa ? *Birs Nimroud*	32.21	44.26	22
Bortina, *Almudevar*	42.0	0.30 w	7
Borysthenes F., *Dnieper*	53.0	30.10	2
Bosa, *Bosa*	40.18	8.30	9
Bospōrus Cimmerius, Strait of Kertsch, or *Jenikaleh*	45.15	36.30	3
Bospōrus Thracius, Channel of Constantinople	41.5	29.4	14
Bostra (Bozrah), *Bosra*	32.27	36.38	21
Bostrēnus F., *Nahr el-Auly*	33.35	35.30	21
BOTTIAEA	40.35	20.25	15
Boviānum, *Bojano*	41.30	14.28	9
Bovillae, n. *Palaverde*	41.46	12.38	11
Bovium, *Bangor*	53.0	2.54 w	5
Bozrah ? *El-Busaireh*	30.52	35.43	21
Bozrah (Bostra), *Bosra*	32.27	36.38	21
Bracăra Augusta, *Braga*	41.34	8.23 w	7
Brachōdes Prom. (or Caput Vada), *C. Kapoudiah*	35.10	11.10	23
Bradanus F., *Bradano*	40.40	16.20	9
Branchīdae, or Didymi	37.21	27.18	19
Brannogenium (or Bravinnium ?) *Leintwardine*	52.22	2.52 w	5
*Brannovices	46.10	4.20	6
Branodūnum, *Brancaster*	52.58	0.39	5
Brasiae, or Prasiae ? *St. Andreas*	37.22	22.47	18
Brattia I., *Brazza*	43.20	16.40	14
Bratuspantium ? *Breteuil*	49.38	2.17	6
Brauron, *Vraona*	37.56	23.57	16
Bravinnium (Brannogenium ?) *Leintwardine*	52.22	2.52 w	5
Bregetio, or Bregentium, r. n. *Szony*	47.45	18.9	14
Bremenium, *Riechester*	55.17	2.15 w	5
Bremetonacae, *Overborough*	54.11	2.35 w	5
Brendice	40.57	25.45	14
Brenthe, *Karytena*	37.29	22.4	18
Brentonicum, *Brentonico*	45.51	10.56	8
*Breuni	46.52	11.30	8
Breviodūrum, *Pont Authon*	49.20	0.36	6
Brevis, *Burres*	42.49	8.10 w	7
*Brigantes	54.0	2.0 w	5
Brigantia, or Brigantium, *Bregenz*	47.30	9.45	25

NAMES.	LAT.	LONG.	MAP.
Brigantīnus L., *L. of Constance*	47°.40'	9°.20'	6
Brigantio, *Briançon*	44.55	6.36	6
Brigantium ? *Betanzos*	43.18	8.12 w	7
Brige, *Broughton*	51.6	1.33 w	5
Brigetium, *Benavente*	42.0	5.40 w	7
Brigiosum, *Briou*	46.10	0.9 w	6
Brilessus, or Pentelicus M., *Penteli, or Mendeli*	38.7	23.53	16
*Briniates	44.24	9.40	8
BRITANNIA, *England*	53.0	2.0 w	2
Britannicae Ins., *British Islands*	55.0	2.0 w	2
Briva Isărae, *Pontoise*	49.3	2.5	6
Brivates Portus ? *Brivain, n. Croisic*	47.20	2.30 w	6
Brivates Portus, or Gesocribate ? *Brest*	48.24	4.29 w	6
Brivodūrum, *Villeneuve, n. Bonny*	47.35	2.52	6
Brixellum, *Brescello*	44.54	10.30	8
*Brixentes	46.40	11.30	8
Brixia, *Brescia*	45.33	10.13	8
Brizana F., *Bunder Dilem*	30.2	50.20	8
Brocavium, *Brougham*	54.39	2.41 w	5
Brocomagus, *Brumath*	48.44	7.42	6
Bromagus, *Promasens*	46.36	6.50	6
Bromiscus ? *Stavros*	40.38	23.41	15
Brovonacae, *Kirkby Thure*	54.37	2.32 w	5
*Bruchi	42.21	44.15	22
Brucla	46.16	23.41	14
*Bructeri	52.0	7.0	25
Brundusium, *Brindisi*	40.38	18.0	9
*Brutii	38.37	16.20	9
Brygias, *Prespa*	41.5	21.4	14
Bryseae, *Sinanbey*	37.1	22.26	18
Brystacia, *Umbriatico*	39.22	16.56	9
Buana, *Van*	38.29	43.10	22
BUBACĒNE ?	37.30	71.0	3
Bubassus, Dulopōlis, or *Acanthus*	36.46	28.11	19
Bubastis, *Tel Basta*	30.34	31.26	24
Bubon	36.59	29.26	20
Buca ? *Punta della Penna*	42.11	14.42	9
Bucephăla ? *Jeloum*	32.55	73.37	3
Bucephăla Prom., *C. Skyli*	37.26	23.31	18
Bucephălus Prom.	37.51	23.7	18
Buchetium ? *Port St. John*	39.16	20.31	15
Bucina I., *Vacca*	38.56	8.25	9
Bucinna, or Phorbantia I., *Levanzo*	38.3	12.19	12
Bucra Pr., *C. Scalambri*	36.46	14.31	12
*Budini ?	53.0	40.0	2
Budōrum Pr.	37.57	23.25	16
Budōrus F.	38.46	23.25	15
Budua ? *Campo Mayor*	39.2	6.54 w	7
Bulis	38.17	22.50	16
Bulla Regia, *Boul.*	36.25	8.44	23
Bullaeum (or Burrium ?), *Usk*	51.42	2.53 w	5
Bumădus F., *Khazeir*	36.30	43.25	22
Buphagium, *Papadha*	37.37	21.56	18
Buphăgus F., *River of Papadha*	37.36	21.55	18
Buporthmus Prom., *C. Musaki*	37.21	23.16	18
Buprasium ?	38.5	21.24	18
Bura	38.10	22.10	18
Burnicus F., *Kalavryta*	38.3	22.8	18
Burbīda ? *Parada*	42.7	8.47 w	7
Burburaca ? n. *Yenikhan*	42.30	23.45	14
Burdigăla, *Bordeaux*	44.51	0.33 w	6
Burginatium, *Schenkenschanz*	51.50	6.8	6
*Buri	50.30	19.0	25
Burnum ?	44.5	16.0	14

NAMES.	LAT.	LONG.	MAP.
Burrium (Bullaeum ?), Usk	51°.42'	2°.53' w	5
Burtudixus? Eski Baba	41.30	27.1	14
Busiris, Abousir	29.54	31.10	24
Busiris (Delta), Abou-sir	30.56	31.11	24
Buthrotum, n. Butrinto	40.44	20.2	15
Buthrotus F., Novito	38.18	16.17	9
Buto?	30.54	30.50	24
Butrium?	44.29	12.12	8
Butua, Budua	42.14	18.51	14
Butuntum, Bitonto	41.7	16.41	9
Buxentum, or Pyxus, Policastro	40.1	15.32	9
Buzaras M.	35.30	5.0	24
Bylazora, Velesa, or Velasso	41.35	21.50	14
Byllis? Gradista, or Graditza	40.33	19.36	15
Byrsa	36.52	10.18	23
Bythias	41.5	29.1	26
BYZACIUM	35.30	10.20	23
Bysantium, aft. Con-stantinopolis, Stam-boul, or Constantino-ple	41.1	28.58	14

C.

NAMES.	LAT.	LONG.	MAP.
CABALIA	37.0	29.40	20
Cabellio, Cavaillon	43.50	5.3	6
Cabillonum, Chalons-sur-Saone	46.47	4.51	6
Cabris?	25.25	63.35	3
Caburro, Cavor	44.47	7.23	8
Cabusa?	30.40	30.57	24
Cabyle, or Calybe? Kar-nabat.	42.40	26.52	14
Cachales F.	38.35	22.40	16
Cacyparis F., Cassibili..	36.58	15.5	12
Cacyrum, Cassaro	37.5	14.57	12
Cadi, Ghedis	39.5	29.35	20
Cadmus M., Baba Dagh	37.40	29.0	20
*Cadurci	44.27	1.28	6
*Cadusii	37.10	49.0	3
Cadyanda?	36.43	29.17	20
Caecina, Cecina	43.22	10.40	8
Caecinum, Satriano	38.43	16.30	9
Caecinus F., Ancinale...	38.44	16.30	9
Caena? Monte Allegro..	37.22	13.20	12
Caenae?	35.25	43.16	22
Caenepolis, or Taena-rum, Kypariso	36.27	22.27	18
Caenina, Ciano	42.2	12.48	11
Caenopolis, Beneghdem..	32.41	21.25	23
Caenys Prom., Punta del Pezzo	38.41	15.40	9
Caepionis Turris, Chi-piona	36.40	6.25 w	7
Caere, for. Agylla, Cervetri	42.1	12.3	11
Caeretanus, Vaccina	42.2	12.4	11
Caesar's Bridge	50.25	7.30	6
Caesar's Wall	46.10	6.0	8
Caesaraugusta, for. Sal-düba, Saragossa	41.46	0.54 w	7
Caesarea I., Jersey	49.14	2.10 w	6
Caesarea, for. Iol, Sher-shell	36.37	2.12	23
Caesarea, for. Mazaca, Kaisariyeh	38.43	39.15	20
Caesarea-Philippi, or Paneas, Banias	33.16	35.42	21
Caesarea, or Tingis, Tangier	35.47	5.48 w	23
Caesarea (for. Turris Stratonis), Kaisari-yeh	32.32	34.54	21
Caesariana, Nagy Var-sony	46.59	17.45	14
Caesariana, Casalnova..	40.12	15.35	8
Caesarodünum, aft. Tu-rones, Tours	47.23	0.42	6

NAMES.	LAT.	LONG.	MAP.
Caesaromagus, aft. Bol-lovnci, Beauvais	49°.27'	2°.4'	6
Caesaromagus, n. Wid-ford	51.43	0.26	5
Caesena, Cesena	44.10	12.15	8
Caete I., S. Theodoro...	35.32	23.56	19
Caetobrix, or Catobriga, Setubal	38.30	8.54 w	7
Caicinus F., Amendolea	37.57	15.54	9
Caicus F., Bakhir Tchai	39.5	27.20	19
Caieta, Gaeta	41.12	13.34	9
Caietanus S., G. of Gaeta	41.14	13.37	9
*Calabri	40.30	18.0	9
Calacte, or Cale Acte, Caronia	37.59	14.25	12
Caladünum?	41.10	7.14 w	7
Calagum, Coulommiers..	48.48	3.5	6
Calagurris, St. Martory	43.9	0.57	6
Calagurris · Fibularia? Loarre	42.20	0.30 w	7
Calagurris Nassica, Ca-lahorra	42.15	2.1 w	7
Calama?	25.20	64.0	3
Calama, Kalat el Wad..	34.57	2.18 w	23
Calamae, Kalami	37.3	22.6	18
Calamon, Kalamun	32.47	34.57	21
Calamyde	35.15	23.34	19
Calanthe, Erdemlu	36.36	34.21	20
Calasarna, Campana....	39.25	16.51	9
Calatia (Campana), Ga-lazze	41.3	14.19	13
Calatia (Samnii), Cai-azzo	41.11	14.21	13
Calauria I., Poro	37.31	23.30	18
Calbis F.? Doloman Tchai	36.50	28.55	19
Calcaria, Tadcaster	53.53	1.15 w	5
Calcaria	43.29	5.16	6
Cale, Oporto	41.9	8.34 w	7
Cale Acte, or Calacte, Caronia	37.59	14.25	12
Cale Acte	38.23	24.0	16
CALEDONIA, Scotland...	57.0	3.0 w	2
Calentes Aquae, Chaudes Aigues	44.52	3.0	6
Caleorsissa...?	39.40	38.52	20
Cales, Calvi	41.12	14.7	9
Cales, or Calex F.?	41.8	31.20	20
*Caletes, or Caleti	49.40	0.30	6
*Calingae	19.0	84.0	2
Calingon Prom.? Ca-lingapatnam Pt.	18.14	24.16	2
Callas F.	38.55	23.6	15
Callatis, or Callatia, Kastalia	43.41	28.36	14
Calleva Atrebatum, Sil-chester	51.22	1.4 w	5
Calliarus, Plain of	38.39	23.3	16
Callichorus, Sunguldaik	41.28	31.50	20
Callidromus	38.45	22.29	26
Callidromus M.	38.45	22.30	16
Callisne, Kalliannes	19.15	73.11	2
Callifae, Calvisi	41.19	14.25	9
Calliga? Coolloo, n. Kuttack	20.26	85.52	2
Callinicum, or Nice-phorium, Rakka	35.56	39.3	22
Callinusa Pr., P. Pomo	35.11	32.33	20
Callipolis, Gallipoli	40.2	17.58	9
Callipolis, Gallipoli	40.24	26.39	19
Callipolis? n. Mascali..	37.42	15.11	12
Callipus F., Sado	38.20	8.20 w	7
Callirhoe (Hot Springs), In Wady Zurka Mayn	31.39	35.40	21
Callirhöe, or Edessa (Ur of the Chaldees?), Urfah	37.10	38.50	22
Callis, Cagli	43.32	12.39	8
Calliste I., or Thera, Santorin	36.25	25.28	19
Callistratia, Merset	42.0	33.19	20

NAMES.	LAT.	LONG.	MAP.
Callium	38°.40'	22°.14'	15
Calor F. (Lucania), Calore	40.30	15.10	9
Calor F. (Samnium), Calore	41.0	14.57	9
Calpe, Kirpeh Liman...	41.10	30.14	20
Calpe, or Carteia, El-Rocadillo, n. San Roque	36.13	5.23 w	7
Calpe M., Rock of Gib-raltar	36.8	5.20 w	7
Calpurniana, Bujalance	37.53	4.22 w	7
Calybe, or Cabyle? Karnabat	42.40	26.52	14
Calycadnus Prom.?	36.19	34.8	20
Calycadnus F., Ghieuk Su	36.37	33.0	20
Calydon, Kurt-aga	38.24	21.34	18
Calymna I., Kalimno...	37.0	27.0	19
Calynda?	36.50	28.55	20
Camala? Castromudarra	42.35	4.55 w	7
Camaracum, Cambray...	50.10	3.14	6
Camarina, Camarana...	36.49	14.29	12
Cambes, Gros Kembs...	47.42	7.30	6
Cambodünum? Slack...	53.39	1.51 w	5
Camboricum? Cam-bridge	52.12	0.8	5
Cambunii M.	40.0	21.50	15
CAMBYSENE	41.20	46.0	22
Cambyses F., Jora	41.26	45.40	22
Cameliomagus, Cigomol	45.4	9.21	8
Cameria, n. Moricone...	42.8	12.47	11
Camerinum, Camerino..	43.6	13.7	8
Camicus? n. Siculiana..	37.19	13.24	12
Camicus F., Fiume delle Canne	37.20	13.24	12
Camirus? Kamera	36.10	27.46	19
Camisa, Keimes	39.45	37.26	20
CAMISENE	39.50	37.30	20
CAMPANIA	41.0	14.15	9
Campanus, Puteolanus, or Cumanus S., B. of Naples	40.40	14.10	12
Campi Falisci.	42.20	12.16	11
Campi Veteres, Vietri..	40.35	15.30	9
Campodünum, Kempten	47.43	10.20	25
Campus Maerae	37.34	22.27	18
Campylus F., Med-ghova	38.53	21.35	15
Camulodünum, or Colo-nia, Colchester	51.53	0.53	5
*Camuni	46.6	10.18	8
Cana, Kana el-Jeleel...	32.49	35.18	21
Cana? Hien Ghoraub...	14.0	48.24	3
Canales, Le Pilelle	40.34	16.53	9
Canalicum, Carcaro	44.22	8.17	8
Canaria I., Grand Ca-nary	28.0	15.30 w	2
*Canarii	27.0	12.0 w	2
Canasida? Ras Tanka..	25.22	59.54	3
Canastraeum Prom., C. Paliouri	39.55	23.46	15
Canate? Kungoon	25.30	59.13	3
Canatha, Kunawat	32.48	36.45	21
Candalicae?	46.55	14.26	14
Candavia	41.16	20.20	14
Candavia M.	41.20	20.34	14
Candidiana, Saorsanlar	44.4	26.45	14
Candidum Prom., C. Bianco	37.20	9.47	23
Candyba, Gendevar	36.19	29.40	20
Cane, or Canae, Aja-nos	39.2	26.51	19
Canethus? Hill of Kara-baba	38.26	23.37	16
Canganorum Prom., Braich-y-Pwll	52.48	4.47 w	5
Canine I., Astola, or Sungadeep	25.6	63 50	3
Cannae, Canne	41.18	16.9	9
Cannarum Pr., C. Qui-lates, or Ras Kirat...	35.20	3.38 w	23
*Canninefates	51.55	4.30	6

NAMES.	LAT.	LONG.	MAP.
Canŏbus, or Canŏpus? r. n. Aboukir	31°.22'	30°.5'	24
Canonium, n. Kelvedon	51.50	0.42	5
Canopic Mouth (of Nile), Madieh Mouth	31.21	30.7	24
*Cantăbri	43.15	4.30 w	7
Cantanus, r. n. Khadros	35.15	23.40	19
Cantharium Prom., C. Katabasis	37.44	26.36	19
Canthi S., G. of Cutch	22.30	70.0	3
*Cantii	51.10	0.45	5
Cantilia, Chantelle	46.15	3.10	6
CANTIUM, Kent	51.10	0.40	6
Cantium Prom., North Foreland	51.23	1.26	5
Canusium, Canosa	41.12	16.4	9
Capara, Ventas de Capana	40.10	6.5 w	7
Caparcotia, Kefr Kood	32.27	35.14 ·	21
Capēna, S. Martino	42.12	12.32	11
Capēnas F.? Grammichia	42.13	12.32	11
Capernaum? Khan Minyeh	32.54	35.33	21
Caphar-dagon, Beitdejan	32.0	34.51	21
Caphăreus Prom., C. Doro, or Xylofago	38.9	24.35	15
Capharsaba (Antipătris), Kefr Saba	32.13	34.59	21
Caphyae	39.45	22.17	18
Capidava?	44.24	28.3	14
Capitium, Capizzi	37.49	14.28	12
Capitolias?	32.44	35.59	21
Capitoniăna? Chiesa di Capella	37.24	14.44	12
Capitŭlum, Il Piglio	41.49	13.7	11
CAPPADOCIA	38.20	36.0	20
Cappădox F.? Kalichisu	39.20	34.0	20
Capraria (or Casperia) I.? Fortaventura	28.30	14.0 w	2
Capraria I.? Gomera	28.10	17.50 w	2
Capraria, or Aegĭlon I., Capraja	43.2	9.50	8
Capraria I., Cabrera	39.5	2.55	7
Caprasia, Tarsia	39.35	16.16	9
Capreae, Capri	40.33	14.13	13
Caprus F., Little Zab	35.30	43.48	22
Caprus L., Kafkana, or Libiada	40.37	23.49	15
Capsa, Ghafsah	34.15	8.54	23
Capua, Santa Maria di Capua	41.6	14.14	13
Caput Anae, Osa la Mantiel	39.0	2.50 w	7
Caput Thyrsi, Orune	40.19	9.22	9
Caput Vada (or Brachōdes Pr.), C. Kapoudiah	35.10	11.10	23
Caput Vada, r. on C. Kapoudiah	35.10	11.10	23
*Carneates	49.45	8.0	6
*Caracēni	41.45	14.10	9
Carae, Carizena	41.25	1.8 w	7
Caralis, Cagliari	39.13	9.7	9
Caralitănum Pr.(Pliny), C. Carbonara	39.6	9.31	9
Caralitănum Pr. (Ptolemy), C. S. Elias	39.11	9.9	9
Caralitănus S., G. of Cagliari	39.5	9.15	9
Caralĭtis L., L. of Beyshehr	37.45	31.45	20
Caralĭtis L., S'urt Ghieul	37.5	29.55	20
Carallia, Kereli	37.55	31.45	20
Carambis Prom., C. Kerembeh	42.1	33.14	20
Carana, or Theodosiŏpolis, Erzeroum	39.55	41.19	22
Caranicum, Guiterli	43.10	7.51 w	7
Carantŏnus F., Charente	45°.45'	0°.30' w	6
Carasa, Garis	43.20	1.2 w	6
Caravi, Mallen	41.59	1.25 w	7
Carbantia (Ad Medias)? Cabiano	45.6	8.25	8
Carbantorigum, Kirkcudbright	54.50	4.1 w	5
Carbia, Alghero	40.33	8.16	9
Carcaso, Carcassonne	43.13	2.21	6
Carcathiocerta, Kharpoot	38.42	39.18	22
Carcavium, Almodovar del Campo	38.48	4.30 w	7
Carchēdon, or Carthăgo, r. n. El-Mersa	36.52	10.18	23
Cardamÿle, Kardamili	38.32	26.5	19
Cardamÿle, Skardhamula	36.54	22.15	18
Cardia, Caridia	40.32	26.45	19
*Cardŭchi, or Cordŭēni	37.15	43.0	22
Careiae, Galera	42.3	12.16	11
CARENĪTIS	39.43	41.0	22
Carentomagus? Villefranche	44.22	2.2	6
CARESĒNE	40.0	27.10	19
Carēsus F.	39.55	27.15	19
CARIA	37.15	28.30	20
Carine, Kirrind	34.19	46.28	22
Carissa	40.24	35.30	20
Caristum, Carosio	44.39	8.46	8
Carmălas F., Churma Su	38.15	36.40	20
Carmăna, Kermaun	29.50	56.28	3
CARMANIA	30.0	58.0	3
Carmel, Kurmul	31.27	35.10	21
Carmēlus M., Jebel Mar Elias	32.50	35.0	21
Carmo, Carmona	37.28	5.33 w	7
Carnasium, or Oechalia	37.16	22.2	18
*Carni	46.12	14.0	8
Carnion F., Xerilla	37·17	22.8	18
Carnuntum, r. n. Hainberg	48.9	16.58	14
Carnūtes, Chartres	48.26	1.29	6
*Carnūtes	48.0	1.30	6
Carocotinum, Harfleur	49.30	0.11	6
Carpasia, Carpas	35.39	34.29	20
Carpātes Mons, Carpathian M	48.0	24.36	14
Carpathium Mare	36.0	27.0	19
Carpăthos I., Scarpanto	35.40	27.10	19
*Carpetăni	40.0	3.30 w	7
*Carpi	49.40	23.0	25
Carpis, Kurbes	36.45	10.33	23
Carrea Potentia, Chieri	45.1	7.49	8
Carrhae (Haran?), Harran	36.52	39.2	22
Carruca?	36.55	4.54 w	7
Carsagis, Bagdetschor	39.58	39.21	20
Carseŏli, Civita, n. Carsoli	42.6	13.1	11
Carsŭlae, Carseoli	42.40	12.32	8
Carsum?	44.31	28.5	14
Cartēia, or Calpe, El-Rocadillo, n. San Roque	36.13	5.23	7
Cartenna, Tennez	36.30	1.20	23
Cartennus F., Wady Tennes	36.28	1.20	23
Carthaea, Port Polais	37.33	24.21	19
Carthaginiensis S., G. of Tunis	37.0	10.30	23
Carthăgo (or Carchēdon), r. n. El-Mersa	36.52	10.18	23
Carthăgo Nova, Cartagena	37.36	0.56 w	7
Cartilis? Dahmousse	36.34	1.47	23
Carula	37.32	5.20 w	7
Carūsa, Gersch	41.48	35.15	20
Carvancas M.?	46.25	15.0	14
Caryae	37.50	22.20	18
Caryae, Khan of Krevata	37°.12'	22°.26'	18
Caryanda?	37.8	27.37	19
Carystus, Karysto	38.1	24.26	15
Carystus (Laconia), Kalyvia of Georgitsi	37.13	22.19	18
Casae, Zoarah, or Eswarah	32.54	12.4	23
Casae Caesariănae, S. Giovanni	43.36	11.34	8
Casae Calventi, Ain Fouka	36.38	2.42	23
Cascantum, Cascante	42.2	1.40 w	7
CASIA REGIO			1
Casilīnum, Capua	41.7	14.12	13
Casīnum, San Germano	41.30	13.50	9
CASIŌTIS	35.30	36.0	20
Casium?	31.4	32.54	24
Casius, or Caesius F., Koi-sou	43.0	46.52	22
Casius Mons, Jebel Okrah	35.55	36.0	20
Casius Mons, C. Kaseroon, or El-Katieh	31.8	32.51	24
Casmĕnae? Scicli	36.47	14.43	12
Casos I., Caxo	35.23	26.55	19
Casos, Polin	35.25	26.56	19
Caspatÿrus?	34.40	73.15	3
Caspeira, Cashmere	34.7	74.43	3
Casperia, or Capraria I.? Fortaventura	28.30	14.0 w	2
Casperia, Aspra	42.23	12.43	11
Caspia, Kasspi	41.57	44.28	22
Caspia, Kadun Seraj	37.33	32.44	20
Caspiae, or Albaniae Pylae, Pass of Derbend	42.0	48.16	22
Caspiae Pylae, Pass of Gaduk	35.50	52.56	3
Caspiēne	39.0	47.30	22
Caspium, or Hyrcănum, Mare, Caspian Sea	40.0	52.0	3
Cassandrīa (Potidaea), Pinaka	40.11	23.20	15
*Cassi	51.45	0.30 w	6
Cassinomăgus, Chassenon	45.51	0.46	6
*Cassiopaei	39.7	20.40	15
Cassiŏpe (Chaonia)?	39.51	20.2	15
Cassiŏpe (Corcyra), Kassopo	39.48	19.55	15
Cassiterĭdes Ins., Scilly Islands	49.55	6.20	6
Cassŏpe, n. Kamarina	39.9	20.40	15
Castabăla? r. n. Demir Kapu	36.54	35.58	20
Castămon, Kastamuni	41.20	33.54	20
Castellum	44.7	11.38	8
Castellum Amerīnum	42.28	12.22	11
Castellum Firmanōrum, Porto di Fermo	43.11	13.47	8
Castellum Menapiōrum, Kessel	51.19	6.3	6
Castellum Morinōrum, Cassel	50.48	2.29	6
Castellum Tingitii?	35.50	1.25	23
Castellum Trajăni, Castel	50.0	8.18	6
Casthanaea?	39.22	23.11	15
Castorum	45.5	10.19	8
Castra Caecilia, Caceres	39.26	6.14 w	7
Castra Constantia, Coutances	49.4	1.26 w	6
Castra Cornelia, Ghellah	37.4	10.4	23
Castra Exploratōrum, Netherby	55.2	2.54 w	5
Castra Hannibălis	38.53	16.34	9
Castra Julia, Truxillo	39.24	5.48 w	7
Castra Nova? El-Kalah	35.32	0.21	23
Castra Puerōrum?	35.34	1.11 w	23

NAMES.	LAT.	LONG.	MAP.
Castra Pyrrhi? *Ostaniji*	40°.10'	20°.51'	15
Castra Trajana	44.48	24.14	14
Castrimonium, *Marino*	41.47	12.41	11
Castrum Cepha? *Hosn Kaifa*	37.43	41.6	22
Castrum Inui?	41.32	12.32	11
Castrum Minervae, *Castro*	40.0	18.26	9
Castrum Novum, *Torre di Chiaruccia*	42.2	11.48	11
Castrum Novum, *Giulia nova*	42.45	13.58	8
Castrum Truentinum, *Porto d'Ascoli*	42.55	13.53	8
Castulo, *Caslona*	38.1	3.45 w	7
Casuaria, *Cesarieux*	45.47	6.14	6
Casuentus F., *Basiento*	40.34	16.20	9
Casystes? *Port Latzata, or Egrylar*	38.15	26.25	19
Catabathmus Major, *Akabah el-Kebir*	31.30	25.0	23
Catabathmus Minor, *Akabah es-Soughair*	31.0	27.45	23
CATACECAUMENE	38.35	28.50	20
Cataea L., *Keish, or Kenn*	26.32	54.0	3
*Catalauni	48.50	4.30	6
CATAONIA	38.0	36.30	20
Cataract (of Nile), Greater, *Wady Halfa*	21.58	31.10	3
Cararact (of Nile), Little	24.0	32.55	3
Cataractonium, *Catterick Bridge*	54.23	1.38 w	5
Catarrhactes F., *Sudsuro, or Zussura*	35.2	25.20	19
*Cathaei	30.30	74.0	3
Catina, or Catăna, *Catania*	37.27	15.3	12
Catobriga, or Caetŏbrix, *Setubal*	38.30	8.54 w	7
*Catti, or Chatti	50.45	10.0	25
*Cattigara? *Cantom*	23.10	113.15	2
Caturiges, *Bar-le-Duc*	48.45	5.10	6
*Caturiges	44.40	6.20	6
Catusiacum, *Chaours*	49.42	4.0	6
*Catyeuchlani	52.0	0.35 w	5
Cauca, *Coca*	41.14	4.28 w	7
Caucana? *Porto Longobardo*	36.46	14.34	12
Caucasa Prom.? *C. Amista*	38.16	25.53	19
Caucasiae Pylae, *Pass of Dariel*	42.44	44.41	22
Caucasus M.	42.30	45.0	22
*Cauci, or Chauci	53.20	9.0	25
*Caucones	41.25	32.0	20
*Caudium?	41.3	14.34	13
Caulon?	38.27	16.30	9
Caunus?	36.50	28.40	19
Caus? *Sariñena*	41.46	0.9 w	7
Caus	37.43	22.0	18
Causennae, *Ancaster*	53.0	0.31 w	5
*Cavares	44.30	4.50	6
Caviclum, *Almunecar*	36.45	3.46 w	7
Caystri Pedion?	38.40	31.2	20
Caystrus F., *Kuchouk Mendere*	38.8	28.0	19
Cea, or Ceos, I., *Zea*	37.35	24.20	19
Ceba, *Ceva*	44.14	8.1	8
Cebrene, r. n. *Baramitch*	39.49	26.41	19
Cebrus, or Ciambrus F., *Zibru, or Zibritza*	43.30	23.25	14
Cebrus, or Cibrus, *Zibru Palanka*	43.47	23.30	14
Cecandros L., *Busheab*	26.48	53.20	3
Cecilionicum?	40.38	5.57 w	7
Ceoryphaleia I., *Kyra*	37.42	23.16	18
Cedris F., *Cedrino*	40.18	9.30	9
Celadussae I^{ae}., *Melada, &c.*	44.15	14.50	14
Celaenae, r. n. *Dineir*	38°.3'	30°.14'	20
Celcia, *Cilli*	46.15	15.18	14
Celendŏris, *Chelendreh*	36.9	33.22	20
Celetrum, *Kastoria*	40.38	21.23	15
Celina? n. *S. Lucia*	46.1	12.32	8
Celius Mons, *Kellmuns*	48.6	10.10	25
Celŏnae? *Sirwan*	33.30	46.37	22
Celsa (Colonia Victrix Julia), *Xelsa*	41.28	0.28 w	7
*Celtae	47.30	2.0	6
Celti?	37.48	5.30 w	7
*Celtibēri	41.0	1.35 w	7
*Celtĭci	37.45	6.0 w	7
Celtĭcum Prom.? *C. Finisterre*	42.53	9.15 w	7
Cenaeum Prom., *C. Lithada*	38.49	22.49	15
Cenchreae (Argeia), *Palea Skofidhaki*	37.34	22.36	18
Cenchreae (Corinthia), *Kekhries*	37.52	23.0	18
Ceneta, *Ceneda*	45.58	12.20	8
*Cenimagni	52.18	1.0	6
Cenion F.? *Falmouth Bay*	50.10	5.3 w	5
Oeno, *Rudera*	41.26	12.41	11
Cenomani, *Le Mans*	48.0	0.11	6
*Cenomani	45.25	10.20	8
Centrītes F., *Bohtan Tchai*	38.0	41.35	22
*Centrŏnes	45.24	6.30	6
Centum-cellae, *Civita Vecchia*	42.6	11.48	9
Centurĭpae (or Centurĭpa), *Centorbi*	37.35	14.45	12
Ceos, or Cea, I., *Zea*	37.35	24.20	19
Cepasiae, *Spresiano*	45.46	12.16	8
Ceperaria, *Kefr Urich*	31.46	34.59	21
Cephălae Prom., *Ras Misratah*	32.26	15.10	23
Cephallenia I., *Cephalonia*	38.15	20.30	15
Cephaloedium, *Cefalu*	38.0	14.2	12
Cepheisia, or Cephisia, *Kivisia*	38.6	23.49	16
Cephissis, or Copais L., *L. Topolias*	38.25	23.5	16
Cephissus F. (Argolis)	37.44	22.33	18
Cephissus F. (Attica)	38.3	23.44	16
Cephissus F. (Attica), *Sarandaforo*	38.9	23.30	16
Cephissus F. (Boeotia)	38.30	22.52	16
Ceramĭcus, or Doris S., *G. of Kos*	36.55	27.45	19
Cerămus? *Keramo*	37.2	27.59	19
Cerăsus	41.4	39.17	20
Cerăta M., *Kerata*	38.3	23.27	16
*Ceraunii	40.10	19.40	15
Cerausius M., *Tetrasi*	37.22	21.58	18
Cerbalus F., *Cervaro*	41.20	15.30	9
Cercas	38.23	23.36	16
Cercasŏra, *El-Arkas*	30.5	31.13	24
Cercetium M., *Khassia*	39.30	21.29	15
Cercidius F.? *Fiume di Porto*	42.15	8.45	9
Cercina I. (Cyraunis?), *Ramlah*	34.45	11.15	23
Cercinītis, or Prasias, L., *Takhyno*	40.55	23.50	19
Cercinītis L., *Gherbah*	34.38	11.0	23
Cerdylium M.	40.48	23.48	15
Ceres, Temple of	37.35	22.27	18
Ceresius L., *Lago di Lugano*	45.58	9.0	8
Ceressus, *Paleopanaghia*	38.12	23.6	16
Ceretapa? *Chardak*	37.51	29.45	20
Cerfennia, *Coll'Armeno*	42.4	13.38	9
Cerillae, *Cirella*	39.38	15.52	9
Cerinthus	38.49	23.30	15
Cerne? *Arguin*	20.30	16.35 w	2
Ceronia, *Kyrenia*	35.21	33.20	20
*Cerretăni	42.15	1.40	7
Certha?	32°.37'	34°.56'	21
Cervaria, *C. Cervera*	42.26	3.11	6
Cerycium M	38.19	23.32	16
Ceryni-a	38.11	22.8	14
Cerynites F., *Bokhusia*	38.8	22.6	18
Cesada? *Brihuega*	40.44	2.50 w	7
Cessero, *St. Tiberi*	43.27	3.26	6
Cestiae, *Cizzengo*	45.7	8.8	8
Cestria (Ilium, or Troja), *Palea Venetia*	39.34	20.23	15
CESTRINE	39.40	20.30	15
Cestrus F., *Ak Su*	37.15	30.45	20
Cetaria? *Torre di Scopello*	38.5	12.49	12
Cetium?	48.19	.16.10	14
Cetius F., *Bergamo Tchai*	39.15	27.20	19
Cetius Mons, *Wiener Wald*	48.0	15.52	14
Cevenna M., *Cevennes*	44.20	3.30	6
Chabŏrras (Chebar) F., *Khabour*	36.30	40.30	22
Chaereum? *El-Keroui*	31.5	30.21	24
Chaeroneia, *Kapurna*	38.29	22.50	16
Chala (Halah?), *Sar Puli Zohab*	34.32	46.8	22
Chalaeum, *Larnaki*	38.27	22.26	16
Chalasar, or Artemīta, *Sheriban*	33.58	44.56	22
Chalastra	40.33	22.41	15
Chalcēdon, *Kadikeui*	40.59	29.2	20
Chalcerītis L. (Aretias), *Kerasunt Ada*	40.56	38.27	20
Chalcia, or Chalce L., *Karki*	36.14	27.35	19
CHALCIDICE	40.21	23.20	15
CHALCIDICE	35.55	37.0	20
Chalcis?	37.57	22.49	13
Chalcis ad Belum? *Majdel Anjar*	33.46	35.54	21
Chalcis (Aetolia), *Ovriokastro*	38.22	21.39	18
Chalcis (Epirus), *Khaliki*	39.44	21.18	15
Chalcis (Euboea), *Egripo, or Negropont*	38.26	23.37	16
Chalcis (Syria), *Kinnesreen*	35.52	37.5	20
CHALDAEA	31.0	46.0	22
Chaldaean Lakes, *Marshes of Lemloom*	31.30	45.15	22
Chaldone Prom., *Ras el-Lur*	29.21	48.1	3
Chalia? *Chalia*	38.17	23.31	16
CHALONITIS	34.36	46.0	22
Chalus F., *Nahr Koweik*	36.10	37.5	20
*Chalÿbes	40.45	37.30	20
*Chalÿbes	40.10	41.0	22
Chalÿbon, or Beroea, *Aleppo*	36.12	37.11	20
CHALYBONITIS	36.15	37.30	20
*Chamavi	51.50	8.0	24
Chammanĕne	39.20	34.0	20
Chaon M.	37.35	22.40	18
CHAONIA	39.50	20.10	15
*Characităni	40.15	2.45 w	7
Charădra, or Charădrus, *Rogus*	39.11	20.51	15
Charadra, *Suvala*	38.37	22.32	16
Charadriae, *Vatopedhi*	40.18	24.13	15
Charadrus, *Kharadran*	36.6	32.36	20
Charădrus F. (Achaia), *River of Velvitza*	38.15	21.49	18
Charădrus F. (Argolis), *Xerias*	37.38	22.40	18
Charadrus F. (Attica), *Marathona*	38.11	23.50	16
Charădrus F. (Cynuria), *Kami*	37.20	22.45	13
Charădrus F. (Epirus), *Rogus, or River of St. George*	39.10	20.46	15

NAMES.	LAT.	LONG.	MAP.
Charădrus F. (Messenia)	37°.15'	22°.0'	18
Charax (Kir of Moab), Kerak	31.15	35.46	21
Charax-spasĭni? Mohammerah	30.23	48.15	22
Charidēmi Prom., C. de Gata	36.43	2.11 w	7
Charmande?	33.29	42.58	22
Charybdis	38.11	15.35	9
*Chasuarii	51.30	8.0	25
*Chatramotītae, Coast of Hadramaut	16.0	50.0	3
*Chatti, or Catti	50.45	10.0	25
*Chauci, or Cauci	53.20	9.0	25
Chebar F. (or Chabŏras), Khabour	36.30	40.30	22
Cheimarrhus F.	37.35	22.40	18
Cheimerium Prom., C. Varlam	39.20	20.18	15
Chelidoniae Iᵐ., Celedoni, or Shelidan	36.9	30.26	20
Chelonātes Prom., C. Tornese	37.54	21.7	18
Chelydoria M., Mavron Oros	38.2	22.26	18
Cleunuis, Ekhmim	26.32	31.45	3
Chersonēsus, Capo Teulada	38.52	8.37	9
Chersonēsus, Khersonesos	35.17	25.21	19
CHERSONĒSUS CIMBRICA, Jutland	57.0	9.0	2
Chersonēsus Magna, Ras et-Tyn	32.35	23.12	23
Chersonēsus Pr. (Aetolia), Point Bakari	38.17	21.31	18
Chersonēsus Pr. (Creta), C. Keronisi	35.27	23.32	19
Chersonēsus Pr. (Euboea), C. Oktonia	38.31	24.12	15
CHERSONĒSUS RHODIORUM	36.40	28.10	19
CHERSONĒSUS (THRACICA)	40.20	26.30	19
*Cherusci	51.30	11.30	25
Chimaera, Kimera	40.4	19.46	15
Chimaera M., Yanar	36.26	30.29	20
Chinalaph F., Shellif	35.52	1.0	23
Chios, Kastro, or Khio	38.22	26.9	19
Chios I., Khio, or Scio	38.25	26.0	19
Chliat? Akhlat	38.46	42.5	22
Choaspes F. (Ariana), River of Ghiznee	34.0	68.50	3
Choaspes F. (Susiana), Kerkhah	33.0	47.35	22
Choatras M.	37.30	44.30	22
Choba? Boujayah, or Bougie	36.46	5.9	23
Chobus, or Cohibus F., Chopius	42.20	41.50	22
Choerădes Iᵐ., S. Pietro e S. Paulo	40.26	17.8	9
Choerius F.	36.57	22 12	18
Choes F.? Alishung	35.10	70.15	3
Cholle? Ain el-Koom	35.10	38.44	20
Chollidae, Grotto of the Nymphs, n. Vari	37.52	23.48	16
Choma?	36.34	29.51	20
*Chorasmii	42.0	57.0	3
Chorazin, Gerazi	32.57	35.34	21
Choriĕnes, Fortress of? Hissar, or Shadman	38.10	69.0	3
Chorsa, Kars	40.37	43.9	22
Chorseus F., Nahr Koradje, or El-Belka	32.40	35.0	21
CHORZĒNE	40.30	43.10	22
Chrysa I., Gardero	34.51	25.41	19
Chrysas F., Dittaino	37.31	14.40	12
Chryse	39.35	26.56	19
Chryse, or Sminthium	39.38	26.10	19
Chrysoceras	41.1	28.58	26
Chrysopŏlis, Scutari	41.0	29.1	20
Chrysos F., Ninfi Tchai	38°.28'	27°.35'	19
Chrysorrhoas F., Wady Burada	33.38	36.15	21
Chydas F., Furiano	38.1	14.32	12
Chytri	38.47	22.28	26
Chytrus, Kythrea	35.15	33.30	20
Ciambrus, or Cebrus F., Zibru, or Zibritza	43.30	23.25	14
Ciănus S., G. of Moudania	40.25	29.0	20
Cibălae, n. Vinkovze	45.16	18.53	14
Cibianum, Hermanstadt	45.48	24.7	14
Cibrus, or Cebrus, Zibru Palanka	43.47	23.30	14
Cibȳra, Choreum, or Horzoom	37.12	29.31	20
Cibȳra	36.43	31.40	20
Cicae Iᵐ., I. de Bayona, or Cies	42.10	8.53 w	7
Ciciliana	38.33	8.42 w	7
*Cioŏnes	41.5	25.10	14
Cicynēthus I., Palea Trikeri	39.9	23.5	15
Cidamis? Ghadamis	30.40	10.25	2
Cierium (Arne), Mataranga	39.23	22.3	15
Ciĕrus, or Prusias, Uskub, or Eski Bagh	40.50	31.21	20
*Cilbiāni	38.8	28.20	19
Cilernum, Walwick Chesters	55.2	0.8 w	5
CILICIA (PEDIAS, or CAMPESTRIS)	37.0	35.30	20
CILICIA (TRACHEIA)	36.30	33.30	20
Ciliconnēsus I., Hoirat Kaleh Adassi	41.5	37.44	20
Ciliza, Killis	36.43	37.9	20
Cilla	39.35	27.0	19
Cillae, Kialik	42.3	25.25	14
Cilniăna, Estepona	36.26	5.7 w	7
Cimarus (or Corȳcus) Pr., C. Buso	35.37	23.35	19
*Cimbri	55.0	9.0	25
Cimbrianae? Veszprim	47.6	17.58	14
Cimbrōrum Prom., The Skawe	57.43	10.40	2
CIMIATĒNE	41.0	34.0	20
Cimĭnus Lacus, Lago di Vico	42.20	12.10	11
Cimĭnus M., Monte di Viterbo	42.41	12.8	11
*Cimmerii			1
Cimōlos, Daskalio	36.47	24.34	19
Cimōlos I., Kimolo, or Argentiera	36.48	24.35	19
Cinăros I., Kinaro	36.58	26.18	19
Cingn F., Cinca	42.15	0.12	7
Cingilia? Civita Retenga	42.12	13.42	8
Cingŭlum, Cingoli	43.23	13.13	8
Cinium, Sineu	39.39	3.3	7
Cinnamomifĕra Regio	10.0	50.0	2
Cinniăna, Ciurana	42.12	2.58	7
Cinōlis, Kinolu	40.57	34.14	20
Cinyps, or Cinȳphus F., Wady Khahan	32.30	14.24	23
Cinyps (town)	32.30	14.24	23
Circaeum Pr., Monte Circello	41.12	13.4	11
Circĕii, San Felice, on Monte Circello	41.12	13.5	11
Circes Templum	41.12	13.3	11
Circesium (Carchemish), Kerkisiyeh	35.9	40.30	22
Cireus F.?	38.34	23.39	15
Cirphis M., Somalesi	38.26	22.36	16
Cirpi Mansio? Visegrad	47.48	19.0	14
Cirrha, Magula	38.26	22.26	16
Cirta, aft. Constantīna, Constantineh	36.19	6.35	23
Cirtisa	45.15	18.38	14
Cisamus, Kalyves	35.26	24.12	19
Cisămus, Kisamos	35°.39'	23°.40'	19
Cissa I., Pago..l	44.28	15.0	14
CISSIA	32.6	48.20	22
Cisterna Nerōnis, Cisterna	41.35	12.58	11
Cisthēne	39.26	26.53	19
Cithaeron M., Elatia	38.11	23.15	16
Citium, Khiti	34.49	33.36	20
Cium, Hirschova	44.40	28.0	24
Cius, Kemlik	40.25	29.12	20
Cladeus F.	33.10	21.39	18
Clambete	44.27	15.44	14
Clanis F., Chiana	42.58	12.0	8
Clanius F., Lagno	41.2	14.6	13
Claropetis, or Lampetia, Amantea	39.12	16.3	9
Claros, Zilleh	38.0	27.14	19
Clastidium, Casteggio	45.1	9.7	8
Claterna, Quaderna	41.27	11.32	8
Claudanum? Ochrida	41.11	20.47	14
Claudias, Alischin	38.25	38.55	20
Claudiopŏlis, Moot	36.36	33.18	20
Claudiopŏlis, for. Bithynium? Boli	40.42	31.47	20
Claudus, or Claude, I., Gozo	34.51	24.6	19
Clausala F., Khiri, or Drinossi	42.10	19.58	14
Clausentum, Bittern, n. Southampton	50.55	1.22 w	5
Claustra Romāna, n. Fogliano	41.21	12.59	11
Clavenna, Chiavenna	46.18	9.24	8
Clasomĕnae, Kelisman	38.23	26.48	19
Cleides I., Klides	35.42	34.37	20
Cleitor	37.54	22.7	18
Cleōnae (Macedonia)	40.12	24.14	15
Cleōnae (Peloponnēsus), Klenes	37.49	22.47	18
Cleōnae (Phocis)	38.37	22.55	16
Cleopătris, or Arsinŏe	30.3	32.34	24
Cleusis F., Chiesa	45.30	10.25	8
Clinax, Tschideh	41.56	33.4	20
Climberris, aft. Ausci, Auch	43.39	0.35	6
Cliternia, Liechiano	41.55	15.17	9
Clitumni Templum and F., la Vene	42.51	12.48	8
Clodiana?	41.8	19.52	14
Clodianus F., Fluvia	42.10	2.40	7
Clota Aestuarium, Firth of Clyde	55.50	4.55 w	5
Cluana, S. Elpidio	43.14	13.41	8
Clunia, r. n. Coruña del Conde	41.43	3.20 w	7
Clusĭna Palus	43.20	11.51	8
Clusium, Chiusi	43.4	11.58	8
Cluso F., Chissone, or Clusone	44.55	7.14	8
Clypĕa, or Aspis, Kalibia	36.50	11.8	23
Clypĕa, or Aspis Prom. (Taphytis), Ras el-Melhr	36.52	11.9	23
Clysma? Tell Kolzoum	29.58	32.30	24
Cnemĭdes	38.46	22.48	16
Cnemides Prom., C. Vromo	38.46	22.49	16
Cnemis M.	38.40	22.45	16
Cnidus, r. n. C. Krio	36.41	27.24	19
Cnopia?	38.23	23.28	16
Cnossus, Makro Teikho	35.20	25.10	19
Cobucla, Pescadores	35.16	4.45 w	23
Cocala?	25.25	66.0	3
Coccium, or Rhigodunum, Ribchester	53.49	2.31 w	5
Cochlearia, Porto Sabatino	40.48	9.40	9
Cocinthum Prom., C. Stilo	38.29	16.37	9
Cocintum, Stilo	38.32	16.30	9
*Cocosātes	44.0	1.0 w	6

NAMES.	LAT.	LONG.	MAP.
Cocussus, or Cucusus, Gogsun	38°.7'	36°.15'	20
Cocytus F., Vuvo	39.17	20.34	15
Codanus S., Kattegat	57.0	11.0	2
Coela	38.35	24.10	19
COELE-SYRIA, El-Bukaa, &c.	34.15	36.10	20
Coelia, Ceglie	41.4	16.52	9
Coelianum, Stigliano	40.25	16.12	9
Coelium, Ceglie	40.39	17.32	9
Coenyra? Kynira	40.50	24.47	19
Coequosa, Caussèque	43.59	1.9 w	6
Coeus F. (Balyra), Mavrozumono	37.15	21.54	18
Cogamus F.	38.28	28.20	19
Cohibus, or Chobus, F.,	42.15	41.35	22
Coidza (Cyiza), Choubar	25.16	60.40	3
Colania, Lanark	55.41	3.48 w	5
*Colchi	40.50	39.40	20
COLCHIS	42.0	42.0	22
Coliacum Prom.			1
Colchicus S.			1
Colias Pr., Trispyrgi	37.56	23.42	16
Collatia, Collatina	41.46	15.25	9
Collatia? Castel del 'Osa	41.54	12.42	11
Collops Magnus, or Cullu, Collo	37.0	6.34	23
Collops Parvus, or Sullucu, Tagodeite	36.59	7.36	23
Colobona, Trubejena	36.50	6.6 w	7
Colonia, Kuleh Hissar	40.9	38.13	20
Colonia, or Camulodunum, Colchester	51.53	0.53	5
Colonia Agrippinensis, or Agrippina, Cologne	50.56	6.57	6
Colonia Equestris, or Noviodunum, Nyon	46.23	6.15	8
Colonia Trajana, Kelln	51.48	6.10	6
Colonides? Kastelia	36.50	21.56	18
Colonis L.? Spezzia Pulo	37.13	23.10	18
Colonos	38.0	23.43	16
COLOPENE	39.46	36.50	20
Colophon	38.2	27.14	19
Colossae, r. n. Khonos	37.50	29.19	20
Colta?	25.13	64.30	3
Colubraria, or Ophiusa I., Columbretes	39.54	0.45	7
Colubraria I. (Ophiusa of Strabo), Formentera	38.42	1.25	7
Columba I., or Balearis Major, Majorca	39.30	3.0	7
Columbaria I., Palmajola	42.42	10.29	8
Columbarium Prom., Capo Figari	40.59	9.39	9
Columna, La Catona	38.11	15.40	9
Colyergia Prom.?	37.24	22.25	18
Comana (Cappadocia)? Al-Bostan	38.6	36.56	20
Comana Pontica, Gumenek	40.19	36.44	20
Comaria (Town and Prom.), C. Comorin	8.4	77.37	2
Comarus Portus, Gomaro	39.0	20.42	15
Combaristum, Combré	47.46	1.0 w	6
Combreia	40.16	23.9	15
Combretonium, Burgh	52.8	1.14	5
Comidava? n. Nyamts	47.10	26.15	24
Cominium Ceritum, Cerreto	41.16	14.33	9
COMMAGENE	37.45	38.30	20
Complitum Anagninum, Osteria della Fontana	41.45	13.10	11
Complutica? Trinidade	41.19	6.56 w	7
Complutum, Alcalá de Henares	40.27	3.25 w	7
Compsa, Conza	40.52	15.19	9
Comum, or Novum Comum, Como	45.48	9.6	8

NAMES.	LAT.	LONG.	MAP.
Conceobar, Kangawar	34°.26'	48°.0'	22
Concordia, Concordia, n. Porto Gruaro	45.45	12.51	8
Concordia? n. Weissenburg	49.3	7.59	6
Concordia Julia, or Nertobriga, Valera la Vieja	36.15	6.29 w	7
Condate, Kinderton, n. Middlewich	53.12	2.26 w	5
Condate, Condé	48.57	0.59 w	6
Condate	45.5	3.32	6
Condate, Seyssel	45.58	5.48	6
Condate, Montereau	48.23	2.57	6
Condate, Cognac	45.41	0.19 w	6
Condate, Cosne	47.25	2.57	6
Condate, aft. Redones, Rennes	48.7	1.40 w	6
Condercum, Benwell Hill	54.59	1.40 w	5
Condivicnum, aft. Namnetes, Nantes	47.13	1.32 w	6
*Condrusi	50.25	5.10	6
Conembrica, Coimbra	40.12	8.24 w	7
Confluentes, Coblenz	50.21	7.36	6
Congavata, Stanwix	54.55	2.54 w	5
Congustus, Tusun Ujuk	38.24	33.28	20
Conistorsis, or Cunistorgis? Silves	37.15	8.19 w	7
Conni, Tschalkeni	39.0	30.9	20
Conope, Angelokastro	38.33	21.18	15
Conope, Hyria, or Lysimachia L., Zygos, or Angelokastro	38.34	21.23	15
Conopium, Koumjas	41.29	36.8	20
Conovium, Caer Rhun, n. Conway	53.13	3.50 w	5
Consabrum, Consuegra	39.29	3.40 w	7
Consentia, Cosenza	39.19	16.15	9
*Consorani	42.48	1.20	6
Constantina, for. Cirta, Constantineh	36.19	6.35	23
Constantinopolis, for. Byzantium, Constantinople, or Stamboul	41.1	28.58	14
*Contestani	38.30	0.40 w	7
Conthyle? r. n. Agios Triada	38.5	23.24	16
Contosolia, Guarena	38.47	5.37 w	7
Contra Acincum (Pessium), Pesth	47.30	19.6	14
Contra Pselcis, for. Tachompso, Kubban	23.11	32.48	3
Contrebia, Cantabria	42.24	2.25 w	7
Contributa?	38.15	6.19 w	7
Convenae, for. Lugdunum, St. Bertrand de Comminges	43.0	0.38	6
*Convenae	43.0	0.30	6
Copae, Topolia	38.29	23.10	16
Copais, or Cephissis L., Topolias	38.25	23.5	16
Cophas?	25.8	61.45	3
Cophen F., Caboul River	34.35	70.0	3
Copiae, for. Thurii	39.40	16.23	9
Coprates F., Dizful	32.0	48.32	22
Coptos, Koft	26.0	32.47	3
Cora, Cora	41.38	12.58	11
Coracae	39.17	23.11	15
Coracesium, Alaya	36.33	32.3	20
Coracium	41.15	29.10	26
Coracodes Portus	40.5	8.25	9
Coralius F.	38.23	22.59	16
Coralla Pr., C. Kereli	41.5	39.10	20
Corassiae I., or Corseae, Fourni, &c.	37.35	26.30	19
Corax F., Kodor	43.0	41.18	22
Corax M., Kisil Dagh	38.18	27.2	19
Corax M., Vardhusi	38.40	22.10	15
Corbia, Rocca Priore	41.48	12.48	11
CORBIANE	33.0	48.0	22
Corbulo, Fossa of	52.10	4.25	6

NAMES.	LAT.	LONG.	MAP.
Corcyra, Corfu	39°.37'	19°.55'	15
Corcyra I., Corfu	39.40	19.45	15
Corcyra Nigra I., Cursola	42.56	17.0	14
Corcura, or Demetrias, Kerkook	35.32	44.10	22
Corda, Lynekirk	55.39	3.17 w	5
Corduba, Cordova	37.53	4.46 w	7
*Cordueni, or Carduchi	37.15	43.0	22
Cordyle, Akcheh Kaleh	41.5	39.30	20
Coreae, Kuriyut	32.8	35.18	21
Coressus, Port St. Nicholas	37.39	24.19	17
Corfinium, S. Pelino, n. Pentima	42.7	13.51	9
Coria, Castle Cary	55.58	3.58 w	5
Coriallum, Cherbourg	49.38	1.38 w	6
Corinium, or Durocornovium, Cirencester	51.43	1.58 w	5
CORINTHIA	37.55	23.0	18
Corinthiacus S., G. of Corinth	38.12	22.30	18
Corinthus, Korinthó (Corinth)	37.54	22.53	13
Corioli? M. Giove	41.40	12.41	11
*Corisopiti	47.55	4.0 w	6
*Coritavi	53.5	1.0 w	5
Corium	35.20	24.19	19
Cormasa?	37.20	30.23	20
Cormones, Cormonso	45.57	13.28	8
Cornacum, Vukovar	45.20	19.6	14
*Cornavii	52.50	2.20 w	5
Corniaspa	39.55	34.54	20
Cornicularia, Mezzogoro	44.53	12.6	8
Cornictilum, S. Angelo	42.3	12.44	11
Cornus? Sindia	40.18	8.39	9
Corobilium, Corbeil	48.37	4.31	6
Coromanis	29.32	48.0	3
Corone (Aepea?), Petalidhi	36.57	21.56	18
Coroneia	38.22	22.57	16
Coronta, n. Prodhromo	38.36	21.10	15
Coronus M.? Demavend	35.52	52.2	3
Coropissus?	38.15	33.52	20
Corsein, Proskyna	38.35	23.10	16
Corsica, or Cyrnos, I., Corsica	42.0	9.0	9
Corsote, Irzah	34.25	41.5	22
Corstopitum, Corbridge	54.59	2.0 w	5
Corte, Korti	23.8	32.45	3
Corterate, Coutras	45.2	0.7 w	6
Cortona, Cortona	43.20	12.6	8
Cortoriacum, Courtray	50.49	3.16	6
Cortovallum, Corten	50.53	5.58	6
Coru, or Trileucum Pr., C. Ortegal	43.46	7.52 w	7
Coryca I., Grabusa	35.38	23.34	19
Corycian Cave	38.31	22.32	16
Corycium Prom., C. Koraka	38.6	26.37	19
Corycus? (Creta)	35.36	23.45	19
Corycus (Cilicia), Korghos Kalaler	36.27	34.10	20
Corycus M., Koraka	38.15	26.37	19
Corycus Pr. (or Cimarus), C. Buso	35.37	23.35	19
Corydallus, Hadjivella	36.20	30.21	26
Corydallus, r. on M. Skarmanga	37.58	23.36	16
Coryphaeus M	37.35	23.5	13
Coryphantia	39.23	26.49	19
Coryphasium, or Pylus, Old Navarino	36.57	21.40	18
Cos, Stanchio, or Kos	36.53	27.20	19
Cos I., Stanchio, or Kos	36.50	27.10	19
Cosa, Cos	44.7	1.25	6
Cosa, or Cossa, Ansedonia	42.13	11.19	8
Cosas F., Cosa	41.43	13.24	11
*Cosetani	41.20	1.20	7
Cosilynum, n. Padula	40.20	15.39	9

NAMES.	LAT.	LONG.	MAP.
Cossa, or Cosa (Etruria), *Ansedonia*	42°.13'	11°.19'	8
Cossa (Lucania), *Civitd, n. Cassano*	39.46	16.18	9
*Cossaei	33.30	49.20	22
Cossio, *Bazas*	44.27	0.12 w	6
Cossyra I., *Pantellaria*	36.47	12.0	23
Cotes, or Ampelusia Pr., *C. Spartel*	35.47	5.56 w	23
Cothon	36.51	10.18	23
Cotilius M., *Zakkuka*	37.28	21.54	18
Cottiae, *Cozzo*	45.12	8.36	8
Cottiära, *Cochin*	9.58	76.19	2
Cottiäris F.? *Si-Kiang*	24.0	110.0	2
Cotyaeum, *Kutayah*	39.24	30.14	20
Cotylaeum M., *Kotylaion*	38.26	23.50	15
Cotyöra, *Ordou*	40.56	37.52	20
Cragus M. (Cilicia)	36.10	32.30	20
Cragus M. (Lycia)	36.23	29.12	20
Crambüsa I. (Cilicia)? *Papadoula*	36.7	33.35	20
Crambusa I. (Lycia), *Garabusa*	36.14	30.31	20
Cranäe I., *Marathonisi*	36.44	22.35	18
Cranae, Macris, or Helöne I., *Makronisi*	37.41	24.7	19
Craneia	39.17	21.10	15
Cranii, *Krania*, n. *Argostoli*	38.9	20.30	18
Cranon, or Crannon, *Palea Larissa*, n. *Hadjilar*	39.29	22.17	15
Crassum Prom.? *Capo di Pecora*	39.27	8.21	9
Crastus?	37.40	13.21	12
Cratas Mons	37.45	13.15	12
Crater, or Campänus S., *B. of Naples*	40.40	14.10	13
Crathis F., *Akrata*	38.4	22.15	18
Crathis F., *Crati*	39.30	16.14	9
Crathis M	37.57	22.15	18
Cratia, aft. Flaviopölis, *Keredi*	40.43	32.20	20
Crauni Prom	36.7	33.36	20
Cremëra F., *Formello*	42.5	12.21	11
Cremna, *Girmeh*	37.32	30.48	20
Cremöna, *Cremona*	45.8	10.2	8
Crennae, *Armyro*	38.54	21.10	15
Crenides, aft. Philippi, *Filibi*	41.4	24.22	19
Crepsa? *Cherso*	44.58	14.24	8
Creta I., *Candia*	35.15	25.0	19
Creticum Mare	36.0	25.0	19
Cretopölis?	37.13	30.31	20
Creusa, or Creusis, r. on Port *Livadostro*	38.12	23.7	16
Crinisa, *Ciro*	39.23	17.5	9
Crimisa F., *Fiumenica*	39.26	17.0	9
Crimisa Prom., *Capo dell' Alice*	39.23	17.10	9
Crimisus F.? *Bellici destro*	37.50	13.5	12
Crissa, *Krisso*	38.28	22.28	16
Crissaeus S., *B. of Salona*	38.23	22.27	16
Crithöte Prom	38.32	21.1	15
Criu-Metöpon Prom., *C. Krio*	35.14	23.34	19
Criu-Metöpon Prom., *C. Aia*	44.25	33.39	3
Crius F., *Vlogokitiko*	38.5	22.21	18
Crocene, n. *Levetzova*	36.52	22.35	18
Crocëla?	24.50	66.57	3
Crociatönum? *Carentan*	49.19	1.15 w	6
Crocodile Lakes, *Birket Temsch*	30.33	32.8	24
Crocodilopölis, or Arsinöe, r. in Valley of *Faioum*	29.25	31.4	24

NAMES.	LAT.	LONG.	MAP.
Crocodilos? *Lahm-el-Himar*	36.35	19.54	23
Crocolanum, *Brough, n. Newark*	53.7	0.45 w	5
Crocylea I.? *Arkudi*	38.33	20.43	15
Cromi, *Samara*	37.19	22.8	18
Crommyon, *St. Theodoro*	37.55	23.9	18
Crommyon Prom., *C. Kormakiti*	35.25	32.56	20
Cromna	41.50	32.42	20
Crotälus F., *Corace*	39.0	16.30	9
Croton, *Cotrone*	39.8	17.10	9
Cruni, or Dionysopölis, *Baljik*	43.25	28.11	14
Crustumerium, *Monte Rotondo*	42.5	12.37	11
Crustumius F., *Conca*	44.0	12.43	8
Crya	36.42	28.55	20
Ctesiphon, *Tauk Kesrah*	33.4	44.40	22
Ctimëne?	39.6	22.4	15
Cuarius F., *Kholo*	39.15	22.45	15
Cuarius F., *Sofadhitiko*	39.12	22.2	15
Cuccium, *Scharengrad*	45.15	19.15	14
Cucülum, *Cuenllo*	42.3	13.44	9
Cucusus, or Cocussus, *Gogsyn*	38.7	36.15	20
Cularo, aft. Gratianopölis, *Grenoble*	45.11	5.43	6
*Culicones	46.10	9.30	8
Cullu, or Collops Magnus, *Collo*	37.0	6.34	23
Cumae, *Cuma*	40.51	14.3	13
Cumaeus S., *B. of Foggia Nova*	38.46	26.53	19
Cumänus, Campänus, or Puteolänus S., *B. of Naples*	40.40	14.10	13
Cume	38.45	26.57	19
Cumerium Pr., *Monte Comero*	43.38	13.31	8
Cunäxa?	33.22	43.48	22
Cunetio, *Mildenhall*	51.26	1.41 w	5
Cunrus, *Algarve*	37.15	8.30 w	7
Cuneus Aureus, *Splugen*	46.33	9.17	7
Cuneus Prom., *C. St. Mary*	36.57	7.50 w	7
Cunici? *Alcudia*	39.50	3.9	7
Cunicularine I., *Santa Maria, Rassoli, &c*	41.18	9.22	9
Cunicularium Pr., *Capo di Pula*	38.59	9.3	9
Cunistorgis, or Conistorsis? *Silves*	37.15	8.19 w	7
Cuppae, *Columbatz*	44.37	21.41	14
Cupra Maritima, *Grottamare*	43.0	13.50	8
Cupra Montäna? *Masaccio*	43.27	13.9	8
Cures, *Corresè*	42.13	12.43	11
Curin, *Borthwick*	55.49	3.0 w	5
Curin, *Chur, or Coire*	46.51	9.31	25
Curianum Pr., *Pointe d'Arcachon*	44.40	1.14 w	6
Curias Prom., *C. Gata*	34.34	33.2	20
Curica? *Cala*	37.59	6.10 w	7
Curicta I., *Veglia*	45.5	14.35	14
*Curiosolitae	48.20	2.30 w	6
Curium, r. n. *Episkopi*	34.40	32.54	20
Curium M	38.29	21.36	15
Curubis, *Kurbah*	36.35	10.55	23
Cusum, *Peterwardein*	45.16	19.57	14
Cutiliae, *Civitd Ducale*	42.23	12.59	8
Cutina, *Aquana*	42.17	13.57	9
Cyämon Pr., *C. Melek*	35.35	24.7	19
Cynamosörus F., *Salso*	37.39	14.35	12
Cyäne Fons, *La Pisma*	37.2	15.10	12
Cyanene	36.16	29.53	20
Cyaneae I	41.14	29.9	14
Cyaneus	42.35	41.26	22

NAMES.	LAT.	LONG.	MAP.
Cybate, *Wasit*	32°.2'	46°.21'	22
Cybistra?	37.30	34.7	20
Cyclädes I	37.0	25.0	19
Cyclops, Rocks of the	37.32	15.8	12
Cydnus F., *Tersoos Tchai*	36.55	34.58	20
Cydonia, *Canea*	35.30	24.1	19
Cyiza (Coidza), *Choubar*	25.16	60.40	3
Cyllëne, *Glarentza*	37.56	21.9	18
Cyllëne M., *Zyria*	37.55	22.25	18
Cyme? *Koumi*	38.38	24.7	15
Cynaetha, *Kalavryta*	38.2	22.7	18
Cynia Lacus, *Anatolico*	38.22	21.20	18
Cynon-pölis, or Cynopölis	28.33	30.54	24
Cynortius M., *Velanidhia*	37.37	23.8	18
Cynoscephälae	39.25	22.31	15
Cynospölis	30.53	31.22	24
Cynossëma Prom., *C. Alepo*	36.33	28.2	19
Cynosüra Prom., *C. Marathon*	38.7	24.4	16
CYNURIA	37.23	22.40	18
Cynus, *Paleopyrgo, n. Livanoti*	38.42	23.3	16
Cyparisseis F., *Arkadhia*	37.15	21.46	18
Cyparissia, *Arkadhia, or Cyparissia*	37.15	21.40	18
Cyparissia, or Asöpus, *Blitra*	36.41	22.51	18
Cyparissia Prom., *C. Arkadhia*	37.13	21.36	18
Cyparissius S., *G. of Arkadhia*	37.25	21.30	18
Cyparissus?	38.27	22.36	16
Cyphanta? *Port of Lenidhi*	37.8	22.53	18
Cyphus M	39.48	31.50	15
Cypriae I., *Trianisi*	36.27	30.35	20
Cyprus I., *Cyprus*	35.0	33.0	20
Cypsöla, *Ipsala*	40.49	26.19	19
Cyptasia, *Erem Boghazi*	41.56	35.9	20
Cyraunis L. (Cercina)? *Ramlah*	34.45	11.15	23
CYRENAICA	31.0	21.30	23
Cyrëne, *Grennah*	32.50	21.49	23
Cyreschäta, or Cyropölis?	41.12	68.15	3
Cyretiae, *Dheminiko*	39.48	22.7	15
Cyrnos, or Corsica, *Corsica*	42.0	9.0	9
Cyropölis? *Enzeli*	37.30	49.19	22
Cyropölis, or Cyreschäta	41.12	68.15	3
CYRRHESTICA	36.45	37.0	20
Cyrrhus, *Khgros*	36.48	36.59	20
Cyrtöne	38.32	23.6	16
Cyrus, *Trikala*	37.59	22.28	18
Cyrus F.? *Presktaf*	28.0	53.0	3
Cyrus F., *Kour*	41.10	45.30	22
Cytaea, *Koutais*	42.16	42.41	22
Cytaeum	35.25	25.4	19
Cythëra I., *Cerigo*	36.15	23.0	15
Cythëra (Upper), *Paleopoli*	36.15	23.5	15
Cytherius F	31.42	21.33	18
Cythnos, *Hebraeokastro*	37.26	24.26	19
Cythnos I., *Thermia*	37.25	24.25	19
Cytinium, *Gravia*	38.44	22.26	16
Cytis I., *Perim*	12.39	43.28	3
Cytörus, *Kidros*	41.54	32.54	20
Cytörus M., *Kidros Dagh*	41.49	33.0	20
Cyzicus, *Bal Kiz*	40.22	37.51	19

D.

NAMES.	LAT.	LONG.	MAP.
*Dnae	40.0	56.0	3
Dabanas, *Dahabaniyeh*	36.34	39.2	22
Daberath, *Deburieh*	32.42	35.23	21
Dables, *Tereklu*	40.24	30.40	20

NAMES.	LAT.	LONG.	MAP.
Drymūsa I., *Tchustan, or Makronisi*	38°.30′	26°.44′	19
•Dryŏpes	39.0	21.50	15
Dubis, or Alduasdubis F., *Doubs*	47.0	5.20	6
•Dulgibini	51.55	9.30	25
Dulopŏlis, Bubassus, or Acanthus	36.46	28.11	19
Dunium, *Maiden Castle, n. Dorchester*	50.42	2.28 w	5
Dunum? *Downpatrick*	54.20	5.41 w	5
Dunum S.?	54.30	0.35 w	5
Dura? *Door*	34.22	43.46	22
Duranius F., *Dordogne*	44.50	0.0	6
Duria F., *Dora*	45.7	7.10	8
Duria Major F., *Dora Baltea*	45.40	7.40	8
Duriae, *Dorno*	45.9	8.58	8
Durius F., *Douro*	41.5	8.20 w	7
Durnovaria, *Dorchester*	50.43	2.26 w	5
Durobrivae, *Water Newton*	52.34	0.22 w	5
Durobrivae, *Rochester*	51.23	0.30	5
Durocasses, *Dreux*	48.44	1.21	6
Durocatalaunum, *Châlons-sur-Marne*	48.58	4.22	6
Durocobrivae, *Maiden Bower, n. Dunstable*	51.53	0.33 w	5
Durocornovium, or Corinium, *Cirencester*	51.43	1.58 w	5
Durocortŏrum, aft. Remi, *Rheims*	49.15	4.1	6
Durolevum, *Judde Hill, n. Ospringe*	51.18	0.51	5
Durolipons, *Godmanchester*	52.20	0.10 w	5
Durolitum, *n. Romford*	51.35	0.13	5
Duronia, *Cività Vecchia, n. Molise*	41.38	14.26	9
Duronum, *Estreung la Chaussée*	50.4	3.58	6
Durostŏrus, or Durostŏlum, *Silistria*	44.10	27.13	14
•Durotriges	50.50	2.30 w	5
Durovernum, *Canterbury*	51.17	1.4	5
Dusae, *Dusdkeh*	40.46	31.21	20
Dyme, or Dymae	38.10	21.28	18
Dyras F., *Gurgo*	38.49	22.20	16
Dyrin, or Atlas Mons, *Mt. Atlas*	31.20	7.0 w	23
Dyrrachium, for. Epidamnus, *Durazzo*	41.21	19.29	14
Dystus, *Dhysta*	38.20	24.11	15

E.

NAMES.	LAT.	LONG.	MAP.
Ebal, Mount	32.16	35.14	21
Ebellinum, *S. Juan de la Peña*	42.26	0.40 w	7
Eblana, *Dublin*	53.21	6.25 w	2
Eboda, *El-Abdeh, or El-Aujeh*	30.52	34.32	24
Ebŏra, *Evora*	38.38	7.39 w	7
Eborācum, or Eburacum, *York*	52.57	1.5 w	5
Ebrodūnum, *Embrun*	44.34	6.28	6
Ebrodūnum, *Yverdun*	46.46	6.39	6
Ebūdae Iᵐ., *Hebrides*	57.0	7.30 w	2
Ebūra, *S. Lucar de Barrameda*	36.43	6.19 w	7
Eburi, *Evoli*	40.36	15.3	9
Eburobriga, *St. Florentin*	48.0	3.44	6
Eburobritium? *Evora*	39.30	8.59 w	7
•Eburŏnes, aft. Tungri	50.50	6.0	6
Eburovices, *Evreux*	49.1	1.9	6
Ebusus, *Iviza*	38.55	1.27	7
Ebusus I., *Iviza*	39.0	1.25	7
Ecbatāna, or Agbatāna (Achmetha), *Hamadan*	34.48	48.33	22
Ecbatāna (of Atropatene)? *Takht-i-Suleimaun*	36.28	47.8	3

NAMES.	LAT.	LONG.	MAP.
Eodippa (Achzib), *Es-zib*	33°.13′	35°.6′	21
Echedameia	38.21	22.35	16
Echelidae?	37.57	23.38	17
•Echetla, *Occhiala*	37.12	14.38	12
Echidŏrus F., *Mana, or Galliko*	40.45	22.48	15
Echinādes Iᵐ., *Petala, &c.*	38.25	21.0	15
Echinus (Acarnania)?	38.54	21.0	15
Echinus (Phthiotis), *Al-chino*	38.53	22.41	16
Eclānum, or Aeculānum, *Le Grotte, n. Mirabella*	41.1	15.0	9
Ecnŏmus M	37.6	13.51	12
Ecregma?	31.8	33.0	24
Edessa, or Aegae, *Vodhena*	40.47	22.2	15
Edessa, or Callirhoe (Ur of the Chaldees?), *Urfah*	37.10	38.50	22
Edeta (Liria), *Liria*	39.37	0.39 w	7
•Edetāni	41.0	0.45 w	7
•Edi			1
Edom	30.20	35.40	24
Edŏnis	40.57	24.0	14
Edrum, *Idro Alto*	45.46	10.27	8
Eetioneia	37.56	23.38	17
Egdavama?	38.37	32.53	20
Egesta, or Segesta, *n. Segesta*	37.59	12.54	12
Egēta, *Gladova*	44.36	22.40	14
Egira, *Banja*	42.10	24.0	14
Eglon, *Ajlân*	31.33	34.46	21
Egnatia, *Torre S. Ignazio*	40.54	17.25	9
Egyptian Copper-mines, *Sarbout el-Khadim*	29.2	33.27	24
Eidomēne	41.12	22.28	14
Eidumania F.? *Mouth of Blackwater*	51.46	0.55	5
Eion, *r. at Mouth of Kara-su*	40.46	23.54	15
Eira?	37.32	23.7	18
Eira M.? *Kutra*	37.21	21.44	18
Eiros M., *C. Monze*	24.48	66.38	3
Ekron, *Akir*	31.50	34.50	21
Elaea (Aeolis)	38.57	27.4	19
Elaea (Epirus)	39.14	20.31	15
Elaea Pr., *C. Elea*	35.19	34.6	20
Elaeum? *Liosia*	38.15	23.35	16
Elaeus (Aetolia), *Meso-longhi*	38.22	21.27	18
Elaeus (Chaonia)? *n. Argiro Kastro*	40.9	20.13	15
Elaeus (Thracia)	40.3	26.14	19
Elaeus S., *G. of Sandarlik*	38.53	27.0	19
Elaeussa, *Alessa*	36.36	28.10	19
Elaeussa I., *St. George*	38.55	26.50	19
Elah, Valley of, *Wady Sumt*	31.42	34.57	21
Elataea, or Elatria?	39.13	20.39	15
Elateia, *Lefta*	38.38	22.47	16
Elateia, *Makrikhori*	39.45	22.26	15
Elath (Aelāna), *Akaba*	29.31	35.1	24
Elātus M., *Mount Skopo*	37.44	20.57	18
Elaver F., *Allier*	45.40	3.12	6
Elĕa, Hyĕle, or Velia, *Castellamare della Bruca*	40.8	15.8	9
Elealeh, *El-Aal*	31.48	35.52	21
Electra F., *Messara*	35.4	24.55	19
Electra F., *Vasiliko*	37.18	21.52	18
Elees, or Heles F., *Alento, or Venere*	40.10	15.7	9
Elegia, *Ilidsha*	39.58	41.12	22
Elephantaria, *Oschiri*	40.43	9.6	9
Elephantine I., *Jeziret el-Sag*	24.6	32.55	3
Elĕphas M., *Ras Filuk*	12.0	50.35	2

NAMES.	LAT.	LONG.	MAP.
Eleusa I., *Peninsula n. Ayash*	36°.29′	34°.14′	20
Eleusiniaous S., *B. of Eleusis*	38.1	23.30	16
Eleusinium	37.45	21.53	18
Eleusis, *Lepsina*	38.3	23.33	16
Eleusis (Thera)? *n. C. Exomiti*	36.21	25.27	19
Eleussa I., *Arsida*	37.42	23.54	18
Eleuthĕrae, *Myupoli*	38.9	23.28	16
Eleuthĕrae, Eleutherna, or Apollonia?	35.19	24.41	19
Eleutheropŏlis (Betogabris), *Beit Jibreen*	31.36	34.55	21
Eleuthĕrus F., *Bagheria*	38.0	13.25	12
Eleuthĕrus F., *Nahr el-Kebir*	34.43	36.5	20
Elim? *Wady Ghurundel*	29.18	32.58	24
Elimeia	40.10	21.40	14
Elis	38.45	21.30	18
Elis, *Paleopoli*	37.53	21.23	18
•Elisii, or Helisii	51.30	17.0	25
Elison F., *Alme*	51.40	8.44	25
Ellepŏrus F.? *Salubro*	38.38	16.34	9
Ellomĕnus, *Klimino*	38.41	20.42	15
Elmantĭca (Salmantĭca?), *Salamanca*	41.6	5.42 w	7
Elŏne, *Selos*	39.50	21.59	15
Elŭsa, *Eause*	43.53	0.5	6
Elusa, *El-Khulasah*	31.5	34.44	24
•Elusates	43.45	0.0	6
Elȳma, *Grevno*	40.11	21.36	14
Elymāis	33.30	48.0	22
Elymia, *Levidhi*	37.41	22.18	18
Elȳrus, *Paleokastro, n. Rhodovani*	35.17	23.46	19
Elysium			1
Emathia	40.40	22.10	15
Emerĭta Augusta, *Merida*	38.51	6.15 w	7
Emŏsa, *Homs*	34.50	36.39	20
Emmāus? *El-Kubeibeh*	31.51	35.8	21
Emmaus, aft. Nicopŏlis, *Amwas*	31.51	35.1	21
Emmaus (Hammath), *Hammâm (hot springs), n. Tiberias*	32.47	35.35	21
Emŏdi Ms., *Himalaya*	29.0	85.0	2
Emŏna, or Aemŏna (aft. Julia Augusta), *Laybach*	46.4	14.31	14
Emporia	33.0	11.0	23
Emporiae, or Emporium, *Ampurias*	42.9	3.4	▾
Emporĭcus S.?	34.14	6.50 w	23
Emporium, *Castellamare*	38.1	12.52	12
Empūlum, *Ampiglione*	41.58	12.55	11
Endidae, *Egna*	46.21	11.13	8
Endor, *Endor*	32.39	35.24	21
En-gannim (Ginaea), *Jeneen*	32.28	35.20	21
En-gedi, *Ain Jidy*	31.29	35.26	21
Engyum, *Gangi*	37.45	14.13	12
Enipeum, or Posidi˜um, Prom., *Punta di Licosa*	40.14	14.53	9
Enipeus F., *r. of Litokhoro*	40.4	22.33	15
Enipeus F.	39.12	22.28	15
Enna, or Henna, *Castro Giovanni*	37.38	14.17	12
Ennea Hodoi, aft. Amphipolis, *Neokhorio*	40.48	23.51	15
Enosis (or Plumbaria?) I., *S. Antioco*	39.0	8.23	9
Entella, *Rocca d'Entella*	37.46	13.6	12
Entella F., *Lavagna*	44.25	9.20	8
Eordaea	40.32	21.41	15
Epacria, *Pikermi*	38.1	23.56	16

NAMES.	LAT.	LONG.	MAP.
Epamanduodūrum, Mandeure	47°.27'	6°.47'	6
•Epanterii	44.10	8.0	8
Epeiacum, *Lanchester*	54.50	1.44 w	5
Epeium, *Smerna*	37.33	21.41	18
Ephēsus, r. n. *Aiasa-look*	37.57	27.23	19
Ephialtium Prom.? *C. Akroteri*	35.23	27.12	19
Ephyra I.? *Spezzia*	37.15	23.8	18
Ephyre, *Monastery of St. John, n. Porto Fanari*	39.16	20.32	15
Epidamnus, aft. Dyrrachium, *Durazzo*	41.21	19.29	14
EPIDAURIA	37.38	23.7	18
Epidaurus, *Epidavro, or Pidhavro*	37.38	23.10	18
Epidaurus, *Ragusa-Vecchia*	42.35	18.13	14
Epidaurus Limēra, *Paleo Monemvasia*	36.44	23.2	18
Epidelium Prom., *C. Kamili*	36.32	23.9	18
•Epidii	56.0	5.30 w	5
Epidium Prom., *Mull of Cantire*	55.17	5.46 w	5
Epidotus?	45.0	15.20	14
Epiphania (Hamath), *Hamah*	35.13	36.38	20
EPIRUS	39.40	20.40	15
Epitalium, *Agulinitza*	37.37	21.30	18
Epōmeus M., *Monte di San Nicola*	40.44	13.54	13
Eporedia, *Ivrea*	45.28	7.51	8
Epusum, *Carignan*	49.38	5.10	6
Equabōna, *Coyna*	38.35	9.4 w	7
Equus Tuticus, *S. Eleuterio*	41.17	15.7	9
Erāna? *Filiatra*	37.9	21.35	18
Erasīnus F., *Kefalari*	37.36	22.42	18
Erbessus, or Herbessus? *Grotte*	37.14	13.41	12
Erbessus, or Herbessus? *Pantalica*	37.8	15.0	12
Erote, or Ercta, M., *Monte Pellegrino*	38.10	13.21	12
Erebantium Prom, *Capo della Testa*	41.14	9.8	9
Erech, *Irak, or Irka*	31.27	45.40	22
Erēsus, r. n. *Eresso*	39.8	25.56	19
Eretenus F., *Agno*	45.20	11.23	8
Eretria, New (Euboea), *Kastri*	38.22	23.49	16
Etretria, Old (Euboea), n. *Vathy*	38.22	23.56	16
Eretria (Thessalia), *Tzangli*	39.15	22.35	15
Erētum? *Rimane*	42.7	12.41	11
Ergasteria, *Kodja Gumisch Maden*	39.42	27.35	19
Ergavica, or Ergavia?	40.23	2.52 w	7
Ergitium, *S. Severo*	41.42	15.23	9
Eriboea?	40.9	21.6	15
Ericūsa I., *Alicudi*	38.33	14.16	9
Ericūsa I., *Merlera*	39.53	19.32	15
Eridānus F. (or Padus), *Po*	45.0	8.45	8
Erigon F., *Tzerna*	41.0	21.47	14
Erineus (Achaia), *Lambirta*	38.13	21.59	18
Erineus (Doris)	38.42	22.24	16
Erineus F., *Fiume di Avola, or Miranda*	36.55	15.7	12
Eriston	37.36	25.10	19
Eritium, *Paleokastro*	39.54	22.3	15
Eriza, *Derekeui*	37.26	29.28	20
Eriza, *Erzingan*	39.32	39.56	20
Ermine Street	52.50	0.35 w	5
Ernodūrum, *St. Ambroise*	46.59	2.8	6
Erucium, *Castel Sardo*	40.55	8.42	9
B. ūli (or Forūli)?	42.26	13.15	9

NAMES.	LAT.	LONG.	MAP.
Erymander, or Erymanthus, F., *Helmund*	31°.0'	62°.0'	3
Erymanthus F., *Doana*	37.40	21.49	18
Erymanthus M., *Kallifoni*	37.59	21.58	18
Erythrae (Boeotia), r. n. *Katzula*	38.14	23.24	16
Erythrae (Ionia), *Ritri*	38.24	26.30	19
Erythrae (Locris)?	38.28	23.16	16
Erythrae (Locri-Ozolae)?	38.23	22.5	18
Erythraea	34.58	26.5	19
Erythraeum Mare	15.0	60.0	2
Erythraeum Prom., *C. Langadha*	34.56	26.3	19
Eryx, or Eryous	38.4	12.34	12
Eryx Mons, *Monte S. Giuliano*	38.4	12.35	12
Esdraëlon (Jezreel), *Zereen*	32.34	35.21	21
Eshtemoa, *Es-Semua*	31.25	35.6	21
Esuris, *Castromarin*	37.11	7.15 w	7
Etanna, *Yenne*	45.43	6.46	6
Eteia, *Settia*	35.13	26.7	19
Eteōnus, or Scarphe?	38.14	23.34	16
Etham, Desert of	29.45	32.45	24
Etham, Thoum, or Pithom (Patumos?), r. n. *Abassieh*	30.28	31.35	24
Etis, *Kyparivia*	36.31	23.4	18
Etocetum, *Wall, n. Lichfield*	52.39	1.51 w	5
Etonia? *Aladsha*	40.8	34.48	20
ETRURIA	43.0	11.35	8
•Etrusci	42.4	12.15	11
Euarchus F., *Kirkgetschid Tchai*	41.43	35.0	20
Euboea? *Licodia*	37.8	14.41	12
Euboea I., *Egripo, or Negropont*	38.30	24.0	19
Eucarpia?	38.37	30.9	20
Eudagina	39.7	36.4	20
•Eudoses	53.35	12.30	25
Eudoxia, *Tokat*	40.15	36.37	20
•Euganei	45.45	10.40	8
Eubydrium	39.21	22.16	15
Eulaeus, or Pasitigris F., *Kuran*	31.0	48.25	22
Eulepa, *Baresma*	38.50	35.26	20
Eumenia, *Ishekli*	38.19	29.55	20
Euonymus I., *Panaria*	38.38	15.3	9
Eupalium	38.24	22.6	15
Eupatoria, *Kozlov, or Eupatoria*	45.11	33.21	3
Eupatoria (Magnopolis)	40.46	36.34	20
Euphorbium, *Emir Hassan Keui*	38.25	30.15	20
Euphrates F. (Phrat), *Euphrates, or Frat*	35.0	40.35	22
Euripus, *Strait of Egripo*	38.26	23.37	16
Euristus	40.58	21.40	14
Euroea	39.30	20.31	15
Eurōmus, r. n. *Iakly*	37.22	27.42	19
Eurōpus (Syria)?	36.49	38.1	22
Eurōpus (Thessalia)	39.42	21.35	15
Eurōtas F., *Vasilo, or Iri*	36.57	22.38	18
Eurymēdon F., *Kopri Su*	37.20	31.14	20
Eurymēnae (Epirus)	39.27	20.48	15
Eurymēnae (Thessalia)	39.44	22.51	15
•Eurytanes	38.50	21.50	15
Eusēne, *Kuru Balur*	41.23	36.15	20
Eutrēsis	38.15	23.9	16
Euxinus Pontus, *Black Sea*	44.0	35.0	2
Eva, *Platano*	37.19	22.41	18
Evandria?	38.54	6.25 w	7
Evaspla F.? *Kooner*	36.0	71.40	3
Evēnus F.	39.15	27.5	19
Evēnus F., *Fidhari*	38.25	21.37	18

NAMES.	LAT.	LONG.	MAP.
Evōras M., *Paximadhi*	37°.2'	22°.20'	18
Excisum, *Villeneuve d'Agen*	44.24	0.42	6
Externum, Atlantīcum, or Magnum Mare, *Atlantic Ocean*	40.0	20.0 w	1
Ezion-geber (aft. Berenice)?	29.33	34.58	24

F.

NAMES.	LAT.	LONG.	MAP.
Fabāris (or Farfārus) F., *Farfa*	42.48	12.40	11
Fabia, or Fapia, *Rocca di Papa*	41.46	12.44	11
Fabrateria, r. n. *Falaterra*	41.32	13.35	11
Faesūlae, *Fiesole*	43.49	11.10	8
Falacrinum, *S. Silvestro in Falacrino*	42.37	13.12	8
Falerii, *Falleri*	42.22	12.18	11
Falernus Ager	41.10	14.10	11
Fanum Carisi, *Orosei*	40.23	9.43	9
Fanum Fortunae, *Fano*	43.51	13.1	8
Fanum Fugitīvi, *Monte Somma*	42.39	12.47	8
Fanum Martis? *Tanie*	48.36	1.26 w	6
Fanum Vacūnae, *Rocca Giovane*	42.3	12.54	11
Fanum Voltumnae? *Viterbo*	42.26	12.6	11
Fapia, or Fabia, *Rocca di Papa*	41.46	12.44	11
Farfārus, or Fabāris, F., *Farfa*	42.48	12.40	11
Faustinopōlis	37.35	34.47	20
Faventia, *Faenza*	44.17	11.54	8
Felicītas Julia (Olisipo), *Lisbon*	38.42	9.9 w	7
Felsina, aft. Bononia, *Bologna*	44.30	11.22	8
Feltria, *Feltre*	46.1	11.56	8
Ferentīnum (Etruria), *Ferento*	42.28	12.9	11
Ferentīnum (Latium), *Ferentino*	41.43	13.17	11
Feritor F., *Bisagno*	44.25	8.56	8
Feronia, or Lucus Feroniae, *Felonica*	42.16	12.31	11
Feroniae Templum, *Torre di Terracina*	41.17	13.13	11
Ferraria, *S. Basilio*	39.17	9.20	9
Ferrātus Mons, *Jebel Jurjura*	36.27	4.0	2
Fescennium, *Civitâ Castellana*	42.21	12.21	11
Fibrēnus F., *Fibreno*	41.42	13.37	11
Ficana, *Dragoncelle*	41.47	12.20	11
Ficaria, *Figari*	41.28	9.3	9
Ficaria I., *Cavoli*	39.4	9.32	9
Ficulea, *Torre Lupara*	42.1	12.38	11
Fidēnae, *Castel Giubileo*	42.0	12.30	11
Figlinae, *Pegli*	44.26	8.47	8
Fines	46.30	0.55	
Fines	45.30	0.59	
Firmum, *Fermo*	43.10	13.42	
Flamonia, *Flagogna*	46.13	13.3	8
Flanatīcus S., *G. of Quarnero, or Fiume*	45.0	14.15	14
Flanōna, *Fianona*	45.8	14.11	8
Flavinium? *Fiano*	42.12	12.36	11
Flaviohriga, for. Amanus Portus, *Portugalete*	43.20	3.3 w	7
Flavionavia, *Aviles*	43.36	6.0 w	7
Flaviopōlis, or Cratia, *Keredi*	40.43	32.20	20
Flenio, *Vlaardingen*	51.55	4.20	25
Flevo L., *Zuyder Zee*	52.30	5.30	25
Flevum Castellum?	53.17	5.0	25
Flevum Ostium?	53.20	5.10	25
Flexum, *Altenburg*	47.53	17.16	14
Florentia, *Fiorenzuola*	44.56	9.58	8

NAMES.	LAT.	LONG.	MAP.
Florentia, *Firenze (Florence)*	43°.47'	11°.15'	8
Floriana?	47.35	18.15	14
Flusor F., *Chienti*	43.17	13.40	8
*Focunātes	46.0	8.20	8
Forentum, *Forenza*	40.50	15.51	9
Formiae, *Mola di Gaeta*	41.15	13.36	9
Forinio F., *Risano*	45.32	13.50	8
Forocrea, *Santa Croce*	42.34	13.10	8
Fortunatae Iᵐ., *Canary Islands*	28.0	15.30 w	2
Forūli (or Erūli)?	42.26	13.15	9
Forum Alliēni, *Ferrara*	44.50	11.37	8
Forum Appii, *Foro Appio*	41.28	13.1	11
Forum Aurelii, n. *Montalto, on R. Fiore*	42.18	11.35	8
Forum Cassii, *Vetralla*	42.21	12.2	11
Forum Cigurrōrum? *Puente Bibey*	42.25	7.24 w	7
Forum Clodii, *Oriuolo*	42.12	12.5	11
Forum Cornelii, *Imola*	44.22	11.43	8
Forum DomIti?	43.30	3.40	6
Forum Flaminii, *S. Giovanni pro Fiamma*	43.2	12.49	8
Forum Fulvii, or Valentinum, *Valenza*	45.1	8.37	8
Forum Gallōrum, *Castel Franco*	44.37	11.4	8
Forum Gallōrum, *Gurrea*	42.4	0.45 w	7
Forum Julii, *Cividad ai Friuli*	46.5	13.25	8
Forum Julii, *Fréjus*	43.26	6.44	6
Forum Licīni? *Lecco*	45.51	9.25	8
Forum Ligneum?	42.54	0.35	6
Forum Livii, *Forli*	44.14	12.3	8
Forum Novum, *Buonalbergo*	41.14	15.0	9
Forum Novum, *Fornovo*	44.42	10.8	8
Forum Novum, *S. Maria di Vescovio*	42.22	12.36	11
Forum Popilii, *Forlimpopoli*	44.13	12.8	8
Forum Segusianōrum, *Feur*	45.28	4.33	6
Forum Sempronii, *Fossombrone*	43.41	12.49	8
Forum Trajāni, *Fordongianus*	39.59	8.49	9
Forum Vibii? *Castel Fiori*	44.41	7.17	8
Forum Voconii? *Le Canet*	43.25	6.19	6
*Fosi	52.15	10.30	25
Fossa I., *Maddalena*	41.14	9.24	9
Fossa of Corbūlo	52.10	4.25	6
Fossa, or Taphros, *Strait of Bonifacio*	41.20	9.10	9
Fossae Cluiliae	41.51	12.34	11
Fossae Mariānae, *Fos les Martigues*	43.26	4.57	6
Fossae Papiriānae, *Viareggia*	43.51	10.15	8
Fossae Philistīnae	45.2	12.8	8
Fosse Way	51.30	2.14 w	5
Fraxīnus	37.59	3.2 w	7
Fraxīnus, *Villa Velha*	39.40	7.37 w	7
Fregellae, r. n. *Ceperano*	41.34	13.35	11
Fregōnae, *Maccarese*	41.52	12.11	11
*Frentāni	42.0	14.40	9
Frento F., *Fortore*	41.40	15.4	9
Frigīdne, *Old Mamora*	35.56	6.18 w	23
Frigīdus F.	45.50	13.50	8
*Friniātes?	44.35	9.18	8
*Frisii	53.0	6.0	25
Frusīno, *Frosinone*	41.39	13.23	11
Frustemae	42.16	13.29	9
Fucīnus L., *Lago di Celano, or Fucino*	42.0	13.30	11
Fulginium, *Foligno*	42.58	12.45	8

NAMES.	LAT.	LONG.	MAP.
Fulsūlae, *Montefusco*	41°.2'	14°.51'	9
Fundi, *Fondi*	41.20	13.25	9
Furcae Caudīnae? *Valley of Arpaja*	41.3	14.33	13

G.

NAMES.	LAT.	LONG.	MAP.
Gabāla, *Jebeileh*	35.20	35.58	20
*Gabali	44.50	3.20	6
Gabāra, *Arrabeh*	32.54	35.23	21
Gabellus, or Secia, F., *Secchia*	44.30	10.42	8
Gabii, *Castiglione*	41.53	12.45	11
Gabrae, *Chabris*	47.15	1.40	6
Gabrantuicorum S.? *Filey Bay*	54.11	0.15 w	5
Gabromāgus?	47.31	14.20	14
Gabrosentum, *Drumburgh*	54.56	3.9 w	5
Gadāra, *Om-keis*	32.41	35.44	21
Gadaum Castra, *Tagudempt*	35.31	0.51	23
Gadda? *Kalat Zurka*	32.5	36.9	21
Gadeira I., *I. de St. Leon*	36.26	6.13 w	7
Gades, *Cadiz*	36.32	6.17 w	7
*Gadēni	55.20	2.40 w	5
Gaditānum, or Herculeum, Fretum, *Strait of Gibraltar*	35.57	5.30 w	7
Gaditānus Portus, *Puerto Real*	36.32	6.10 w	7
Gaetara, or Gangara? *Baku*	40.25	49.53	22
*Gaetūli	32.0	5.0	2
GAETULIA	34.0	4.0	23
Gaganae, *Szlatina*	45.15	22.21	14
GALAADĪTIS (MOUNT GILEAD)	32.20	35.46	21
Galacum, n. *Kendal*	54.18	2.44 w	5
Galaria, *Gagliano*	37.41	14.34	12
Galāta, *Galati*	37.59	14.46	12
Galata I., *Galita*	37.31	8.55	23
GALATIA	40.0	34.0	20
Galava, *Keswick*	54.36	3.9 w	5
Galepsus?	40.5	23.48	15
Galēsus F., *Galeso*	40.32	17.15	9
GALILAEA	33.0	32.20	21
Galilee, Sea of (Tiberias L., or Gennesaret), *Bahr Tubariyeh*	32.50	35.36	21
*Gallaeci Bracarii	41.40	8.0 w	7
*Gallaeci Lucenses	42.45	7.30 w	7
GALLIA, *France*	46.0	2.0	2
GALLIA CISALPĪNA	45.0	10.0	8
GALLIA TRANSALPĪNA	45.0	6.0	8
Gallīca Flavia, *Fraga*	41.35	0.18	7
Gallīcum, *Zuera*	41.56	0.48 w	7
Gallīcus F., *Gallego*	42.0	0.46 w	7
Gallīcus S., *G. of Lyons*	43.0	4.0	6
Galliuaria L., *Galinara*	44.2	8.12	8
Gallinaria Silva?	40.0	14.2	13
Gallus F.	40.8	30.0	20
Gāmala? *El-Hum*	32.48	35.41	21
Gamarga, *Maraghah*	37.19	46.14	22
GANDARĪTIS	34.0	72.0	3
Gandhara, *Candahar*	31.38	65.30	3
Gangara? *Ganja, or Elisavetpol*	40.36	46.21	22
Gangara, or Gaetara? *Baku*	40.25	49.53	22
*Gangarīdae	22.0	88.0	2
Gange Regia? *Rajmahal*	25.1	87.51	2
Ganges F., *Ganges*	27.0	80.0	2
Ganges F. (Ceylon), *Gunga*	8.0	81.15	2
Gangeticus S., *Bay of Bengal*	20.0	90.0	2
Gangra, or Germanicopōlis, *Kankari*	40.35	33.40	20
Garāma, *Germa*	26.34	13.57	2
*Garamantes	26.0	12.0	2

NAMES.	LAT.	LONG.	MAP.
Gargānum Pr., *Punta di Viesti*	41°.52'	16°.11'	9
Gargānus Mons, *Monte Gargano, or S. Angelo*	41.50	16.0	9
Gargāra	39.33	26.38	19
Gargāra M., *Kas Dagh*	39.41	26.50	19
Gargettus	38.2	23.54	16
Gariannonum, *Burgh Castle*	52.35	0.40	5
Garium, *Sarpana*	41.59	33.35	20
Garnace? *Gorun*	38.51	36.56	20
Garryenus, or Gariennus F., *Yare*	52.35	1.43	5
GARSAURĪTIS	38.10	34.20	20
Garumna F., *Garonne*	44.40	0.20 w	6
Gath?	31.47	34.51	21
Gatheae, *Khiradhes*	37.16	22.6	18
Gath-hepher? *El-Meshad*	32.46	35.20	21
Gaugamēla	36.15	43.28	22
GAULANĪTIS, or GAULONĪTIS (ARGOB), *Jaulān*	32.54	35.45	21
Gaulita? *Orbeth, or Samechwilde*	41.31	44.30	22
Gaulos I., *Gozo*	36.2	14.15	4
Gaurion, or Gaurelēon, *Gavrion*	37.53	24.45	19
Gaurus Mons, *Monte Barbaro*	40.51	14.6	13
Gaza, *Ghuzzeh*	31.28	34.29	21
Gaza? *Ghaz*	42.0	67.0	3
Gaza, Gazāca, or Pharaspa, *Takht-i-Suleimaun*	36.28	47.8	22
GAZAOĒNE	40.30	36.0	20
Gazēlon, *Vizir Kupri*	41.8	35.27	20
GAZELONĪTIS	41.10	35.20	20
Gasorum, *Aksu Tchai*	41.41	35.27	20
GEBALĒNE	31.0	35.50	21
GEDROSIA	27.30	62.0	3
Gēla, *Terranova*	37.3	14.15	12
Gēlas, or Gēla, F., *F. di Terranova*	37.6	14.20	12
Geldūba, *Gellep, or Gelb*	51.16	6.41	6
Gelōi Campi	37.5	14.15	12
Gemellae, *Jijel*	35.47	5.30	23
Gemellae, *Lugo Santo*	41.3	9.12	9
Gemestarium	42.30	7.4 w	7
Geminae?	42.20	8.6 w	7
Geminae? *Mens*	44.49	5.45	6
Geminiacum? *Vieuville*	50.26	4.20	6
Genābum, aft. Aureliāni, *Orleans*	47.54	1.55	6
*Genauni	46.4	9.0	8
Genesium? *Paleokiveri*	37.32	22.43	18
Genēva, or Genua, *Geneva*	46.12	6.11	8
Gennesaret L. (Sea of Galilee, or Tiberias L.), *Bahr Tubariyeh*	32.50	35.36	21
Genua, *Genoa*	44.25	8.55	8
Genua, or Geneva, *Geneva*	46.12	6.11	8
Genusium, *Genosa*	40.35	16.45	9
Genusus F., *Scombi*	41.9	20.0	14
Gephȳra	40.39	22.40	15
Ger? *Wady Ghir*	32.30	2.40 w	23
Geraestus Prom., *C. Mandili*	37.57	24.30	15
Geraneia M., *Makriplaghi*	38.1	23.7	18
Gerar, *Khirlet-el-Gerar*	31.22	34.33	21
GERARITICA	31.20	34.35	21
Gerasa, *Jerash*	32.19	36.0	21
Gerasus, or Grissia, F., *Koros*	46.52	21.0	14
Gerenia, *Kitries*	36.46	22.9	18
Gergithus, or Gergītha	40.1	27.0	19
Gergovia, *Gergovia*	45.43	3.10	6
Gerizim, M.	32.14	35.14	21
Germa, *Germa*	39.19	32.0	20
GERMANIA (MAGNA)	52.0	15.0	2

NAMES.	LAT.	LONG.	MAP.
Germania Inferior, or Secunda	51°.0'	6°.0'	25
Germania Superior, or Prima	49.0	7.30	25
Germanicia, *Marash*	37.36	36.56	20
Germanicopŏlis, *Ermenek*	36.41	32.51	20
Germanicopŏlis, or Gangra, *Kankari*	40.35	33.40	20
Germe	39.6	27.35	19
Geronthrae, *Gheraki*	36.59	22.43	18
Gerontia I.? *Ioura*	39.23	24.10	19
Gerrha, *El-Katiff*	26.33	50.3	3
*Gerrhaei	27.30	48.30	3
Gerrum	30.57	32.34	24
Gerunda, *Gerona*	42.1	2.49	7
Geruvium, *Girone*	41.45	14.54	9
Gesdae, *Sezanne*	44.58	6.45	8
Gesoriacum, aft. Benonia, *Boulogne*	50.44	1.36	6
*Getae	45.40	28.0	14
Gibeon, *El-Jeeb*	31.51	35.11	21
Gichthis, or Gitbis, *Jeress*	33.30	10.44	23
Gigŏnus	40.22	22.56	15
Gigŏnus Pr., *Panomi, or Apanomi Point*	40.22	22.55	15
Gilboa, Mount, *Jebel Fukua*	32.31	35.26	21
Gilgal?	31.50	35.30	21
Gilva? *Takumbrit*	35.19	1.29 w	23
Ginaea (En-gannim), *Jeneen*	32.28	35.20	21
Gindărus, *Jindaris*	36.23	36.40	20
Gir F			1
Girba I. (Lotophagitis, or Meninx), *Jerbah*	33.45	11.0	23
Girgiri M., *Mountains of Tarkournah*	32.20	14.0	23
Gischăla, *El-Jish*	33.2	35.26	21
Gitanae? *Margariti*	39.25	20.25	15
Glanoventa, *Ellenboro'*	54.43	3.28 w	5
Glaucus F., *Lafka*	38.12	21.45	18
Glaucus F.? *Olti-su*	40 30	41.45	20
Glaucus F., *Rion*	42.32	43.0	22
Glaucus S., *G. of Makri*	36.40	29.0	20
Glemona, *Gemona*	46.16	13.9	8
Glevum, *Gloucester*	51.52	2.14 w	5
Glisas, r. at foot of *Mount Siamata*	38.22	23.25	16
Glycys Portus, *Porto Fanari*	39.14	20.31	15
Glympia, or Glyppia, *Kastro Lymbiada*	37.11	22.42	18
Gobaeum Pr., *Pointe St. Matthieu*	*48.20	4.46 w	6
Gobannium, *Abergavenny*	51.49	3.0 w	5
Gogana, *Congoon*	27.48	52.10	3
Gogarene	41.0	43.0	22
Golan?	32.55	35.50	21
Gomphi, *Episkopi*	39.26	21.43	15
Gonnus, or Gonni, *Lykostomo*	39.48	22.27	15
Gophna, *Jafna*	31.57	35.12	21
Gophnitica	32.0	35.15	21
Gorditănum Pr., *Capo Falcone*	40.59	8.10	9
Gordium, aft. Juliopolis	40.4	31.35	20
Gordyaei M., *Jebel Judi*, &c.	37.40	42.0	22
Gorgon, or Urgo I., *Gorgona*	43.26	9.55	8
Gorneas, *Karhni*	40.7	44.45	22
Gortyna	35.5	24.56	19
Gortynius F., *River of Dhimitzana*	37.33	22.3	18
Gortys, n. *Atzikolo*	37.32	22.3	18
*Gothini	50.0	18.0	25
*Gothŏnes	54.0	18.0	25
Graecia	38.0	22.0	2
Graecŭris, *Corella*	42.7	1.54 w	7
*Grafocŏli	45.14	6.30	6
Grandimirum, *Muros*	42°.45'	9°.2' w	7
Graniacum Pr., *Punta Chiape*	41.36	9.22	9
Granicus F., *Kodscha Tchai*	40.15	27.12	19
Granis F., *Khisht*	29.30	51.12	3
Granua F., *Graan*	48.15	19.0	25
Gratianopŏlis, or Cularo, *Grenoble*	45.11	5.43	6
Graviscae? *Torre di Carneto*	42.11	11.41	9
Grissia, or Gerasus, F., *Koros*	46.52	21.0	14
Grius M	37.25	27.30	19
*Grudii	51.18	3.30	6
Grumentum, n. *Saponara*	40.7	15.53	9
Grumum, *Grumo*	41.0	16.42	9
Gryneium	38.51	27.3	19
Gudgodah? *Ain el-Ghudhyan*	29.51	35.5	24
*Gugerni	51.40	6.10	6
Guntia, *Gunzburg*	48.27	10.20	25
Guraeus F.? *Lundye*	35.0	71.52	3
Gyăros I., *Jura*	37.37	24.43	19
Gygaea Palus, *Lake of Mermereh*	38.37	28.5	19
Gymnesiae, or Baleares Iᵐ., *Majorca, &c.*	39.30	3.0	7
Gymnias? *Gumish Khaneh*	40.24	39.28	20
Gyndes F. (Delas, or Silla)? *Diyalah*	34.20	45.10	22
Gyrton, *Tatari*	39.40	22.20	15
Gythium, n. *Marathonisi*	36.46	22.34	18

H.

NAMES.	LAT.	LONG.	MAP.
Habitancum, *Risingham*	55.10	2.9 w	5
Hactarn, *Pozoalcon*	37.38	3.2 w	7
Haditha?	32.11	35.16	21
Hadranum, or Adranum, *Aderno*	37.38	14.49	12
Hadria, or Atria, *Adria*	45.3	12.3	8
Hadria, or Adria, *Atri*	42.34	14.1	8
Hadriăni, r. n. *Edranos*	39.52	29.1	20
Hadrianopŏlis (Bithynia)? *Viran Shehr*	41.8	32.27	20
Hadrianopŏlis (Epirus), *Libokhovo*	40.1	20.24	15
Hadrianopŏlis (Thracia), *Adrianople*	41.43	26.32	14
Hadriănum, *Ariano*	44.57	12.6	8
Hadriănus, or Tartărus, F., *Tartaro*	45.5	11.20	8
Hadriaticum (or Superum) Mare, *Adriatic Sea*	44.0	14.0	8
Haemus M., *Balkan*	42.45	26.0	14
Hafa, *Budduso*	40.35	9.15	9
Ha-biroth(Heroopolis)? r. in Valley of the Seven Wells (Seba Biyar)	30.33	31.53	24
Halae	38.39	23.11	16
Halae Aexonĭdes, *Aliki*	37.51	23.45	16
Halae Araphenĭdes, by C. Velani	37.59	24.2	16
Halah, or Chala? *Sar Puli Zohab*	34.32	46.8	22
Hales, Heles, or Elees, F., *Alento, or Venere*	40.10	15.7	9
Halĕsa, or Alaesa, n. *Tusa*	37.57	14.14	12
Halĕsus (or Alaesus) F., *Pettineo*	37.55	14.16	12
Halex F., *Alice*	37.58	15.50	9
Haliacmon F., *Indjeh Kara-su*	40.24	22.8	15
Haliartus, r. n. *Mazi*	38.21	23.6	16
Halias	37.22	23.10	18
Halicarnassus, *Boo-droom*	37.3	27.28	19
Halice, or Halieis, r. on Port Kheli, or *Bizati*	37°.19'	23°.9'	18
Halicyae, *Salemi*	37.49	12.46	12
Halicyrna	38.23	21.31	18
Halimus, on C. Kallimakhi, or *Kosmas*	37.53	23.43	16
Halisarna (Aeolis)	39.2	27.2	19
Halisarna (Cos)	36.44	27.0	19
Haliussa I	37.26	23.33	18
Halmўrae?	30.50	29.25	24
Halmўris, or Salmorudis?	44.50	28.49	14
Halmўris L., *L. of Raselm*	44.45	29.0	14
Halŏne I., *Liman Pasha*	40.28	27.36	19
Halonnēsus I.? *Khelidromi*	39.12	23.55	19
Halonnēsus I., *Tavates*	38.12	26.27	19
Halos, or Alos, *Kefalosi*	39.9	22.47	15
Halus, or Oryx? n. *Podhogora*	37.46	22.3	15
Halyattis Tumŭlus, *Bin Tepeh*	38.35	28.3	17
Halўcus F., *Platani*	37.25	13.20	12
Halys F., *Kizil-Irmak*	40.30	34.20	20
Hamath (Epiphania), *Hamah*	35.13	36.38	20
Hamaxia	36.35	31.58	20
Hamaxĭtos	39.32	26.6	19
Hanes, or Tahpanes (Daphne), *Tell Defenneh*	30.52	32.3	24
Hannibălis Portus, *Portimao*	37.11	8.27 w	7
Hara? *Zarnah*	33.54	46.8	22
Harne? *Erek, or Yareka*	34.27	38.35	20
Haran (Carrhae)? *Harran*	36.52	39.2	22
*Harii, or Arii	51.0	20.30	25
Harma L., *Paralimni, or Moritza*	38.26	23.22	16
Harma (Attica), r. n. *Phyle*	38.9	23.37	16
Harma (Boeotia)?	38.22	23.31	16
Harmĕ̆ne (or Armĕ̆ne), *Ak Liman*	42.3	35.5	20
Harmozeia	27.0	57.10	3
Harmozĭca? *Armassi*	41.49	44.39	22
Harmŏzon Prom.? *C. Bombareek, or Ras el-Khore*	25.47	57.20	3
Harpagium	40.20	27.22	19
Harpăsa, *Arpas Kaleh*	37.47	38.21	19
Harpăsus F., *Arpa Su*	37.45	28.21	19
Harpăsus F. (Lycus)? *Joruk Su*	40.26	41.0	20
Harpessus F., *Arda*	41.30	25.30	14
Harpinna, *Miraka*	37.39	21.39	18
Hasta, *Voltri*	44.16	8.43	8
Hatera, *Katerina*	40.14	22.30	15
Hatra, *Al-Hadhr*	35.33	42.49	22
Hazeroth? *Ain el-Hudherah*	28.51	34.27	24
Hebron (or Kirjath-arba), *El-Khuleel*	31.33	35.9	21
Hebrus F., *Maritza*	41.15	26.30	14
Hebŭdes, or Ebŭdae, Iᵐ., *Hebrides*	57.0	7.30 w	5
Hecăle?	38.12	23.59	16
Hecatombaeum?	38.8	21.27	18
Hecatompĕdum?	40.15	20.9	15
Hecatompўlos? *Jah Jerm*	36.50	56.34	3
Hecatonnēsi Iᵐ., *Mosko, &c.*	39.20	26.40	19
Hedylium M	38.33	22.52	17
Hedўphon F., *Jerrahi*	31.0	49.20	22
Heldua, *Khan Khulda*	33.45	35.28	21
Helĕna (or Illibĕris), *Elne*	42.36	2.58	6

NAMES.	LAT.	LONG.	MAP.
Helĕne. Macris, or Cranae I., *Makronisi*	37°.41′	24°.7′	19
Helenŏpolis, for. Drepane	40.41	29.33	20
Heles, Hales, or Elees, F., *Alento, or Venere*	40.10	15.7	9
Helevetones, or Helvecones	51.45	20.30	25
Helĭce	38.13	22.9	18
Helĭce, *Ichliman*	42.19	24.0	14
Helĭcon F., *Oliveri*	38.2	15.0	12
Helĭcon M., *Paleovouni*	38.18	22.54	16
Helĭcranum, *Delvino*	39.56	20.13	15
Heliopŏlis (Baalath), *Baalbek*	33.57	36.1	21
Heliopŏlis (Rameses, or Beth-shemesh), *Matarieh*	30.8	31.20	24
Helisii, or Elisii	51.30	17.0	25
Helisson F.	37.58	22.40	18
Helisson F., *Davia*	37.27	22.13	18
Helium Ostium, *Mouth of Meuse, or Maas*	51.57	4.10	25
Hellana, *Agliana*	43.55	11.2	8
Hellespontus, *Dardanelles*	40.15	26.30	19
Helŏrus, or Helŏrum	36.51	15.5	12
Helŏrus F., *Abisso*	36.52	15.0	12
Helos ?	36.49	22.46	18
Helvecones, or Helvetones	51.45	20.30	25
Helvetii	47.0	7.40	6
Helvii	44.38	4.30	6
Helvillum, or Suillum, *Sigillo*	43.20	12.45	8
Helvinus F., *Salinello*	42.47	13.55	8
Henna, or Enna, *Castro Giovanni*	37.33	14.17	12
Hephaestia (Lemnos)	39.54	25.21	19
Hephaestiădae, *Arakli*	38.4	23.46	16
HEPTANŎMIS, *Vostani, or Middle Egypt*	29.0	31.0	24
Heraclĕa (Aeolis)	39.17	26.42	19
Heraclĕa (Athamania)	39.16	21.10	15
Heraclĕa (Cephallenia)? *Rakli*	38.10	20.42	18
Heraclĕa (Chalcidice)	40.35	23.19	15
Heraclĕa (Ionia)	37.31	27.33	19
Heraclĕa (Lucania), *Policoro*	40.12	16.39	9
Heraclĕa-Lyncestis, n. *Filurina, cr Florina*	40.50	21.27	15
Heraclĕa Minŏa	37.22	13.16	12
Heraclĕa (Pieria), *Platamona*	39.38	22.36	15
Heraclĕa (Pisatis), *Streft*	37.40	21.34	18
Heraclĕa-Pontĭca, *Erekli*	41.17	31.29	20
Heraclĕa-Sintĭca, *Zervokhori*	40.54	23.30	14
Heraclĕa (Syria)	35.36	35.45	20
Heraclĕa (Trachinia)	38.47	22.23	16
Heracleius F.	38.16	22.52	16
Heracleopŏlis Magna, r. n. *Anasieh*	29.10	31.8	24
Heracleopŏlis Parva, or Heracleum ?	30.59	32.2	24
Heracleotic Mouth (of Nile), *Rosetta Mouth*	31.29	30.27	24
Heraclĕum	35.21	25.13	19
Heraclĕum, or Heracleopŏlis Parva	30.59	32.2	24
Heraclĕum Prom	41.18	36.58	20
Heraea	37.36	21.52	18
Hernei Montes ?	37.10	15.35	12
Heræum	37.42	22.47	18
Heraeum Pr., *C. Melangavi*	38.2	22.51	18
Herbănum, *Orvieto*	42.44	12.9	8
Herbessus, or Erbessus? *Grotte*	37.14	13.41	12
Herbessus, or Erbessus? *Puntal·ca*	37.8	15.0	12
Herbĭta ? *Citadella*	37°.25′	14°.29′	12
Herculanĕum, n. *Resina*	40.49	14.21	13
Herculeum, or Gaditănum, Fretum, *Strait of Gibraltar*	35.57	5.30 w	7
Hercŭlis Arēnae	31.0	20.20	23
Hercŭlis Castra ? *Gran*	47.48	18.45	14
Hercŭlis Fanum, *Massarosa*	43.52	10.20	8
Hercŭlis I., or Scombraria, *Escombrera*	37.34	0.55 w	7
Hercŭlis I., *Asinara*	41.5	8.15	9
Hercŭlis Portus	38.41	20.58	15
Hercŭlis Prom., *Capo Spartivento*	37.56	16.3	9
Hercŭlis Prom., *Hartland Point*	51.1	4.32 w	20
Hercŭlis Templum ? n. *C. Roche*	36.19	6.8 w	7
Hercўna Fons	38.26	22.52	16
Hercynia Silva	50.40	15.0	25
Herdonia, *Ordona*	41.18	15.37	9
Hermaeum Prom., *Capo della Caccia*	40.34	8.5	9
Hermaeum Prom., *Point Placo*	35.11	23.57	19
Hermaeus S., *G. of Smyrna*	38.40	26.40	19
Herminius Mons, *Sierra d'Estrella*	40.10	8.0 w	7
Hermĭŏne, or Hermion, *Kastri*	37.23	23.15	18
Hermionicus S	37.23	23.25	19
HERMĬŎNIS	37.26	23.12	18
Hermon, Mount, *Jebel esh-Sheikh*	33.28	35.29	21
Hermonassa, *Platana*	41.2	39.34	20
Hermopŏlis, *Eshmounein*	27.45	30.50	3
Hermopŏlis Parva? *Rhamanieh*	31.6	30.39	24
*Hermundŭri	50.0	11.20	25
Hermus, r. n. *Khaidari*	38.1	23.40	16
Hermus F., *Gedis Tchai*	38.32	28.0	20
*Hernĭci	41.50	13.10	11
Herodium, *Frank Mountain*	31.40	35.16	21
Heroopŏlis (Hahiroth?), r. in *Valley of the Seven Wells (Seba Biyar)*	30.33	31.53	24
Heroopolĭtes S., *G. of Suez*	29.0	32.50	24
Heshbon, *Hesbân*	31.46	35.52	21
Hesperĭdes, aft. Berenice, *Benghasi*	32.7	20.3	23
*Hesperii Aethiŏpes	8.0	5.0	2
HESTIAEŌTIS, or HISTIAEŌTIS	39.31	21.40	15
Hesudrus, or Zaradrus, F., *Sutlej*	31.0	76.0	3
Hetricŭlum. *Lattarico*	39.28	16.8	9
HIBERNIA, *Ireland*	53.0	8.0 w	2
Hicesia I., *Basiluzzo ?*	38.39	15.8	9
Hiĕra, Therasia, or Vulcāni I., *Vulcano*	38.23	14.56	9
Hiĕra, or Maritĭma, I., *Maretimo*	38.0	12.1	12
Hiĕra Sycamĭnos, *Wady Maharrakah*	23.4	32.43	3
Hierăcon	27.16	31.9	3
Hierapŏlis, *Pambouk-Kaleh*	37.55	29.10	20
Hierapŏlis, or Bambyce, *Membidj, or Bambouj*	36.32	37.57	20
Hierapytna, *Hierapetra*	35.3	25.44	19
Hierăsus, or Porata, F., *Pruth*	47.0	28.0	14
Hieratis ?	28.48	51.0	3
Hierĭcus (Jericho), n. *Er-Riha*	31.51	35.28	21
Hieromiax F., *Yarmouk, or Sheriat el-Mandhour*	32.46	35.50	21
Hieron	41°.7′	29°.7′	26
Hiĕron Pr., *C. Yoros*	41.7	39.24	20
Hierosolўma (Jerusalem), *El-Koods*	31.47	35.14	21
Hiĕrum	37.36	23.5	18
Himella F., *L'Aia*	42.22	12.30	11
Himĕra	37.58	13.38	12
Himĕra F., *S. Leonardo*	37.55	13.36	12
Himĕra F., *Salso*	37.10	14.0	12
Hippăris F., *Fiume di Camarana*	36.54	14.31	12
Hippi Pr., *Ras el-Hamrah, or C. Maverah*	36.58	7.48	23
Hippo Diarrhўtus (or Zaritus), *Benzert*	37.17	9.49	23
Hippo Regius, *Bonah*	36.53	7.47	23
Hippo Zaritus (or Diarrhўtus), *Benzert*	37.17	9.49	23
Hippoi I., *Goui*	38.27	26.22	19
Hippŏla, *Kipula*	36.31	22.21	18
Hipponensis S., *G. of Bonah*	37.10	8.30	23
Hipponiătes, Terinaeus, or Vibonensis S., *G. of S. Eufemia*	38.55	16.0	9
Hipponĭtis Palus, *Lake of Benzert*	37.10	9.50	23
Hipponium (aft. Vibo, or Vibo Valentia), *Monteleone*	38.42	16.10	9
Hipponon? *Sheikh Embarak*	28.42	30.58	24
Hippos, *Khurbet es-Sumrah*	32.46	35.39	21
Hippŏtae	38.20	22.59	16
Hippurius F., *Banas Tchai*	38.26	29.30	20
Hippus F., *Galisga*	42.40	41.25	22
Hippus Pr., *Point Ali*	30.32	18.39	23
Hira, or Alexandria	32.0	44.30	22
Hirminius F.? *Ragusa*	36.50	14.41	12
*Hirpĭni	41.7	15.0	9
Hispălis, *Sevilla*	37.25	5.49 w	7
HISPANIA, *Spain*	40.0	5.0 w	2
HISPANIA CITERIOR, or TARRACONENSIS	42.0	5.0 w	4
HISPANIA ULTERIOR, or BAETICA	37.0	5.0 w	4
Hispellum, *Spello*	43.0	12.42	8
Histiaea (Oreus), *Oreos*	38.57	23.6	15
HISTIAEŌTIS, or HESTIAEŌTIS	39.31	21.40	15
Histonium, *Vasto d'Ammone*	42.7	14.43	9
HISTRIA, or ISTRIA	45.15	14.0	8
*Homerītae	14.0	46.0	3
Homōle M	39.50	22.42	15
Homōle, or Homolium, *St. Demetrius*	39.52	22.40	15
Hoplias, or Isomantus, F.	38.22	22.54	16
Hor, Mount, *Jebel Neby Haroun*	30.25	35.37	24
Horeb	28.40	34.0	24
Hormah, or Zephath? *Nukb es-Sufah*	30.59	35.13	21
Horrea Caelia, *Herklah*	35.59	10.30	23
Horreum Margi, *Devibagherdan*	43.55	21.9	14
Horta, or Hortanum, *Orte*	42.28	12.23	11
Hostilia, *Ostiglia*	45.3	11.8	8
Hunnum, *Halton Chesters*	55.1	2.0 w	5
Hyaea ?	38.31	22.12	15
HYAMIA	36.55	21.55	18
Hyampŏlis, r. n. *Vogdhani*	38.35	20.54	16
Hybla Heraea ?	37.1	14.39	12
Hybla Major, *Paterno*	37.32	14.53	12
Hybla Megarensis	37.8	15.9	13
Hyccăra? *Grazia*	38.11	13.9	12
Hyda, or Hyla	36.43	28.11	19
Hydaspes F., *Jeloum*	32.0	72.10	3

NAMES.	LAT.	LONG.	MAP.
Hydra Prom., *Utch-Keucheh*	38°.49'	26°.54'	19
Hydramum, *Dhramia*	35.21	24.21	19
Hydraōtes F., *Ravee*	31.0	73.30	3
Hydrea I., *Hydra*	37.20	23.30	18
Hydrus F., *Idro*	40.8 .	18.26	9
Hydrus, or Hydruntum, *Otranto*	40.8	18.29	9
Hydrussa I., *Prasso*	37.50	23.45	16
Hyčle, Elša, or Velia, *Castelamare della Bruca*	40.8	15.8	9
Hyettus	38.31	23.5	16
Hyctussa I., *Gaidaro*	37.28	27.0	19
Hyla, or Hyda	36.43	28.11	19
Hylaethus F., *Morno*	38.30	22.10	18
Hyle? *Paleokastro*	38.25	23.15	16
Hylias F.?	39.34	16.42	9
Hyllca L., *Senzina, or Livadhi*	38.23	23.15	16
Hyllaicus Portus	39.35	19.55	15
*Hylli	44.0	15.35	14
Hyllis Peninsula? *Sabioncello*	42.53	17.30	14
Hymettus Mons, *Telovuni*	37.58	23.49	16
Hypaea I., *Titan*	43.1	6.27	8
Hypaipa, *Tepaya*	38.13	27.54	19
Hypǎnis F., *Boug*	48.20	30.0	2
Hypǎnis F., *Kouban*	45.5	39.0	3
Hyparodes	41.8	29.2	26
Hypǎta, *Neopatra*	38.52	22.12	15
Hypǎtus M., *Samata*	38.23	23.25	16
Hyperborei (or Riphaei) Montes, *S. part of Ural*	58.0	60.0	2
Hyperteleǎtum	36.39	22.54	18
Hyphanteium M	38.33	22.55	16
Hyphǎsis F., *Garra, or Sutlej*	30.0	73.0	3
Hypia M., *Tschila Dagh*	41.0	31.30	20
Hypius F., *Milan Su*	41.0	31.0	20
Hypocremnos	38.19	26.40	19
Hypsas F., *Bellici*	37.40	12.52	12
Hypsas F., *Drago*	37.16	13.34	12
Hypsi?	38.41	22.29	18
Hypsirisma I., *Kappari*	36.56	27.10	19
Hypsus, *Stemnitza*	37.33	22.5	18
HYRCANIA	36.20 ·	56.0	3
Hyrcǎnum (or Caspium) M., *Caspian Sea*	40.0	52.0	3
Hyria, Conōpe, or Lysimachia, L., *Zygos, or Angelokastro*	38.34	21.23	15
Hyria, or Urin, *Oria*	40.29	17.38	9
Hyrmīna, *Khlemutsa, or Kastro (Castel Tornese)*	37.53	21.9	18
Hysaeea F.			1
Hysiae (Argolis)	37.31	22.35	18
Hysiae (Boeotia)	38.13	23.22	16
HYSPRIĀTIS	40.20	41.0	22
Hyssus Portus, *Surmeneh*	40.57	40.5	20

L

NAMES.	LAT.	LONG.	MAP.
Iadera, *Zara*	44.6	15.13	14
Ialysus, *Paleo-Rhodos*	36.24	28.11	19
Iambo, *Yembo*	24.5	38.5	3
Iamnium Pr., *St. John's Point*	54.14	5.40 w	5
Iapis F	38.3	23.26	16
*Iapydes	45.0	15.20	14
IAPYGIA, or MESSAPIA	40.30	17.40	9
Iapygium, or Salentinum, Prom., *Capo di Leuca*	39.48	18.22	9
Iapygum tria Prom., *C. Onstella, C. Rizzuto, C. della Nave*	38.56	17.0	9
Iardǎnus F	35.27	23.53	19
Jasius, or Bargyliŏtes S., *G. of Mundelyah*	37.15	27.25	19

NAMES.	LAT.	LONG.	MAP.
Iassiorum Municipium? *Jassy*	47°.5'	27°.24'	14
Iasus, or Iassus	37.17	27.36	19
Iatinum, *Meaux*	48.58	2.53	6
Iatrippa, *Yathrib, or Medina*	25.0	39.58	3
Iatrus F., *Jantra*	43.12	25.20	14
*Iaxÿges Metanastae	47.30	20.0	14
*Iberi			1
IBERIA	42.10	44.0	22
Iberiae Pylae? *n. Mecheta, N. of Tiflis*	41.50	44.45	22
Ibērus F., *Ebro*	41.18	0.0	7
Ibes, *Ibi*	38.36	0.35 w	7
Ibium?	28.15	30.44	24
Ibliodūrum, *Hannonville au Passage*	49.17	5.48	6
Ibora	39.53	35.45	20
Icaria I., *Nikaria*	37.35	26.10	19
Icarium Mare	37.12	26.30	19
Icarthon M.	38.7	23.58	26
Icauna F., *Yonne*	47.50	3.30	6
*Icēni, or Simēni	52.25	1.0	5
Ichana? *Ichana, or Scibino*	36.45	15.6	12
Ichnae	40.41	22.33	15
Ichnae, *Konais*	36.10	39.1	22
*Ichthyophǎgi	25.45	60.0	3
*Ichthyophǎgi Aethiōpes	8.0	10.0 w	2
Ichthys Prom., *C. Katakolo*	37.38	21.19	18
Icidmagus, *Yssingeaux*	45.9	4.7	6
Iconium, *Koniyeh*	37.53	32.49	20
Icos I., *Peristeri*	39.10	23.58	19
Icosium, *Algiers*	36.48	3.4	23
Ictis I. (of Diodōrus), *St. Michael's Mount*	50.7	5.28 w	5
Ictumulorum Vicus?	45.46	8.4	8
Iculisma, *Angoulême*	45.38	0.10	6
Ida Mons (Creta), *Psiloriti*	35.13	24.50	19
Ida Mons (Troas)	40.0	26.45	19
Idex F., *Idice*	44.27	11.30	8
Idimum, *Hassan Pasha Palanka*	44.16	20.55	14
Idomēne, *Paleokulia*	39.3	21.7	15
Idrias, aft. Stratonicēa, *Eski-hissar*	37.17	28.11	19
Idubēda Mons, *Sierra Moncayo, &c*	41.0	1.40 w	7
IDUMAEA	31.0	35.17	21
Idyros, *Egder*	36.36	30.36	20
Iena Aest., *Wigton Bay*	54.50	4.20	5
Ierabriga, or Arabrica, *Alenquer*	39.2	8.56 w	7
IERNE, or IVERNIA			1
Iētae?	37.53	13.7	12
Igilgilis, *Jiljel, or Jijeli*	36.50	5.45	23
Igilium I., *Giglio*	42.20	10.58	8
Iguvium, *Gubbio*	43.21	12.34	8
Ila? *Jilla Abad.*	26.46	53.57	3
Ildum, *Torre Blanca*	40.16	0.14	7
Ilei	37.25	23.19	18
*Ilercaōnes	40.40	0.10	7
Ilerda, *Lerida*	41.40	0.30	7
*Ilergētes	41.40	0.30	7
Ilici, *Elche*	38.18	0.39 w	7
Ilicitǎnus S.	38.0	0.20 w	7
Illpa	37.40	5.18 w	7
Illpa, *Niebla*	37.24	6.30 w	7
Ilipūla M., *Sierra Nevada*	37.8	4.0 w	7
Ilissus F	37.58	23.44	16
Ilium, or Troja (Cestria), *Palea Venetia*	39.34	20.23	15
Ilium-novum, *Hissarjik*	39.57	26.15	10
Illibēris, *n. Granada*	37.18	3.51 w	7
Illibēris, aft. Helēna, *Elne*	42.36	2.58	6
Illibēris, or Tichis, F., *Tech*	42.35	2.50	6
Illiturgis, *Andujar*	38.1	4.3 w	7

NAMES.	LAT.	LONG.	MAP.
ILLYRICUM	41°.40'	18°.0'	14
Ilorci, *Lorca*	37.42	1.54 w	7
Iluro, *Alora*	36.53	4.44 w	7
Iluro, *Mataro*	41.33	2.28	7
Iluro, *Oléron*	43.11	0.37 w	6
Ilva, or Aethalia I., *Elba*	42.47	10.15	8
Imachǎra, *Cerami*	37.46	14.32	12
Imǎus M., *Beloortagh, Altai, &c*	38.0	72.0	2
Imbarus M., *Gurengli Dagh*	36.25	32.50	20
Imbrǎsus F.	37.43	26.55	19
Imbros, *Kastro*	40.14	25.54	19
Imbros I., *Imbro*	40.10	25.50	19
Imus Pyrenaeus, *St. Jean Pied de Port*	43.9	1.13	6
Inachorium	35.19	23.31	19
Inǎchus F., *Banitza*	37.43	22.37	15
Inǎchus F., *River of Ariadha*	38.55	21.11	15
In Apennino, *Matarana*	44.16	9.38	8
Inarīme, Aenaria, or Pithecūsa I., *Ischia*	40.44	13.54	13
Inatus	35.4	25.20	19
Indenea	44.21	16.25	14
INDIA extra Gangem, *Indo-Chinese Peninsula*	20.0	100.0	2
INDIA intra Gangem, *Hindoostan*	25.0	78.0	2
Indīcus Oceǎnus, *Indian Ocean*	0.0	70.0	2
*Indigētes	42.15	2.50	7
Indus F., *Indus*	31.0	70.54	3
Indus F.? *Doloman Tchai*	37.10	29.10	20
Industria, *Monteu*	45.10	7.59	8
*Ingauni	44.0	8.5	8
Ingena, *Avranches*	48.42	1.20 w	6
Inicerum, *Posega*	45.21	17.43	14
In Monte Haemo	42.44	25.24	14
Insǎni Montes, *Monti di Limbara*	40.54	9.12	9
*Insubres	45.30	4.0	6
*Insūbres	45.35	9.0	8
INSULĀRUM PROVINCIA	37.0	26.0	4
*Intemelii	43.50	7.45	8
Interamna, *Teramo*	42.41	13.42	8
Interamna (ad Lirim)	41.15	13.41	9
Interamna(Umbrorum), *Terni*	42.35	12.41	8
Interamnium	39.40	16.18	9
Interamnium, *Villaroane*	42.22	5.30 w	7
Interamnium Flavium? *Bembibre*	42.36	6.35 w	7
Intercatia?	42.1	5.20 w	7
Interocrea, *Interdoco, or Antrodoco*	42.25	13.6	8
Interpromium, *S. Valentino*	42.11	14.2	9
Intibīli, *Torre del Sol*	40.31	0.30	7
Iol, aft. Caesarēa, *Shershell*	36.37	2.12	23
Iolcus, *Volo*	39.24	22.57	15
Iomnium? *Marsa Fahm*	36.54	4.20	23
Ion, or Ios, *Kolines*	37.17	22.22	18
IONIA	38.0	27.0	19
Ionopōlis, for. Aboniteichos, *Ineboli*	41.57	33.46	20
Ios, *Nio*	36.43	25.17	19
Ios I., *Nio*	36.43	25.20	19
Ios, or Ion, *Kolines*	37.17	22.22	18
Ipagrum, *Baena*	37.41	4.25 w	7
Ipnoi? *Zagora*	39.29	23.5	19
Ipsus	38.41	30.52	20
Irenopōlis, for. Beroea? *Eski Sagra*	42.30	25.44	14
Iria, *Voghera*	44.59	9.1	8
Iria F., *Staffora*	45.0	9.2	8
Iria Flavia, or Pria, *El Padron*	42.38	8.38 w	7

NAMES.	LAT.	LONG.	MAP.
rine L., *Ypsili*	37°.26'	23°.0'	18
ris F., *Yeshil Irmak*	41.0	36.38	20
rrhesia I.? *Psathoura*	39.29	24.10	19
.s, or Aeopolis, *Hit*	33.36	42.52	22
.sica F., *Exe*	50.38	3.27 w	5
.annavatin, or Bena- venta, *Burrow Hill*, n. *Daventry*	52.16	1.8 w	5
.ara F., *Indre*	45.5	5.10	6
.ara F., *Oise*	49.30	2.50	6
*isarci	45.46	8.45	8
.aurus F., *Isar*	48.30	12.0	25
ISAURIA	37.30	32.30	20
.aurus, or Pisaurus, F., *Foglia*	43.47	12.30	8
sca Damnoniorum, *Exeter*	50.43	3.32 w	5
sca (Silurum), *Caer- leon*	51.37	2.57 w	20
.chalis, *Ilchester*	51.0	2.40 w	5
scina, r. at *Ras Benja- wad*	30.50	18.10	23
sinisca, *Aschbach*	48.5	11.55	25
.ionda	36.57	30.22	20
sis F., *Tscholoki*	41.54	41.50	22
sium	29.23	31.15	24
sium M.	21.10	36.30	3
smarus			1
smenus F.	38.20	23.19	16
somantus, or Hop- lias, F.	38.22	22.54	16
ssa, *Lissa*	43.4	16.10	14
ssicus S., G. of Scan- deroon	36.40	35.50	20
ssus ?	36.56	36.8	20
ster (or Danubius) F., *Donau*, or *Danube*	44.0	26.20	14
sthmus, *Isthmus of Co- rinth*	37.57	23.0	18
sthmus (Doris)	36.47	28.5	19
stone M.?	39.44	19.50	15
ISTRIA, or HISTRIA, *Istria*	45.15	14.0	8
stron	35.8	25.44	19
stropolis, *Kargaliuk*	44.25	28.48	14
stros I., *Yali*	36.40	27.10	19
.aurium, *Aldborough*	54.6	1.22 w	5
sus ?	38.27	23.28	16
tabyrium, or Ataby- rium (Mt. Tabor), *Jebel et-Tuor*	32.42	35.25	21
ITALIA, *Italy*	43.0	12.0	2
talica, *Santiponce*	37.29	5.51 w	7
tanum Pr.? C. Sula- mon, or *Salmone*	35.10	26.19	19
tanus, *Itagnia*	35.8	26.16	19
thaca I., *Ithaca*	38.25	20.40	18
thome, *Fanari*	39.24	21.27	15
thoria, *St. Elias*	38.30	21.16	18
tium Prom., C. Gris Nez	50.52	1.35	6
tius Portus, *Wissant*	50.53	1.40	6
ton, or Itonus	39.8	22.41	15
tuce, or Utica, *Bou- shater*	37.9	10.2	23
tuna Aest., *Solway Firth*	54.55	3.25 w	5
ITURAEA, *El-Jeidoor*	33.10	36.0	21
ulis, *Zea*	37.38	24.21	19
IVERNIA, or IERNE... vin, or Juvia, F., *Jubia*	43.32	8.5 w	7
xia, *Lanathi*	36.1	27.58	19

J.

NAMES.	LAT.	LONG.	MAP.
abadii, or Sabadii, I..? *Jara*, &c.	7.0	110.0	2
abbok F., *Nahr Zurka*	32.14	35.50	21
.besh-gilead? In Wady *Yabes*	32.29	35.44	21
.eca, *Jara*	42.31	0.31 w	7
Jaccetani	42.30	0.20 w	7
unnia, *Yebna*	31.51	34.45	21

NAMES.	LAT.	LONG.	MAP.
Jamno, or Jamna, *Ciu- dadela*	39°.59'	3°.53'	7
Japhia, *Yafa*	32.41	35.18	21
Jarmuth, *Yarmook*	31.42	34.58	21
Jasonium Pr., *C. Jason*	41.7	37.39	20
Jattir, *Atteer*	31.21	35.5	21
Jaxartes F., *Sir*, or *Sihoon*	44.0	68.25	3
Jazer, n. *Ain Hazeir*	32.3	35.46	21
Jenysus, *Khan Yunas*	31.18	34.18	24
Jericho (Hiericus), n. *Er-Riha*	31.51	35.28	21
Jerusalem, *El-Koods*	31.47	35.14	21
Jezreel (Esdraelon), *Zereen*	32.34	35.21	21
Jonnaria	44.7	16.25	14
Joppa, *Jaffa*	32.3	34.45	21
Jordan F., *Nahr el- Kebir*	32.10	35.36	21
Jordan, Plain of (Aulon, or Magnus Campus), *El-Ghor*	32.20	35.35	21
Jotapata, *Jefat*	32.51	35.17	21
Jovia, *Apathia*	46.16	16.30	14
Jovis Urii Templum	41.9	29.10	20
Jovisura, *Eggenfelden*	48.24	12.47	14
JUDAEA	31.40	35.0	21
Julia, *Tschai*	38.38	31.5	20
Julia Augusta (for. Ae- mona), *Laybach*	46.4	14.31	14
Julia Constantin, or Zilis, *Arzilla*	35.29	6.1 w	23
Julia Fidentia, *Borgo S. Donino*	44.53	10.6	8
Julia Gemella (Acci), *Guadix el-Viejo*	37.22	3.19 w	7
Julia Gordus, *Gordis*	38.55	28.28	20
Julia Joza, aft. Trans- ducta, *Tarifa*	36.0	5.37 w	7
Julia Libyca? *Puig- cerda*	42.26	1.56	7
Julia Myrtilis, *Mertola*	37.40	7.28 w	7
Juliacum, *Juliers*	50.56	6.21	6
Julias (Bethsaida), *Et- Tell*	32.58	35.40	21
Juliobona, *Lillebonne*	49.31	0.31	6
Juliobriga, *Reynosa*	43.0	3.57 w	7
Juliomagus, aft. Ande- cavi, *Angers*	47.28	0.33 w	6
Juliopolis, *Ibol*	38.10	39.15	20
Juliopolis, or Gordium	40.4	31.35	20
Julium Carnicum, *Zu- glio*	46.27	13.3	8
Juncaria, *Junquera*	42.24	2.53	7
Junonia I.? *Palma*	28.45	17.50 w	2
Junonis Fontes, *Cal- diero*	45.23	11.14	8
Junonis Laciniae Tem- plum	39.5	17.11	9
Junonis Pr., *C. Trafal- gar*	36.11	6.1 w	7
Jupiter, Temple of (Aegina)?	37.45	23.32	18
Jupiter Palenius, Tem- ple of, *Campo di Giove*	42.0	14.3	9
Jura (or Jurassus) Mons, *Mt. Jura*	47.0	6.40	6
Justinopolis, for. Aegida, *Capo d'Istria*	45.32	13.44	8
Juttah, *Yutta*	31.28	35.9	21
Juvavum, *Salzburg*	47.48	13.4	14
Juvia, or Ivia, F., *Jubia*	43.32	8.5 w	7

K.

NAMES.	LAT.	LONG.	MAP.
Kadesh (in Paran), or Kadesh-barnea, *Ain Kudes*	30.34	34.28	24
Kadesh (in Zin)? *Ain- el-Weibeh*	30.41	35.22	24
Kaloi Limenes, *Fair Havens*	34.56	24.48	19
Kanah, *Kana*	33.15	35.18	21

NAMES.	LAT.	LONG.	MAP.
Kanah F., *Nahr el- Arsouf*	32°.18'	34°.55'	21
Kedesh, *Kedes*	33.9	35.31	21
Kerioth, *El-Kuryetein*	31.22	35.11	21
Kersus F., *Merkez Su*	36.39	36.11	20
Kidron, or Cedron, F., *Wady er-Rahib*	31.44	35.20	21
Kir of Moab (Charax), *Kerak*	31.15	35.46	21
Kirjath-arba (Hebron), *El-Khuleel*	31.33	35.9	21
Kirjath-jearim, or Baa- lah, *Kuryet el-Enab*	31.49	35.7	21
Kishon F., *Nahr Mu- kutta*	32.47	35.6	21

L.

NAMES.	LAT.	LONG.	MAP.
*Labeates	42.0	19.40	14
Labeatis L., *L. of Sku- tari*	42.5	19.20	14
Labicum, *Colonna*	41.51	12.46	11
Labranda	37.25	27.50	19
Lacedaemon, or Sparta, n. *Mistra*	37.5	22.26	18
*Lacetani	42.0	1.50	7
Laceter Pr., *C. Kephala*, or *Krokilo Pt.*	36.40	27.0	19
Lachish ?	31.32	34.59	21
Laciacum, *Vöcklamarkt*	48.0	13.51	14
Laciadae?	37.59	23.43	17
Lacinium Prom., *Capo delle Colonne*, or *C. Nao*	39.5	17.13	9
Lacipea, *Deleitosa*	39.35	5.35 w	7
Lacippo, Alecippe, n. *Casares*	36.25	5.18 w	7
Lacmon M., *Metzovo*	39.53	21.30	15
Lacobriga, *Lagos*	37.9	8.38 w	7
Lacobriga, *Villa Laco*	42.30	4.34 w	7
LACONIA	37.30	22.40	18
Laconicus S., G. of *Kolokythia*	36.40	22.40	18
Lacotene? *Viran Shehr*	38.5	38.9	20
Lacron F., *Lezero Vedra*	42.26	8.36 w	7
Lactodorum, *Towcester*	52.8	0.59 w	5
Lactura, *Lectoure*	43.56	0.38	6
Lacus Lausonius, *Lau- sanne*	46.32	6.38	6
Lacus Prilis, *Lago di Castiglione*	42.46	11.0	8
Lade I.	37.32	27.14	19
Ladoceia	37.24	22.10	18
Ladon F.	37.50	21.32	18
Ladon F., *Rufia*	37.40	21.51	18
Laea, or Aphrodite, I., *Al-Hiera*	32.50	22.34	23
Laerta	36.28	32.11	20
*Laevi	45.15	8.50	8
Lagana F., *Lahn*	50.20	8.0	25
Lagania	40.4	32.1	20
Lagaria, *Nocara*	40.6	16.27	9
Lagina, *Lakina*	37.21	28.18	20
Lagusae I..?	39.56	26.5	19
Laii	38.21	26.0	19
Laish, or Dan, *Tell el- Kady*	33.17	35.38	21
LALASSIS	36.40	32.30	20
*Laletani	41.40	2.30	7
Lamate?	44.36	17.20	14
Lambasa, *L'erba*, or *Tezout*	35.1	6.15	23
Lambrus F., *Lambro*	45.20	9.21	8
Lametia, *S. Eufemia*	39.3	16.14	9
Lametus F., *Lamato*	38.55	16.17	9
Lamia, *Zeitouni*	38.54	22.24	16
Laminium, *Don Sancho*	38.57	3.4 w	7
Lamos, *Lamas*	36.34	34.17	20
LAMOTIS	36.37	34.0	20
Lampe, or *Lappa*	35.19	24.20	19
Lampeia M., *Olonos*	37.58	21.51	18
Lampsacus, *Lamsaki*	40.20	26.40	19
Lamptra inferior	37.49	23.51	16

NAMES.	LAT.	LONG.	MAP.
Hydra Prom., *Utch-Keucheh*	38°.49'	26°.54'	19
Hydramum, *Dhramia*	35.21	24.21	19
Hydraötes F., *Ravee*	31.0	73.30	3
Hydrea I., *Hydra*	37.20	23.30	18
Hydrus F., *Idro*	40.8 .	18.26	9
Hydrus, or Hydruntum, *Otranto*	40.8	18.29	9
Hydrussa I., *Prasso*	37.50	23.45	16
Hyele, Elea, or Velia, *Castelamare della Bruca*	40.8	15.8	9
Hyettus	38.31	23.5	16
Hyetussa I., *Gaidaro*	37.28	27.0	19
Hyla, or Hyda	36.43	28.11	19
Hylaethus F., *Morno*	38.30	22.10	18
Hyle? *Paleokastro*	38.25	23.15	16
Hylias F.?	39.34	16.42	9
Hyllica L., *Senzina, or Livadhi*	38.23	23.15	16
Hyllaïcus Portus	39.35	19.55	15
*Hylli	44.0	15.35	14
Hyllis Peninsula? *Sabioncello*	42.53	17.30	14
Hymettus Mons, *Telovuni*	37.58	23.49	16
Hypaea L., *Titan*	43.1	6.27	8
Hypaipa, *Tepaya*	38.13	27.54	19
Hypänis F., *Boug*	48.20	30.0	2
Hypänis F., *Kouban*	45.5	39.0	3
Hyparodes	41.8	29.2	26
Hypäta, *Neopatra*	38.52	22.12	15
Hypätus M., *Samata*	38.23	23.25	16
Hyperborei (or Riphaei) Montes, *S. part of Ural*	58.0	60.0	2
Hyperteleätum	36.39	22.54	18
Hyphanteium M	38.33	22.55	16
Hyphäsis F., *Garra, or Sutlej*	30.0	73.0	3
Hypia M., *Tschila Dagh*	41.0	31.30	20
Hypius F., *Milan Su*	41.0	31.0	20
Hypocremnos	38.19	26.40	19
Hypsas F., *Bellici*	37.40	12.52	12
Hypsas F., *Drago*	37.16	13.34	12
Hypsi?	36.41	22.29	18
Hypsirisma L., *Kappari*	36.56	27.10	19
Hypsus, *Stemnitza*	37.33	22.5	18
HYRCANIA	36.20	56.0	3
Hyrcanum (or Caspium) M., *Caspian Sea*	40.0	52.0	3
Hyrin, Conöpe, or Lysimachia, L., *Zygos, or Angelokastro*	38.34	21.23	15
Hyria, or Uria, *Oria*	40.29	17.38	9
Hyrmina, *Khlemutza, or Kastro (Castel Tornese)*	37.53	21.9	18
Hysaees F.			1
Hysine (Argolis)	37.31	22.35	18
Hysiae (Boeotia)	38.13	23.22	16
HYSPRIÄTIS	40.20	41.0	22
Hyssus Portus, *Surmeneh*	40.57	40.5	20

L

NAMES.	LAT.	LONG.	MAP.
Iadera, *Zara*	44.6	15.13	14
Ialysus, *Paleo-Rhodos*	36.24	28.11	19
Iambo, *Yembo*	24.5	38.5	3
Iaunium Pr., *St. John's Point*	54.14	5.40 w	5
Iapis F.	38.3	23.26	16
*Iapydes	45.0	15.20	14
IAPYGIA, or MESSAPIA	40.30	17.40	9
Iapygium, or Salentinum, Prom., *Capo di Leuca*	39.48	18.22	9
Iapygum tria Prom., *C. Castella, C. Rizzuto, C. della Nave.*	38.56	17.0	9
Iardänus F.	35.27	23.53	19
Iasius, or Bargyliëtes S., *G. of Mendelyah*	37.15	27.25	19

NAMES.	LAT.	LONG.	MAP.
Iassiorum Municipium? *Jassy*	47°.5'	27°.24'	14
Iasus, or Iassus	37.17	27.36	19
Iatinum, *Meaux*	48.58	2.53	6
Iatrippa, *Yathrib, or Medina*	25.0	39.58	3
Iatrus F., *Jantra*	43.12	25.20	14
*Iazyges Metanastae	47.30	20.0	14
*Iberi			1
IBERIA	42.10	44.0	22
Iberiae Pylae? *n.Mscheta, N. of Tiflis*	41.50	44.45	22
Ibērus F., *Ebro*	41.18	0.0	7
Ibes, *Ibi*	38.36	0.35 w	7
Ibium?	28.15	30.44	24
Ibliodürum, *Hannonville au Passage*	49.17	5.48	6
Ibora	39.53	35.45	20
Icaria I., *Nikaria*	37.35	26.10	19
Icarium Mare	37.12	26.30	19
Icarthon M.	38.7	23.58	26
Icauna F., *Yonne*	47.50	3.30	6
*Icēni, or Simēni	52.25	1.0	5
Ichana? *Ichana, or Scibino*	36.45	15.6	12
Ichnae	40.41	22.33	15
Ichnae, *Konais*	36.10	39.1	22
*Ichthyophägi	25.45	60.0	3
*Ichthyophägi Aethiöpes	8.0	10.0 w	2
Ichthys Prom., *C. Katakolo*	37.38	21.19	18
Icidmagus, *Yssingeaux*	45.9	4.7	6
Iconium, *Koniyeh*	37.53	32.49	20
Icos I., *Peristeri*	39.10	23.58	19
Icosium, *Algiers*	36.48	3.4	23
Ictis I. (of Diodörus), *St. Michael's Mount*	50.7	5.28 w	5
Ictumulorum Vicus?	45.46	8.4	8
Iculisma, *Angoulême*	45.38	0.10	6
Ida Mons (Creta), *Psiloriti*	35.13	24.50	19
Ida Mons (Troas)	40.0	26.45	19
Idex F., *Idice*	44.27	11.30	8
Idimum, *Hassan Pasha Palanka*	44.16	20.55	14
Idomēne, *Paleokulia*	39.3	21.7	15
Idrias, aft. Stratonicēa, *Eski-hissar*	37.17	28.11	19
Idubēda Mons, *Sierra Moncayo, &c*	41.0	1.40 w	7
IDUMAEA	31.0	35.17	21
Idyros, *Egder*	36.36	30.36	20
Iena Aest., *Wigton Bay*	54.50	4.20	5
Icorabriga, or Arabrica, *Alenquer*	39.2	8.56 w	7
IERNE, or IVERNIA			1
Iētae?	37.53	13.7	12
Igilgilis, *Jiljel, or Jijeli*	36.50	5.45	23
Igilium I., *Giglio*	42.20	10.58	8
Iguvium, *Gubbio*	43.21	12.34	8
Ila? *Jilla Abad.*	26.46	53.57	3
Ildum, *Torre Blanca*	40.16	0.14	7
Ilei	37.25	23.19	18
*Ilercaönes	40.40	0.10	7
Ilerda, *Lerida*	41.40	0.30	7
*Ilergētes	41.40	0.30	7
Ilici, *Elche*	38.18	0.39 w	7
Ilicitänus S.	38.0	0.20 w	7
Ilipa	37.40	5.18 w	7
Ilipa, *Niebla*	37.24	6.30 w	7
Ilipüla M., *Sierra Nevada*	37.8	4.0 w	7
Ilissus F.	37.58	23.44	16
Ilium, or Troja (Cestria), *Palea Venetia*	39.34	20.23	15
Ilium-novum, *Hissarjik*	39.57	26.15	19
Illibēris, n. *Granada*	37.18	3.51 w	7
Illibēris, aft. Helēna, *Elne*	42.36	2.58	6
Illibēris, or Tichis, F., *Tech*	42.35	2.50	6
Illiturgis, *Andujar*	38.1	4.3 w	7

NAMES.	LAT.	LONG.	MAP.
ILLYRICUM	41°.40'	18°.0'	14
Ilorci, *Lorca*	37.42	1.54 w	7
Iluro, *Alora*	36.53	4.44 w	7
Iluro, *Mataro*	41.33	2.28	7
Iluro, *Oléron*	43.11	0.37 w	6
Ilva, or Aethalia I., *Elba*	42.47	10.15	8
Imachära, *Cerami*	37.46	14.32	12
Imäus M., *Belvortagh, Altai, &c.*	38.0	72.0	2
Imbarus M., *Gurengli Dagh.*	36.25	32.50	20
Imbräsus F.	37.43	26.55	19
Imbros, *Kastro:*	40.14	25.54	19
Imbros I., *Imbro*	40.10	25.50	19
Imus Pyrenaeus, *St.Jean Pied de Port*	43.9	1.13	6
Inachorium	35.19	23.31	19
Inächus F., *Banitza*	37.43	22.37	18
Inächus F., *River of Ariadha*	38.55	21.11	15
In Apennino, *Matarana*	44.16	9.38	8
Inarïme, Aenaria, or Pithecüsa I., *Ischia*	40.44	13.54	13
Inatus	35.4	25.20	19
Indenea	44.21	16.25	14
INDIA extra Gangem, *Indo-Chinese Peninsula*	20.0	100.0	2
INDIA intra Gangem, *Hindoostan*	25.0	78.0	2
Indïcus Oceänus, *Indian Ocean*	0.0	70.0	2
*Indigētes	42.15	2.50	7
Indus F., *Indus*	31.0	70.54	3
Indus F.? *Doloman Tchai*	37.10	29.10	20
Industria, *Monteu*	45.10	7.59	8
*Ingauni	44.0	8.5	8
Ingena, *Avranches*	48.42	1.20 w	6
Inicerum, *Posega*	45.21	17.43	14
In Monte Haemo	42.44	25.24	14
Insäni Montes, *Monti di Limbara*	40.54	9.12	9
*Insubres	45.30	4.0	6
*Insübres	45.35	9.0	8
INSULÄRUM PROVINCIA	37.0	26.0	4
*Intemelii	43.50	7.45	8
Interamna, *Teramo*	42.41	13.42	8
Interamna (ad Lirim)	41.15	13.41	9
Interamna (Umbrorum), *Terni*	42.35	12.41	8
Interamnium	39.40	16.18	9
Interamnium, *Villaroane*	42.22	5.30 w	7
Interamnium Flavium? *Bembibre*	42.36	6.35 w	7
Intercatia?	42.1	5.20 w	7
Interocrea, *Interdoco, or Antrodoco*	42.25	13.6	8
Interpromium, *S. Valentino*	42.11	14.2	9
Intibïli, *Torre del Sol*	40.31	0.30	7
Iol, aft. Caesarēa, *Shershell*	36.37	2.12	23
Iolcus, *Volo.*	39.24	22.57	15
Iomnium? *Marsa Fahm*	36.54	4.20	23
Ion, or Ios, *Kolines*	37.17	22.22	18
IONIA	38.0	27.0	19
Ionopölis, for. Aboniteichos, *Ineboli*	41.57	33.46	20
Ios, *Nio*	36.43	25.17	19
Ios I., *Nio*	36.43	25.20	19
Ios, or Ion, *Kolines*	37.17	22.22	18
Ipagrum, *Baena*	37.41	4.25 w	7
Ipnoi? *Zagora*	39.29	23.5	19
Ipsus	38.41	30.52	20
Irenopölis, for. Beroea? *Eski Sagra*	42.30	25.44	14
Iria, *Voghera*	44.59	9.1	
Iria F., *Staffora*	45.0	9.2	
Iria Flavia, or Pria, *El Padron*	42.38	8.38 w	7

NAMES.	LAT.	LONG.	MAP.
rine L., *Ypsili*	37°.26′	23°.0′	18
ris F., *Yeshil Irmak* ...	41.0	36.38	20
rrbesia I.? *Psathoura*	39.29	24.10	19
s, or Aeopŏlis, *Hit*	33.36	42.52	22
sXca F., *Exe*	50.38	3.27 w	5
sannavatia, or Bena-			
venta. *Burrow Hill,*			
n. Daventry	52.16	1.8 w	5
sàra F., *Isère*	45.5	5.10	6
sàra F., *Oise*	49.30	2.50	6
'Isarci	45.46	8.45	8
surus F., *Isar*	48.30	12.0	25
SAURIA	37.30	32.30	20
saurus, or Pisaurus, F.,			
Foglia	43.47	12.30	8
sca Damnoniorum,			
Exeter	50.43	3.32 w	5
sca (Silurum), *Caer-*			
leon	51.37	2.57 w	20
schälis, *Ilchester*	51.0	2.40 w	5
scinn, r. at *Ras Benja-*			
wad	30.50	18.10	23
sinisca, *Aschbach*	48.5	11.55	25
sionda	36.57	30.22	20
sis F., *Tscholoki*	41.54	41.50	22
sium	29.23	31.15	24
sium M	21.10	36.30	3
smarus			1
smēnus F	38.20	23.19	16
somantus, or Hop-			
lias, F	38.22	22.54	16
ssa, *Lissa*	43.4	16.10	14
sslcus S., *G. of Scan-*			
deroon	36.40	35.50	20
ssus ?	36.56	36. 8	20
ster (or Danubius) F.,			
Donau, or *Danube*	44.0	26.20	14
sthmus, *Isthmus of Co-*			
rinth	37.57	23.0	18
sthmus (Doris)	36.47	28.5	19
stŏne M.?	39.44	19.50	15
STRIA, or HISTRIA,			
Istria	45.15	14.0	8
stron	35.8	25.44	19
stropŏlis, *Kurgaliuk* ...	44.25	28.48	14
stros I., *Yali*	36.40	27.10	19
surium, *Aldborough*	54.6	1.22 w	5
sus ?	38.27	23.28	16
tabhyrium, or Ataby-			
rium (Mt. Tabor),			
Jebel et-Toor	32.42	35.25	21
TALIA, *Italy*	43.0	12.0	2
tallca, *Santiponce*	37.29	5.51 w	7
tänum Pr.? *C. Sala-*			
mon, or *Salmone*	35.10	26.19	19
tänus, *Itagnia*	35.8	26.16	19
thäca I., *Ithaca*	38.25	20.40	18
thŏme, *Fanari*	39.24	21.27	15
thoria, *St. Elias*	38.30	21.16	18
tium Prom., *C. Gris*			
Nez	50.52	1.35	6
tius Portus, *Wissant* ...	50.53	1.40	6
ton, or Itŏnus	39.8	22.41	15
tüce, or Utica, *Bou-*			
shater	37.9	10.2	23
tünn Aest., *Solway*			
Firth	54.55	3.25 w	5
TURAEA, *El-Jeidoor*	33.10	36.0	21
ülis, *Zea*	37.38	24.21	19
VERNIA, or IERNE			
vin. or Juvia, F.,			
Jubia	43.32	8.5 w	7
xia, *Lanathi*	36.1	27.58	19

J.

NAMES.	LAT.	LONG.	MAP.
nbadii, or Sabadii, I?			
Java, &c.	7.0	110.0	2
nbbok F., *Nahr Zurka*	32.14	35.50	21
hesh-gilead? *In Wady*			
Yabes	32.29	35.44	21
icca, *Jaca*	42.31	0.31 w	7
Jaccetáni	42.30	0.30 w	7
imnia, *Yebna*	31.51	34.45	21

NAMES.	LAT.	LONG.	MAP.
Jamno, or Jamna, *Ciu-*			
dadela	39°.59′	3°.53′	7
Japhia, *Yafa*	32.41	35.18	21
Jarmuth, *Yarmook*	31.42	34.58	21
Jasonium Pr., *C. Jason*	41.7	37.39	20
Jattir, *Atteer*	31.21	35.5	21
Jaxartes F., *Sir,* or			
Sihoon	44.0	68.25	3
Jazer, *n. Ain Hazeir*	32.3	35.46	21
Jenysus, *Khan Yunas* ...	31.18	34.18	24
Jericho (Hierīcus), *n.*			
Er-Riha	31.51	35.28	21
Jerusalem, *El-Koods* ...	31.47	35.14	21
Jezreel (Esdraelon),			
Zereen	32.34	35.21	21
Jonnaria	44.7	16.25	14
Joppa, *Jaffa*	32.3	34.45	21
Jordan F., *Nahr el-*			
Kebir	32.10	35.36	21
Jordan, Plain of (Aulon,			
or Magnus Campus),			
El-Ghor	32.20	35.35	21
Jotapäta, *Jefât*	32.51	35.17	21
Jovia, *Apathia*	46.16	16.30	14
Jovis Urii Templum....	41.9	29.10	20
Jovisura, *Eggenfelden* ...	48.24	12.47	14
JUDAEA	31.40	35.0	21
Julia, *Tschai*	38.38	31.5	20
Julia Augusta (for. Ae-			
mŏna), *Laybach*	46.4	14.31	14
Julia Constantia, or			
Zilis, *Arzilla*	35.29	6.1 w	23
Julia Fidentia, *Borgo*			
S. Donino	44.53	10.6	8
Julia Gemella (Acci),			
Guadix el-Viejo	37.22	3.19 w	7
Julia Gordus, *Gordis* ...	38.55	28.28	20
Julia Joza, aft. Trans-			
ducta, *Tarifa*	36.0	5.37 w	7
Julia Libўca? *Puig-*			
cerda	42.26	1.56	7
Julia Myrtĭlis, *Mertola*	37.40	7.28 w	7
Juliacum, *Juliers*	50.56	6.21	6
Julias (Bethsaida), *Et-*			
Tell	32.58	35.40	21
Juliobŏna, *Lillebonne* ...	49.31	0.31	6
Juliobriga, *Reynosa*	43.0	3.57 w	7
Juliomägus, aft. Ande-			
cavi, *Angers*	47.28	0.33 w	6
Juliopŏlis, *Ibol*	38.10	39.15	20
Juliopŏlis, or Gordium...	40.4	31.35	20
Julium Carnĭcum, *Zu-*			
glio	46.27	13.3	8
Juncaria, *Junquera,*	42.24	2.53	7
Junonia I.? *Palma*	28.45	17.50 w	2
Junōnis Fontes, *Cal-*			
diero	45.23	11.14	8
Junōnis Laciniae Tem-			
plum	39.5	17.11	9
Junōnis Pr., *C. Trafal-*			
gar	36.11	6.1 w	7
Jupiter, Temple of			
(Aegina)?	37.45	23.32	18
Jupiter Palenius, Tem-			
ple of, *Campo di*			
Giove	42.0	14.3	9
Jura (or Jurassus) Mons,			
Mt. Jura	47.0	6.40	6
Justinŏpolis, for. Aegida,			
Capo d'Istria	45.32	13.44	8
Juttah, *Yutta*	31.28	35.9	21
Juvavum, *Salzburg*	47.48	13.4	14
Juvia, or Ivia, F., *Jubia*	43.32	8.5 w	7

K.

NAMES.	LAT.	LONG.	MAP.
Kadesh (in Paran), or			
Kadesh-barnes, *Ain*			
Kudes	30.34	34.28	24
Kadesh (in Zin)? *Ain-*			
el-Weibeh	30.41	35.22	24
Kaloi Limĕnes, *Fair*			
Havens	34.56	24.48	19
Kanah, *Kâna*	33.15	35.18	21

NAMES.	LAT.	LONG.	MAP.
Kanah F., *Nahr el-*			
Areouf	32°.18′	34°.55′	21
Kedesh, *Kedes*	33.9	35.31	21
Kerioth, *El-Kuryetein* ..	31.22	35.11	21
Kersus F., *Merkes Su* ...	36.39	36.11	20
Kidron, or Cedron, F.,			
Wady er-Rahib	31.44	35.20	21
Kir of Moab (Charax),			
Kerak	31.15	35.46	21
Kirjath-arba (Hebron),			
El-Khuleel	31.33	35.9	21
Kirjath-jearim, or Baa-			
lah, *Kuryet el-Enab* ..	31.49	35.7	21
Kishon F., *Nahr Mu-*			
kutta	32.47	35.6	21

L.

NAMES.	LAT.	LONG.	MAP.
*Labeätes	42.0	19.40	14
Labeätis L., *L. of Sku-*			
tari	42.5	19.20	14
Labĭcum, *Colonna*	41.51	12.46	11
Labranda	37.25	27.50	19
Lacedaemon, or Sparta,			
n. Mistra	37.5	22.26	18
*Lacetäni	42.0	1.50	7
Lacēter Pr., *C. Kephala,*			
or *Krokilo Pt.*	36.40	27.0	19
Lachish ?	31.32	34.59	21
Laciacum, *Vöcklamarkt*	48.0	13.51	14
Laciädae?	37.59	23.43	17
Lacinium Prom., *Capo*			
delle Colonne, or *C.*			
Nao	39.5	17.13	9
Lacipea, *Deleitosa*	39.35	5.35 w	7
Lacippo, *Alecippe, n.*			
Casares	36.25	5.18 w	7
Lacmon M., *Metzovo*	39.53	21.30	15
Lacobriga, *Lagos*	37.9	8.38 w	7
Lacobriga, *Villa Laco* ..	42.30	4.34 w	7
LACONIA	37.30	22.40	18
Laconĭcus S., *G. of*			
Kolokythia	36.40	22.40	18
Lacotēne? *Viran Shehr*	38.5	38.9	20
Lacron F., *Lezero*			
Vedra	42.26	8.36 w	7
Lactodŏrum, *Towcester*	52.8	0.59 w	5
Lactura, *Lectoure*	43.56	0.38	6
Lacus Lausonius, *Lau-*			
sanne	46.32	6.38	6
Lacus Prilis, *Lago di*			
Castiglione	42.46	11.0	8
Lade I	37.32	27.14	19
Ladoceia	37.24	22.10	18
Ladon F	37.50	21.32	18
Ladon F., *Rufia*	37.40	21.51	18
Laea, or Aphrodīte, I.,			
Al-Hiera	32.50	22.34	23
Laerta	36.28	32.11	20
*Laevi	45.15	8.50	8
Lagana F., *Lahn*	50.20	8.0	25
Lagania	40.4	32.1	20
Lagaria, *Nocara*	40.6	16.27	9
Lagina, *Lakina*	37.21	28.18	20
Lagūsae Iᵐ?	39.56	26.5	19
Laii	38.21	26.0	19
Laish, or Dan, *Tell el-*			
Kady	33.17	35.38	21
LALASSIS	36.40	32.30	20
*Laletäni	41.40	2.30	7
Lamate?	44.36	17.20	14
Lambasa, *L'erba,* or			
Texout	35.1	6.15	23
Lambrus F., *Lambro*	45.20	9.21	8
Lametia, *S. Eufemia* ...	39.3	16.14	9
Lamētus F., *Lamato*	38.55	16.17	9
Lamia, *Zeitouni*	38.54	22.24	16
Laminium, *Don Sancho*	38.57	3.4 w	7
Lamos, *Lamas*	36.34	34.17	20
LAMŎTIS	36.37	34.0	20
Lampe, or *Lappa*	35.19	24.20	19
Lampeia M., *Olonos*	37.58	21.51	18
Lampsäcus, *Lamsaki* ...	40.20	26.40	19
Lamptra inferior	37.49	23.51	16

NAMES.	LAT.	LONG.	MAP.
Lamptra superior, *La-morika*	37°.52′	23°.52′	16
Lancia? *Castro*	42.38	5.27 w	7
*Langobardi	52.45	11.0	25
Langobriga, *Sobral*	41.3	8.36 w	7
Lanuvium, *Città La-vinia*	41.39	12.43	11
Laodicēa, *Eski Hissar*	37.49	29.9	20
Laodicēa, *Latikiyeh*	35.30	35.47	20
Laodicēa (ad Libanum)? *Jusy*	34.22	36.21	20
Laodicēa Combusta, *Ladik*	38.13	32.39	20
LAODICĒNE	34.10	36.30	20
Lapathus, *n. Rapsani*	39.54	22.29	15
Lapēthus, *r. n. Lapta*	35.21	33.12	20
Laphystium M., *Gra-nitsa*	38.25	22.54	16
Lapidaria, *n. Zillis*	46.38	9.26	8
Lapīthus M., *Smerna*	37.33	21.41	18
Lappa, or Lampe	35.19	24.20	19
Lapurdum? *Bayonne*	43.29	1.30 w	
Laranda, *Karaman*	37.11	33.23	20
Largiana?	47.11	24.0	14
Larīnum, *Larino*	41.48	14.53	9
Larisium M.	36.45	22.34	18
Larissa (Acrop. of Argos)	37.38	22.43	18
Larisssa (Aeolis), *Bu-rundjik*	38.38	27.1	19
Larissa Cremaste, *n. Gardhiki*	38.58	22.50	16
Larissa (Ionia)	38.7	27.39	19
Larissa (Resen?), *Nim-roud*	36.0	43.23	22
Larissa (Syria), *Kalat Seijar*	35.17	36.33	20
Larissa (Thessalia), *Yeni-shehr, or La-rissa*	39.37	22.22	15
Larissus F., *Mana*	38.7	21.25	18
Larius L., *Lago di Como*	46.0	9.17	8
Larnum F., *Tordera*	41.48	2.48	7
Larymna, *r. on Port Larmes*	38.32	23.16	16
Larymna (Upper)	38.31	23.17	16
Las	36.43	22.30	18
Lasea?	34.57	24.48	19
Lasion, *Lala*	37.42	21.43	18
Latēra	43.33	3.54	6
Lathon F.	32.7	20.5	23
*Latini	41.45	12.35	11
LATIUM	41.40	13.0	9
Latmus M.	37.25	27.50	19
Latmus S., *Akis Tchai, or L. Denizli*	37.30	27.30	19
Lato	35.14	25.37	19
*Latobrigi	47.53	8.20	6
Latopōlis, *Esneh*	25.17	32.35	3
Latris L., *Zealand*	55.30	12.0	2
Laumellum, *Lumello*	45.7	8.47	8
Laurentum, *Torre Pa-terno*	41.39	12.23	11
Lauriacum, *Enns*	48.13	14.30	14
Laurium M., *St. Elias*	37.42	23.59	18
Lauron	39.8	0.8 w	7
Laus	39.43	15.51	9
Laus F., *Lao*	39.45	15.54	9
Laus, or Laus Pompeia, *Lodi Vecchia*	45.18	9.25	8
Laus S., *G. of Poli-castro*	39.50	15.35	9
Lautūlae	41.17	13.17	11
Lavatrae, *Bowes*	54.32	2.0 w	5
Lavinium, *Pratica*	41.39	12.29	11
Lavinius F., *Lavino*	44.35	11.15	8
Lavisco, *Lannen, n. Yenne*	45.43	5.45	6
Lebadeia, *Livadhia*	38.26	22.52	16
Lebēdos	38.5	26.59	19
Lebēna	34.55	24.54	19
Lebinthos I., *Levitha*	37.0	26.30	19
Lebonah, *El-Lubbân*	32.5	35.13	21

NAMES.	LAT.	LONG.	MAP.
Lechaeum	37.56′	22°.53′	18
Lectum Pr., *C. Baba*	39.29	26.4	19
Ledon?	38.37	22.38	16
Ledus F., *Les*	43.40	3.52	6
*Legae	42.30	46.0	22
Legedia, *Villebaudon*	48.58	1.9 w	6
Legio (Megiddo), *El-Lejjoon*	32.35	35.12	21
Legio Septīma Gemīna, *Leon*	42.30	5.35 w	7
Legiolium, *Castleford*	53.43	1.20 w	5
Leibethrium M., *Za-gara*	38.20	22.57	16
Leipsydrium, *Monastery of St. Nicholas*	38.8	23.15	16
Lelantus F.	38.27	23.45	15
Lemannonius S., *Loch Fyne*	56.0	5.25 w	5
Lemannus Lacus, *L. of Geneva, or Leman*	46.27	6.30	8
Lemnos I., *Lemno, or Stalimeni*	39.55	25.10	19
Lemovīces, or Augusto-ritum, *Limoges*	45.50	1.16	6
*Lemovices	45.50	1.0	6
*Lemovii	54.0	16.0	25
Lentulae, *Virje*	46.4	17.0	14
Leon	37.7	15.12	13
Leon, or Leontes, F., *Nahr Kasimiyeh, or Liettani*	33.51	35.30	21
Leon Pr., *C. Matala*	34.55	24.44	19
Leontarne	38.19	23.4	16
Leontīni, *Lentini*	37.16	14.59	12
Leontium, *Aghios Ianni*	38.7	21.55	18
Leontopōlis?	30.35	31.21	24
Lepethymnus M.	39.20	26.17	19
Lepīnus M., *Monte Lupone*	41.35	13.5	11
*Lepontii	46.30	8.40	8
Lepreum, *n. Strovitsa*	37.27	21.44	18
Lepsia I., *Lipso*	37.18	26.46	19
Lepte, or Syrias Prom., *C. Indjeh*	42.7	34.59	20
Leptis Magna (or Nea-pōlis), *Lebdah*	32.38	14.13	23
Leptis Minor, *r. n. Lamta*	35.40	10.52	23
Lerina I., *St. Honorat (I. de Lerins)*	43.31	7.3	8
Lerna, *Myli*	37.33	22.43	18
Leron I., *St. Marguerite (I. de Lerins)*	43.32	7.3	8
Leros I., *Lero*	37.10	26.50	19
Lesbos I., *Mityleni*	39.15	26.15	19
Lessa, *Ligurio*	37.37	23.3	18
Lesūra M., *La Lozère*	44.24	3.52	6
Letandros I., *Denusa*	37.7	25.50	19
Lethaeus Fl., *Deresi, or Trikkalino*	39.33	21.54	15
Letōa I	38.8	20.25	18
Letōa I., *Paximadi*	35.0	24.34	19
Letopōlis?	29.59	30.57	24
Letrini, *Aiannis*	37.41	21.23	18
Letrini Lacus	37.39	21.24	18
Leuca, *S. Maria di Leuca*	39.48	18.22	9
Leucadia (or Leucas) I., *Santa Maura*	38.45	20.40	15
Leucae, *Lefkes*	38.34	26.52	19
Leucae Campi	36.45	22.52	18
Leucarum, *Lluchwr, or Lloughor*	51.40	4.4 w	5
Leucas, *Kaligoni, n. Amarikhi*	38.48	20.42	15
Leucas, or Leucadia, I., *Santa Maura*	38.45	20.40	15
Leucas			1
Leucasia F.	37.18	21.56	18
Leucasium	37.50	22.10	18
Leucaspis Portus, *Mak-taarai*	30.59	28.48	23
Leucāte Pr., *C. Ducato*	38.33	20.33	15

NAMES.	LAT.	LONG.	MAP
Leuce Acte, *Ras el-Kanais*	31°.16′	27°.51′	21
Leuce Come?	25.10	37.15	3
Leuce I.? *Fort Suda*	35.29	24.9	19
Leuce I., *Lassa, or Elasa*	35.15	26.20	19
Leuce, or Achillis, I., *Oulan Adassi, Fido-nisi, or Serpents' I.*	45.15	30.15	14
Lenceris, *Lovere*	45.50	10.6	5
*Leuci	48.30	8.0	6
Leuciāna, *Madronera*	39.45	5.15 w	
Leucimne Pr., *Alefkimo Point*	39.27	20.4	15
Leuconum, *n. Verpolje*	45.10	18.25	14
Leucopētra (or Petra) Pr., *Capo dell'Armi*	37.57	15.40	9
Leucos Portus, *E'Shoona*	25.37	34.40	3
Leucosia, *Lefkosia*	35.10	33.23	20
Leucosia I., *Licosa*	40.14	14.53	9
Leuctra	38.16	23.11	16
Leuctra, *Leftro*	36.51	22.16	15
Leuctrum	37.20	22.5	18
Leusaba?	44.25	17.20	14
*Levaci	51.7	3.30	6
*Lexovii	49.14	0.10	6
Libānus Mons, *Jebel Libnān, &c.*	34.10	36.0	20
Libarna, *Arquata*	44.40	8.52	8
Libero, *Viverone*	45.26	8.2	8
Libia	42.30	3.4 w	7
*Libicii, or Libui	45.16	8.0	8
Libisosia, or Libisōna, *Lesusa*	39.8	2.43 w	7
Libnah?	31.35	35.2	21
*Libui, or Libicii	45.16	8.0	8
LIBURNIA	45.0	15.0	14
Libya Palus? *L. Tchad*	14.0	16.0	
*Libyphoenicis			1
Libyssa	40.46	29.35	20
Lichādes I., *Lithada*	38.48	22.48	16
Licias F., *Lech*	48.30	10.54	25
Lida M.	37.7	28.0	19
Liger, or Ligēris, F., *Loire*	47.30	1.10	6
LIGURIA	44.33	9.0	8
Ligustīcum Mare	43.30	8.0	8
Lilaea, *Paleokastro*	38.37	22.31	16
Lilybaeum, *Marsala*	37.49	12.25	12
Lilybaeum Prom., *C. Boeo*	37.48	12.24	12
Limenia	35.6	32.58	20
Limia, *Ponte da Lima*	41.45	8.32 w	7
Limia F., *Lima*	41.46	8.30 w	7
Limnae? *Nisi*	37.3	22.2	15
Limnaea, *Kortikhi*	39.30	21.54	15
Limnaea, *n. Kervasara*	38.51	21.10	15
Limnias, *Lamloudeh*	32.44	22.14	23
Limōnum, aft. Pictāvi, *Poitiers*	46.35	0.20	6
Limyra	36.24	30.14	20
Lindum, *Ardoch*	56.27	3.51 w	5
Lindum, *Lincoln*	53.14	0.32	5
Lindus, *Lindo*	36.5	28.7	19
*Lingōnes	47.55	5.0	6
*Lingōnes	44.45	11.30	8
Lipāra I. and Town, *Lipari*	38.28	14.58	9
Liparaeae, Aeoliae, or Vulcaniae, Iᵃᵉ., *Lipari Islands*	38.30	15.0	9
Lipaxus	40.15	23.13	15
Liquentia F., *Livensa*	46.0	12.40	8
Liria, or Edeta, *Liria*	39.37	0.39 w	7
Liris F., *Garigliano*	41.15	13.45	9
Lisae	40.19	23.3	15
Lisae, *Gabra-khan*	42.11	24.5	14
Lissus, *Alessio*	41.46	19.35	14
Lissus, *Selino Kastelli*	35.14	23.41	19
Lissus F.	41.0	55.42	19
Lissus F., *Rettore*	37.16	14.50	12
Lista	42.11	13.13	11
Litana Silva	44.33	10.15	8

NAMES.	LAT.	LONG.	MAP.
Litanobriga, *Pont S. Maxence*	49°.18'	2°.31'	6
Liternum, *Patria*	40.56	14.1	13
Litubium (Ritubium ?), *Retorbio*	44.56	9.5	8
Livias (Beth-haran), *Er-Rameh*	31.49	35.39	21
Lixus, *Al-Araish*	35.13	6.7 w	23
Lixus F., *Wady al-Khos*	35.4	6.0 w	23
Locanus F.? *Locano*	38.21	16.20	9
Locaricum? *Calatafimi*	37.55	12.50	12
Locra F., *Talavo*	41.46	8.55	9
Locri Epicnemidii	38.42	22.45	16
Locri Epizephyrii	38.15	16.15	9
Locri Opuntii	38.35	23.5	16
Locri Ozolae	38.30	22.15	15
LOCRIS	38.40	23.0	16
Logia F., *Mouth of R. Lagan*	54.35	5.56 w	5
Londinium, aft. Augusta, *London*	51.31	0.6 w	5
Longanus F., *F. dell' Aranci*	38.5	15.10	12
Longaticum, *Lohitsch*	45.55	14.13	8
Longianum, *Lugnano*	41.47	12.54	11
Longones, *Ozieri*	40.35	9.0	9
Lorium, *Lorio*	41.54	12.15	11
Loryma	36.34	28.5	19
Losa, *Bois de Licogne*	44.25	1.0 w	6
Lotophagi			1
Lotophagitis, or Meninx, I. (aft. Girba), *Jerbah*	33.45	11.0	23
Loucopibia? *Wigton*	54.53	4.27 w	5
Luca, *Lucca*	43.51	10.30	8
LUCANIA	40.16	16.0	9
Lucentum, *Alicante*	38.22	0.27 w	7
Luceria, *Lucera*	41.30	15.20	9
Lucretilis M., *Monte Genaro*	42.5	12.50	11
Lucrinus L., *Lago Lucrino*	40.50	14.5	13
Lucus Angitiae, *Luco*	41.57	13.29	11
Lucus Asturum (Ovetum?), *Oviedo*	43.22	5.57 w	7
Lucus Augusti, *Luc-en-Diois*	44.38	5.26	6
Lucus Augusti, *Lugo*	43.1	7.36 w	7
Lucus et Oraculum Fauni, *Solfatara*	41.42	12.32	11
Lucus Feroniae, *Pietra Santa*	43.57	10.14	8
Lucus Feroniae, or Feronia, *Felonica*	42.16	12.31	11
Lucus Jovis Indigetis	41.37	12.28	11
Luentinum, *Llanioisaf, n. Tregaron*	52.11	3.59 w	5
LUGDUNENSIS	48.0	0.0	4
Lugdunum, *Leyden*	52.9	4.30	6
Lugdunum, *Lyons*	45.46	4.50	6
Lugdunum, aft. Convenae, *St. Bertrand de Comminges*	43.0	0.38	6
Luguido, *Monti*	40.48	9.18	9
Luguvallium, *Carlisle*	54.54	2.56 w	5
Luna, *Luni*	44.4	10.1	8
Lunae Portus, *Golfo di Spezzia*	44.4	9.53	8
Lunarium Pr., *C. Carvoeiro*	39.21	9.25 w	7
Lupiae, *Lecce*	40.22	18.11	9
Luppia F., *Lippe*	51.40	7.0	25
Lusi, *Sudhena*	37.59	22.9	18
Lusitani	40.0	8.20 w	7
LUSITANIA	39.0	8.0 w	7
Lussunum, *Foldvar*	46.49	18.57	14
Lutetia, *Paris*	48.52	2.20	6
Luteva, or Forum Neronis, *Lodève*	43.45	3.19	6
Luxia F., *Odiel*	37.25	6.48 w	7
Lycabettus M. (or Anchesmus), *Hill of St. George*	37.59	23.45	17

NAMES.	LAT.	LONG.	MAP.
Lycaeus M., *Dhiaforti*	37°.28'	22°.0'	18
LYCAONIA	38.0	33.0	20
Lycastus?	35.11	25.0	19
Lycastus F., *Merd Irmak*	41.7	36.0	20
Lychnidus	41.2	20.52	14
Lychnitis L., *Goukcha, or Sevan*	40.20	45.20	22
Lychnitis L., *L. of Ochrida*	41.5	20.48	14
LYCIA	36.25	30.0	20
Lycopolis, *Siout*	27.10	31.10	3
Lycoreia M., *Liakhoura*	38.31	22.37	16
Lycosura	37.23	22.3	18
Lyctus, or Lyttus	35.10	25.19	19
Lycuria? *Lykuria*	37.51	22.13	18
Lycus, or Zabatus, F., *Great Zab*	36.10	43.40	22
Lycus F. (Bithynia), *Kilij Su*	41.17	31.30	20
Lycus F. (Harpasus of Xenophon?), *Joruk Su*	40.26	41.0	20
Lycus F. (Pontus), *Germeili Tchai*	40.17	37.30	20
Lycus F. (Syria), *Nahr el-Kelb*	33.43	35.40	21
Lydda, aft. Diospolis, *Lood*	31.56	34.55	21
LYDIA	38.30	28.0	19
Lydias F., *Vistritza*	40.40	22.20	15
*Lygii	51.40	19.0	25
LYNCESTIS	40.45	21.25	15
Lyrcea, *Skala*	37.42	22.39	18
Lyrceium M	37.45	22.30	18
Lyrnatea	36.45	30.36	20
Lyrnessus	39.32	27.12	19
Lysa, *r. in Wady Lusan*	30.24	34.27	24
Lysias? *Khosru Pasha Khan*	39.10	30.56	20
Lysimachi~a, *Examili*	40.35	26.54	19
Lysimachia, Conope, or Hyria, L., *Zygos, or Angelokastro*	38.34	21.23	15
Lystra? *Bin-birkilissa*	37.25	33.25	20

M.

NAMES.	LAT.	LONG.	MAP.
Maarsares F.?	32.10	44.30	22
Macaras F. (Bagradas), *Mejerdah*	36.22	9.0	23
Macareae?	37.24	22.5	18
MACEDONIA	41.0	22.0	14
Macella	37.57	13.16	12
Macestus F., *Suserlu Tchai*	39.30	28.4	20
Maceta Pr., *Ras Mussendom*	26.22	56.30	3
Machaerus?	31.43	35.45	21
Macistus, *Mofkitza*	37.27	21.45	18
Macomada?	31.15	16.18	23
Macomada, or Macomades, *Sidi Maharess*	34.31	10.21	23
Macoraba, *Mecca*	21.25	40.10	3
Macra F., *Magra*	44.15	10.0	8
Macri Campi	44.37	10.30	8
Macris, Cranae, or Helene, I., *Makronisi*	37.41	24.7	19
Macron Teichos	41.12	28.18	14
*Macrones	40.46	40.10	20
Mactorium, *Butera*	37.11	14.11	12
Macynia	38.21	21.43	18
Madaura (Admedera)? *Ayedrah*	35.30	8.27	23
Madian, *n. Mukna*	28.23	34.46	24
Madrenae, *Muderli*	40.28	31.27	20
Madytus, *Maitos*	40.11	26.21	19
Maeander F., *Mendere Su*	37.46	28.0	20
Maenalus M	37.34	22.18	18
Maenoba, *Velez Malaga*	36.47	4.9 w	7
Maenoba F., *Velez*	37.0	4.20 w	7
MAEONIA	38.45	29.20	20

NAMES.	LAT.	LONG.	MAP.
Maeonia, *Henneh*	38°.34'	28°.37'	19
Maeotis Palus, *Sea of Azoe*	46.0	37.0	2
MAESOLIA	17.0	80.0	2
Maesolia, *Masulipatam*	16.10	81.12	2
Maesolus F., *Kistna, or Krishna*	16.10	78.0	2
Magalassus, *Scharkiela*	39.15	36.25	20
Magdala, *El-Mejdel*	32.51	35.31	21
Magdolon	30.52	32.18	24
*Magelli	44.0	11.20	8
Magetobriga? *Broye, or Moigte-Broye*	47.19	5.30	6
Magiovintum, *Fenny Stratford*	52.0	0.43 w	5
Magnae, *Carvorran*	54.59	2.31 w	5
Magnae, *Kentchester*	52.5	2.48 w	5
Magnana, *Tchewislik*	40.49	39.37	20
MAGNESIA	39.28	23.0	15
Magnesia, *Manisa*	38.36	27.26	19
Magnesia (ad Maeandrum), *Aineh Basar*	37.49	27.31	19
Magnum, Externum, or Atlanticum Mare, *Atlantic Ocean*	40.0	20.0 w	2
Magnum Prom., *C. Romania*	1.23	104.18	2
Magnum Prom., *C. Roca*	38.45	9.30 w	7
Magnus Campus, or Aulon (Plain of Jordan), *El-Ghor*	32.20	35.35	21
Magnus Portus? *Bay of Ferrol*	43.25	8.20 w	7
Magnus S.? *China Sea*	10.0	112.0	2
Magnus S., *G. of Guinea*	0.0	0.0	2
Mago, *Port Mahon*	39.53	4.20	7
Maguliānus F	42.0	12.40	11
Magydus, *n. Laara*	36.50	30.50	20
Mahanaim?	32.23	35.50	21
Makkedah?	31.36	35.3	21
Malaca, *Malaga*	36.45	4.25 w	7
Malaca F	36.48	4.21 w	7
Malana? *Ras Malan*	25.20	65.10	3
Malanga? *Mahabalipoor*	12.37	80.15	2
Malao, *Berberah*	10.28	45.0	2
Malatha, *El-Milh*	31.16	35.5	21
Malceca? *Palma*	38.28	8.27 w	7
Malea	37.20	22.11	18
Malea Pr., *C. Malea*	36.26	23.12	18
Malea Pr. (Lesbos), *C. Zeitin*	39.1	26.37	19
Maliacus S., *G. of Zeitouni*	38.50	22.30	16
MALIS	38.47	22.23	16
*Malli	30.15	71.30	3
Malliae?	38.16	15.50	9
Malliana, *Miliana*	36.19	2.19	23
Malloea, *r. n. Mologhusta*	39.45	22.0	15
Mallus	36.35	35.22	20
Maloitas F	37.40	22.11	18
Malthace I., *Samotraki*	39.46	19.28	15
Malva, Mulucha, or Molochath, F., *Mulwia*	34.0	2.51 w	23
Mamertium, *Oppido*	38.18	16.2	9
Mancunium, *Manchester*	53.29	2.15 w	5
Mandela, *Bardella*	42.2	12.56	11
*Mandubii	47.27	4.30	6
Manduessedum, *Mancester, n. Atherstone*	52.34	1.31 w	5
Manduria, *Manduria*	40.23	17.39	9
*Manini	52.40	16.45	25
Manliana? *n. Fullonica*	42.57	10.48	8
Mantala, *n. St. Pierre d'Albigny*	45.34	6.8	6
Manthurium, *n. Kapareli*	37.25	22.23	18
Mantiane L. (Spauta?), *L. Urumiyah*	37.30	45.30	22
Mantineia, *Paleopoli*	37.37	22.24	18
Mantinorum Oppidum, *Bastia*	42.42	9.27	9

NAMES.	LAT.	LONG.	MAP.
Mantua, Mantua	45°.9'	10°.49'	8
Maon, Ma'in	31.25	35.11	21
Maracanda, Samarcand	39.56	66.55	3
Marah? Ain Hawarah	29.23	32.57	24
Marandara	39.11	36.9	20
Marātha	37.32	21.58	18
Marathesium, Skala Nuova	37.52	27.17	19
Marāthon, Vrana	38.7	23.57	16
Marāthon, Plain of	38.13	23.58	16
Marāthus, n. Ain el-Hya	34.48	35.58	20
Marāthus, Sidhiro-Kaf-khio	38.22	22.42	16
Marcelliāna, La Sala	40.23	15.35	9
Marcianopōlis?	43.15	27.29	14
Marcina, Vietri	40.39	14.43	9
Marcomagus, Marmagen	50.34	6.32	6
*Marcomanni, for. Boii	49.30	14.30	25
*Mardi	36.20	51.0	3
Mare Aegaeum, Archipelago	38.0	25.30	19
Mare Atlanticum, or Externum, Atlantic Ocean	40.0	20.0 w	2
Mare Azanium, or S. Barbaricus	0.0	50.0	2
Mare Carpathium	36.0	27.0	19
Mare Caspium (or Hyrcanum), Caspian Sea	42.0	50.0	2
Mare Creticum	36.0	25.0	19
Mare Erythraeum, Indian Ocean	15.0	60.0	2
Mare Germanicum, or Oceanus Germanicus, German Ocean	55.0	5.0	2
Mare Hadriaticum, or Superum, Adriatic Sea	44.0	14.0	8
Mare Internum, Mediterranean Sea	35.0	20.0	2
Mare Myrtōum	37.20	24.0	19
Mare Pigrum (Oceānus Septentrionālis)	66.30	5.0	2
Mare Suevicum, Baltic Sea	56.0	18.0	2
Mare Thracium	40.0	25.0	19
Mare Tyrrbēnum, or Infērum	40.0	14.0	9
Marēa, or Palaemaria, El-Rasheat	30.56	30.3	24
Mareōtis L.	31.10	30.0	24
Maresba (Marissa)	31.35	34.55	21
Margăna? Pyrgo	37.40	21.27	18
MARGIĀNA	38.0	62.0	3
Margidūnum, n. East Bridgeford	52.58	0.58 w	5
Margus	44.40	21.8	14
Margus F., Moorghaub	37.0	62.25	3
Margus F., Morava	44.0	21.15	14
Mariaba, Mareb	15.45	45.40	3
Mariāna, Alcubillas	38.58	3.32 w	7
*Mariandȳni	41.0	31.0	20
Mariānae Fossae, Fos les Martigues	43.26	4.57	6
Mariānum?	41.35	8.48	9
Mariānum, Marano	45.45	13.10	8
Mariānus M., Sierra Morena	38.20	5.0 w	7
Maride, Mardin	37.20	40.38	22
Maridūnum (or Muridūnum), Caermarthen	51.51	4.19 w	5
Marinianae	45.46	18.0	14
Marissa (Mareshah)	31.35	34.55	21
Marisus F., Maros	46.4	22.0	14
Maritima, or Hiēra, I., Maretimo	38.0	12.1	12
Marius, Kato Mari	37.1	22.51	18
Marmăra? r. n. Tchandeer	36.47	30.30	20
MARMARĬCA	31.30	24.0	23
*Marmaridae			1
Marmarium, Marmari	38.4	24.18	15
Marōnēa, Marrah	35.41	36.43	20

NAMES.	LAT.	LONG.	MAP.
Maronēa, Campo Marano	41°.50'	14°.36'	9
Maronēa, Marona	40.53	25.30	19
Marpessa, Mt. Elias	37.3	25.10	19
Marrubium, or Marruvium, S. Benedetto	41.59	13.36	11
*Marrucini	42.15	14.10	9
*Marsi	41.54	13.30	11
*Marsi	52.10	7.40	25
*Marsigni	51.0	15.30	25
Marsȳas F., Tschinar Tchai	37.36	28.0	19
Marta F., Marta	42.20	11.50	8
Marthula, Vitzeh	41.16	41.18	20
Martia (Pons Nartias)? Monteceda	42.58	7.46 w	7
Martīlus S., G. of Kisamos	35.35	23.50	19
Martyropōlis, Meiafarakin	38.11	40.47	22
Marus F., March, or Morava	48.30	17.0	25
Masada, Sebbeh	31.20	35.25	21
Mascas F.	34.25	41.5	22
Masciacum, Schwaz	47.21	11.44	25
Masclianae, Karansebes	45.24	22.17	14
*Massaesyli			1
Mases? St. Dimitrias	37.25	23.9	18
Masius M., Jebel Toor, &c.	37.34	41.0	22
Massa Veternensis, Massa	43.2	10.53	8
*Massaesylii	36.0	1.0	23
Massaga? Hushtnagar	34.17	71.46	3
Massagētae	43.0	65.0	3
Massicus Mons, Mt. Massico	41.10	13.55	9
Massiēnus S.	37.20	1.30 w	7
Massilia, Marseilles	43.17	5.23	6
Mastaura, Mastavro	37.59	28.22	19
Mastusia Prom., C. Helles	40.3	26.11	19
Matalia	34.58	24.44	19
Mateola, Matera	40.39	16.38	9
Maternum, Farnese	42.30	11.41	8
Maternum, Maderno	45.38	10.37	8
Mathia (or Temathia) M., Lykodhimo	36.55	21.51	18
MATIĒNE	35.0	47.0	22
Matilica, Matelica	43.15	13.1	8
Matīnum Littus, Matinata	41.43	16.5	9
Matisco, Macon	46.19	4.50	6
Matium	35.23	25.5	19
Matrīnum	42.31	14.11	8
Matrīnus F., Piomba	42.31	14.8	8
Matrōna F., Marne	49.0	3.45	6
*Mattiaci	50.15	8.20	25
Mattiacum? Marburg	50.49	8.47	25
Mattium? Metz	51.12	9.20	25
Matusarum, Ponte do Soro	39.15	7.56 w	7
*Matycetae			1
MAURITANIA CAESARIENSIS	36.0	3.0	23
MAURITANIA TINGITĀNA	33.0	6.0 w	23
*Maureusii			1
Maximianopōlis	32.34	35.10	21
Maxula, Aradis	36.45	10.14	23
Mazăca, aft. Caesarēa, Kaisariyeh	38.43	39.15	20
Mazăra, Mesara	38.33	39.8	22
Mazăra, or Mazăras, F., Fiume di Mazzara	37.45	12.37	12
Mazaras F.? Goorkan	37.10	55.0	3
Mazărum, Mazzara	37.40	12.32	12
Mearus F., Mero	43.15	8.13 w	7
Mecyberna, Molivo-pyrgo	40.17	23.26	15
Medeba, Madeba	31.43	35.54	21
Medeon, Dhesfina	38.24	22.34	16
Medeon, n. Katuna	38.47	21.10	15
MEDIA	35.40	48.30	22

NAMES.	LAT.	LONG.	MAP.
MEDIA MINOR, or ATROPATĒNE	37°.0'	47°.0'	22
Mediae (or Zagri) Pylae, Tak-i-Girrah	34.25	46.20	22
Mediolānum, Chateau-Meillant	46.33	2.12	6
Mediolānum, Gueldres	51.30	6.20	6
Mediolānum, Meylieu	45.38	4.15	6
Mediolānum, Milan	45.28	9.12	8
Mediolānum, aft. Eburovices, Evreux	49.1	1.9	6
Mediolānum, aft. Santōnes, Saintes	45.45	0.36 w	6
Mediolānum (Britannia, It. II.), Clawdd Goch	52.46	3.6 w	5
Mediolānum (Britannia, It. X.), Chesterton	53.3	2.13 w	5
*Mediomatrici	49.0	7.0	6
Medma?	38.30	15.59	9
*Medoaci	45.56	11.35	8
Meduacus Major F., Brenta	45.40	11.42	8
Meduacus Minor F., Bacchiglione	45.40	11.34	8
Meduana F.? Mayenne	47.50	0.43 w	6
*Medulli	45.0	6.10	6
*Medulli	45.20	1.0 w	6
Medullia, n. Monte Verde	42.3	12.48	11
Medus F., Shamier, or Palwar	30.45	53.10	3
Megalassus	39.53	38.6	20
Megalopōlis	37.25	22.9	18
Meganītas F.	38.13	22.0	18
Megăra, Megara	38.0	23.21	16
Megăra Hyblaea	37.15	15.10	12
MEGĂRIS	38.3	23.35	16
Megarsus Prom., C. Karatash	36.32	35.20	20
Megerthis? Tojourah	32.54	13.19	23
Megiddo (Legio), El-Lejjoon	32.35	35.12	21
Megiste I., Kastelorizo	36.8	29.38	20
Mela F., Mella	45.25	10.8	9
Melaena Pr., C. Kara Bournou	38.40	26.23	19
Melaena Pr., Kara Burun	41.15	29.25	20
Melaenae, Convent of St. Meletius	38.11	23.28	16
Melaeneae, n. Kokora	37.34	21.56	18
*Melanchlaeni			1
Melangeia	37.40	22.27	18
Melania	36.7	33.9	20
Melanthius F., Melet Irmak	40.50	37.57	20
Melantīae I.? Stapodia	37.25	25.35	19
Melas F.	36.15	33.30	20
Melas F., Kara Su	38.50	35.2	20
Melas F., Kavatch	40.40	26.55	19
Melas F., Mavraneria	38.48	22.23	16
Melas F., Mavropotami	38.31	23.0	16
Melas F., Nocito	38.10	15.15	12
Melas F., River of Manavgat	37.0	31.37	20
Melas F., Tochmah Su	38.30	37.40	20
Melas S., G. of Xeros	40.30	26.30	19
*Meldi?	51.10	3.0	6
*Meldi	48.50	3.10	6
Meldia, Kalkali	42.47	23.9	14
Meles F.	38.28	27.12	19
Melibocus M.? Brocken	51.47	10.38	25
Melibocus M.? Melibocus	49.44	8.40	25
Meliboea, Kastri, n. Dhemata	39.34	22.57	15
Melīte L., Trikardho	38.27	21.12	18
Melita I., Malta	35.52	14.25	4
Melita I., Meleda	42.45	17.30	14
Melitaea? Tjeutma	39.6	22.25	15
MELITĒNE	38.20	38.15	24
Melitēne, Malatia	38.27	38.26	24
Mellaria	36.5	4.42 w	7

NAMES.	LAT.	LONG.	MAP.
Iollaria, Hinojosa (de Cordoba)	38°.25'	5°.4' w	7
Iellisurgis, Mellisurgus	40.37	23.12	15
Ielodunum, Melun	48.31	2.40	6
Ielos, Milo	36.42	24.29	19
Ielos I., Milo	36.40	24.30	19
IELOTIS	40.7	20.48	15
Ielphes F., Molpa	40.5	15.7	9
Ielsus F., Narcea	43.17	6.30 w	7
Ielta, Loftcha	43.12	24.49	14
Iemnonis Tumulus	40.18	27.35	19
Iemphis, Metrakenny	29.52	31.15	24
Ienae, Mineo	37.14	14.41	12
Ienapia, Porthmawr, n. St. David's	51.54	5.17 w	5
Ienapia, Wexford	52.21	6.27 w	2
Menapii	51.25	4.30	6
Ienaria I., Melora	43.34	10.12	8
Iende, n. C. Posidhi	39.58	23.22	15
Iendes?	31.4	31.33	24
Iendesian Mouth (of Nile), Dibe Mouth	31.20	31.59	24
Iendiculeia? Alcolea	41.42	0.5	7
Ienelaus Portus	31.54	24.56	23
Ienesthei Portus, Harbor of Cadiz	36.34	6.20 w	7
Ieninx, or Lotophagitis, I. (aft. Girba), Jerbah	33.45	11.0	23
Ienlascus F., Bidassoa	43.15	1.40 w	7
Ienneianae, Bodegraje	45.25	17.12	14
Ienoba F.	37.25	6.5 w	7
Ientosa Bastia, S. Tomé	38.6	3.20 w	7
Ieutonomon S.			1
Ienuthias I., Zanzibar	6.0	39.18	2
Iercurii Pr., C. Bon.	37.5	11.4	23
Iergablum, Conil	36.17	6.4 w	7
Iergana?	37.46	13.31	12
Ierinum, S. Merino	41.54	16.6	9
Ierobrica, or Mirobriga? Santiago de Cacem	38.3	8.44 w	7
Ieroe? El-Bekrauwiyah	16.50	33.42	3
Ieroe I.	16.0	35.0	3
Ierom, Waters of (Samochonitis L.), Bahr el-Houle	33.5	35.38	21
Ierula F., Arosia	44.4	8.0	8
Iesambria	40.51	25.42	19
Iesambria, Bushire	29.0	50.47	3
Iesanites S., Khor Abdullah	29.55	48.15	22
Iese I., Porteros	43.0	6.24	8
Iesembria, Missivri	42.40	27.45	14
IKSENE	33.55	44.0	22
Meslates	46.17	9.7	8
AESOBATENE	33.30	46.45	22
Iesochorion?	40.27	17.27	9
IESOGARA	38.0	23.55	18
IESOLA	37.4	22.0	18
IESOPOTAMIA, Al-Jezireh	36.0	41.0	22
Iespila (Ninus), Nebbi Yunus	36.21	43.11	22
Iessa, Mezapo	36.33	22.23	18
Iessana, Messina	38.11	15.34	12
IESSAPIA, or IAPYGIA	40.30	17.40	9
Iessapia, Mesagne	40.33	17.50	9
Iessapium M., Kiypa	38.26	23.30	16
Iessene	37.10	21.56	18
IESSENIA	37.8	21.50	18
Iesseniacus S. (Asinaeus S.), G. of Kalamata	36.45	22.5	18
Iessogis M., Kestane Dagh, &c.	38.0	28.0	19
Iestriana?	47.10	17.2	14
Iesyla	36.21	43.11	26
Ietagonites (or Metagonium) Pr.	35.15	2.45 w	23
Ietalla, Iglesias	39.19	8.32	9
Ietapa?	38.36	21.31	15
Metapontum, Torre a Mare	40°.21'	16°.46'	9
Metaris Aest., The Wash	53.0	0.20	5
Metaurum, Gioja	38.25	15.56	9
Metaurus F., Marro	38.25	15.56	9
Metaurus F., Metauro	43.50	13.1	8
Metolis?	31.15	30.32	24
Metellinum, Medellin	38.54	5.57 w	7
Methana, or Methone, Megalo Khorio	37.35	23.21	18
Methone, or Mothone, Mothoni	36.49	21.43	18
Methone (Pieria), Eleftero-khori	40.25	22.34	15
Methone (Thessalia)	39.20	23.5	15
Methurides I^m., Revitouza, &c.	37.58	22.24	16
Methydrium, n. Nemnitza	37.38	22.11	18
Methymna	35.30	23.43	19
Methymna, Molivo	39.22	26.11	19
Metropolis (Acarnania), Lygovitzi	38.38	21.14	15
Metropolis (Amphilochia)	38.58	21.11	15
Metropolis (Ionia), Yenikeui	38.5	27.22	19
Metropolis (Phrygia)? Dughan Arslan	39.13	30.30	20
Metropolis (Thessalia), Paleokastro	39.18	21.47	15
Mettis, Metz	49.7	6.10	6
Mevania, Bevagna	42.56	12.38	8
Mevaniola, Galeata	44.0	11.56	8
Miacum, Torre Lodones	40.35	3.55 w	7
Michmash, Mukhmas	31.53	35.17	21
Midaium, Harab Ewren	39.30	31.2	20
Midea	37.36	22.52	18
Mideia	38.25	22.51	16
*Midianites	28.30	34.20	24
Miletopolis, Mualitsch	40.12	28.22	20
Miletopolis L., L. Maniyas	40.10	28.0	20
Miletus, Palatia	37.32	27.18	19
Miletus (Creta), Milata	35.17	25.35	19
Miletus F.	35.16	25.36	19
Milichus F., River of Sykena	38.16	21.44	18
MILYAS	36.50	30.10	20
Milyas, Milli	37.23	30.43	20
Mimas M., Kara Bournou Dagh	38.39	26.30	19
Mina? in Wady Mina	35.42	0.30	23
Minariacum? Merville	50.39	2.37	6
Mincius F., Mincio.?	45.20	10.44	8
Minervae Pr., Campanella Point	40.34	14.20	13
Minervium, Manerbio	45.21	10.10	8
Minio F., Mignone	42.12	11.50	9
Minius, or Baenis, F., Minho	42.0	8.36 w	7
Minnodunum, Moudon	46.41	6.49	6
Minoa (Amorgos), Ta Katapola	36.50	25.53	19
Minoa (Creta)	35.30	24.11	19
Minoa (Creta)? Castel Mirabello	35.11	25.44	19
Minoa (Laconia), Monemvasia	36.41	23.3	18
Minoa (Siphnos)	36.59	24.41	19
Minthe M., Alvena	37.30	21.46	18
Minturnae	41.15	13.45	9
Mirobriga, Puebla de Alcocer	38.43	5.5 w	7
Mirobriga, or Merobrica? Santiago de Cacem	38.3	8.44 w	7
Misenum Pr., C. Miseno	40.47	14.5	13
Misio F., Muscone	43.26	13.30	8
Misus F., Miso	43.36	13.0	8
Mizpeh, Neby Samweel	31.49	35.10	21
Mnemium Pr., Ras Roway, or C. Calmez	21.0	37.12	3
Mnizus, Ajasch	40.2	32.30	20
MOABITIS	31°.15'	35°.56'	21
Mocissus? Mujur	39.8	34.18	20
Modicia, Monza	45.35	9.17	8
Modura, Madura	9.56	78.10	2
Moenus F., Mayn	50.0	9.7	25
Moeris Lacus	29.20	30.55	24
MOESIA (LOWER)	43.0	24.0	14
MOESIA (UPPER)	43.30	21.0	14
Mogetiana?	46.59	17.11	14
Mogontiacum, Mayence, or Mains	50.0	8.17	6
Mogrus F., Supsaa	42.0	42.0	22
Molaria, Bottida	40.24	9.3	9
Molochath, Mulucha, or Malva F., Mulwia	34.0	2.51 w	23
MOLOSSIS	39.45	21.0	15
Molycreia, or Molycreium, n. Roumeli	38.20	21.45	18
Momemphis?	30.56	30.34	24
Mona (of Tacitus), I. of Anglesey	53.20	4.25 w	5
Mona I. (of Caesar), Isle of Man	54.15	4.30 w	5
Monalus F., Fiume di Pollina	37.55	14.11	12
Monaoeda I. (Mona of Caesar), Isle of Man	54.15	4.30 w	5
Monate?	47.11	14.40	14
Monilia, Moneglia	44.14	9.32	8
Mons Brisiacus, New Breisach	48.1	7.31	6
Mons Feretrus, S. Leo.	43.55	12.21	8
Mons Sacer	41.56	12.32	11
Mons Seleucus, Mont Saléon	44.29	5.44	6
Mons Silicis, Monselice	45.14	11.45	8
Mopsucrene, Mezarluk Khan	37.8	34.54	20
Mopsuestia, Missis	36.58	35.38	20
Morbium? Templeborough, n. Rotherham	53.25	1.22 w	5
Morginnum, Moiran	45.20	5.33	6
Moricambe Aest., Morecambe Bay	54.5	3.0 w	5
MORIMENE	39.40	35.10	20
*Morini	50.45	2.9	6
Morius F., River of Mera	38.29	22.48	16
Morunda, Mehrand	38.27	45.40	22
Mosa, Meury	48.3	5.33	6
Mosa F., Maas, or Meuse	50.45	5.40	6
Mosa, or Mosella, F., Moselle	50.0	7.0	6
Mosarna, Passeenoe	25.16	63.25	3
Moscha Portus, Muscat	23.38	58.40	3
Maschici Montes, Katschar Dagh, &c.	40.40	41.0	20
Moschius F., West Morava	43.20	21.0	14
Mosconnum, Mixe	43.57	0.54 w	6
Mosella, or Mosa, F., Moselle	50.0	7.0	6
Mosomagus, Mouzon	49.36	5.5	6
Mostene? Mermereh	38.41	27.58	19
Mosyllum? Bunder Ghasim	11.18	49.17	2
*Mosynoeci	40.50	38.40	20
Mothone, or Methone, Mothoni	36.49	21.43	18
Motya I., Longa.	37.53	12.26	12
Motyca, Modica	36.52	14.45	12
Motycanus F., Scicli	36.45	14.39	12
MOXOENE	38.0	43.0	22
Mucrae, Morcone	41.21	40.38	9
Mugilla? r. n. Ponte della Streghe	41.46	12.36	11
Mulidus, or Munda, F., Mondego	40.10	8.40 w	7
Mulucha, Molochath, or Malva, F., Mulwia	34.0	2.51 w	23
Munda, Monda	36.44	4.53 w	7

NAMES	LAT.	LONG.	MAP.
Mocha, w. Mt. Sinai F., Hindugu	46.14	9.14 w	7
M[illegible]ya Portulegre	20.12	7.15 w	7
M[illegible], Moyet	11.4	47.17	2
M[illegible]yma, Panvaro[illegible]	44.24	21.15	14
M[illegible]a Portus	27.56	22.29	17
M[illegible]a Portus, Mara[illegible]ishi	27.56	22.29	17
M[illegible] M.	44.78	65.8	3
M[illegible], Murnau	20.47	16.6	9
M[illegible] (Turn.A.g?)	42.40	4.0 w	7
M[illegible]a, Brasiles	41.24	15.0	9
M[illegible], Murgu	27.23	16.3	12
M[illegible] Guardina Viejas	36.41	2.52 w	7
M[illegible] (or Mari-[illegible]), Cuormar-khen	51.51	4.19 w	5
M[illegible]num, Konten	50.43	3.4 w	5
Muria V., Mur	47.0	15.30	14
Murmax Rock, Leftari	39.8	23.21	15
Mursa, Esek	45.34	18.42	14
Mursella, Egyed	47.31	17.21	14
Mursia, La Porta	45.25	9.40	8
Mursia, Quesada	39.15	8.16 w	7
Musagura I., Pundura, or N. Antonia	35.85	23.28	19
Muscabanus, Capital of? Aloro	27.38	69.0	3
Muscabanus, Kingdom of	27.30	69.0	3
Museum? Neale Sheikh Hasson	26.21	30.49	24
Musti, Hidi Abd el-Rubbu	36.2	9.11	23
Musua F., Murt	40.10	42.15	22
Mutenum? Wiener Neustadt	47.49	16.15	14
Mutila, Modulinn	44.49	13.56	8
Mutilum, Modigliana	44.10	11.47	8
Mutina, Modena	44.39	10.55	8
Muza, Muschid	13.48	48.15	3
Musiris? Mangalore	12.53	74.54	2
Mycale M., Samsun Dagh	37.40	27.10	19
Mycalessus?	38.25	23.32	16
Mycenae	37.44	22.16	18
Mychus Portus, Kalitza	38.16	22.48	16
Myclaeum	41.0	20.8	26
Myconos	37.27	25.24	19
Myconos I., Mykoni	37.27	25.25	19
Myonnus M.	38.30	21.51	15
Mygdonia	40.45	23.0	15
Mygdonia	37.0	41.0	22
Mydonius F., Jakjak-juh	36.21	41.0	22
Myla F., Marcellino	37.18	15.5	12
Mylae, Agha Limon	36.17	33.51	20
Mylae, Ghemuel	30.43	22.5	15
Mylae, Milazzo	38.13	15.14	12
Mylasa, Melasso	37.19	27.49	19
Myndus, Gumishlu Li-men	37.3	27.16	19
Myonia?	38.38	32.23	16
Myonnesus Chersonnesus	38.3	20.53	19
Myra, Dembra, Abu Nhsar	37.20	33.12	3
Myra, Dembre	36.17	30.3	20
Myrae	30.40	22.48	13
Myrciuus	40.04	23.33	19
Myrlandra, Godfrey's Castle	36.34	36.8	20
Myrina	38.49	27.0	19
Myrina? Anatea	30.32	23.4	19
Myrtilus, w. Myrtum Mare?	37.40	21.22	18
Myrtoum Mare	37.20	24.0	19
Myrtuntium, w. Myrtum Mare?	37.40	21.22	18
Mysacum, w. Pitiolo	38.0	22.23	18
Mysia	30.40	25.0	20
Mysella, Messerino	38.11	16.43	9
Mysiana Messena	30.7	84.84	19
Mysa Parchus	37.38	2.29	19

NAMES	LAT.	LONG.	MAP.
*Nabathaei	30.20	35.50	24
Nabius F. (or Navia?), Navia	43.15	7.0 w	7
Narthea, Bakir	38.58	27.44	19
Nabius F., Cavado	41.32	8.30 w	7
Nagidus	36.7	32.56	20
*Nahanarvali, or Naharvali	52.25	18.30	25
Nain, Nein	32.39	35.22	21
Naissus, Nissa	43.18	22.5	14
Namadus F., Nerbudda	22.5	75.0	2
Namnetes, or Portus Namnetum (for. Condivicnum), Nantes	47.13	1.32 w	6
*Nannetes, or Namnetes	47.25	1.45 w	6
*Nantuates	46.13	7.0	6
Napkris F., Jalomnitza	44.34	27.0	14
Napata? Jebel Berkel	18.30	31.50	3
Napetia, Pizzo	38.47	16.13	9
Napoca (Colonia), Klausenburg	46.45	23.31	14
Nar F., Nera	42.35	12.40	8
Narbo Martius, Narbonne	42.11	3.0	6
NARBONENSIS	44.0	5.0	4
*Narcsii	43.20	17.20	14
*Narisci	49.15	13.0	25
Narnia, Narni	42.31	12.32	8
Naro F., Narento	43.45	18.0	14
Narona, Opus	43.2	17.36	14
Narthacium	39.11	22.26	15
Naryx?	38.38	23 0	16
*Nasamones	30.0	18.0	2
Nasi, n. Dara	37.47	22.12	18
Nasium, Naix	48.38	5.23	6
Natidlum, Bisceglia	41.15	16.31	9
Natiso F., Natisone	46.0	13.23	8
Natron Lakes	30.20	30.20	24
Naucratis?	31.0	30.40	24
Nauldchus	38.15	15.25	12
Nauldchus, on C. Emineh	42.43	27.56	14
*Naunos	46.25	11.0	8
Naupactus, Epakto, or Lepanto	38.24	21.50	18
Nauplia, Nauplia (or Napoli di Romania)	37.34	22.48	18
Nauportus, Ober Laybach	45.59	14.20	14
Naustathmus	41.34	36.9	20
Naustathmus, Marsa el-Halal	32.55	22.11	23
Naustathmus Portus, Porto del Cane	36.57	15.9	12
Nautaca, Kurshee	38.52	66.10	3
Nava F., Nahe	49.40	7.35	6
Navalo, Bivona	38.45	16.10	9
Navalia, Arezzano	44.24	8.40	8
Navia, or Nabius, F., Naria	43.15	7.0 w	7
Navilubio F.? Nalon	43.25	6.5 w	7
Naxos, Naria	37.16	25.24	19
Naxos I., Naria	37.0	25.30	19
Naxos (Sicilia), n. Capo di Schiso	37.47	15.15	12
Naxuana, Nakshevan	39.13	45.20	22
Nazareth, En-Nasirah	32.43	35.19	21
Nasianzus, Vi[illegible]uhehr	38.8	34 18	20
Neae I., Stati	39.30	25.0	19
Neaethus F., Neto	39.12	17.0	9
Neandria? Iuch, or Eneieh	39.47	26.22	19
Neapolis (Apulia), Polignano	41.0	17.13	9
Neapolis (Kolonia), Ka[illegible]	46.56	24.25	14
Neapolis (Ionia), n. [illegible] N[illegible]a	37.49	27.15	19
Neapolis (or Lepsis Magna), Lebida	32.58	14.13	23

NAMES	LAT.	LONG.	MAP
Neapolis (Pallene), Polykromo	40.1'	23.32'	15
Neapolis (or Parthenope), Naples	40.51	14.15	13
Neapolis (Sardinia), S. Maria de Nabui, or Nabui	39.41	8.34	9
Neapolis (Sychar, or Shechem). Nabloos	32.15	35.14	21
Neapolis (Zeugitana), Nabal	36.27	10.46	23
Neapolitanus S., G. of Hammamet	36.10	11.0	23
Nebo, Mount?	31.48	35.43	21
Nebrissa, Nabrissa	36.55	6.2 w	7
Nebrodes M.	37.46	14.0	12
Nechesia, in Wady Nukkaree	24.54	35.0	3
Necho's Canal, in Wady Toomilat	30.32	31.50	24
Neda F., Buzi	37.23	21.44	15
Nedon F., River of Kalamata	37.3	22.8	15
Neleia, n. Agria	39.21	23.1	15
Nemausus, Nismes	43.50	4.21	6
Nemea	37.48	22.43	15
*Nemetes	49.10	8.15	6
Nemetobriga?	42.22	7.44 w	7
Nemetocenna, or Nemetacum, aft. Atrebates, Arras	50.17	2.45	5
Nemossus, aft. Augustonemetum, Clermont	45.47	3.4	6
Nemus, or Nemorensis, L., Lago di Nemi	41.42	12.44	11
Neo-Caesarea (Cabira Diopolis), Niksar	40.35	37.5	22
Neon Teichos	38.39	27.6	17
Neon, aft. Tithorea, Velitza	38.34	22.41	15
Neoptana	26.50	57.0	3
Nepete, Nepi	42.16	12.18	11
Nephelis Prom.	36.9	32.25	20
Neretum, Nardo	40.9	18.4	9
Nericum, Nardo	38.50	20.40	15
Nericos?	60.0	7.0	1
Neris?	37.20	22.38	15
Neritum M., Anoi, or Neritos	38.25	20.40	15
Nerium Pr., C. Finisterre	42.53	9.15 w	7
Neronia, Codigoro	44.50	12.6	8
Nertobriga, Ricla	41.35	1.19 w	7
Nertobriga, or Concordia Julia, Valera la Vieja	36.15	6.29 w	7
Nerulum, Rotondo	39.55	16.2	9
*Nerusi	43.46	7.0	6
Nerva F., Nervion	43.19	3.0 w	7
*Nervii	50.40	3.50	6
Nesactium, Castel Nuovo	44.59	14.2	8
Nessonis L., Karatjair	39.40	22.39	15
Nestane, Luka	37.34	22.28	15
Nestus F., Kara-su	41.30	24.15	14
Nesus, Asso	38.23	20.33	15
Netindava?	44.44	26.20	14
Netum, Noto Vecchio	36.56	14.59	12
Neve, Nowa	32.56	36.1	21
Nias F., Rio Grande	11.40	15.0 w	2
Nicaea (Bactriana), Begram	34.59	69.20	3
Nicaea (Bithynia), Iznik	40.22	29.45	20
Nicaea (Gallia Transalpina), Nice	43.42	7.16	6
Nicaea (India)? n. Jelaipoor	32.40	73.15	3
Nicaea (Locris)	38.47	22.36	16
Nicasia I.? Makari	37.5	25.42	19
Nicephorius M.	35.40	43.50	26
Nicephorium, aft. Callinicum, Rakka	35.56	39.3	22
Nicer F., Neckar	49.27	9.0	25
Nicia F., Enza	44.49	10.27	8

NAMES.	LAT.	LONG.	MAP.
Nicium? *Mit Salameh*..	30°.20'	30°.51'	24
Nicomedia, for. Olbia, *Ismid*	40.48	29.58	20
Nicopolis (Aegyptus)...	31.14	29.59	24
Nicopolis (Epirus), *Paleo-prevesa*	39.0	20.44	15
Nicopolis (Pontus), *Enderes*	39.57	38.24	20
Nicopolis	41.6	29.3	26
Nicopolis (Thracia), *Nikopoli*	41.7	24.38	14
Nicopolis ad Istrum, *Nikup*	43.20	25.33	14
Nicopolis (ad Istrum), *Nikopol*	43.45	24.53	14
Nicotera, *Nicotera*	38.32	15.58	9
Nidum, *Neath*	51.40	3.58 w	5
Nigama, *Negapatam*	10.48	79.54	2
Niger F., *Joliba*	13.0	7.0 w	2
Nigira? *Timbuctoo*	17.22	2.56 w	2
*Nigritae	14.0	5.0	2
Nileus F.?	38.33	24.0	15
Nilopolis	29.7	31.10	24
Nilus F., *Nile*	21.20	31.0	3
Nineveh, *Nebbi Yunus, Kouyunjik*	36.21	43.11	22
Ninus (Mespila of Xenophon), or Nineveh, *Nebbi Yunus*	36.21	43.11	22
Niphates M., *Ali-Dagh, &c.*	38.30	42.0	22
Nisaea, *Nissa*	37.50	58.35	3
Nisaea, r. n. *S. Nikolao*	37.59	23.21	16
Nisaean Plains	34.0	48.0	22
Nisibis, or Antiochia Mygdonia, *Nisibin*	37.1	41.10	22
Nisyros?	35.42	27.4	19
Nisyros I., *Nisero*	36.35	27.12	19
Nithine?	30.49	30.46	24
*Nithones, or Vithones	52.50	13.0	25
*Nitiobriges	44.30	0.30	6
Nivaria, *Mojados*	41.27	4.33 w	7
Nivaria I., *Teneriffe*	28.15	16.30 w	2
Nivernum, *Nevers*	46.58	3.10	6
Noae, *Noara*	37.58	15.6	12
Noega, *Gijon*	43.35	5.44 w	7
Nola, *Nola*	40.55	14.32	13
Nomentum, *Mentana*	42.4	12.39	11
Nonacris, *Solo*	38.1	22.15	18
Norba, *Conversano*	40.57	17.7	9
Norba, *Norma*	41.34	13.3	11
Norba Caesarea, *Alcantara*	39.41	6.43 w	7
Noreia? *Neumarkt*	47.4	14.25	14
Noricum	47.30	14.0	14
Notium Prom., *Misen Head*	51.26	9.50 w	2
Nova, *Dobra*	44.36	21.57	14
Nova Sparsa	35.43	5.53	23
Novae, *Gourabeli*	43.39	25.4	14
Novana, *Novi*	42.59	13.36	8
*Novantae	55.15	4.20 w	5
Novantum Chersonesus	54.50	5.0 w	5
Novantum Pr., *Mull of Galloway*	54.38	4.51 w	5
Novaria, *Novara*	45.27	8.37	8
Novesium, *Neuss*	51.11	6.42	6
Noviodunum, *Karlstadt*	45.30	15.35	14
Noviodunum? *Neuvy sur Baranjon*	47.19	2.10	6
Noviodunum? *Toultcha*	45.10	28.47	14
Noviodunum, aft. Diablintes, *Jubleins*	48.17	0.25 w	6
Noviodunum, aft. Nivernum, *Nevers*	46.58	3.10	6
Noviodunum, aft. Augusta Suessionum, *Soissons*	49.24	3.20	6
Noviodunum, or Colonia Equestris, *Nyon*	46.23	6.15	8
Noviomagus? *Holwood Hill, n. Keston*	51.21	0.3	5
Noviomagus, *Neumagen*	49.53	6.54	6
Noviomagus, *Nimeguen*	51°.50'	5°.51'	6
Noviomagus, *Noyon*	49.35	3.0	6
Novioregum, *Royan*	45.37	1.1 w	6
Novius F., *Nith*	55.20	3.50 w	5
Novum Comum, or Comum, *Como*	45.48	9.6	8
*Nubae	20.0	27.0	2
Nuceria, *Luzzara*	44.57	10.42	8
Nuceria, *Nocera*	40.44	14.38	13
Nuceria, *Nocera*	43.7	12.49	8
Numana, *Umana*	43.31	13.38	8
Numantia, *Garray*	41.46	2.26 w	7
Numicius, or Numicus F., *Torto*	41.38	12.34	11
NUMIDIA	36.0	7.0	23
Numistro, n. *Muro*	40.46	15.20	9
Nura?	40.40	8.18	9
Nura, *Nurri*	39.43	9.14	9
Nura F., *Nura*	44.45	9.38	8
Nura I., or Baleāris Minor, *Minorca*	40.0	4.0	7
Nymbaeum	36.26	23.11	18
Nymphaea I.? (Phintonis?), *Caprera*	41.13	9.27	9
Nymphaeum, *Medua*	41.47	19.31	14
Nymphaeum Pr., *Capo Santo*	40.7	24.22	15
Nymphaeus F., *Ninfa*	41.30	13.0	11
Nymphaeus Portus	40.40	8.6	9
Nymphalum, *Ninfi*	38.26	27.28	19
Nymphius F., *Batman Su*	38.0	40.50	22
Nysa? *Nicetta*	34.10	71.47	3
Nysa, *Sultan-hissar*	37.53	38.9	19
Nysaeum M	38.23	22.49	16

O.

NAMES.	LAT.	LONG.	MAP.
Oanus F., *Frascolari*	36.50	14.32	12
Oaracta I., *Kishm*	26.50	56.0	3
Oaxes F., *Axus*	35.20	24.41	19
Oaxus, or Axus, *Acus*	35.16	24.50	19
Oblimum, *La Batie*	45.38	6.22	8
Ocalea	38.22	23.3	16
Oceanus Britannicus, *English Channel*	50.0	2.0 w	5
Oceanus Cantabrius, *Bay of Biscay*	46.0	5.0 w	2
Oceanus Gaditanus	36.0	15.0 w	2
Oceanus Gallicus	49.0	4.0 w	2
Oceanus Germanicus, or Mare Germanicum, *German Ocean*	55.0	5.0	2
Oceanus Hesperius (Mare Atlanticum, Externum, or Magnum), *Atlantic Ocean*	40.0	20.0 w	2
Oceanus Hibernicus, *Irish Sea*	53.40	5.0 w	5
Oceanus Indicus, *Indian Ocean*	0.0	70.0	2
Oceanus Sarmaticus, or Mare Suevicum, *Baltic Sea*	57.0	20.0	2
Oceanus Septentrionalis (Mare Pigrum)	66.30	5.0	2
Oceanus Vergivius, *Bristol Channel*	51.20	5.0 w	20
Ocellodurum, *Toro*	41.36	5.27 w	7
Ocellum Pr., *Flamborough Head*	54.7	0.4 w	5
Ocelum? *Uxeau, n. Fenestrelles*	45.3	7.2	8
Oche, or Ocha, M., *Okhi*	38.4	24.28	15
Ochus, *Nackiloo*	26.55	53.31	3
Ochus F.?	39.0	56.0	3
Ochus F.? *Kokcha*	37.10	70.0	3
Ocra Mons	45.50	14.30	14
Ocriculum, *Otricoli*	42.27	12.27	11
Ocrinum, or Damnonium Prom., *The Lizard*	49.58	5.11 w	5
Octapitarum Prom., *St. David's Head*	51.54	5.19 w	5
Octodurus, *Martigny*	46°.6'	7°.4'	8
Octogesa? *La Granja*	41.25	0.23	7
Odessus, *Varna*	43.13	27.56	14
*Odomanti	41.12	23.40	14
*Odrysae	42.0	26.0	14
Odysseae Portus and Pr., *P... d'Ulysse*	36.42	15.0	12
Oea? *...amari*	36.22	25 29	19
Oea? n. *Stefani*	38.2	23.38	16
Oea, *Palea-Khora*	37.44	23.29	18
Oea (Augusta Felix), *Tripoli*	32.54	13.11	23
Ocantheia, *Galaxidi*	38.22	22.23	16
Oeaso, or Olarso, *Oyarsun*	43.18	1.52 w	8
Oechalia (Aetolia)?	38.54	21.47	15
Oechalia (Euboea)?	38.27	24.8	15
Oechalia, aft. Carnasium	37.16	22.2	18
Oechardes F.			1
Oenanthia, *Bambora*	43.6	46.31	22
Oeneum?	41.37	20.5	14
Oeneum? *Magula*	38.25	21.56	18
Oeniadae, *Trikardho*	38.25	21.14	18
Oenoanda, *Uludscha*	36.48	29.35	20
Oenoe?	37.37	22.35	18
Oenoe, *Ghysto Kastro*	38.11	23.24	16
Oenoe, *Inoi*	38.9	23.57	16
Oenoe, *Port Skhino*	38.3	23.2	16
Oenoe, *Unieh*	41.8	37.17	20
Oenoe (Icaria)	37.36	26.11	19
Oenotrides Insulae?	40.6	15.6	9
Oenophyta, *Inia*	38.17	23.39	16
Oenus, *Tzitzina*	37.10	22.36	18
Oenus, or Aenus, F., *Inn*	47.30	12.0	25
Oenus F. (Laconia), *Kelefina*	37.6	22.27	18
Oenussae I., *Spalmatori*	38.32	26.15	19
Oenussae I**., *Sapienza and Capri*	36.45	21.45	18
Oeroe F.	38.13	23.12	16
Oescus, *Glava*	43.20	24.19	14
Oescus, or Oius, F., *Isker*	42.55	24.0	14
Oeta M., *Katavothron*	38.48	22.16	15
Oetylus, *Vitylo*	36.43	22.23	18
Oeum, r. n. *Varibopi*	38.9	23.46	16
Oeum Cerameicum?	37.58	23.42	17
Oglasa I., *Monte Christo*	42.20	10.20	8
Ogygia			1
Oisyme	40.49	24.18	19
Oius, or Oescus, F., *Isker*	42.55	24.0	14
Olabus I., *Hadisah*	34.5	42.28	22
Olarso, or Oeaso, *Oyarsun*	43.18	1.52 w	7
Olbasa, *Belenglu*	37.22	30.0	20
Olbia?	36.52	30.45	20
Olbia, aft. Nicomedia, *Ismid*	40.48	29.58	20
Olbia, r. n. *Nicolaef*	46.40	32.1	2
Olbia? *St. Vincent de Carquairanne*	43.6	6.5	6
Olbia, *Terranova*	40.55	9.29	9
Olbianus Portus, *Golfo di Terranova*	40.57	9.35	9
Olbius, or Aroanius, F.	37.57	22.20	18
Olenchites S., *Bay of Storah*	37.10	7.0	23
Olcinium, *Dulcigno*	41.53	19.12	14
Oleastrum, *Coll de Balaguer*	40.59	0.56	7
Olenacum, *Old Carlisle*	54.49	3.10 w	5
Olenus, *Kato Akhaia*	38.8	21.34	18
Olerus, *Castel Messeleri*	35.7	25.48	19
Olgassys M., *Alkas Dagh*	41.6	34.0	20
Oliaros I., *Antiparo*	37.0	25.3	19
Olicana, *Ilkley*	53.55	1.47 w	5
Oligyrtus, *Lafka*	37.50	22.23	18
Olisipo (Felicitas Julia), *Lisbon*	38.42	9.9 w	7

NAMES.	LAT.	LONG.	MAP.
Olives, Mount of, *Jebel Toor*	31°.47'	35°.15'	21
Olizon	39.7	23.14	15
Ollius F., *Oglio*	45.55	10.14	8
Olmeius F.? *Zagara*	38.20	23.4	16
Olmiae Pr., *C. Olmia*	38.4	22.58	18
Olmōnes?	38.28	23.6	16
Oloetodariza	40.2	38.49	20
Olophyxus, *Khilandari*	40.20	24.8	15
Olpae, *Arapi*	38.57	21.9	15
Olpae (Locris)	38.26	22.12	15
Oltis F., *Lot*	44.40	2.30	6
Olūrus, *Xylo-kastro*	38.4	22.38	18
Olus? *Porto di Spina Longa*	35.16	25.44	19
OLYMPĒNE	39.45	29.0	20
Olympia, *Tschiraly*	37.38	21.38	18
Olympus, *Tschiraly*	36.24	30.30	20
Olympus M. (Bithynia), *Kheshish Dagh*	40.0	29.20	20
Olympus M. (Cyprus), *Oros Troados*	34.56	32.52	20
Olympus M. (Ionia), *Ninfi Dagh*	38.22	27.22	19
Olympus M. (or Orminium), *Ala Dagh*	40.20	32.0	20
Olympus M. (Thessalia), *Lacha*	40.5	22.21	15
Olynthus, *Agia Maria, or Aio Mamas*	40.16	23.21	15
*Omanītae, *Omaun*	23.30	57.0	3
Ombi, *Koom Ombo*	24.28	32.59	3
Omirras F. (Euphrates?), *Murad Tchai*	38.50	40.30	22
Omphalium	35.13	25.6	19
Omphalium?	39.56	20.28	15
On, or Onion? (Vicus Judaeorum), *Tell el-Yehud*	30.22	31.28	24
Onceium?	37.41	21.52	18
Onchesmus, *Santa Quaranta*	39.53	20.2	15
Onchestus	38.21	23.9	16
Onchestus F	39.33	22.31	15
Oneia M	37.52	22.56	18
Oneum?	43.29	16.39	14
Onisia I.?	35.11	26.18	19
Onoba, *Huelba*	37.15	6.50 w	7
Onobālns F. (Acesines, or Asines), *Cantara*	37.50	15.10	12
Onochōnus F.?	39.23	22.6	15
Onthis L., *L. of Bokhori*	38.21	21.35	18
Onugnāthus I., *Cervi, or Elafonisi*	36.28	22.58	18
Onūphis? *Mit Ghamr*	30.44	31.14	24
*Ophionenses	38.37	22.0	15
Ophir?	13.20	45.0	3
Ophius, *Of*	40.59	40.19	20
Ophiūsa, or Colubraria I. (of Strabo), *Formentera*	38.42	1.25	7
Ophiūsa, or Colubraria, I., *Columbretes*	39.54	0.45	7
Ophiussa I., *Afsia*	40.30	27.30	19
Ophrynium	40.1	26.21	26
Opinum, *Oppido*	40.44	15.59	9
Opis?	34.10	43.52	22
Opitergium, *Oderzo*	45.47	12.31	8
Opizus?	42.2	25.32	14
Oplonti, *Torre dell' Annunciata*	40.45	14.27	13
Opōne, *Hafoon*	10.26	51.18	2
Oppidum Novum, *El-Kadurah*	36.9	2.9	23
Oppidum Novum, *Naye*	43.11	0.16 w	6
Optatiana, *Szamosujvar, or Armenienstadt*	47.1	23.50	14
Opuntii Ms., *Mt. Khlomo, &c.*	33.35	23.0	16
Opus (Elis), n. *Skiadha*	37.52	21.41	18
Opus (Locris), *Kardhenitsa*	38.36	23.4	16
Opus Prom	38°.19'	22°.32'	16
Ora?	34.12	72.23	3
ORBALISĒNE	40.0	38.25	20
Orbēlus M	41.16	23.40	14
Orcādes Iˢᵐ., *Orkney Islands*	59.0	3.0 w	2
Orcas, or Tarvēdum, Pr., *Dunnet Head*	58.41	3.24 w	2
Orchoe, *Mogeiyer*	30.47	46.4	22
Orchomēnus (Arcadia), *Kalpaki*	37.44	22.19	18
Orchomēnus (Boeotia), r. n. *Skripu*	38.29	22.59	16
Orcistus, *Alekiam Jaila*	39.14	31.21	20
Ordessus, or Ardiscus, F., *Arjisch*	44.23	26.0	14
*Ordovices	52.48	3.30 w	5
Ordymnus M	39.14	25.57	19
ORESTIS	40.31	21.20	15
Orestium, *Marmaria*	37.23	22.14	18
*Oretāni	38.30	3.0 w	7
Orethus F., *Oreto*	38.6	13.20	12
Orētum	38.50	3.40 w	7
Orēus (Histiaea), *Oreos*	38.57	23.6	15
Orexis M	37.51	22.21	18
Orgia, *Organya*	42.13	1.18	7
Orgus F., *Orco*	45.25	7.20	8
Oricum, or Oricus, *Erikho*	40.22	19.27	15
Orippo, *Alcala de Guadaira*	37.16	5.45 w	7
*Oritae	26.0	65.40	3
Oriundus F., *Boyana*	41.50	19.20	14
Oriza? *Es-Sukhneh*	34.44	38.47	20
Orminium M. (Olympus), *Ala Dagh*	40.20	32.0	20
Orneae	37.47	22.39	18
Ornithopōlis? *Adlān*	33.24	35.18	21
Oroanda? *Arwan*	37.14	32.6	20
Oroatis, or Arōsis, F., *Tab*	30.20	49.52	22
Orobine, *Rovies*	38.48	23.14	15
*Orobii	45.55	9.20	8
Orōbis, or Orbis, F., *Orb*	43.30	3.0	6
Orolaunum, *Arlon*	49.40	5.50	6
Orontes F., *Nahr El-Ahsy*	35.50	36.25	20
Orontes M., *Elwound*	34.45	48.30	22
Orōpus, *Oropo*	38.17	23.47	16
Orospēda Mons, *Sierra Alcaraz, &c.*	39.0	2.20 w	7
Orra, or Uria Locrōrum, *Palazzi*	38.8	16.10	9
ORSĒNR	39.20	38.0	20
Orthopāgum, or Thurium, M	38.28	22.52	16
Orthosia?	34.38	36.2	20
Ortōna, *Ortona*	42.21	14.24	9
Ortopula, *S. Marco*	44.16	15.29	14
Ortospana? *Cauhool*	34.28	69.5	3
Ortygia, *Siracusa*	37.3	15.15	13
Ortygia I. (or Delos), *Delos*	37.23	25.17	19
Orvium Prom., *C. Silleiro*	42.5	8.52 w	7
Oryx, or Halus, n. *Podhogora*	37.46	22.3	18
Osa F., *Osa*	42.32	11.15	8
Osaea? *Bocca dello Stagno*	39.49	8.33	9
Osca, or Vesca, *Huesca*	42.9	0.20 w	7
Oscēla, *Domo d'Ossolo*	46.7	8.17	8
Oscelis, *Orihuela*	38.8	1.0 w	7
Oscineium, *Moulin d'Escinjot*	44.13	0.0	6
*Osi	49.30	19.0	25
*Osismii	48.20	3.40 w	6
Osmus F., *Osma*	43.0	24.45	14
Osopum, *Osopo*	46.15	13.6	8
OSROĒNE	37.20	39.0	22
Ossa M., *Kissovo*	39.48	22.42	15
Osset	37.25	5.51 w	7
Ossonōba, *Faro*	36.59	7.54 w	7
Ostadizus, *Khofsa*	41°.42'	27°.0'	14
Osteōdes I.? *Ustica*	38.42	13.10	9
Ostia, *Ostia*	41.43	12.16	11
Ostra, *Corinaldo*	43.40	13.2	8
Ostracīne?	31.3	32.22	24
*Otadēni	55.25	2.0 w	5
Othoca, *Oristano*	39.54	8.34	9
Othrōnus I., *Fano*	39.50	19.20	15
Othrys M., *Ierako*	39.3	22.42	15
Ovetum, (or Lucus Asturum?) *Oviedo*	43.22	5.57 w	7
Ovilaba, *Wels*	48.10	14.2	14
Oxinas, *Kuchuk Oksina*	41.22	31.39	20
Oxus F., *Amoo, or Jihon*	39.0	64.0	3
Oxus L., *Sir-i-kol*	37.25	73.45	3
*Oxybii	43.30	6.40	6
Oxycānus, Kingdom of	26.35	69.0	3
Oxydrācae, or Sudracae	28.40	72.0	3
Oxyneia?	39.47	21.38	15
Oxyrynchus, *Bahnesch*	28.33	30.45	24
Ozēne, *Oojein*	23.10	75.48	2

P.

NAMES.	LAT.	LONG.	MAP.
Pacciana Matidiae? r. n. *Marsa Zeitoun*	36.58	6.17	23
Pachnamūnis?	31.27	31.9	24
Pachȳni Portus, *Porto di Palo*	36.40	15.6	12
Pachȳnus, or Pachȳnum Pr., *Capo Passaro*	36.41	15.7	12
Pactōlus F	38.25	28.3	19
Pactȳa, *Doghan Arslan*	40.32	26.51	19
Pactȳas M	37.55	27.28	19
PADAN-ARAM, or ARAM-NAHARAIM, *Al-Jezireh*	36.0	41.0	22
Padinum, *Bondeno*	44.42	11.24	8
Pādus, or Eridānus, F., *Po*	45.0	8.45	8
Padūsa F., *Primaro*	44.38	11.45	8
Paeania, n. *Karela*	37.56	23.50	16
*Paemāni	50.15	5.0	6
PAEONIA	41.45	22.0	14
Pneonīdae, *Menidhi*	38.6	23.43	16
*Paesīci	43.30	6.0 w	7
Paestānus (or Posidoniātes) S., *G. of Salerno*	40.20	14.40	9
Paestum, or Posidonia	40.23	15.0	9
Pagae, *Psatho*	38.6	23.14	16
Pagala?	25.25	66.20	3
Pagāsae	39.23	22.55	13
Pagasaeus S., *G. of Volo*	39.12	23.0	13
Pagrae, *Bagras*	36.25	36.11	20
Palaea, n. *Apidhia*	36.53	22.48	18
Palaea Paphos, *Koulia*	34.42	32.34	20
Palaemaria, or Marēa, *El-Rasheat*	30.56	30.3	24
Palacrus, or Palirus	38.45	20.54	15
Palaeste	40.11	19.34	15
Palanta, *Bologna*	42.32	8.54	9
Palantia, *Palencia*	42.1	4.27 w	7
Pale, *Polikata*	38.13	20.26	18
Palfuriāna, *Villarodona*	41.22	1.20	7
Palica?	37.18	14.43	12
Palimbothra? *Patna*	25.37	85.15	3
Palindrōmus Prom., *C. Bab-el-Mandeb*	12.40	43.34	3
Palinūrus Prom., *Capo di Palinuro*	40.0	15.16	9
Palirus, or Palnerus	38.45	20.54	15
Palisscius, *Rakhamytes*	37.27	22.14	18
Paliūrus	32.19	23.10	23
Palla, *Bonifacio*	41.23	9.9	9
Pallacōpas	30.40	46.40	22
Pallantia? *Reliejos*	42.23	5.17 w	7
Pallantias F., *Palancia*	39.53	0.30 w	7
Pallantium	37.27	22.20	18
Pallānum, *Pallano*	42.10	14.30	9
Pallēne	38.2	23.51	16
PALLĒNE	40.0	23.30	15

NAMES.	LAT.	LONG.	MAP.
Palma, *Palma*	39°.35'	2°.39'	7
Palmaria I., *Palmarola*	40.56	12.52	9
Palmyra(Tadmor), *Tadmor*	34.18	38.14	20
PALMYRĒNE	34.40	38.30	20
Palus Maeōtis, *Sea of Azov*	46.0	37.0	2
Palus Stentōris, *G. of Enos*	40.43	26.5	19
Palus Tritōnis, *Al-Sibkah*	33.30	8.45	23
Pambōtis L., *L. of Ianina*	39.50	21.0	15
Pamisus F. (Messenia), *Pirnatza*	37.6	22.0	18
Pamisus F. (Thessalia), *Bliuri, or Piliuri*	39.27	21.50	15
PAMPHYLIA	37.0	31.0	20
Panachaïcus Mons, *Voidia*	38.12	21.52	18
Panactum?	38.11	23.35	16
Panaetolium M., *Viena*	38.40	21.30	15
Pandataria I., *Vandotena*	40.47	13.25	9
Pandosia (Bruttiorum), *n. Mendocino*	39.17	16.11	9
Pandosia(Epirus), *Kastri*	39.18	20.36	15
Pandosia (Lucania), *Anglona*	40.16	16.31	9
PANEAS	33.15	35.47	21
Paneas, or Caesarēa-Philippi, *Banias*	33.16	35.42	21
Panephysis?	31.8	31.50	24
Pangaeus M., *Pilaf Tepeh*	40.53	24.6	19
Panhormus, or Panormus, *Palermo*	38.7	13.21	12
Panionium?	37.44	27.17	19
Panium	33.17	35.41	21
PANNONIA, LOWER	47.0	16.0	14
PANNONIA, UPPER	46.0	18.0	14
Panōpeus	38.29	22.48	16
Panormus, or Panhormus), *Palermo*	38.7	13.21	12
Panormus (Achaia)	38.19	21.49	18
Panormus(Cephallenia), *Port Viskardho*	38.27	20.34	15
Panormus (Creta)	35.25	24.29	19
Panormus (Ionia)	37.56	27.18	19
Panormus Portus, *Karajia Agatach*	36.50	28.30	19
Panormus Portus, *Marsa Sollum*	31.29	25.11	23
Panormus Portus, *Panorimo*	37.41	24.4	18
Panormus Portus, *Port Palermo*	40.5	19.42	15
Pantagias F., *Porcari*	37.18	15.10	12
Pantanus L., *Lago di Lesina*	41.53	15.25	9
Panticapaeum, *Kertsch*	45.22	36.28	3
Pantichium, *Pandik*	40.54	29.16	20
Panysus F., *Pravadi*	43.10	27.30	14
PAPHLAGONIA	41.10	34.0	20
Paphos, *Baffo*	34.45	32.25	20
Pappa?	37.28	32.12	20
Papua M.?	37.3	7.20	23
Parachoathras M., *Chain of El-Burz, or Caspian Mts*	36.0	52.0	3
PARAETACĒNE?	38.30	70.0	3
Paraetacēni	33.0	51.0	3
Paraetonium, *Marsa Labeit*	31.21	27.12	23
PARALIA	37.50	23.55	18
Paran, Desert of, *El-Tih*	30.30	34.45	24
Parapotamii, *r. n. Belimi*	38.33	22.48	16
Paracopia, Plain of	38.15	23.20	16
PARAVAEA	40.26	20.40	15
Parduaca	39.50	35.21	20

NAMES.	LAT.	LONG.	MAP.
Pardua, *Slano*	42°.48'	17°.52'	14
Parembōle, *Debod*	23.55	32.52	3
Parentium, *Parenzo*	45.14	13.35	8
*Paricanii?	27.35	58.0	3
Parietina, *Mostasa*	35.8	4.27 w	23
Parietini?	39.24	2.31 w	7
*Parisii	54.0	0.20 w	5
*Parisii	48.42	2.15	6
Parium M	36.50	35.40	26
Parium, *Kamares*	40.25	27.4	19
Parma, *Parma*	44.48	10.21	8
Parma F., *Parma*	44.40	10.19	8
Parnassus? *Koj Hissar*	38.52	33.34	20
Parnassus M., Range of *Liakhoura*	38.34	22.30	16
Parnes M., *Nozia*	38.11	23.43	16
Parnon M., *Malevo, or Kani*	37.17	22.37	18
Paropamīsus M., *Seffeid Koh*	34.0	70.0	3
Parōpus, *Collesano?*	37.54	13.55	12
PAROREIA	39.45	21.17	15
Parōreia, *Paleomiri*	37.29	22.10	18
PARORĒUS	38.30	31.0	20
Paros, *Parekhia*	37.5	25.10	19
Paros I., *Paro*	37.5	25.12	19
Parthanum, *Partenkirch*	47.29	11.8	25
Parthenicum, *n. Partenico*	38.56	13.4	12
Parthenium, *Bartan*	41.40	32.17	20
Parthenius F., *Bartan Tchai*	41.30	32.25	20
Parthenius M., *Partheni*	37.30	22.32	18
Parthenōpe (Neapōlis), *Naples*	40.51	14.15	13
PARTHIA	35.50	57.0	3
*Parthini	41.45	20.30	14
Paryadres Mons	40.40	39.0	20
Parysātis, Villages of?	35.15	43.27	22
Pasargādae? *Deh Minair*	28.31	53.20	3
Pasira?	25.20	64.40	3
Pasitigris, or Eulaeus, F., *Kuran*	31.0	48.25	22
Passaron	39.40	20.57	15
Patāra	36.15	29.22	20
Patavium, *Padua*	45.24	11.51	8
Patavinae Aquae, or Apōni Fons, *Bagni d'Abano*	45.22	11.46	8
Patavissa (Colonia), *Thorda*	46.33	23.45	14
Pathmetic, see Phatnitic			
Patmos I., *Patino*	37.20	26.34	19
Patrae, *Patras*	38.15	21.44	18
Patrocli I., *Gaidharo*	37.39	23.57	18
Pattāla? *Hyderabad*	25.23	68.21	3
Patūmos (Thoum, or Pithom), *r. n. Abassich*	30.28	31.35	24
Patyous, *Paola*	39.22	16.2	9
Pauca, *Porto Polo*	41.43	8.49	9
Paura, *Puhra*	27.58	60.30	3
Paus	37.51	21.57	18
Pausilypus Mons, *Hill of Posilipo*	40.49	14.13	13
Pax Julia, *Beja*	38.5	7.41 w	7
Paxus I., *Paxo*	39.11	20.10	15
Pedalium Pr., *C. Grego*	34.57	34.6	20
Pedalium Pr., or Artemisium, *C. Suvela*	36.35	28.53	19
Pedāsus? *Paitechin*	37.15	27.54	19
Pedāsus?	39.32	26.17	19
Pediaios F.	35.10	33.45	20
Pedieia?	38.37	22.41	16
PEDIUM	38.0	23.41	16
Pednelissus	37.31	31.19	20
Pedona, *Borgo S. Dalmazzo*	44.20	7.31	8
Pēdum, *Gallicano*	41.53	12.51	11
Pegae, *Kapsomati*	37.22	22.11	18

NAMES.	LAT.	LONG.	MAP.
Pegella?	38°.30'	33°.10'	20
Peiraeum, *Perakhora*	38.2	22.57	16
Peiraeus	37.56	23.39	17
Peiraeus Portus, *Dhrako, or Porto Leone*	37.56	23.38	17
Peiraeus Portus (Corinthia), *Porto Franco*	37.50	23.8	18
Peirus F., *Kamenitsa*	38.8	21.37	18
Peiso L.? *Balaton, or Platten See*	46.53	18.0	14
PELAGONIA	41.6	21.30	14
Pelagonia, *Bitoglia, or Monastir*	40.58	21.15	14
PELASGIŌTIS	39.30	22.25	15
*Pelendōnes	41.50	2.40 w	7
Pelendova, *Krajova*	44.20	23.44	14
*Peligni	41.58	14.0	9
Pelinnaeum, or Pelinna, *Kardhiki*	39.35	21.54	15
Pelion M., *Zagora*	39.26	23.3	15
Pella, aft. Apamēa, *Famieh*	35.29	36.24	20
Pella (Macedonia), *Alakliei, or Apostolus*	40.44	22.27	15
Pella (Palaestina), *Kefr Beel*	32.35	35.44	21
Pellana	37.10	22.22	18
Pellēne	38.3	22.32	18
Pelōdes Portus, *Harbor of Butrinto*	39.44	20.0	15
PELOPONNĒSUS, *Morea*	37.30	22.0	15
Pelōrum, Pelōrus, or Pelorias, Pr., *Capo di Faro*	38.16	15.40	12
Pelōrus F.? *Ksia, or Chram*	41.30	44.30	22
Peltae?	38.12	29.52	20
Pelusiac Mouth (of Nile), *Tineh Mouth*	31.4	32.25	24
Pelusium (Sin?), *Tineh*	31.2	32.21	24
Pelva?	43.52	17.8	14
Peme?	29.39	31.16	24
Peneius F., *Gastouni*	37.53	21.20	18
Peneius F., *Selembria*	39.45	22.24	15
Penni-lucus	46.22	6.55	6
Pennocrucium, *Stretton, n. Penkridge*	52.42	2.9 w	5
PENTAPŌLIS	32.40	21.0	23
Pentaschoenon?	31.1	32.37	24
Pentēle, *Mendeli*	38.4	23.54	16
Pentelicus M., or Brilessus, *Penteli, or Mendeli*	38.7	23.53	16
*Pentri	41.27	14.25	9
Peparēthos I., *Piperi*	39.20	24.19	19
Pephnus, *St. Dhimitri*	36.49	22.18	18
PERAEA (Caria)	36.54	28.30	19
PERAEA (Palaestina)	32.0	35.50	21
Peraetheae, *Valtetsi*	37.28	22.16	18
Perceiāna?	38.31	6.13 w	7
Percōte, *Bourgas*	40.13	26.38	19
Percri, *Peigir Kalah*	39.1	43.40	22
Pergāmos?	35.29	23.51	19
Pergāmum, or Pergāmos, *Bergamo*	39.6	27.14	19
Perge	37.1	30.55	20
Pergus L., *Lago Pergusa*	37.29	14.18	12
Perimulicus S., *Strait of Malacca*	4.0	100.0	2
Perinthus, aft. Heraclea, *Erekli*	40.59	27.58	19
Peripolium?	37.59	15.50	9
Permessus F.?	38.14	23.5	16
Perniciacum	50.37	4.52	6
*Perorsi	22.0	15.0 w	2
Perre, *Adiaman*	37.45	38.26	20
PERRHAEBIA	39.50	22.10	15
Persepōlis, *Istakhr*	29.58	53.0	3
Persicae Pylae? *Kaleh Sefeed*	30.16	51.50	3
Persicus S., *Persian Gulf*	28.0	50.0	3

NAMES.	LAT.	LONG.	MAP.
PERSIS	30°.0'	52°.0'	3
Perta, *Ujak Basaat*	38.21	33.36	20
Pertusa, *Portus*	41.57	0.1 w	7
Perusia, *Perugia*	43.7	12.23	8
Pessinus, *Bala Hissar*	39.20	31.45	20
Pessium (Contra Acincum), *Pesth*	47.30	19.6	14
Petaliae I^æ., *Petalies P.*	38.0	24.18	15
Petavonium?	42.5	6.30 w	7
Peteon?	38.24	23.21	16
Petilia, *Strongoli*	39.17	17.5	9
Petiliana	37.21	14.0	12
Petinesca, *Bienne*	47.8	7.15	6
Petitarus F.	38.52	21.19	15
Petra (Arabia), r. in *Wady Mousa*	30.25	35.38	24
Petra (Colchis), *Zichedshari*	41.44	41.43	22
Petra (Illyricum), on *C. Pali*	41.25	19.25	14
Petra (Macedonia), *Petrovitsch*	41.26	23.15	14
Petra (Pieria)	40.11	22.16	15
Petra (Sicilia), *Buonpietro*	37.44	14.6	12
Petra Magna	31.45	25.6	23
Petra Parya, *Ras el-Toum*	32.14	23.38	23
Petra Pertusa, *Pietra Pertusa*	42.2	12.30	11
Petra Pertusa, or Intercisa, *Il Furlo*	43.36	12.41	8
Petrae	45.50	23.4	14
Petriana, *Castlesteads*	54.57	2.45 w	5
Petrina?	37.41	14.1	12
*Petrocorii	45.0	0.40	7
Petrocorii, for. Vesunna, *Perigueux*	45.11	0.44	6
Petromantalum, *St. Clair*	49.12	1.40	6
Petuaria? *Brough on Humber*	53.44	0.33 w	5
Peuce L, *Moish*	45.0	29.30	24
Peucela? *Pushkalavati*	34.12	72.16	3
PEUCETIA	41.0	16.40	9
*Peucini	45.15	29.15	14
*Peucini, or Bastarnae	48.30	21.0	25
Phacium?	39.35	22.0	15
Phacusa, *Tell Fakhous*	30.46	31.44	24
Phacussa I., *Karo*	36.53	25.40	19
Phaedriades	38.30	22.30	16
Phaedrias?	37.21	22.4	18
Phaestus	35.3	24.49	19
Phaestus? *Alifaka*	39.34	22.10	15
Phaestus, *Vithari*	38.21	22.21	16
Phalacrium Prom., *Capo Rasocolmo*	38.18	15.31	12
Phalacrum Prom., *C. Drasti*	39.48	19.38	15
Phalanna, n. *Karajoli*	39.45	22.20	15
Phalara	38.53	22.30	16
Phalarus F.	38.24	22.58	16
Phalasarna	35.31	23.34	19
Phalerum	37.56	23.39	17
Phalerum Portus, *Porto Fanari*	37.56	23.40	17
Phaloria	39.36	21.38	15
Phamothis, *El-Khreit*	31.2	29.51	24
Phanae Prom., *C. Mastiko*	38.9	26.1	19
Phanagoria, n. *Tuman*	45.15	36.45	3
PHANAROEA	40.46	36.30	20
Phara	38.38	20.37	15
Pharae	38.5	21.44	18
Pharae, or Pherae, *Kalamata*	37.2	22.8	18
Pharaga, *Makam*	31.8	66.8	3
Pharan, *Feiran*	28.42	33.38	24
Pharan Prom. (or Posidium)? *Ras Mohammed*	27.44	34.15	24
Pharaspa, *Gaza*, or (Iazaca, *Takht-i-Suleimaun*	36.28	47.8	22

NAMES.	LAT.	LONG.	MAP.
Pharax, *Koudiah*	30°.45'	18°.20'	23
Pharia, see Pharus			
Pharis, *Vafio*	27.1	22.29	18
Pharmacussa I., *Farmako*	37.17	27.7	19
Pharmatenus	40.56	38.11	20
Pharnacia, *Kerasoun*	40.56	38.24	20
Pharos I., *Faro*, or *Lighthouse of Alexandria*	31.12	29.55	24
Pharsalus, *Fersala*	39.16	22.23	15
Pharus, or Pharia, I., *Lesina*	43.10	16.40	14
*Pharusii	16.0	15.0 w	2
Pharygium Prom., *C. Punda*	38.20	22.41	16
Phaselis, *Tekrova*	36.32	30.36	20
PHASIANE	40.6	42.0	22
Phasis, *Poti*	42.8	41.38	22
Phasis F., *Rion*	42.10	41.50	22
Phasis F.(of Xenophon)? *Aras*	40.14	43.0	22
Phatisane, *Fatsa*	41.3	37.27	20
Phatnitic, or Pathmetic, Mouth (of Nile), *Damietta Mouth*	31.30	31.41	24
Phaura I., *Phleva*	37.46	23.46	16
PHAZANIA, *Fezzan*	27.0	14.0	2
Phazemon, *Mersiwan*	40.50	35.36	20
PHAZEMONITIS	40.50	35.40	20
Pheia, *Pondiko Kastro*	37.39	21.19	18
Phelleus M., *Mavronoro*	38.14	23.56	16
Phelloe, *Zakhuli*	38.5	22.24	18
Pheneus, *Fonia*	37.54	22.19	18
Pherae?	38.18	23.35	16
Pherae, *Velestino*	39.24	22.43	15
Pherae, *Verria*	37.11	22.32	18
Pherae, or Pharae, *Kalamata*	37.2	22.8	18
Pherendis? *Piran*	38.21	40.5	22
Phiala L.	33.15	35.50	21
Phicium, Phoenicium, or Sphingium, M., *Faga*	38.23	23.12	16
Phigalia, or Phigaleia, n. *Pavlitza*	37.24	21.51	18
Phigamus F., *Dscherwis Dere*	41.0	37.30	20
Phila?	39.55	22.40	15
Philadelphia (Rabbathammon, or Rabbah), *Amman*	31.58	36.0	21
Philadelphia, *Allahshehr*	38.21	28.35	19
Philae I., *Jeziret Anas-el-Wojoud*	24.1	32.54	3
Philia Prom., *C. Kalionjik*	41.26	28.28	14
Philippi, for. Crenides, *Filibi*	41.4	24.22	19
Philippopolis, *Filippopoli*	42.2	24.55	14
Philippopolis, *Oermaun*	32.34	36.54	21
*Philistines	31.35	34.40	21
Philocalia	41.3	39.5	20
Philomelium, *Ak Shehr*	38.23	31.36	20
Philotera, *Old Cosseir*	26.13	34.14	3
Philyreis I	40.59	38.36	20
Phinea, or Phinopolis	41.10	29.4	26
Phintias, *Alicata*, or *Licata*	37.4	13.55	12
Phintonis I.? *Caprera*	41.13	9.27	9
PHLIASIA	37.50	22.37	18
Phlius, *Polyfengo*	37.50	22.39	18
Phlya, *Kucara*	37.49	23.58	18
Phocae, *Port Skroponeri*	38.29	23.20	16
Phocaea, *Fouges*, or *Foggia*	38.41	26.46	19
PHOCIS	38.30	22.40	16
Phocusae I^æ., *Moulrou Rocks*	31.25	27.6	23

NAMES.	LAT.	LONG.	MAP.
Phoeliae, or Phytia, *Porta*	38°.41'	21°.11'	15
PHOENICE	34.0	35.40	20
Phoenice (Chaonia), *Finiki*	39.50	40.12	15
Phoenice (Creta), *Lutro*	35.12	24.6	19
Phoenicium, Phicium, or Sphingium, M., *Faga*	38.23	23.12	16
Phoenicum Oppidum, *Mowilah*	27.40	35.30	3
Phoenicus (Cythera), *Arlemona*	36.13	23.5	15
Phoenicus (Ionia)? *Tcheemeh*	38.20	26.20	19
Phoenicus Portus	36.49	21.49	18
Phoenicus Portus	36.15	29.26	20
Phoenicus Portus, *Ghatta Bay*	31.8	27.55	23
Phoenicus Portus, *Porto Vindicari*	36.58	15.5	12
Phoenicusa I., *Filicuri*	38.35	14.30	9
Phoenix F.? *Salmeniko*	38.15	21.56	18
Phoenix M.	36.39	28.10	19
Phoezon	37.36	22.26	18
Pholegandros I., *Polykandro*	36.38	24.55	19
Pholoe M.	37.45	21.45	18
Phorbantia, or Bucinna, I., *Levanzo*	38.3	12.19	12
Phorbia Pr., *Pt. Euro*	37.28	25.28	19
Phorcys Portus? *Afrikie Bay*	38.28	20.38	15
Phoron Portus	37.57	23.36	17
Photinopolis	41.25	26.33	14
Phra, *Furrah*	32.23	62.8	3
Phricius M.	38.45	22.26	26
Phrixa, *Paleo Fanaro*	37.38	21.43	15
PHRYGIA	39.0	30.45	20
PHRYGIA-EPICTETUS	39.36	30.30	20
Phrygius, or Hyllus, F.	38.46	27.40	19
PHTHIOTIS	39.6	22.35	15
Phycus	32.56	21.38	23
Phycus Pr., *Ras Sem*, or *El-Razat*	32.56	21.38	23
Phylace (Laconia), *Krya Vrysi*	37.20	22.26	18
Phylace (Pieria), *Servia*, or *Volustana*	40.13	21.58	15
Phylace (Thessalia), r. n. *Ghidek*	39.13	22.38	15
Phyle	38.9	23.39	16
Phyllus	37.37	22.58	18
Phyrites F.	38.10	27.20	19
Physcus, *Marmaras*, or *Marmarice*	36.52	28.19	19
Physcus F., *Adhem*	34.20	44.29	22
Phyteum, *Kuvelo*	38.36	21.35	15
Phytia, or Phoeliae, *Porta*	38.41	21.11	15
Picentia, *Vicenza*	40.37	14.54	9
*Picentini	40.40	15.0	9
Picentinum, *Brod*	45.9	18.2	14
PICENUM	43.0	13.35	8
Piciniana?	37.24	13.35	12
Pictavi, *Poitiers*	46.35	0.20	6
*Pictones, or Pictavi	46.40	1.0 w	6
PIERIA	36.30	36.0	20
PIERIA	40.15	22.20	15
Pierus M.	40.10	22.5	15
Pietas Julia, for. Pola, *Pola*	44.52	13.50	8
Pinara	36.30	29.17	20
Pinarus F., *Deli Tchai*	36.50	36.10	20
Pindus M.	40.0	21.25	15
Pineptimi (False Mouth of Nile	31.34	31.10	24
Pinetus? *Pinhel*	40.46	7.1 w	7
Pinna, *Civitá di Penne*	42.25	13.59	8
Pintia?	41.45	4.20 w	7
Piquentum, *Pinguente*	45.25	13.59	8
Pirae? n. *Bedroni*	38.7	21.36	18
Piresiae, *Vlokho*	39.30	22.1	15

NAMES.	LAT.	LONG.	MAP.
Pirina?	37°.51′	13°.51′	12
Pirum, *Bukharest*	44.28	26.8	14
Pisa	37.40	21.39	18
Pisae, *Pisa*	43.43	10.23	8
PISAEA, or PISĀTIS	37.43	21.38	18
Pisaurum, *Pesaro*	43.55	12.55	8
Pisavae, *Pellisane*	43.38	5.10	6
PISIDIA	37.30	31.0	20
Pisaurus, or Isaurus, F., *Foglia*	43.47	12.30	8
Pisoraca F., *Pisuerga*	41.50	4.30 w	7
Pistorium, or Pistoria, *Pistoja*	43.58	10.56	8
Pistyros	40.52	24.38	19
Pitāne, *Sandarlik*	38.56	26.27	19
Pitch Springs (of Zacynthus)	37.41	20.50	18
Pithecusa, Aenaria, or Inarīme, I., *Ischia*	40.44	13.54	13
Pithom, Thoum, or Etham, (Patūmos?) r. n. *Abasseih*	30.28	31.35	24
Pitonius F., *Giovenco*	41.59	13.40	11
Pitya	40.26	27.10	19
Pityonnēsus I., *Angistri*	37.42	23.21	18
Pityus, *Pitzunda*	43.10	40.17	22
Pityūsae I., *Iviza and Formentera*	39.0	1.25	7
Pityussa I.	37.26	23.32	18
Pityussa I., *DanaAdassi, or Provençal I.*	36.11	33.48	20
Placentia, *Piacenza*	45.3	9.43	8
Plagiaria? *El-Comandante*	39.7	6.45 w	7
Planasia I., *Pianosa*	42.33	10.8	8
Planesia I., *Pluna*	38.10	0.27 w	7
Plataeae, *Kokla*	38.12	23.16	16
Platamōdes Prom.	37.9	21.34	18
Platanistus	36.3	32.42	20
Platanistus Prom., C. *Spathi*	36.23	22.57	18
Platănum	33.41	35.28	21
Platĕa I., *Bomba*	32.23	23.15	23
Plateia, *Plaka*	36.4	26.26	19
Plavis F., *Piave*	46.20	12.22	8
Pleistus F., *Xeropotamo*	38.28	22.30	16
Plemmyrium	37.1	15.17	13
Pleraei	43.0	18.15	14
Plera, *Gravina*	40.46	16.24	9
Plestinia? *Peschio Asserolo*	41.49	13.44	11
Pleuron, *Castle of Irene*	38.25	21.26	18
Plinii Villa, *Pliniana*	45.52	9.10	8
Plinthine?	30.54	29.28	24
Plinthinētos S., *Arabs Gulf*	31.0	29.20	24
Plumbaria I.	38.46	0.14	7
Plumbaria (or Enosis?) I., *S. Antioco*	39.0	8.23	9
Plumbinaria, *Pimpinara*	41.44	13.2	11
Pluvialia L.? *Ferro, or Hierro*	27.45	18.0 w	2
Podalia	36.47	29.54	20
Podandus	37.22	34.54	20
Poecilasium	35.14	23.48	19
Poecīle Petra	36.24	34.2	20
Poediculi	41.10	16.30	9
Poetovio, *Pettau*	46.25	15.51	14
Pogla, *Fulla*	37.16	30.19	20
Pogon, *Port Vidhi*	37.31	23.25	18
Poiessa	37.35	24.18	19
Pola, aft. Piĕtas Julia, *Pola*	44.52	13.50	8
Polaticum Pr., C. *Promontoire*	44.46	13.54	8
Polemonium, *Puleman*	41.1	37.30	20
Polichne, *Reonda*	37.15	22.46	18
Polichne	37.17	21.54	18
Polichne? *Skala*	38.22	26.47	19
Polimartium, *Bomarzo*	42.30	12.14	11
Politorium, *La Giostra*	41.46	12.35	11
Pollentia, *Pollenza*	44.41	7.55	8
Pollentia, *Pollenza*	39.52	3.5	7
Pollentia (Picenum), *Monte Moline*	43°.16′	13°.22′	8
Polynaegos L., *Polino*	36.45	24.39	19
Polyanthes F., *River of Livizza*	40.16	19.43	15
Polybōtus, *Buluodun*	38.43	31.7	20
Polyrrhenia	34.27	23.41	19
Polytimētus F., *Zerafshan*	40.0	66.0	3
Pompeii	40.45	14.29	13
Pompeiopŏlis, or Soli, *Mezetli*	36.44	34.34	20
Pompeiopŏlis, *Tash Kupri*	41.28	34.23	20
Pompĕlo, *Pamplona, or Pampeluna*	42.48	1.40 w	7
Pomptīnae Paludes, *Pontine Marshes*	41.25	13.5	11
Pons Aelii, *Newcastle on Tyne*	54.58	1.36 w	5
Pons Alutae, *Slatina*	44.25	24.18	14
Pons Aufīdi, *Ponte S. Venere*	41.5	15.32	9
Pons Augusti	45.29	22.43	14
Pons Aureoli, *Pontiruolo*	45.35	9.34	8
Pons Drusi	46.31	11.21	8
Pons Dubis	46.55	5.9	6
Pons Liquentiae, *La Motta*	45.46	12.39	8
Pons Milvius, *Ponte Molle*	41.57	12.27	11
Pons Nartiae (Martia?), *Monteceda*	42.58	7.46 w	7
Pons Naviae, *Navia de Suarna*	43.9	7.7 w	7
Pons Oeni, *Wasserburg*	48.4	12.15	14
Pons Saravi, *Sarrebourg*	48.44	7.4	6
Pons Servilii, n. Sturga, or *Strugo*	41.13	20.40	14
Pons Sociorum?	46.22	18.8	14
Pons Vetus, *Kosia*	45.16	24.18	14
Pontes, *Ponche*	50.20	1.51	6
Pontes, *Staines*	51.26	0.30 w	5
Pontes Tessenii, on *River Loisach*	47.43	11.23	25
Pontia I., *Ponza*	40.54	12.58	9
Pontīnus M.	37.33	22.40	18
PONTUS	40.30	39.0	20
Pontus Euxīnus, *Black Sea*	44.0	35.0	2
Pontus F., *Radovitz*	41.26	23.0	14
PONTUS POLEMONIĀCUS	41.0	38.0	4
Populonium	43.0	10.30	8
Populonium Pr., *Capo di Campana*	42.57	10.30	8
Porata, or Hierasus, F., *Pruth*	47.0	28.0	14
Porcifĕra F., *Polcevera*	44.26	8.53	8
Porolissus, *Bistrita*	47.8	24.26	14
Porphyrion, *Nebi Yunas*	33.37	35.26	21
Porsulae	40.58	25.20	19
Porticenses	39.32	9.38	9
Portus Adurni? *Aldrington*	50.50	0.12 w	5
Portus Argōus, *Porto Ferrajo*	42.48	10.20	8
Portus Augusti, *Porto*	41.46	12.15	11
Portus Brundŭlus, *Brondolo*	45.10	12.16	8
Portus Classis?	44.22	12.17	8
Portus Cossānus, or Hercŭlis, *Porto d'Ercole*	42.12	11.16	8
Portus Delphīni, *Porto Fino*	44.19	9.14	8
Portus Divīnus?	35.44	0.55 w	23
Portus Domitiānus, *Porto S. Stefano*	42.26	11.10	8
Portus Dubris, *Dover*	51.8	1.19	5
Portus Edro	45.15	12.9	8
Portus Faleria, *Porto Falese*	42.56	10.34	8
Portus Favonii, *Porto Favone*	41°.47′	9°.23′	9
Portus Garnae	41.55	15.17	9
Portus Hercŭlis, Labronis, or Liburni, *Livorno (Leghorn)*	43.34	10.19	8
Portus Hercŭlis Monoeci, *Monaco*	43.43	7.27	6
Portus Hercŭlis, or Cossānus, *Porto d'Ercole*	42.12	11.16	8
Portus Lemanis, *Lympne, n. Hythe*	51.4	1.1	5
Portus Luguidonis, *Posada*	40.38	9.44	9
Portus Magnus? *Oran*	35.41	0.40 w	23
Portus Magnus, *Porchester Castle*	50.51	1.7 w	5
Portus Mauricii, *Porto Maurizio*	43.55	8.0	8
Portus Namnētum (Condivicnum, aft. Namnetes), *Nantes*	47.13	1.32 w	6
Portus Novus? *Rye Harbor*	50.56	0.47	5
Portus Parthenius	39.47	15.51	9
Portus Pisānus, *Mouth of Arno*	43.42	10.14	8
Portus Rhusibis, *Saffee*	32.20	9.14 w	23
Portus Romatīnus	45.41	12.50	8
Portus Sasina, *Porto Cesareo*	40.13	17.56	9
Portus Sulcitānus, *G. of Palmas*	39.0	8.30	9
Portus Syracusānus, *Porto di S. Mansa*	41.26	9.14	9
Portus Telamōnis, *Talamone*	42.32	11.11	8
Portus Tiliānus, *Porto Tizzano*	41.32	8.50	9
Portus Trajānus, *Torre di Troja*	42.48	10.48	8
Portus Venĕris, *Port Vendre*	42.31	3.7	6
Portus Venĕris, *Porto Venere*	44.4	9.51	8
Portus Velīni	40.8	15.6	9
Poseidon, Temple of	37.55	23.1	18
Posidium (Carpathos), *Pigadin, or Posin*	35.34	27.12	19
Posidium (Macedonia)	40.38	23.45	15
Posidium (Syria), *Bosseda*	35.53	35.51	20
Posidium (or Enipium) Prom., *Punta di Licosa*	40.14	14.53	9
Posidium, or Posidonium, Prom., C. *Posidhi, or Kassandra*	39.57	23.21	15
Posidium Prom., *Bos Burun*	40.33	28.47	20
Posidium Prom., C. *Skala*	39.45	19.58	15
Posidium Prom., C. *Gatos*	37.44	27.6	19
Posidium Prom., C. *Helena*	38.20	26.11	19
Posidium Prom., C. *Kiz-liman*	36.4	33.8	20
Posidium Prom., C. *Marmarice*	36.44	28.21	19
Posidium Prom., C. *Mondendri*	37.21	27.13	19
Posidium Prom. (or Pharan?), *Ras Mohammed*	27.44	34.15	24
Posidium Prom., C. *Stavros*	39.1	23.4	15
Posidium Prom., *Tchaush Aghizi*	41.22	31.32	20
Posidonia, or *Paestum*	40.23	15.0	9
Posidoniātes, or Paestānus, S., *G. of Salerno*	40.20	14.40	9

NAMES.	LAT.	LONG.	MAP.
Posidonium, or Posidi~um Pr., C. Posidhi, or Kassandra	39°.57'	23°.21'	15
Posidonium, Port Kisternes, or Asomata	36.24	22.29	18
Potămi	41.58	34.50	20
POTAMIA	40.50	33.0	20
Potămos, Paleo Kastro	37.47	24.2	18
Potentia, Potenza	40.37	15.47	9
Potentia, S. Maria di Potenza	43.24	13.39	8
Potentia F., Potenza	43.25	13.39	8
Potidaea, aft. Cassandria, Pinaka	40.11	23.20	15
Potniae?	38.17	23.18	16
Praeneste, Palestrina	41.51	12.55	11
Praesidium?	41.58	9.24	9
Praesidium?	41.8	7.45 w	7
Praesidium? S. Estevan	42.26	7.48 w	7
Praesidium, S. Lucar de Guadiana	37.20	7.16 w	7
Praesidium Julium, or Scalabis, Santarem	39.16	8.38 w	7
Praesidium Pompeii, Boulovan	43.30	21.32	14
Praesus	35.7	26.7	19
Praetoria Augusta	45.56	27.0	14
Praetorium	45.7	22.21	14
Praetorium	46.4	1.35	6
Praetorium, Bossigliana	43.31	16.7	14
Praetorium, Granollers	41.38	2.20	7
Praetorium? n. Hunmanby	54.11	0.18 w	5
Praetorium, Rimnik	45.4	24.23	14
Praetorium Agrippinae, n. Zwieten	52.8	4.32	6
Praetorium Latovicŏrum, Neustadtl	45.48	15.13	14
*Praetutii	42.35	13.35	8
Pramnos M., Melissa	37.33	26.5	19
Prasiae, r. on Porto Rafti	37.52	24.2	18
Prasiae, or Brasiae? St. Andreas	37.22	22.47	18
Prasias, or Cercinltis, L., Takhyno	40.55	23.50	19
*Prasii	26.0	83.0	2
Prasum Prom., C. Delgado	10.20 s	40.20	2
Premnis, Ibrim	22.40	32.0	3
Propesinthos I., Despotiko	36.57	25.0	19
Pria, or Iria Flavia, El-Padron	42.38	8.38 w	7
Priansus?	35.1	25.18	19
Priăpus	40.25	27.20	19
Priëne, Samsoun	37.40	27.19	19
Prifernum, Assergio	42.23	13.32	8
Privernum, n. Piperno	41.29	13.11	11
Probalinthus	38.6	23.59	16
Probatia F.	38.26	22.51	16
Prochyta I., Procida	40.45	14.1	13
Procolitia, Carrawburgh	55.2	2.11 w	5
Proconnesus L., Marmora	40.37	27.35	19
Proerna, Ghynekokastro	39.13	22.16	15
Prolaqueum, Pioracco	43.8	13.1	8
Promŏna	44.0	16.12	14
Proni, n. Limenia	38.8	20.47	18
Prophthasia, Peshawuroon	31.50	61.48	3
Propontis, Sea of Marmora	40.45	28.0	20
Proschium	38.28	21.22	18
Prosymna	37.35	22.57	18
Prote I., Porquerolles	43.0	6.13	8
Prote I., Proti	37.3	21.34	18
Prusa, Brusa	40.10	29.8	20
Prusias, or Ciĕrus, Uskub, or Eski Bagh	40.50	31.21	20
Prymnessus? Seid el-Ghazy	39.23	30.55	20
Prytanis F., Kala Dere	41.0	41.10	20

NAMES.	LAT.	LONG.	MAP.
Psaeon Pr., C. Spada	35°.41'	23°.44'	19
Psamăthus Portus, Port Kaio	36.26	22.30	18
Psaphăra, or Antigonĕa	40.20	23.6	15
Psaphis, Kalamo	38.16	23.53	16
Pselcis, Dakke	23.12	32.46	3
Psilis	36.42	28.44	19
Psilis F.	41.5	30.0	20
Psophis, Tripotamo	37.52	21.54	18
Psychium	35.6	24.41	19
Psygmos, Gulwaini (or Great L.)	11.59	50.45	2
Psylli			1
Psyra I., Psara	38.35	25.36	19
Psyttaleia I., Lipso	37.56	23.35	16
Pteleum?	38.30	26.25	19
Pteleum, Pteleo	39.1	22.57	15
Ptolemăis (Accho), St. Jean d'Acre	32.56	35.5	21
Ptolemăis (Cyrenaica), Tolmeita	32.43	20.55	23
Ptolemăis Hermii, El-Menshieh	26.28	31.48	3
Ptolemăis Theron? Erih Island	18.8	38.30	3
Ptoum M., Strutsina	38.27	23.17	16
Ptychia I., Vido	39.38	19.55	15
Pucinum, Castel Duino	45.46	13.27	8
Pulchrum Prom.? C. Zebeeb	37.17	10.1	23
Pullariae Iᵐᵃ., Brioni, &c.	44.54	13.45	8
Pullopice, Finale	44.11	8.20	8
Pulŏra I., Polior	26.17	54.38	3
Pumentum, Cerenza	39.16	16.49	9
Pupulum, Villamasargia	39.17	8.38	9
Puteolănus (or Campănus) S., Bay of Naples	40.40	14.10	13
Puteŏli, Puzzuoli	40.49	14.7	13
Pycnus F.	35.36	23.58	19
Pydna, Kitro	40.22	22.33	15
Pygĕla	37.54	27.18	19
Pygmaei			1
Pylae Albaniae, or Caspiae, Pass of Derbend	42.0	48.16	22
Pylae Amanlcae (of Arrian)	37.0	36.23	20
Pylae Caspiae, Pass of Gaduk	35.50	52.56	3
Pylae Caucasiae, Pass of Dariel	42.44	44.41	22
Pylae Ciliciae, Golek Boghaz	37.14	34.50	20
Pylae (of Mesopotamia)? Anbar	33.30	42.59	22
Pylae Persicae? Kaleh Sefeed	30.16	51.50	3
Pylae (Pontus), Kulabat Boghas	40.37	39.36	20
Pylae Syriae, Pass of Beilan	36.29	36.10	20
Pylae Syriae-Ciliciae, Sakal Tutan	36.39	36.11	20
Pylae Zagri (or Mediae), Tak-i-Girrah	34.25	46.20	22
PYLUS	37.0	21.40	18
Pylus, or Coryphasium, Paleo Avarin	36.57	21.40	18
Pylus (Elis), n. Kulugli	37.50	21.33	18
Pylus (Tryphylia), Biskini	37.29	21.41	18
Pyra M.	38.50	22.1	26
Pyramis (Great)	29.58	31.5	24
Pyrămus F., Jaihăn	37.18	36.0	20
Pyranthus, Pyrathi	35.6	25.11	19
Pyrenaei Ms., Pyrenees	42.40	0.0	6
Pyrenaeum Prom., C. Creuse	42.19	3.20	7
Pyrgi	37.24	21.42	18
Pyrgi, Santa Severa	42.1	11.55	11
Pyrrha (Ionia)	37.30	27.22	19

NAMES.	LAT.	LONG.	MAP.
Pyrrha (Lesbos)	39°.9'	26°.18'	19
Pyrrha Prom., C. Anghistri	39.19	22.57	15
Pyrrhăsus, n. Kokkina	39.18	22.50	15
Pyrrhĭchus, n. Karaloe	36.39	22.26	15
Pythis Prom., Ras el-Hazeit	31.23	27.24	23
Pythium	40.3	22.14	15
Pytho (Delphi), Kastri	38.28	22.31	15
Pyxītes F., Vitzeh Su	41.10	41.16	20
Pyxus, or Buxentum, Policastro	40.1	15.32	9
Pyxus F., Bucento	40.5	15.31	9
Pyxus Pr., Capo degl' Infreschi	39.56	15.25	9

Q.

NAMES.	LAT.	LONG.	MAP.
*Quadi	49.0	16.30	25
Quadrăta, Verginmost	45.21	15.53	14
Quaetis F., Quieto	45.20	13.40	8
Querquetŭla? Cappannello	41.56	12.47	11
Quintiana, Landau	48.40	12.44	25
Quiza?	35.50	0.28 w	23

R.

NAMES.	LAT.	LONG.	MAP.
Rabbah, or Rabbatn-ammon (Philadelphia), Ammăn	31.58	36.0	21
Rabbath-moab (Areopŏlis, or Ar of Moab), Rabba	31.22	35.45	21
Radis, or Ratis, I., I. de Ré	46.10	1.25 w	6
Ragandum, Windisch Feistritz	46.25	15.35	14
Rama, Rame	44.45	6.32	3
Ramah, Er-Ram	31.51	35.15	21
Rambacla?	26.10	66.20	3
Ramĕses, or Beth-shemesh (Heliopŏlis), Matarieh	30.8	31.20	24
Ramidava? Rimnik	45.17	27.9	14
Ramoth-gilead, Jelaad	32.10	35.48	21
Raphia, Refah	31.17	34.14	24
Rarapia, Ferreira	38.6	8.0 w	7
Ratae, Leicester	52.38	1.8 w	5
Rataneum	43.15	17.5	14
Ratiaria, or Rhaetiaria, Widin	43.57	22.55	14
Ratiatum	47.0	1.53 w	5
Rauda, Roa	41.43	3.58 w	7
Raudii Campi?	45.27	9.0	8
*Rauraci	47.40	7.20	8
Rauranum, Rom	46.17	0.5	6
Ravenna, Ravenna	44.25	12.14	8
Reăte, Rieti	42.24	12.53	8
*Redŏnes	48.0	1.40 w	6
Redŏnes, Rennes	48.7	1.40 w	6
Regama? Ras al-Khaima	25.47	56.5	3
Regeta	41.19	13.10	11
Regia? Armagh	54.21	6.39 w	2
Regia Altĕra, Limerick	52.41	8.38 w	2
Regiăna, Reyna	38.11	6.2 w	7
Regillus L., Cornufelle	41.50	12.43	11
Reginum, Reyensburg, or Ratisbon	49.1	12.6	25
Regium Lepĭdi, Reggio	44.42	10.36	8
*Regni	51.0	0.0	5
Regnum, Chichester	50.50	0.46 w	5
Regulbium, Reculver	51.23	1.11	5
Reii, Riez	43.50	6.5	6
Remesinna, Mousa Pasha Palanka	43.12	22.26	14
*Remi	49.30	4.0	6
Remi, Rheims	49.15	4.1	6
Rephidim? in Wady Sheikh	28.41	34.1	24
Rerigonium? Stranraer	54.54	5.1 w	5
Rerigonius S., Loch Ryan	55.0	5.4 w	5

NAMES.	LAT.	LONG.	MAP.
Resaena, aft. Theodosiopolis, Ras el-Ain..	36°.52'	40°.1'	22
Resapha, Resafah	35.34	38.45	20
Resen (Larissa)? Nimroud	36.0	43.23	22
Respa, Molfetta	41.12	16.35	9
Retina, n. Resina	40.48	14.21	13
Reudigni	53.20	13.30	25
Revessium, S. Paulien	45.8	3.50	6
Rha F., Volga	50.0	45.30	2
Rha F.(East branch of), Kama	56.0	53.0	2
Rhabon F., Schyl	44.30	23.32	14
Rhaedestus, or Bisanthe, Rodosto	40.59	27.31	14
RHAETIA	47.0	11.0	25
Rhaetiaria, or Ratiaria, Widin	43.57	22.55	14
Rhagae, Veramin	35.37	51.46	3
Rhamnus, Ovriokastro	38.12	24.3	16
Rhamnus Portus, Stomio	35.23	23.33	19
Rhaptum Prom.?	2.0 s	41.0	2
Rhaptus F.?	2.0 s	40.50	2
Rhatostathybius F., Taff	51.30	3.13 w	5
Rhaucus	35.15	25.4	19
Rhausium	42.42	18.0	14
Rhebas, Riva Kaleh	41.14	29.15	20
Rhegium, Reggio	38.6	15.40	9
Rheiti	38.1	23.36	16
Rheitrum Portus, G. of Molo	38.23	20.42	18
Rheitus, n. Galataki	37.51	23.0	18
Rhenea I., Rhenea	37.25	25.14	19
Rhenus F., Rhine	49.0	8.20	6
Rhenus F., Reno	44.15	11.5	8
Rhesus F., Karatli	40.11	27.0	19
Rhezius, Riza	41.4	40.34	20
Rhigodunum, or Coccium, Ribchester	53.49	2.31 w	5
Rhinocolura, or Rhinocorura? El-Arish	31.6	33.47	24
Rhipaei			1
Rhium	36.50	21.50	18
Rhium Prom., Capo di Feno	41.58	8.36	9
Rhium Prom., Kastro Morea	38.18	21.47	18
Rhizon, Risano	42.32	18.46	14
Rhizus?	39.40	22.48	15
Rhoda, Rosas	42.18	3.9	7
Rhodanus F., Rhone	44.20	4.40	6
Rhodius F	40.8	26.30	19
Rhodope M., Despoto Dagh	41.30	24.40	14
Rhodos, Rhodes	36.26	28.16	19
Rhodos I., Rhodes	36.10	28.0	19
Rhoduntia	38.45	22.27	26
Rhodussa I., Linosa	36.46	28.29	19
Rhoeteum	39.59	26.16	19
Rhoeteum Prom	40.	26.16	26
Rhoge I., St. George	36.9	29.24	20
Rhossus, Arsoos	36.25	35.52	20
Rhossus Mons, Jebel Keserik	36.20	36.0	20
Rhotanus F., Tavignano	42.13	9.20	9
Rhudiae (Iapygia)?	40.29	18.15	9
Rhudiae (Peucetia), Andria	41.12	16.17	9
Rhygmana	36.5	32.55	20
Rhyndacus F., Mualitsch	40.18	28.30	19
Rhyphae (or Rhypes)?	38.16	22.2	18
Ricina, Recco	44.23	9.9	8
Riduna I., Alderney	49.43	2.12 w	6
Rigomagus, Reinmagen	50.34	7.14	6
Rigomagus, Rinco	45.3	8.10	8
Riobe, Orby	48.30	2.58	6
Ripa Alta?	46.31	18.56	14
Riphaei (or Hyperborei) Montes, S. part of Ural	58.0	60.0	2
Rithymna, Retimo	35°.22'	24°.28'	19
Rittium, Szurduk	45.9	20.20	14
Ritubium (or Lituvium?), Retorbio	44.56	9.5	8
River of Egypt, or Sihor? Wady el-Arish	30.45	33.40	24
Roboraria, Molara	41.47	12.45	11
Roboretum?	41.11	6.55 w	7
Robrica, Longué	47.21	0.5 w	6
Rodumna, Roanne	46.2	4.4	6
Rogonis, Gonarra	29.32	50.35	3
Roma, Rome	41.54	12.29	11
Romatinus F., Lemene	45.50	12.54	8
Romechium? Romechi	38.22	16.26	9
Romula Castra?	45.16	15.33	14
Romulea, or Sub Romula? n. Andretta	40.57	15.17	9
Roscianum, Rossano	39.33	16.41	9
Rossulum, Monte Rosi	42.14	12.16	11
Rostrum Nemaviae, Buchloe	48.2	10.45	25
Rotomagus, Rouen	49.27	1.5	6
Rubi, Ruvo	41.7	16.28	9
Rubico F.? Fiumicino	44.11	12.27	8
Rubra, Porto Nuovo	41.30	9.16	9
Rubricatus F., Llobregat	41.30	1.55	7
Rubricatus, or Ubus, F., Seibous	36.27	7.30	23
Rubrum Mare, or Arabicus S., Red Sea	20.0	39.0	3
Rudiae, or Rhudiae (Iapygia)?	40.29	18.15	9
Rudiae, or Rhudiae (Peucetia), Andria	41.12	16.17	9
Ruffrium, S. Angelo	41.22	14.14	9
Rufrae, Ruvo	40.51	15.33	9
*Rugii	54.10	13.0	25
*Rugusci	46.0	10.0	8
Rura F., Ruhr	51.23	7.0	25
Rusadir, Melilla	35.20	2.55 w	23
Rusadir Prom., C. Tres Forcas, or Ras al-Deir	35.28	2.57 w	23
Rusazus? Sidi Daoud	36.52	4.41	23
Ruscino, Perpignan	42.42	2.54	6
Ruscino, or Tetis, F., Tet	42.44	3.0	6
Rusellae, Roselle	42.48	11.13	8
Rusgunia, r. on C. Matifou	36.48	3.15	23
Rusicada	36.54	7.8	23
Ruspina? Es-Sahalin	35.46	10.42	23
Russicana, Galisteo	39.59	6.3 w	7
Rusubbicari, Sarab Velrab	36.47	3.35	23
Rusuccurrum? Sidi Ferej	36.46	2.51	23
*Ruteni	44.21	2.35	6
Rutuba F., Roya	44.0	7.36	8
*Rutuli	41.35	12.32	11
Rutunium, Rowton	52.43	2.54 w	5
Rutupiae, Richborough Castle	51.18	1.19	5
Ryknield Way	52.20	1.55 w	5
S.			
Saba?	16.45	43.20	3
*Sabaei	15.10	45.0	3
Sabara? Martaban	16.38	97.32	2
Sabarkeus S., G. of Martaban	15.0	96.0	2
Sabaria, Stein-am-Anger	47.13	16.38	14
Sabate, S. Marciano	42.7	12.7	11
Sabatinca?	47.20	15.1	14
Sabatinus L., Lago di Bracciano	42.8	12.12	11
Sabatus F., Sabato	41.0	14.50	9
Sabatus F.(Bruttiorum), Savuto	39.8	16.0	9
*Sabini	42.15	12.45	11
Sabis F., Sambre	50.15	4.0	6
Sabium, Sabbio	45.39	10.26	8
Sablones, Venloo	51°.23'	6°.7'	6
Sabrata, Tripoli-Vecchia	32.48	12.25	23
Sabrina, or Sabriana, Aest., Mouth of Severn	51.30	2.50 w	5
Sabrina F., Severn	52.25	2.20 w	5
Sabus	39.5	38.17	20
*Sacae	39.0	72.0	3
Sacamaza, Medina es-Sultan	31.9	17.15	23
SACARUM REGIO			1
SACASENE	39.40	46.30	22
Sacer F., Arbo	42.6	9.20	9
Sacer F., Uras	39.44	8.40	9
Sacer Mons.	41.56	12.32	11
*Sachalitae?	18.0	55.0	3
Sacra I., Isola Sacra	41.44	12.15	11
Sacred Bay, B. of Korein, or Grane	29.25	48.0	3
Sacri-portus? Valle Sacco	41.46	13.0	11
Sacrum Prom.	36.22	29.10	20
Sacrum Prom., C. Khelidonia	36.13	30.26	20
Sacrum Prom., C. St. Vincent	37.2	9.0 w	7
Sadame? Devlet Aghaj	42.11	26.59	14
Saeprus F., Flumendosa	39.40	9.20	9
Saetabis?	39.0	0.42 w	7
Sagalassus, r. n. Aghtasan	37.38	30.38	20
*Sagartii?	26.45	64.0	3
Sagis? n. Migliaro	44.48	11.59	8
Sagras F.? Alaro	38.27	16.25	9
Sagrus F., Sangro	41.54	14.15	9
Saguntum, Murviedro	39.41	0.15 w	7
Sais, Sa el-Hajar	30.57	30.44	24
Saittae, Sidas Kaleh	38.45	28.45	20
Sala F., Saale	51.45	11.40	25
Sala F., Wady Bou Regreb	34.0	6.40 w	23
Sala, r. of Shella, n. Rabat	34.4	6.49 w	23
Salacia, Alcazar do Sal	38.22	8.22 w	7
Salacia, Pombeiro	41.23	8.12 w	7
Salamis, Ambelaki	37.57	23.32	16
Salamis (Cyprus), r. n. Costanza	35.10	33.55	20
Salamis I., Kuluri, or Salamis	37.55	23.30	16
Salaminias, Salamiyeh	34.47	37.11	20
Salapia, Salpi	41.25	16.0	9
Salapina Palus, Lago Salpi	41.35	16.0	9
*Salassi	45.40	7.30	8
Salbacum M., Bos Dagh	37.10	29.0	20
Salchah, Sulkhad	32.31	36.51	21
Saldae?	36.53	3.51	23
Salduba, aft. Caesaraugusta, Saragossa	41.46	0.54 w	7
Salduba, Tower of Bovedas	36.28	5.0 w	7
Salduba F	36.35	5.1 w	7
Salebro?	42.52	10.53	8
Salenae, Chesterfield, n. Sandy	52.7	0.17 w	5
*Salentini	40.13	18.0	9
Salentinum (or Iapygium) Prom., Capo di Leuca	39.48	18.22	9
Salernum, Salerno	40.40	14.46	13
Salganeus	38.28	23.35	16
Salia F., Sella	43.24	5.30 w	7
Salice, or Taprobane, I., Ceylon	7.0	81.0	2
Salientes? Orense	42.22	7.57 w	7
Salinae	42.30	14.12	8
Salinae	31.50	14.23	23
Salinae, Felrincz	46.24	23.46	14
Salinae, n. Cecina	43.18	10.31	8
Salle, Szala Egerszeg	46.50	16.52	14
Salluntum	42.47	18.14	14

NAMES.	LAT.	LONG.	MAP.
Salmantīca (Elmantīca?), Solamanca....	41°.6'	5°.42' w	7
Salmōne, Krekuki..	37.40	21.36	18
Salmorudis, or Halmyris?.........	44.50	28.49	14
Salmydessus, Midiah...	41.40	28.6	14
Salo F., Xalon..........	41.30	1.30 w	7
Salodūrum, Soleure.....	47.13	7.32	6
SALON	40.40	32.0	20
Salōna, Salona.........	43.32	16.28	14
Salsovia, Baba Dagh..	44.55	28.40	24
Salsūlae, Salces........	42.50	2.55	6
Salsum Flumen....	37.20	5.5 w	7
Salt, Valley of, El-Ghor	31.5	35.30	21
Saltici, Sisante....	39.30	2.14 w	7
Saltus Castulonensis....	38.40	3.0 w	7
Salurnum, Salurno....	46.17	11.10	8
*Salyes....	43.30	5.40	6
Samāra F., Somme......	50.0	2.0	6
SAMARIA.........	32.10	35.15	21
Samaria, aft. Sebaste, Sebustieh..............	32.18	35.9	21
Samarobriva, aft. Ambiāni, Amiens..........	49.54	2.17	6
Sambina? Seimarrah...	32.57	47.26	22
Sambracitānus S., St. Tropez, or Grimaud B.	43.17	6.40	8
Sambulos M., Sunbulah	34.15	46.5	22
Same, Samos............	38.14	20.37	18
Samicum............	37.32	21.37	18
Saminthus? Kutzopodhi	37.41	22.43	18
SAMNIUM............	41.30	14.20	9
Samochonītis L. (Waters of Merom), Bahr el-Houle............	33.5	35.38	21
Samonium Prom., or Salmōne? C. Sidero..	35.20	26.19	19
Samos............	37.42	26.57	19
Samos I., Samo............	37.45	26.50	19
Samos, or Cephallenia, I., Cephalonia............	38.15	20.30	15
Sampsāta, Samosat......	37.32	38.36	20
Samothrāce, Paleopoli..	40.30	25.32	19
Samothrāce I., Samothraki............	40.26	25.35	19
Sanderva............	42.42	18.35	14
Sane............	40.6	23.19	15
Sane (Uranopōlis?)......	40.22	23.56	15
Sangāla?	31.0	74.0	3
Sangarius F., Sakaria..	40.0	30.54	20
Sanina, Moghan............	39.38	49.0	22
Sanisera, Alajor............	39.53	4.10	7
Sanora, Schemkur............	40.43	46.5	22
Santicum, n. Villach....	46.38	13.51	14
*Santōnes, or Santōni..	45.45	0.36 w	6
Santōnes, Saintes............	45.45	0.36 w	6
Santōnum Portus, La Rochelle............	46.10	1.9 w	6
Santōnum Prom............	46.16	1.13 w	6
Sapianae, Fünfkirchen, or Pecs............	46.5	18.16	14
Sapis F., Savio............	43.54	12.5	8
Sapphe, or Bezabde, Jezireh Ibn Omar..	37.17	41.59	22
Saragana, Sinkar.........	36.54	45.5	22
SARAMĒNE	41.20	36.0	20
SARANGA	26.0	67.0	3
Sarapana, Scharopani..	42.6	43.6	22
Sardīca, Sophia.........	42.37	23.27	14
Sardis, Sart.........	38.28	28.5	19
SARDO, or SARDINIA, Sardinia............	40.0	9.0	9
Sarepta (Zarephath), Surāfend............	33.57	35.19	21
SARGARAUSĒNE..........	39.23	36.0	20
SARMATIA..............	54.0	30.0	2
SARMATIA ASIATICA..	46.0	45.0	2
Sarmatīci Ms............	49.0	20.0	14
Sarmatīcus Oceānus, or Mare Suevīcum, Baltic Sea............	57.0	20.0	2
Sarmizegetūsa (Col. Ulpia Trajana)............	45.30	22.50	14
Sarnade?......................	44°.16'	17°.19'	14
Sarnius F., Atrek..........	37.40	55.0	3
Sarnus F., Sarno............	40.44	14.30	13
Saron Campus (Plain of Sharon)............	32.15	34.56	21
Saronīcus S., G. of Egina	37.48	23.30	18
Sarpēdon Prom., C. Gremsa..............	40.35	26.7	19
Sarpēdon Prom., Lissan el-Karpeh..............	36.14	33.59	20
Sarraca, Sarche..............	46.5	10.55	8
Sarrum, Houme, or Oum	45.34	0.14	6
Sarsīna, Sarsina............	43.57	12.11	8
Sarus F., Seihoon..........	37.30	35.25	20
Sasima?..............	38.2	34.36	20
Sason I., Sassena............	40.30	19.18	15
Satāla..............	40.6	40.3	20
Saticūla, S. Agata dei Goti..............	41.6	14.30	13
Satnioeis F., Touzla....	39.35	26.8	19
Satricum, Conca............	41.31	12.46	11
Saturium, Saturio............	40.21	17.19	9
Saturni Prom., or Scombraria, C. Palos......	37.38	0.37 w	7
Saturnia, Saturnia............	42.41	11.27	8
Sauconna, or Arar, F., Saône..............	46.20	4.50	6
Saunium F.? Saja............	43.20	4.0 w	7
Sauromatae..............			1
Savatra?..............	38.11	33.21	20
Savo, Savona..	44.18	8.28	8
Savo F., Savone............	41.10	14 0	9
Savus F., Save............	45.48	16.0	14
Saxa Rubra, or Rubrae (Ad Gallinas), Prima Porta............	42.1	12.29	11
Saxetānum, or Sex, n. C. Sacratif..............	36.42	3.30 w	7
*Saxōnes..............	53.40	10.0	25
Saxula..............	41.59	12.56	11
Scaidava, Sistova..........	43.39	25.13	14
Scalābis, or Praesidium Julium, Santarem.....	39.16	8.38 w	7
Scaldis F., Schelde, or Escaut..............	51.0	4.0	6
Scamander F., Bunarbashi Tchai..............	39.54	26.14	19
Scamander F. (Sicilia)	37.58	12.50	12
Scamnum, Latiano..........	40.33	17.43	9
Scampae, El-bassan....	41.10	20.2	14
Scandaria Prom., Koum Point..............	36.55	27.19	19
Scandeia? Kapsali..........	36.9	23.0	15
Scandīle I., Skantzoura	39.4	24.6	19
SCANDINAVIA, or SCANDIA?............	60.0	15.0	2
Scaptia, Passerano......	41.54	12.47	11
Scarabantia, Oedenburg	47.42	16.36	14
Scarcopi..............	39.20	9.33	9
Scardōna, Scardona.....	13.50	15.55	14
Scardōna I., Grossa, or Lunga..............	44.0	15.1	14
Scardus M., Sharra-dagh, or Tchardagh..	42.0	21.0	14
Scarphe, or Eteōnus?...	38.14	23.34	16
Scarpheia..............	38.47	22.40	16
Scenae Mandrārum....	29.46	31.19	24
Scenae (Succoth), r. n. Shibbeen..............	30.16	31.22	24
Scepsis..............	39.48	27.17	19
Scetis..............	30.19	30.15	24
Schinussa I., Skinosa..	36.52	25.31	19
Schiste..............	38.27	22.34	16
Schoenus, Kalamaki....	37.55	23.1	18
Schoenus F.? Kanavari	38.17	23.13	16
Schoenus Portus, B. of Kalamaki..............	37.55	23.1	16
Schoenus S., B. of Loxa	36.44	28.7	19
Sciāthis M., Snita.......	37.51	22.17	18
Sciāthos I., Skiatho......	39.10	23.28	15
Scidrus, Sapri..............	40.1	15.49	9
Scillium, Kazareen......	34.57	8.47	23
Scillus, n. Makrysia.....	37°.36'	21°.36'	18
Seingomāgus? Siguin...	44.56	6.50	8
Sciōne..............	39.57	23.31	15
Sciradium	37.59	23.26	16
SCIRĪTIS..............	37.15	22.23	18
Scironīdes Petrae........	37.58	23.15	16
Scodra, n. Skutari......	41.56	19.33	14
Scoedises Mons, Kepan Dagh..............	39.50	39.45	20
Scollis M., Sandameri..	37.58	21.34	18
Scolus..............	38.15	23.25	16
Scombraria (or Saturni) Prom., C. Palos......	37.38	0.37 w	7
Scombraria, or Herculis I., Escombrera......	37.34	0.55 w	7
Scomius M., Argentaro	42.15	22.40	14
Scopēlos I., Skopelo....	39.7	23.43	19
Scopūlus Rhossīcus, Ras el-Khanzir	36.18	35.45	20
Scotane..............	37.50	22.0	18
Scotussa	40.58	23.36	14
Scotussa, r. n. Supli....	39.21	22.32	15
Scultenna F., Panaro...	44.29	11.0	8
Scupi, Uskup, or Skopia	41.55	21.43	14
Scylax F., Tschoterlek..	40.12	35.0	20
Scylla, Rock of..........	38.14	15.44	9
Scyllaeum, Scylla........	38.14	15.44	9
Scyllaeum Prom., C. Spadi..............	37.28	23.31	18
Scylletīcus S., G. of Squillace..............	38.45	16.50	9
Scylletium, Scylacium, or Scylacaeum, Squillace	38.50	16.30	9
Scyros..............	38.53	24.32	19
Scyros I., Skyro..........	38.50	24.35	19
Scyras F..............	36.41	22.30	18
SCYTHIA (of Herodotus)..............	50.0	35.0	2
SCYTHIA extra Imaum.	40.0	90.0	2
SCYTHIA intra Imaum.	50.0	60.0	2
SCYTHIA PARVA....	44.40	28.30	14
*Scythini..............	40.20	40.0	22
Scythopōlis (Bethshan), Bysān..............	32.33	35.32	21
Sebaste (Samaria), Sebustieh..............	32.18	35.9	21
Sebastīa, Sivas..............	39.40	37.3	20
Sebastopōlis, for. Dioscurias, Iskuria........	42.48	41.17	22
Sebastopōlis, Kisiljeh...	37.26	29.5	20
Sebastopōlis, Turkhal..	40.17	36.15	20
Sebatum, Sabs..............	46.47	11.40	8
Sebennytic Mouth (of Nile), Boorlos Mouth	31.34	30.58	24
Sebennytus? Semenhoud	31.0	31.13	24
Sebēthus F., Maddalona..............	40.52	14.18	13
Sebīnus L., Lago d'Iseo	45.45	10.5	8
Secerrae, S. Celoni......	41.44	2.31	7
Secia, or Gabellus, F., Secchia	44.30	10.42	8
Securisca, Tcherezelan..	43.39	24.39	14
Secusia, or Segusio, Susa	45.7	7.1	8
*Sedūni..............	46.15	7.40	8
Segantiorum (or Setantiorum) Portus? Lancaster B..............	54.0	3.0 w	5
Segedūnum, Cousens House............	55.0	1.30 w	5
Segeia (or Seteia), Aest.?..............	53.25	3.10 w	5
Segelocum, Littleboro'..	53.20	0.46	5
Segessera, Bar-sur-Aube	48.14	4.42	6
Segesta, or Egesta, n. Segesta..............	37.59	12.54	12
Segeste, Sestri Levante	44.17	9.26	8
Segisamo, Sasamon......	42.38	4.12 w	7
Segisamunculum, Balluercanes..............	42.32	3.11 w	7
*Segni..............	50.14	5.50	6

NAMES.	LAT.	LONG.	MAP.
Segobodium, *Seveux*	47°.34'	5°.45'	6
Segobriga, *Segorbe*	40.24	2.19 w	7
Segodūnum, aft. Ruteni, *Rhodez*	44.21	2.35	6
Segontia, *Epila*	41.41	1.13 w	7
Segontia, *Siguensa*	41.4	2.41 w	7
*Segontiaci	51.6	1.30 w	6
Segontium, *Caer Seiont* (*Caernarvon*)	53.9	4.15 w	5
Segora, *Segré*	47.42	0.52 w	6
Segosa, *Escourse*	44.10	1.1 w	6
*Segovēllauni	44.50	4.52	6
Segovia, *Segovia*	41.1	4.8 w	7
*Segusiāni	45.40	4.30	6
Segusio, *Susa*	45.7	7.1	8
Segustero, *Sisteron*	44.12	5.55	6
Seir Mt., *Jebel esh-Sherah*	30.30	35.35	24
Seïrae, *Loperi*	37.52	21.55	18
Sela	37.6	21.35	18
Sela F., *Langovardho...*	37.6	21.38	18
Selambina, *Solobrena...*	36.45	3.39 w	7
Selemnus F.	38.16	21.50	18
Seleucia	33.4	44.39	22
Seleucia?	33.3	35.40	21
Seleucia (Cilicia), *Selef-keh*	36.23	33.57	20
Seleucia (Pamphylia)...	36.51	31.19	20
Seleucia in Pieria, n. *Suadeiah*	36.6	35.56	20
Seleucia Sidēra, *Eger-dir*	37.54	30.57	20
SELEUCIS	36.15	38.15	20
Selge, *Surk*	37.19	31.10	20
*Selgōvae	55.20	3.30 w	5
Seliniāna? *Estrica*	41.56	8.23 w	7
SELINITIS	36.20	32.30	20
Selinus, *Kosmas*	37.5	22.45	18
Selinus, *Pileri*	37.36	12.48	12
Selinus, or Trajanopō-lis, *Selinty*	36.16	32.19	20
Selinus F., *Madiani...*	37.36	12.46	12
Selinus F., *Vostitza...*	38.5	22.1	18
Selinus Portus, *Esmarh*	31.29	26.30	23
Sellasia, *St. Saranda...*	37.7	22.59	18
Sellium, *Seijo*	39.46	8.36 w	7
Selymbria	41.5	28.16	14
Semirus F., *Simmari*	39.0	16.37	9
*Semnōnes	52.10	13.0	25
Sena F., *Cesano*	43.39	13.0	8
Sena Gallica, *Sinigag-lia*	43.43	13.13	8
Sena Iᵐ., *I. de Sein.*	48.4	4.50 w	6
Sena Julia, *Sienna*	43.22	11.21	8
*Senōnes	48.0	2.45	6
*Senōnes	43.50	12.40	8
Senōnes, *Sens*	48.11	3.17	6
Sentice, *Castroverde...*	40.51	5.51 w	7
Sentīnum, *Sentina*	43.26	12.50	8
Senus F., *Shannon*	53.15	8.0 w	2
Sepelaci, *Castellon de la Plana*	39.59	0.4 w	7
Sepia M.	39.54	22.21	18
Sepias Prom.	39.10	23.21	15
Sepinum, *Sepino*	41.26	14.36	9
Sepomana, *Omago*	45.25	13.31	8
Sepphōris, aft. Diocae-sarēa, *Sefurieh*	32.45	35.17	21
Septem Maria	45.0	12.15	8
Septem Fratres, *Jebel Mousa*	35.54	5.25 w	23
Septempēda, *S. Severino*	43.15	13.12	8
Septimauca, *Simancas..*	41.35	4.50 w	7
Sequāna F., *Seine*	49.0	1.40	6
*Sequāni	47.0	5.40	6
Seranūra	40.27	36.48	20
Serapaeum	41.9	29.3	26
Serapēum (Baal-zephon?), r. below *Birket Temsah*	30 24	32.10	24
Serāpis I., *Massera*	20.30	58.50	3
Serbōnis Lacus, *Subakat Bardowal*	31.5	33.0	24
Seriphos, *Livathi*	37°.9'	24°.31'	19
Seriphos I., *Serfo*	37.10	24.30	19
Seriane, *Esrieh*	35.18	37.48	20
SERICA, *China*	35.0	110.0	2
Sermanicomagus, *St. Laurent de Séris*	45.56	0.29	6
Sermo, *Maxalocha*	41.35	4.3 w	7
Sermyle, *n. Ormylia*	40.15	23.34	15
Serota, *Verocae*	45.52	17.26	14
Serpa, *Serpa*	37.59	7.24 w	7
Serrhae, *Kara Bambouj*	36.22	38.11	20
Serus F.? *Sang-koi*	31.30	105.0	2
Servittium?	44.57	17.23	14
Sesāmus, aft. Amastris, *Amasserah*	41.45	32.24	20
Sessites F., *Sesia*	45.30	8.23	8
Sestīnum, *Sestino*	43.44	12.16	8
Sestos	40.13	26.25	19
*Sesuvii	48.40	0.10 w	6
Setantiorum (or Segan-tiorum) Portus? *Lancaster B.*	54.0	3.0 w	5
Seteia (or Segeia) Aest.?	53.25	3.10 w	5
Sethrum?	30.55	32.3	24
Setia, *Sezza*	41.30	13.5	11
Setius M., *Cette*	43.24	3.39	6
Seumara? *Gartiskalak...*	41.51	44.46	22
Sevo M., *Mt. Sevo, n. Gottenburg*	57.41	12.0	2
Sex, or Saxitānum, *n. C. Sacratif.*	36.42	3.30 w	7
Sex Insūlae? *Hajarou en-Nekkor, &c.*	35.16	3.48 w	23
Sexantaprista, *Birgos...*	43.41	25.44	14
Sextantio, *r. n. Castelnau (on the Lez)*	43.39	3.53	6
Shalem, *Salim*	32.16	35.19	21
Shechem, or Sychar (Neapōlis), *Nablous..*	32.15	35.14	21
Shiloh, *Seiloun*	32.5	35.16	21
Shunem, *Solām*	32.37	35.21	21
Shur, Desert of	30.45	34.0	24
Shusban (Susa), *Soos...*	32.0	48.25	22
Siagul, *Kasr ez-Zeit...*	36.26	10.38	23
Siazūros, *Shahrizoor....*	35.20	45.49	22
*Sibae	31.40	71.30	3
Sibaria, *Zamocina*	41.26	6.45 w	7
Siberena, *S. Severino...*	39.12	16.53	9
*Sibuzates	43.35	1.15 w	6
*Sibyllates	43.15	0.50 w	6
*Sicambri	50.50	7.30	25
Sicca Veneria, *Kassir Jebir*	36.0	8.28	23
Sicinos I. and Town, *Sikino*	36.42	25.8	19
Sicor Portus, *Baie de Bourgneuf*	47.0	2.5 w	6
Sicōris F., *Segre*	42.0	1.12	7
Siculum Fretum, *Strait of Messina*	38.10	15.36	9
Sicyon, *Vasiliko*	37.58	22.44	18
SICYONIA	37.57	22.42	18
Side?	36.29	23.9	18
Side?	38.13	23.30	16
Side, *Eski Adalia*	36.47	31.24	20
Side, or Sidus, *Sousaki*	37.55	23.4	16
Sidēna, *Boghazhehr....*	40.14	27.12	19
SIDĒNE	40.55	37.30	20
Sidēnus F., *Puleman Tchai*	40.55	37.29	20
Sidērus Pr., *C. Adrat-schan*	36.20	30.35	20
*Sidicīni	41.14	14.10	9
Sidolocum, *Saulieu*	47.16	4.14	6
Sidon, *Saida*	33.33	35.22	21
Sidōne? *Shenas*	26.33	54.52	3
Sidȳma	36.24	29.15	20
Siga, *Honain*	35.8	1.51 w	23
Siga F., *Tewants*	35.8	1.51 w	23
Sigēum	39.59	26.12	19
Sigēum Prom.	40.	26.12	26
Signia, *Segna*	44.59	14.53	14
Signia, *Segni*	41°.42'	13°.5'	11
Sigrium Pr., *C. Sigri...*	39.11	25.50	19
Sigus? *Summah*	36.11	6.49	23
Sihor (or River of Egypt)? *Wady el-Arieh*	36.45	33.40	24
Sila Silva	38.50	16.20	9
Silandus, *Selendi*	38.43	28.59	20
Silārus F., *Sele*	40.30	15.0	9
Silārus F., *Silaro*	44.25	11.40	8
Sile	30.45	32.9	24
Silis F., *Sile*	45.40	12.15	8
Silla, or Delas, F., (Gyndes?), *Diyalah..*	34.0	44.50	22
*Silures	52.0	3.10 w	5
Silva Laurentia	41.42	12.25	11
Silva Teutobergiensis...	51.50	9.0	25
Silvanectes, *Senlis*	49.12	2.35	6
Silvia? *Kupris*	44.2	17.11	14
Silvium, *Garagnone*	40.54	16.10	9
Simbrivīni Montes	42.0	13.5	11
*Simēni, or Iceni	52.25	1.0	5
Simois F., *Mendere Tchai*	39.55	26.15	19
Simois F. (Sicilia), *Freddo*	38.0	12.54	12
Simȳra, *Jahmura*	34.50	36.0	20
Sin, Desert of, *Wady Mokatteb*	28.50	33.24	24
Sin (Pelusium)? *Tineh*	31.2	32.21	24
*Sinae	30.0	115.0	2
Sinai, Mt., *Jebel Mousa, Jeb. Katerin, &c*	28.30	34.0	21
Sinarum S.			1
Sinda, *Agelan*	37.18	29.36	20
Sinda, *Anapa*	44.55	37.17	3
Sindocanda? *Candy*	7.18	80.47	2
Sindomana? *Schwan...*	26.20	67.55	3
Sindus	40.37	22.50	15
Sinerva, *Seni Beli*	39.45	39.19	20
Singa	37.30	38.15	20
Singames	42.26	41.32	22
Singāra, *Sinjar*	36.17	41.51	22
Singas F., *Araban Tchai*	37.38	37.40	20
Singidūnum, *Belgrade..*	44.48	20.37	14
Singitīcus S., *G. of Monte Santo*	40.10	24.6	15
Singos	40.11	23.48	15
Singūlis F., *Xenil*	37.32	5.0 w	7
Sinna, *Zabliak*	42.14	19.10	14
Sinnus F., *Senio*	44.15	11.40	8
Sinonia I., *Zannone*	40.58	13.3	9
Sinōpe, *Sinoub*	42.2	35.11	20
Sintha, *Sennah*	35.20	47.20	22
Sinuessa, *Mondragone..*	41.7	13.54	9
Sinus ad Gradus	43.25	4.30	6
Siphnos L., *Sifano*	37.0	24.42	19
Sipin, *Visseiche*	47.58	1.20 w	6
Sipontum (or Sipus), *Siponto*	41.37	15.53	9
Sipus (or Sipontum), *Siponto*	41.37	15.53	9
Sipȳlus M., *Manisa Dagh, &c*	38.34	27.25	19
Sirenum I.			1
Sirenūsae Iᵐ., *Galli*	40.35	14.26	13
Siricis? *Sis*	37.26	35.50	20
Sirio, *Cerons*	44.38	0.20 ▼	6
Siris	40.9	16.37	9
Siris F., *Sinno*	40.14	16.30	9
Sirmio, *Sermione*	45.29	10.37	8
Sirmium, *Mitrovitz*	45.0	19.36	14
Sisapon, *Almaden*	38.40	4.48 ▼	7
Sisar, or Usar F.? *Ajeby*	36.10	4.45	23
Sisarn Palus, *L. of Jebel Ishkel*	37.10	9.35	23
Siscia, *Siszek*	45.30	16.22	14
Sitacus F., *Sita Rhe-gian*	28 10	51 30	3
SITHONIA	40.5	23.55	15
Sitifis, *Setif*	35.59	5.15	23

NAMES.	LAT.	LONG.	MAP.
Sitomăgus, *Dunwich*....	52°.17′	1°.36′	5
Sittăce	33.17	44.26	22
SITTACĒNE	33.20	44.30	22
Sivel, or Suel, *Cast. de Frangerola*	36.33	4.37 w	7
Smenus F., *Arna*	36.43	22.33	18
Sminthium, or Chryse..	39.38	26.10	19
Smyrna, *Smyrna*	38.25	27.10	19
Smyrna Antiqua	38.28	27.10	19
Soastris, *Keuprikeui*....	43.1	27.26	14
Socoh, *Esh-Shuweikeh*..	31.25	35.4	21
SODUCĒNE	39.40	45.30	22
*Sogdi	28.20	69.30	3
SOGDIĀNA	40.0	64.0	3
Solentii Iᵃᵉ., *Zirone, &c.*	43.26	16.10	14
Soli, *Solia*	.35.9	32.51	20
Soli, or Pompeiopŏlis, *Mezetli*	36.44	34.34	20
Solia, or Arae Hespĕri, *S. Lucar la Mayor*...	37.24	6.2 w	7
Solimariaca, *Soulosse*..	48.24	5.44	6
Solimnia I., *Pelago*	39.20	24.5	19
Sollium	38.48	20.52	15
Soloeis Pr.? *C. Spartel*	35.47	5.56 w	23
Soloeis Pr.? *C. Cantin*..	32.35	9.15 w	2
Soloeis, or Solventia, Pr.? *C. Blanco*	20.50	17.8 w	2
Solomacum?	44.34	0.51 w	6
Solonna, *Città del Sole*...	44.13	12.0	8
Solonium? *Sullonza*	45.50	5.28	6
Solus, or Soluntium, *Castello di Solanto*...	38.5	13.31	12
Solygia, *Galata*	37.51	22.59	18
Solŷma M., *Taktalu*	36.40	30.30	20
Sontia, *Sanza*	40.13	15.24	9
Sontius F., *Isonzo*	46.0	13.40	8
Sonus F., *Sone*	24.30	83.0	2
SOPHĒNE	38.30	39.30	22
Sophon, *Sabandscha*....	40.43	30.15	20
Sora, *Sora*	41.43	13.38	11
Sorabile, *Mamojada*	40.13	9.17	9
Soracte M., *Monte S. Oreste*	42.17	12.30	11
Sorbiodūnum, *Old Sarum*	51.6	1.48 w	5
*Sordi, or Sordones	42.30	2.30	6
Sorek, Valley of, *Wady es-Surar*	31.48	34.50	21
Soroba, *Sarumenk*	38.52	35.37	20
Sossius F., *Fiume di Marsala*	37.48	12.30	12
Sostomagus, *Castelnaudary*	43.20	1.59	6
Sostra?	42.58	25.11	14
*Sotiātes	44.6	0.0	6
Sotium, *Sos*	44.3	0.9	6
Southern Horn (of Hanno)? *Sherboro' Sound*	7.40	12.50 w	2
Sozopŏlis, for. Apollonia, *Sizeboli*	42.26	27.44	14
Spalathrae	39.11	23.14	15
Sparta, or Lacedaemon, *n. Mistra*	37.5	22.26	18
Spartarius Campus	37.45	1.0 w	7
Spauta (or Mantiăne) L.? *L. Urumiyah*	37.30	45.30	22
Spelunca, *Sperlonga*....	41.14	13.25	9
Speluncae, *Grotta Rossa*	40.44	17.46	9
Speos Artemīdos? *Beni Hassan*	27.55	30.53	24
Sperchiae	38.55	22.5	15
Sperchius F., *Ellada*....	38.56	22.5	15
Sphaeria? *Poro*	37.30	23.28	18
Sphagia, or Sphacteria I.	36.56	21.41	18
Sphendale, *Malakasa*	38.13	23.49	16
Sphettus, *Spata*	37.57	23.55	16
Sphingium, Phicium, or Phoenicium, M.,*Faga*	38.23	23.12	16
Spina? *n. Mezzano*	44.82	12.8	8
Spinae, *Speen, n. Newbury*	51.25	1.21 w	5
Spiraeum Prom., *C. Spiri*	37°.48′	23°.11′	18
Spoletium, *Spoleto*	42.45	12.48	8
Stabatio, *Monsetier*	44.58	6.30	8
Stabiae, *Castellamare*....	40.41	14.29	13
Stabŭla, *Ottmarsheim*...	47.47	7.30	6
Stabŭlum Novum, *Sitjas*	41.15	1.49	7
Stachir, or Trachir, F., *Gambia*	13.30	15.0 w	2
Stageirus, or Stageira?	40.35	23.48	15
Stanacum?	48.26	13.51	14
Staneclum?	43.28	18.47	14
*Statielli	44.37	8.25	8
Steiria, *r. on Porto Rafti*	37.53	24.1	18
Stelae	35.5	25.13	19
Stenae, *Rotherthurm*....	45.35	24.14	14
STENYCLĒRUS	37.13	22.0	18
Stephăne, *Istifan*	41.57	34.34	20
Stiris, *r. n. Kyriaki*	38.22	22.46	16
Stobi, *Stobi*	41.10	21.50	14
Stoechădes Iᵃᵉ., *Isles d'Hieres*	43.0	6.25	8
Stomalimne	36.46	27.2	19
*Stoni	46.5	10.45	8
Stratae-burgus, *Strasbourg*	48.35	7.45	6
Stratonicĕa, or Idrias, *Eski-hissar*	37.17	28.11	19
Stratus, *r. n. Lepenu*..	38.40	21.22	15
Stravianae, *Nassicz*	45.20	18.8	14
Strongŷle I., *Stromboli*	38.47	15.13	9
Strophădes Iᵃᵉ.,*Strofadhia*	37.15	21.0	18
Struthus Portus, *Vourlia Bay*	37.28	23.2	18
Stryme	40.52	25.36	19
Strymon F., *Struma, or Kara-su*	42.0	23.17	14
Strymonīcus S., *G. of Rufani*	40.35	24.0	19
Stucia F., *Dovey*	52.33	4.0 w	5
Stura F., *Stura*	44.19	7.20	8
Stymphālus, *n. Khionia*	37.52	22.27	18
Styra, *Stoura*	38.9	24.13	15
Styx F., *Mavro Neria*..	37.59	22.14	18
Suana, *Sovana*	42.38	11.36	8
*Suanetes	46.0	9.47	8
*Suani	42.55	42.30	22
*Suardones	54.0	10.30	25
Sub Lanuvium, *San Gennarello*	41.40	12.45	11
Sub Lupatia, *Anticaglie*	40.40	16.43	9
Sub Murănum, *Castro Villari*	39.46	16.11	9
Sub Radice	42.39	25.10	14
Sub Romŭla, or Romŭlea? *n. Andretta*	40.57	15.1	9
Sub Sabione, *Clausen*..	46.39	11.32	8
Subis F., *Gaya*	41.8	1.22	7
Sublaqueum, *Subiaco*...	41.57	13.5	11
Subur F., *Wady Sebou*	34.25	6.0 w	23
Suburbanum Commŏdi, *Roma Vecchia*	41.49	12.34	11
Suburbanum Hadriăni, *Sette Bassi*	41.51	12.36	11
Subzapara, *Hirmanli*...	41.55	26.0	14
Succoth (Scenae), *r. n. Shibbeen*	30.16	31.22	24
Sucidava, *Kouzgoun*	44.9	27.43	14
Sucro, *Sueca*	39.12	0.19 w	7
Sucro F., *Xucar*	39.14	1.0 w	7
Sucronensis S.	39.20	0.0	7
Sudĕti M., *Sudeten Gebirge*	50.10	17.0	25
*Sudrăcae, or Oxydrăcae	28.40	72.0	3
Suel, or Sivel, *Cast. de Frangerola*	36.33	4.37 w	7
Suessa, *Sessa*	41.15	13.54	9
Suessa Pometia?	41.25	13.8	11
*Suessetăni?	39°.30′	0°.30′ w	7
*Suessiones	49.10	3.20	6
Suessŭla, *Sessola*	41.1	14.22	11
*Suetri	43.50	6.30	6
*Suēvi	51.20	14.0	25
Suevīcum Mare, or Sarmatīcus Oceănus, *Baltic Sea*	57.0	20.0	2
Sufasar? *Medeya*	36.17	2.45	23
Sufes, *Esbibah*	35.22	9.7	23
Sufetŭla, *Sbeitlah*	35.1	9.15	23
Suillum, or Helvillum, *Sigillo*	43.20	12.45	8
Suindinum, aft. Cenomani, *Le Mans*	48.0	0.11	6
Suīnus F., *Salino*	42.22	14.0	8
*Sulones	60.0	15.0	2
Suissa	39.55	39.53	20
Suissatio? *Vittoria*	42.52	2.42 w	7
Sulcense Prom., *Punta Sperone*	38.58	8.23	9
Sulci? *Bari*	39.51	9.38	9
Sulci, *Porto Botte*	39.3	8.33	9
Sulgas F., *Sorgue*	44.0	5.0	6
Sulia Prom., *C. St. Paul*	35.7	24.31	19
Sulis?	47.45	3.15 w	6
Sulloniacae, *Brockley Hill, n. Stanmore*	51.38	0.18 w	5
Sullucu, or Collops parvus? *Tagodeite*	36.59	7.36	23
Sulmo, *Sermoneta*	41.33	13.3	11
Sulmo, *Sulmona*	42.3	13.56	9
Summuntorium, *Kuhbach*	48.30	11.15	25
Summus Lacus, *Samolaco*	46.15	9.24	8
SummusPennīnus,*Great St. Bernard*	45.53	7.9	8
Summus Pyrenaeus	42.46	0.33 w	6
Summus Pyrenaeus, *Bellegarde*	42.30	2.50	7
Summus Pyrenaeus, *Roncesvaux*	43.1	1.19 w	6
Suna? *Nerola*	42 13	12.49	11
Sunium, *r. on C. Colonna*	37.39	24.2	18
Sunium Prom., *C. Colonna*	37.39	24.2	18
Sunium Prom. (Paros)..	37.18	25.19	19
Supĕrum, or Hadriaticum, Mare, *Adriatic Sea*	44.0	14.0	8
Sura	31.50	45.0	22
Sura, *Suram*	42.2	43.36	22
Sura, *Surich*	35.54	38.48	20
Surius F., *Tchenisskali*	42.21	42.20	22
Surrentum, *Sorrento*....	40.37	14.22	13
Susa (Shushan), *Soos*...	32.0	48.25	22
Susia? *Zuzan*	34.20	60.45	3
SUSIĀNA, *Khuzistan*	31.30	48.0	22
Sutrium, *Sutri*	42.16	12.12	11
Syagros Prom., *Ras el-Had*	22.33	60.0	3
Sybăris	39.41	16.28	9
Sybăris F., *Coscile*	39.40	16.20	9
Sybŏta, *Murtzo, or Murto*	39.24	20.15	15
Sybŏta I., *Sivota*	39.24	20.14	15
Sybritia	35.13	24.36	19
Sycamīnos, *Athleet, or Castel Pelegrino*	32.43	34.56	21
Syce	41.2	28.59	26
Sychar, or Shechem (Neapŏlis), *Nablous*...	32.15	35.14	21
Syēne, *Essouan*	24.5	32.56	3
Syia	35.14	23.45	19
Sylleum, *Assarkeui*	37.4	31.2	20
Symaethus, *Regalbuto*..	37.37	14.39	12
Symaethus F., *Simeto*...	37.30	14.52	12
Symbŏlum	41.0	24.24	19
Syme I., *Symi*	36.35	27.53	19
Synaus, or Synnaus, *Simaul*	39.7	29.5	20

NAMES.	LAT.	LONG.	MAP.
Synnăda, *Afioum Karahissar*	38°.45'	30°.38'	20
Syphaeum, *Montalto*	39.25	16.8	9
Syracellae, *Migalgara*	40.52	26.51	14
Syracūsae, *Siracusa*	37.5	15.15	13
SYRASTRENE	22.0	71.30	2
Syrias, or Lepte, Prom., *U. Indjeh*	42.7	34.59	20
Syrnae I., *Joannes*	36.20	26.41	19
Syros, *Syra*	37.27	24.57	19
Syros I., *Syra*	37.25	24.55	19
Syrtis Major, *G. of Sidra*	32.0	18.0	23
Syrtis Minor, *G. of Kabes*	34.15	11.0	23
Sys, or Sythas, F.	38.0	22.40	18

T.

NAMES.	LAT.	LONG.	MAP.
Taanach, *Taanuk*	32.31	35.14	21
Tabae, *Davas*	37.26	28.50	20
Tabae? *Bannah*	11.11	51.5	2
Tabula, *Durala*	38.34	28.57	20
Tabellaria, *Castelluccio*	42.16	11.38	8
Taberna Frigida, *Frigido*	43.59	10.9	8
TABIENE	35.0	51.0	3
Tabor M. (Atabyrium, or Itabyrium), *Jebel et-Tuor*	32.42	35.25	21
Tabrāca, *Tubarkah*	36.55	8.45	23
Tabuda, or Tabulla, F.? *Aas*	51.0	2.7	6
Taburnus Mons, *Monte Taburno*	41.8	14.30	13
Tacupe, *Khabs, or Kabes*	33.53	10.4	23
Tacona?	28.54	31.3	24
Tader F., *Segura*	38.15	1.40 w	7
Tadinum, *S. Maria Tadina, n. Gualdo*	43.14	12.48	8
Tadmor, or Palmyra, *Tadmor*	34.18	38.14	20
Tadutti, *Tattubt*	35.31	6.8	23
Taenārum, or Taenarium, Prom., *C. Matapan*	36.23	22.29	18
Taenārum, or Caenepŏlis, *Kypariso*	36.27	22.27	18
Taenia Longa, *Fagasah, or Tagasah*	35.19	4.57 w	23
Taguba, *Tubukah*	31.31	34.43	21
Tagara, r. of Deoghir, *n. Aurungabad*	20.0	75.13	2
Tagonius F., *Tajuna*	40.15	3.20 w	7
Tagus F., *Tajo (or Tagus)*	39.28	8.20 w	7
Tahapanes, Tabpanes, or Hanes, (Daphne), *Tell Defenneh*	30.52	32.3	24
Taizalum Prom., *Kinnaird's Head*	57 42	2.0 w	2
Talabriga? *Salten*	40.43	8.34 w	7
Taletum M., *St. Elias, or Makryno*	36.57	22.22	18
Taliata, *Gagersinlik*	44.30	22.14	14
Talmena? *Ras Godem*	25.20	60.10	3
Tamāre? *Tamerton*	50.25	4.11 w	5
Tamaris F., *Tambre*	42.40	9.0 w	7
Tamārus F., *Tamar*	50.26	4.12 w	5
Tamarus F., *Tamaro*	41.17	14.45	9
Tamasseus	35.9	33.13	20
Tamesis, or Tamēsa, F., *Thames*	51.30	1.3 w	5
Tamissa Aest., *Mouth of Thames*	51.30	0.40	5
Tamnum?	45.27	0.47 w	6
Tamÿnae	38.24	24.3	16
Tamÿras, or Damūras, F.. *Nahr ed-Damour*	33.41	35.30	21
Tanāger F., *Tangro, or Negro*	40.30	15.30	9
Tanagra, *Grimadha*	38.17	23.36	16
Tanais F., *Don*	50.35	50.0	2
Tanarus F., *Tanaro*	44.50	8.10	8

NAMES.	LAT.	LONG.	MAP.
Tanis (Zoan?), *San*	30°.59'	31°.48'	24
Tanitic Mouth (of Nile), *Om Faradjeh*	31.10	32.20	24
Tannētum, or Tanētum, *Taneto*	44.46	10.27	8
Tanus (or Tanaus) F., *River of Luku*	37.25	22.37	18
*Taōchi	39.50	41.30	22
Taōke, *Khor Gassair*	29.13	50.40	3
Tape? *Nooserabad*	36.50	53.24	3
Taphiae I*., *Telboides I.*	38.35	20.50	15
Taphiassus M., *Kakiscala*	38.25	21.44	18
Taphis, *Tafah*	23.37	32.30	3
Taphos I., *Meganisi*	38.39	20.46	15
Taphros, or Fossa, *Strait of Bonifacio*	41.20	9.10	9
Taphus, *Tafio*	38.13	20.23	18
Taphytis Prom. (Aspis, or Clypĕa), *Ras el-Melhr*	36.52	11.9	23
Taposīris (or Apis?), *Arabs Tower*	30.47	29.34	24
Taprobane, or Salice I., *Ceylon*	8.0	81.0	2
*Tapȳri	36.20	53.0	3
Tarabenorum Vicus, *Vico*	42.11	8.47	9
Taras F., *Tara*	40.35	17.10	9
Taras, or Tarentum, *Taranto*	40.28	17.14	9
Tarasco, *Tarascon*	43.48	4.39	6
*Tarbelli	43.30	1.20 w	6
Tarbellĭcae, or Aquae Augustae, *Dax*	43.43	1.2 w	6
Tarentīnus S., *G. of Taranto*	40.0	17.0	9
Tarentum, or Taras, *Taranto*	40.28	17.14	9
Targines F., *Tacina*	39.6	16.50	9
Taricheae, *El-Kerak*	32.44	35.36	21
Tarichiae I*., *Alkuriyah*	35.45	11.0	23
Tarnadae, *St. Maurice*	46.12	7.0	8
Tarnis F., *Tarn*	43.50	1.40	6
Tarphe	38.44	22.37	16
Tarpodizus?	42.1	26.58	14
Tarquinii, *Trachina*	42.16	11.46	8
Tarracīna, or Anxur, *Terracina*	41.16	13.15	11
Tarrāco, *Tarragona*	41.7	1.16	7
TARRACONENSIS	41.0	3.0 w	7
Tarras, *Tramuzza*	40.0	8.39	9
Tarrha	35.14	23.52	19
Tarsatica, *Tarsatch*	45.19	14.27	8
Tarsaticum, *n. Fiume*	45.21	14.27	14
Tarsie Prom., *Ras Djrd*	26.38	54.30	3
Tarsius F., *Kara Dere Su*	40.0	27.50	19
Tarsus, *Tersoos*	36.56	34.58	20
Tartārus, or Hadriānus, F., *Tartaro*	45.5	11.20	8
Tartessus (Calpe?), *El Rocadillo, n. S. Roque*	36.13	5.23 w	7
Taruenna, *Terouenne*	50.39	2.7	6
Tarus F., *Taro*	44.39	10.0	8
*Tarusātes	44.0	0.20 w	6
Tarvēdum, or Orcas, Prom., *Dunnet Head*	58.41	3.24 w	2
Tarvessedum, *Madese*	46.26	9.20	8
Tarvisetum, *Tarvis*	46.29	13.35	14
Tarvisium, *Treviso*	45.39	12.16	8
Tasacarta?	30.42	31.52	24
Tasaccora? *Mascara*	35.25	0.6	23
Tusciaca, *Thesée, n. Montrichard*	47.20	1.19	6
Tataium	40.32	30.23	20
Tutta Palus, *L. of Kodj Hissar, or Touz Ghieul*	38.40	33.30	20
*Taulantii	41.0	19.35	14
Taunus M., *Taunus*	50.10	8.20	25

NAMES.	LAT.	LONG.	MAP.
Taurasium? *Taurasi*	40°.59'	14°.58'	9
TAURĪCA, *Crimea*	45.0	34.0	3
Tauroentum, *Tarente*	43.11	5.41	6
Tauromenium, *Taormina*	37.49	15.16	12
Tauriāna, *Traviano*	38.22	15.55	9.
*Taurini	45.0	7.45	8
Taurunum, *Semlin*	44.51	20.32	14
Taurus Mons, *Allah Dagh, Bulghar Dagh, &c.*	37.0	34.0	20
Taurus M. (Sicilia), *Mount Venerella*	37.51	15.14	12
Taurus Prom., *Capo S. Croce*	37.15	15.15	12
Taus, or Tava, Aest., *Firth of Tay*	56.27	3.0 w	5
Tava? *Tantah*	30.50	30.59	24
Tavae, *Tavi, n. Leonforte*	37.37	14.22	12
Tavium, *Boghas Keui*	40.0	34.34	20
Tavola F., *Golo*	42.30	9.10	9
Taxila, *Manikyala*	33.29	73.0	3
Taygĕtus M.	36.57	22.22	18
Teănum, *Teano*	41.15	14.3	9
Teănum Apŭlum, *Civitate*	41.46	15.14	9
Teăte, *Chieti*	42.20	14.11	9
Teăte Apŭlum, *Chieuti*	41.50	15.10	9
Tecmon?	39.46	20.56	15
*Tectosăges	39.50	32.40	20
Tedanius F., *Zermagna*	44.10	15.50	14
Tegĕa, *Paleo Episkopi*	37.28	22.26	18
Tegiănum, *Diano*	40.22	15.31	9
Teglicium, *Vetrena*	44.7	26.59	14
Tegŭla, *Siliqua*	39.18	8.49	9
Tegyra	38.32	22.58	16
Teichiussa	37.25	27.26	19
Teichos, *Kastro Kalogria*	38.9	21.54	18
Tekoah, *Tekua*	31.39	35.15	21
Tela?	41.57	4.50 w	7
Telebōas F., *Kara Su*	38.45	41 40	22
Telesia, *Telese*	41.13	14.30	9
Telethrius M., *Ploko*	38.52	23.7	15
Tellēnae, *Toretta*	41.44	12.28	11
Tellonum?	44.18	0.51 w	6
Telmissus, *Makri*	36.36	29.10	20
Telo Martius, *Toulon*	43.8	5.54	6
Telonius F., *Turano*	42.44	12.56	11
Telos I., *Piskopi, or Tilo*	36.25	27.25	19
Telphūsa, *n. Vanena*	37.44	21.53	18
Temathia M. (or Mathia), *Lykodhimo*	36.55	21.51	18
Temenium	37.35	22.45	18
Temēsa, or Tempsa? *Torre del Piano del Casale*	39.6	16.6	9
Temnus, *Menimen*	38.36	27.5	19
Tempe, Valley and Pass, *Valley of Lykostomo, or Dereli*	39.50	22.35	15
Temple of Apollo Corynthus	36.51	21.56	18
Temple of Ceres	37.35	22.27	18
Temple of Jupiter (Aegina)?	37.45	23.32	18
Temple of Jupiter Palenius, *Campo di Giove*	42.0	14.3	9
Temple of Poseidon	37.55	23.1	18
Temple of Venus (Cyprus)	34.51	32.22	20
Templum Circes	41.12	13.3	11
Templum Feroniae	41.17	13.13	11
Templum Hercŭlis? *n. C. Roche*	36.19	6.8 w	7
Templum Jovis Urii	41.7	29.7	20
Templum Junōnis Laciniae	39.5	17.11	9
Tempsa, or Temēsa? *Torre del Piano del Casale*	39.6	16.6	9

NAMES.	LAT.	LONG.	MAP.
*Tenotheri	51°.10′	7°.30′	25
Tenča, Klenia	37.47	22.52	18
Tenědos	39.50	26.5	19
Tenědos I., Tenedos	39.50	26.0	19
Teneric Plain	38.20	23.18	16
Tenos, Tino	37.32	25.11	19
Tenos I., Tino	37.35	25.10	19
Tentyra, Denderah	26.9	32.41	3
Teos, r. n. Sighajik	38.11	26.49	19
Tephrice, Divriki	39.21	38.15	20
Terēdon, or Diridōtis, Jebel Sinam	30.15	47.45	22
Tergedum?	18.0	41.0	2
Tergeste, Trieste	45.39	13.47	8
Tergestinus S., Golfo di Trieste	45.40	13.40	8
Terias F., S. Leonardo	37.17	15.0	·12
Terina? n. Nocera	39.8	16.7	9
Terinaeus, Hipponiātes, or Vibonensis, S., G. of S. Eufemia	38.55	16.0	9
Terioli, Tirol	46.43	11.6	8
Termerium Pr., Petra Termera	36.57	27.20	19
Termes?	41.31	2.24 w	7
Termessus	36.55	30.26	20
Termus F., Fiume Temo, or F. di Bosa	40.18	8.29	9
Testrina, Tomasso	42.21	13.18	8
Tetis, or Ruscino, F., Tet	42.44	3.0	6
Tetraphylia?	39.15	21.29	15
TETRAPOLIS	38.8	23.57	26
Taucheira, aft. Arsinoe, Taukra	32.32	20.32	23
Teudūrum, Tudder	51.3	5.55	6
Teumessus	38.21	23.24	16
Teumessus M.	38.18	23.24	16
Teuthea? Upper Akhaia	38.6	21.34	18
Teutheas F.?	38.5	21.33	18
Teuthis, Dhimitsana	37.36	22.4	18
TEUTHRANIA	39.10	27.30	20
Teuthrania, or Thymena, Timteh	41.58	33.9	20
Teuthrōne, n. Kotorna	36.37	22.30	18
Teutlussa I., Limniona	36.16	27.45	19
Teutoburgium	45.32	19.0	14
Teutria, Pianosa	42.14	15.45	9
Thagura? Tajeilt	36.16	8.20	23
Thalāmae?	37.51	21.42	18
Thalāmae, Platzo	36.48	22.19	18
Thamara (Tamar), Kurnub	31.8	35.6	21
Thamnath, El-Burj	31.54	35.1	21
THAMNITICA	31.55	35.0	21
Thamusida? Mehediah	34.18	6.39 w	23
Thantia?	32.16	39.22	21
Thapsācus (Tiphsah)? El-Hamn'am	35.55	38.54	20
Thapsus, Baltah	35.35	11.3	23
Thapsus, Magnisi	37.9	15.12	13
Thasos	40.46	24.45	19
Thasos I., Thaso	40.40	24.40	19
Thaumāci, Dhomoko	39.8	22.16	15
Thaumacia?	39.17	23.14	15
Thaubasium?	30.31	32.10	24
Thebae (Aegyptus), Karnak, &c	25.43	32.40	3
Thebae (Boeotia), Thiva	38.18	23.19	16
Thebae (Thessalia), r. n. Ak-Kedjel	39.17	22.45	15
Thebe	39.39	27.1	19
Theoches Mons? Tekieh Dagh	40.25	39.45	20
Theganūsa I., Venetiko	36.42	21.54	18
Thelopte, Feriana	34.41	8.40	23
THEMISCYRA	41.5	37.0	20
Themiscyra, Thermeh	41.11	37.1	20
Themisonium? Tefenii	37.23	29.43	20
Thenae, Castel Temenos	35.13	25.7	19

NAMES.	LAT.	LONG.	MAP.
Thenae, In Wady Theny	34°.40′	10°.35′	23
Theodosiopōlis, for. Carana, Erzeroum	39.55	41.19	22
Theodosiopōlis, for. Resaena, Ras el-Ain	36.52	40.1	22
Thera? r. on Messa Vouno	36.21	25.29	19
Thera L. (Calliste), Santorin	36.25	25.28	19
Therambus	39.57	23.41	15
Theranda	42.0	20.46	14
Therapne	37.3	22.28	18
Therapne?	38.16	23.22	16
Therasia, Theraeia	36.26	25.21	19
Therasia, Hiēra, or Vulcāni I., Vulcano	38.23	14.56	9
Thermae, Lutraki	37.59	22.59	16
Thermae (Phazemonitis), Kawsa	40.58	35.39	20
Thermae Agrippae	41.59	12.44	11
Thermae Himerenses, Termini	37.58	13.41	12
Thermae Selinuntiae, Sciacca	37.28	13.5	12
Thermaïcus S., G. of Saloniki	40.15	22.45	15
Therme, aft. Thessalonica, Saloniki	40.38	22.58	15
Thermi, or Thermum, Vlokho	38.40	21.34	15
Thermōdon F.	38.20	23.30	16
Thermōdon F., Termeh Tchai	40.50	37.0	20
Thermopylae	38.47	22.29	16
Thespiae (or Thespia), Lefka, n. Rimokastro	38.16	23.9	16
THESPROTIA	39.25	20.40	15
THESSALIA	39.30	22.20	15
THESSALIŌTIS	39.18	22.0	15
Thessalonica, Saloniki	40.38	22.58	15
Theudoria, Thodhoriana	39.22	21.11	15
Theveste, Tebesah, or Tipsa	35.19	8.8	23
Thinae			1
Thiar	37.58	0.48 w	7
Thimonepsi?	29.7	31.11	24
Thisbe, Kakosia	38.15	22.58	16
Thisōa, or Theisōa	37.38	22.5	18
Thisōa, or Theisōa, Lardha	37.31	21.58	18
Thius F., Kutufarina	37.18	22.12	18
Thmuis? Tell Muit	30.59	31.30	24
Thoantium Prom.? (Carpathos), C. Bonandrea	35.51	27.11	19
Thoantium Prom. (Rhodos), C. St. George	36.7	27.45	19
Thoaris F., Tureh Tchai	41.8	37.11	20
*Thomani	40.40	59.0	3
Thorae? Thinika	37.47	23.54	18
Thorax M., Gumusch Dagh	37.48	27.25	19
Thoricus, Mandri	37.44	24.3	18
Thornax M.	37.21	23.13	18
Thornax M.	37.8	22.26	18
Thospītis L. (Arsissa, or Arsēne)? L. of Van	38.40	42.40	22
Thoum, Etham, or Pithom (Patūmos?), r. n. Abassieh	30.28	31.35	24
THRACIA	41.40	26.0	14
Thraustus	37.50	21.49	18
Thria	38.4	23.33	16
Throni Prom., C. Pila	34.56	33.53	20
Thronium	38.46	22.41	16
Thronium? Krisilio	40.30	19.30	15
Thubactis, Marsa Zouraik	32.27	14.51	23
Thubuna, Tubnah	35.10	4.49	23

NAMES.	LAT.	LONG.	MAP.
Thule, Shetland Islands	60°.30′	1°.20′ w	2
Thumāta?	29.30	41.0	3
Thuria, n. Veisaga	37.6	22.4	13
Thurii, aft. Copiae	39.40	16.23	9
Thurium, or Orthopāgum, M	38.28	22.52	16
Thyamia	37.54	22.41	18
Thyāmis F., Calamas	39.33	20.25	15
Thyāmis Pr., Mt. Mavronoro	39.34	20.11	15
Thyāmus M., Spartovuni	38.47	20.15	15
Thyatira, Ak-hissar	38.53	27.53	19
Thybarna, Kassaba	38.31	27.45	19
Thymbris F., Pursek Tchai	39.43	30.40	20
Thymbrium, Derekeui	38.28	31.29	20
Thymena, or Teuthrania, Timteh	41.58	33.9	20
Thymnias S., G. of Symi	36.38	28.0	19
Thymoetādae, Keratsini	37.58	23.37	17
*Thyni	41.0	30.0	20
Thynias I., Kefken Adassi	41.14	30.16	20
Thynias Pr., C. Ainada, or Kouri	41.53	28.4	14
Thyrēa? n. Astro	37.24	22.45	18
Thyrīdes Prom., Capo Grosso	36.29	22.21	18
Thyrium?	38.52	20.58	15
Thyrsus F., Tyrsi	39.55	8.35	9
Thysdrus, or Tusdra, El-Jemm	35.21	10.39	23
Thyssus	40.16	24.10	15
*Tibarēni	40.50	38.15	20
Tiberias, Tubariyeh	32.48	35.34	21
Tiberias L. (Sea of Galilee, or L. of Gennesaret), Bahr Tubariyeh	32.50	35.36	21
Tibēris, or Tihris, F., Tevere, or Tiber	42.12	12.40	11
Tibiscum, or Tibiscus? Temeswar	45.43	21.20	14
Tibiscus F.? Theiss	46.0	20.6	14
Tibiscus F.? Temes	45.21	21.0	14
Tibisis F.? Ak Lom	43.38	26.0	14
Tibūla, Longo Sardo	41.14	9.11	9
Tibur, Tivoli	41.59	12.49	11
Tiburnia	46.50	13.29	14
Ticarius F., Valinco	41.39	9.0	
Tichis, or Illibēris, F., Tech	42.35	2.50	6
Tichius	38.44	22.25	16
Ticinum, Pavia	45.11	9.10	8
Ticinus F., Ticino	45.30	8.46	8
Tierna? Alt Orsova	44.43	22.26	14
Tifāta Mons, Monte Maddaloni	41.5	14.20	13
Tifernum, n. Limosani	41.37	14.39	9
Tifernum Metaurense, S. Angelo in Vado	43.40	12.24	8
Tifernum Tiberinum, Città di Castello	43.28	12.15	8
Tifernus F., Biferno	41.40	14.40	9
Tifernus Mons, Monte Matese	41.25	14.27	9
Tigauda?	35.58	1.42	23
Tigava Castra	36.10	2.10	23
Tigra, Ruschouk	43.50	26.1	14
Tigrana?	38.27	47.25	22
Tigranocerta? Sert	38.1	41.36	22
Tigris F., Dijel, or Tigris	35.0	43.32	22
Tigulia, Tregosa	44.16	9.28	8
TIGURĪNUS PAGUS	46.40	7.20	6
Tilavemptus F., Tagliamento	46.0	12.56	8
Tilis, Thil le-Châtel	47.31	5.10	6
Tillium, Porto S. Nicolo	40.44	8.9	9

NAMES.	LAT.	LONG.	MAP.
Venedĭcus S., *G. of Danzig*	54°.30′	19°.0′	2
*Venĕti	47.45	2.40 w	6
VENETIA	45.40	12.0	8
Venĕtus, or Acronius, L., *L. of Constance*	47.40	9.20	6
Voniatia? *Vinhaes*	41.53	6.56 w	7
*Vennŏnes	46.14	10.0	8
Venonae, *High Cross*	52.30	1.18 w	5
*Venostes	46.41	10.45	8
Venta Belgărum, *Winchester*	51.4	1.19 w	5
Venta Icenŏrum, *Caistor, n. Norwich*	52.35	1.17	5
Venta Silurum, *Caerwent*	51.37	2.45 w	5
Ventisponte?	37.24	4.47 w	7
Ventium, *Vence*	43.43	7.7	8
Venus, Temple of (*Cyprus*)	34.51	32.22	20
Venusia, *Venosa*	40.57	15.50	9
*Veragri	46.0	7.10	8
Veratinum, *Warrington*	53.24	2.35 w	5
Verbănus L., *Lago Maggiore*	46.0	8.43	8
VERBIGENUS PAGUS	47.10	7.30	6
Vercellae, *Borgo Vercelli*	45.21	8.27	8
Verene, *Sohaze-Miholaes*	45.44	18.20	14
Vereasueca?	43.27	3.53 w	7
Verela, or Varia, *Varea*	42.22	2.26 w	7
Verĕtum, or Baris, *S. Maria di Vereto*	39.52	18.21	9
Vergae, *Ruggiano*	39.34	16.15	9
Vergilia, *Murcia*	38.0	1.15 w	7
Verisa	40.6	36.40	20
Verlucio? *Sandy Lane, n. Devizes*	51.24	2.1 w	5
Vernosol, *Vernos*	0.0	0.0	6
*Veromandui	49.55	3.30	6
Verometum, *n. Willoughby*	52.49	1.2 w	5
Verŏna, *Verona*	45.26	11.1	8
Verterae, *Brough*	54.31	2.19 w	5
Vertinae, *Versine*	39.18	16.46	9
Verŭlae, *Veroli*	41.43	13.28	11
Verulamium, *St. Albans*	51.45	0.21 w	5
Vervedrum Pr., *Duncansby Head*	58.38	3.1 w	2
Vesca, or Osca, *Huesca*	42.9	0.20 w	7
VESCITANIA?	42.15	0.0	7
Vesontio, *Besançon*	47.14	6.2	6
Vesperies, *Bermeo*	43.25	2.48 w	7
*Vestini	42.20	13.50	9
Vesulus Mons, *Monte Viso*	44.40	7.5	8
Vesunna, aft. Petrocorii, *Perigueux*	45.11	0.44	6
Vesuvius M., *Mount Vesuvius*	40.49	14.26	13
Vetĕra, *Xanten*	51.39	6.29	6
Vettona, *Bettona*	43.0	12.30	8
*Vettŏnes	40.30	6.30 w	7
Vetulonii?	43.5	10.41	8
Vetussalina? *Hanselbek*	47.21	18.59	14
Vexalla Aest., *Bridgewater Bay*	51.15	3.5 w	5
Via Aemilia	44.55	10.0	8
Via Amerina	42.26	12.21	11
Via Appia	41.33	12.57	11
Via Aquillia	40.30	15.30	9
Via Ardeatina	41.42	12.32	11
Via Aurelia	41.53	12.20	11
Via Casperia	42.46	12.40	11
Via Ciminia	42.24	12.8	11
Via Claudia (or Clodia)	42.15	12.4	11
Via Collatina	42.55	12.40	11
Via Cornelia	41.55	12.22	11
Via Cossia	42.20	12.5	11
Via Domitiana	41.0	13.58	13
Via Egnatia	40.36	23.25	15
Via Flaminia	42.5	12.28	11
Via Gabina	41°.54′	12°.40′	11
Via Labicana	41.52	12.40	11
Via Latina	41.48	12.38	11
Via Laurentina	41.47	12.28	11
Via Nomentana	41.58	12.36	11
Via Ostiensis	41.45	12.25	11
Via Portuensis	41.48	12.22	11
Via Postumia	45.4	10.30	8
Via Praenestina	41.53	12.47	11
Via Salaria	42.10	12.45	11
Via Severiăna	41.40	12.23	11
Via Sublacensis	42.0	13.1	11
Via Tiberina	42.4	12.32	11
Via Tiburtina	42.57	12.40	11
Via Valeria	42.0	12.52	11
Via Velentăna	42.0	12.26	11
Via Vitellia	41.52	12.24	11
Viadrus F., *Oder*	51.20	16.30	25
*Viberi	46.25	8.0	8
Vibo, or Vibo Valentia (Hipponium), *Monteleone*	38.42	16.10	9
Vibonensis, Hipponiātes, or Terinaeus S., *G. of S. Eufemia*	38.55	16.0	9
Vicentia, or Vicetia, *Vicenza*	45.32	11.34	8
Vicinianum, *n. Pristina*	42.20	21.12	14
Vicinium, *n. Cattaro*	42.24	18.50	14
Victoria, *Dealgin Ross*	56.21	3.57 w	5
Victoriae Portus? *Santander*	43.10	3.43 w	7
Victrix Julia (Celsa), *Xelsa*	41.26	0.28 w	7
Vicumniae, *Vicomuni*	45.2	9.15	8
Vicus Alexandrinus	41.51	12.29	11
Vicus Aquarius? *Belver*	41.47	5.26 w	7
Vicus Aurelii, *Vicarello*	42.11	12.10	11
Vicus Cuminarius, *Ocana*	39.56	3.31 w	7
Vicus Judaeŏrum, On, or Onion? *Tell el-Yehud*	30.22	31.28	24
Vicus Matrini, *La Campanaccia*	42.19	12.6	11
Vicus Mendicolco, *Lago Negro*	40.5	15.45	9
Vicus Novus, *Ostia Nuova*	42.16	12.49	11
Vicus Spacorum, *Vigo*	42.13	8.44 w	7
Vicus Variănus, *Bariano*	45.2	11.16	8
Vicus Virginis, *Varaggio*	44.31	8.33	8
Vidotara (or Vindogara) S.	55.30	4.45 w	5
Vidrus F.? *Vecht*	52.35	6.20	25
Viducassis, *Vieux, n. Caen*	49.5	0.27 w	6
Vienna, *Vienne*	45.31	4.53	6
Villa Hadriăni, *Colle S. Stefano*	41.56	12.48	11
Villa Horatii, *n. Licensa*	42.5	12.54	11
Villa Rostrăta, *Rignano*	42.14	12.27	11
Viminacium, *Kleisevats*	44.43	21.22	14
Viminiacum, *Beceril*	42.25	4.46 w	7
Vincela, *Semendria*	44.37	21.1	14
Vindalum, *Sorgues*	44.1	4.52	6
Vindeleia, *Pancorbo*	42.40	3.10 w	7
VINDELICIA	48.15	11.0	25
Vinderius F.? *Lough Strangford*	54.20	5.31 w	5
Vindilis, *Belle Isle*	47.20	3.10 w	6
Vindius M., *Vindhya Mts.*	22.30	76.0	2
Vindobala, *Rutchester, or Rud-chester*	55.0	1.49 w	5
Vindebona, *Vienna*	48.13	16.17	14
Vindogara (or Vidotara) S.	55.30	4.45 w	5
Vindogladia, *Gussage*	50.54	2.0 w	5
Vindolana, *Little Chesters*	55.0	2.21 w	5
Vindomis, *n. Whitchurch*	51°.15′	1°.23′ w	5
Vindomora, *Ebchester*	54.53	1.50 w	5
Vindonissa, *Brugg*	47.30	8.10	6
Vineas? *Jenne*	41.54	13.9	11
Viniŏlae	37.58	2.57 w	7
Viniolae, *Torre di Vignola*	41.13	9.3	9
Vinnius Mons (or Vindius), *Mountains of Asturias*	43.0	6.0 w	7
Vinovia, *Binchester*	54.41	1.39 w	5
Vipitenum, *Sterzing*	46.54	11.25	25
Viracelum, *Verrucola*	44.8	10.22	8
Viriballum Pr., *Punta di Gargalo*	42.22	8.33	9
*Virodunenses	49.10	5.15	6
Virodūnum, *Verdun*	49.10	5.24	6
Virovesca, *Bribiesca*	42.33	3.23 w	7
Viroviacum, *Werwick*	50.47	3.2	6
Virunum, *n. Klagenfurt*	46.42	14.22	14
Virus F.	43.11	8.42 w	7
Vistula F., *Weichsel, or Vistula*	52.0	21.10	25
Visurgis F., *Weser*	52.30	9.10	25
Vitellia, *Valmontone*	41.47	12.57	11
*Vithones, or Nithones	52.50	13.0	25
Vitodūrum, *Winterthur*	47.30	8.42	6
Vitricium, *Verres*	45.41	7.41	8
Viviscus, *Vevay*	46.28	6.50	6
Vobarna, *Vobarno*	45.39	10.30	8
*Vocates, or Vasates	44.30	0.15 w	6
*Vocontii	44.30	5.15	6
Volana F., *Volano*	44.50	11.50	8
Volaterrae, *Volterra*	43.24	10.51	8
*Volcae-Arecomici	43.50	4.0	6
*Volcae-Tectosăges	43.20	2.0	6
Volci, *Piano di Volci*	42.23	11.39	8
Volenes, *Volagnia*	45.32	10.51	8
Vologesias, *Kufa*	32.3	44.41	22
*Volsci	41.31	13.0	11
Volsiniensis L., *L. di Bolsena*	42.35	11.56	8
Volsinii, *Bolsena*	42.39	11.58	8
Voluba? *Lostwithiel*	50.24	4.39 w	5
Volubilis? *Mequinez*	33.58	5.32 w	23
Voluce, *Valecha*	41.36	2.38 w	7
Vomanus F., *Vomano*	42.38	14.0	8
Vorganium, *Concarneau?*	47.53	3.54 w	6
Vosalia, *Ober Wesel*	50.6	7.43	6
Vosĕgus (or Vogĕsus) M., *Vosges*	48.20	7.0	6
Vulcăni L (Hiĕra, or Therasia), *Vulcano*	38.23	14.56	9
Vulcaniae, Aeoliae, or Liparaeae, I., *Lipari Islands*	38.30	15.0	9
Vulceium, *Buccino*	40.37	15.21	9
*Vulgientes	44.0	5.30	6
Vultur Mons, *Monte Vulture*	40.48	15.40	9
Volturnum, *Castel Volturno*	41.2	13.56	13
Vulturnus F., *Volturno*	41.7	14.10	9

W.

NAMES.	LAT.	LONG.	MAP.
Wall of Agricola and Antoninus, *Grimes Dyke*	56.0	3.51 w	5
Wall of Hadrian and Severus	55.0	2.30 w	5
Watling Street	52.10	1.0 w	5
Western Horn (of Hanno)? *Bissagos B.*	11.15	16.0 w	2
White Mountains (Creta)	35.18	24.0	19

X.

NAMES.	LAT.	LONG.	MAP.
Xanthus, *Gunik*	36.20	29.23	20
Xanthus F., *Kodsha Tchai*	36.20	29.23	20
Xenippa?	41.0	65.0	3
Xerxes, Canal of	40.22	26.56	15